HAZING

HAZING

DESTROYING YOUNG LIVES

edited by

HANK NUWER

Indiana University Press

This book is a publication of

Indiana University Press
Office of Scholarly Publishing
Herman B Wells Library 350
1320 East 10th Street
Bloomington, Indiana 47405 USA

iupress.indiana.edu

Library of Congress Cataloging-in-Publication Data

Names: Nuwer, Hank, editor.
Title: Hazing : destroying young lives / edited by Hank Nuwer.
Description: Bloomington, Ind. : Indiana University Press, 2018. |
    Includes bibliographical references.
Identifiers: LCCN 2017051097 (print) | LCCN 2017057864 (ebook) |
    ISBN 9780253030252 (e-book) | ISBN 9780253029386 (hardback) |
ISBN 9780253030047 (pbk)
Subjects: LCSH: Hazing—United States. | College students—United
    States—Conduct of life. | Greek letter societies—United States. |
    Initiations (into trades, societies, etc.)
Classification: LCC LA229 (ebook) | LCC LA229 .H39 2018 (print) |
    DDC 371.5/80973—dc23
LC record available at https://lccn.loc.gov/2017051097

1 2 3 4 5   23 22 21 20 19 18

In memory of Harrison Kowiak and all others who have perished due to hazing.
To all the Hank Nuwer Anti-Hazing Hero Award recipients recognized by HazingPrevention.Org.
To my wife, Gosia Wroblewska-Nuwer, for her unflagging support of my research on hazing.

And that is why I swore never to be silent whenever and wherever human beings endure suffering and humiliation. We must always take sides. Neutrality helps the oppressor, never the victim. Silence encourages the tormentor, never the tormented. Sometimes we must interfere.

—Elie Wiesel, Nobel Prize Acceptance Speech

[The hazers'] code of honor exalts perjury as a virtue.

—Julian Hawthorne, "The Crime of Hazing," *Munsey's Magazine*, March 1905

Contents

Acknowledgments

I THANK FRANKLIN College President Thomas J. Minar, Vice President Tim Garner, and the Franklin Steering Committee for approving my sabbatical in 2016 that enabled me to complete this book. My colleagues in the Pulliam School of Journalism under Director John Krull made the sabbatical possible by dividing my advising and teaching load. Franklin colleagues in other disciplines also have been especially encouraging.

James Wiggins, Adele Cooke, John Cirilli, Gary Eller, Dennis Cripe, Diane Raines, Max Aguilera-Hellweg, Jim Garlits, Joe Jansen, the recently deceased Ben Pesta, late Fraser Drew, Maryruth Glogowski, Muriel A. Howard, and many more friends have been in my corner ever since I tackled hazing four decades ago as my area of expertise. My students and former students over the years have been supportive, none more so than James Garlits, Cody Federmann, and Shelby Mullis.

I thank the library staffs at Cornell University, Indiana University, Ball State University, the History Center in Tompkins County (Ithaca, New York), and, especially, Franklin College for assistance with reference questions.

I am grateful to Buffalo State College's Butler Library archivist Dan DiLandro and special collections staff for housing the Hank Nuwer Hazing Collection to provide research materials for current and future scholars. The Hank Nuwer Collection has celebrated its twentieth anniversary.

In addition to the authors and hazing experts included in this volume whom I counted on for advice and criticism, I have received longtime loyalty from school safety and hazing experts educator Chad Ellsworth; NFHS executive Elliot Hopkins; NCAA hazing expert Mary Wilfert; HazingPrevention .Org executives Emily Pualwan, Michael Gordon, Gretchen Barton, and Lenny Sancilio; the StopHazing.org team; and campus security authority S. Daniel Carter. I also received support over the years from many parents of students killed in hazing incidents, and I am particularly indebted to Lianne and Brian Kowiak, Eileen Stevens, and Julie DeVercelly of the Clery Center for Security on Campus. Other antihazing activists to thank include Alice Haben, Maisie Ballou, Edith Heideman, Ruth Harten, Valerie Bisanz, Charles Eberly, Rita Saucier, Debbie Smith, George Starks, Kelly Henson, Jerry Meredith, William Henson, Andy Robison, David Bianchi, Diane Dhanen, Brian Rahill, Fran Becque, and Julia and Scott Starkey.

Finally, I am indebted to my wife, Gosia Wroblewska-Nuwer, for her patience when I needed time to work on this volume in our Indiana and Warsaw, Poland, residences. I also wish to thank editors Peggy Solic, Ashley Runyon, Mary Jo Rhodes, Jamie Armstrong, and David Hulsey for being one email away if I had questions or they had suggestions to make this book better.

Thank you, all.

Credits

CHAPTERS 1, 3–10, and the Debbie Smith portion of chapters 12–19, 21, 23, 25, and 26 were commissioned for this book and are appearing in print for the first time.

Hank Nuwer's review of the Joe Bisanz cold case (chapter 22) was originally published as "Why Did Joe Die," *Nuvo Newsweekly* 11, no. 13 (2000): 1, 14–16.

James F. Keenan's essay (chapter 20) was reprinted from Keenan's *University Ethics: How Colleges Can Build and Benefit from a Culture of Ethics* (Lanham, Maryland: Rowman and Littlefield, 2015), 105–112.

David M. Hovde's Purdue Tank Scrap article (chapter 24) was originally published as "A Manly Spectacle: Purdue University's Tank Scrap," in *Traces of Indiana and Midwestern History* 26.1 (Winter 2014): 14–25.

Sections of chapter 27 appeared in Hank Nuwer, *Broken Pledges* (Atlanta: Longstreet Press, 1990), 201–206.

The Stacey Kennelly section of chapter 12 first appeared as "In the Basement No One Can Hear You Scream," *Diablo Magazine*, 36, 8 (August 4, 2015): 50–53, 110.

Chapter 2 first appeared in Hank Nuwer, "Hazing in Fraternities and Sororities," in *International Encyclopedia of the Social & Behavioral Sciences*, 2nd ed., vol. 10, ed. James D. Wright, 554–561, (Oxford: Elsevier, 2015).

Chapter 11 is excerpted from a much longer version published as "Warriors, Machismo, and Jockstraps: Sexually Exploitative Athletic Hazing and Title IX in the Public School Locker Room," *Western New England Law Review* 35, no. 2 (2013): 377–423.

HAZING

Introduction

The Perils of Hazing, a Few Thoughts on Forty Years of Writing about Hazing

Hank Nuwer

REVISING YET ANOTHER volume on hazing has been a challenging undertaking made all the more fulfilling for me as I worked with this book's team of Indiana University Press editors and contributors that include the nation's best-known academics on hazing, hazing legal experts, Greek and student affairs professionals, and antihazing activists. A new volume dedicated to hazing research and prevention was necessary because hazing behaviors themselves have changed so dramatically in the last decade.

Having written about hazing ever since 1978 with an investigative journalism piece back then on hazing deaths for *Human Behavior*, I have watched attitudes toward the practice change with the times. In 1978 academics scoffed at the idea that hazing behaviors and practices were a matter of worthwhile academic research. This was part of a long-standing pattern. Back then, even more so than today, faculty, staff, and administrators turned their heads away from hazing humiliations and tragedies. One need only look at campus yearbooks through the first three quarters of the twentieth century to see hazing treated by students as a lark instead of as a degrading, and occasionally dangerous, affront to civility.

At present a generation of new scholars is completing graduate theses and dissertations on hazing in numbers unheard of back in 1978. During the Jimmy Carter administration, quality hazing scholarship predominately existed in abnormal psychology journals, but today it is an expertise, even a passion, for researchers in gender studies, minority studies, law enforcement, folklore, education, psychology, behavior studies, sociology, literary journalism, and on and on. Buffalo State College's Butler Library Special Collections decision to create the Hazing Collection, stocked with scholarly works in part by me, offers a sanctuary for visiting researchers intent on finding new ways to counter hazing around the world.

What has changed is that some of the most demeaning hazing incidents now occur in sports teams, particularly at the secondary-school level. While collegiate deaths from hazing in the United States are as common today as they were forty to forty-eight years ago, there now occur similar tragic losses worldwide, particularly in the Philippines and India. Back in 1978, there existed one antihazing organization; today several well-known organizations and untold thousands of people battle hazing all year and many, many thousands more observe National Hazing Prevention Week. HazingPrevention.Org, StopHazing.org, the Clery Center for Security on Campus, the AHA! (Antihazing) Movement, 32 National Campus Safety Initiative, and smaller antihazing groups dedicate resources and time to eradicating hazing.

What also has changed is that researchers and reporters have made the public aware that hazing happens, not just in fraternities and the military, but in bands, sports teams, occupations, honor societies, church groups, camps, and even professional and honor societies. Hazing has become what I called on National Public Radio an "equal opportunity disgrace," prevalent among whites, blacks, Asians, and brown-skinned people.

What has not changed is that despite full awareness, Greek hazing continues to be an odious form of abuse—a type that I call "domestic abuse" because it occurs in a fraternity or sorority house. Such cult-like abuse targets pledges and associate members without status of full membership that live in a single chapter household. What has not changed is that the deaths from hazing have continued unabated. There now has been one death every year (and many years multiple deaths) in our colleges from hazing in the 1961–2017 time frame, according to the verifiable statistics I keep. These continuing deaths, but also less-publicized indignities and scurrilous conduct during hazing incidents, have spurred me on to recruit an impressive team of essayists contributing to this anthology.

In addition, I see other bright lighthouses now erected on the formerly dark, wave-tossed shores. Where once fraternity and sorority hazing practices seemed to continue unchecked, there now is a buy-in from nearly all national and international Greek organizations to stamp out this "Weed in the Garden of Academe," as hazing was called in 1866.[1] Unfortunately, many of their chapters lack all their admirable resolve and continue to haze. The dry house initiatives of Phi Delta Theta and numerous sororities have shown them to be a viable strategy to keep houses safer. Out of necessity, Sigma Alpha Epsilon has ended pledging after numerous hazing and post-party deaths had inspired *Bloomberg News* to label the organization America's Deadliest Fraternity.

Reporters once in a while ask about my personal experience with hazing. My own experience being hazed and hazing others in a fraternity was minimal in comparison with all the deadly incidents that I chronicle. What has motivated me was a tragedy at the University of Nevada, Reno. I was a bystander at two alcohol-inflamed initiations put on by a then-suspended student club for athletes called the Sundowners; one hazing was on campus and one was at a college bar hangout. True, I stepped up as a bystander at the bar and successfully requested Sundowner acquaintances to walk an intoxicated, frothing pledge outside until he sobered up, but I did not call 911, although fortunately the lucky hazee survived. Because that near death went unpunished by school authorities who had no knowledge of it, the Sundowners in October of 1975 felt entitled to perform a third senseless initiation (that I did not witness). Wolfpack football player John Davies died of an alcohol overdose in the back of the pickup where he'd been tossed, unconscious, with other pledges. That single death led to the greater part of my life given over to researching and writing about hazing behaviors.

The Death of Harrison Kowiak

Flash forward to the present. A letter given to me one year ago has been a driving inspiration for me to finish this book. The letter was written to Brian and Lianne Kowiak after their son perished with a head injury following physical hazing by the Theta Chi chapter at Lenoir-Rhyne University. To me, the contents of the letter should be enough to stop every Greek, athlete, or band member from hazing, as well as to assure those committed to ending hazing to know that they are doing the right thing. Their son was a golfer, abstainer from drugs and alcohol, and in perfect shape when the chapter's senior members piled on him during a traditional hazing ritual in darkness, and then failed to immediately call 911 as Harrison lay dying of a massive blow to the head.

> Dear Mr. and Mrs. Kowiak:
>
> Please allow me to extend my sincere sympathy to you in the loss of your son at Carolinas Medical Center. Your willingness to consider the needs of others at a time when your own grief was so great will always serve as a special tribute to Harrison.
>
> I wanted to share with you the outcome of your generous gift with the hope that this information can bring some comfort to you.
>
> His liver and one of his kidneys went to a sixty-five-year-old man from South Carolina who is married and has one adult son. He is a minister who loves to travel, read Biblical history, study Civil War history, and collect stamps. He also enjoys art and politics. He has a doctorate in the ministry and was working until he became too ill. His transplant center reports that he had excellent function in his transplanted organs.
>
> His other kidney and his pancreas went to a forty-nine-year-old married father of one from North Carolina. He had been on dialysis for a year and a half. He is an engineer who enjoys shooting, skiing, and golfing. His transplant center reports that his organ function is good.
>
> [Harrison's] heart was transplanted into a thirty-nine-year-old married man who is also from North Carolina. Prior to becoming ill, he was a truck driver. He enjoyed his work and hopes to return to it. He enjoys watching sports. . . .

Both lungs went to a seventeen-year-old girl in Missouri. She is in high school and enjoys spending time with her new friends. She lives with her grandparents and her mother. Her new lungs functioned well immediately and she is currently recovering at home. She looks forward to just being a "normal teen." She and her family are so grateful for the gift given to them.

One of his corneas enabled a twenty-two-year-old man in Mexico to see and the other one gave the gift of sight to a twenty-nine-year-old woman who lives in the mountains of North Carolina.

You also graciously consented to tissue donation. We were able to recover tissue, and numerous lives will be enhanced as a result. . . .

Mr. and Mrs. Kowiak, your generosity has touched so many lives. What an incredible blessing Harrison has been and continues to be in the lives of these recipients. What an amazing family you are to have said yes to donation.

The letter was signed by a "Lifeshare of the Carolinas" family support coordinator. As this book appears, I can predict that from all the research and evidence that school hazing deaths will not end in my lifetime. I can, however, hope that hazing will end before the last recipients of Harrison's precious body are buried in graves of their own with his organs.

With the much-publicized, horrific death of Tim Piazza at Penn State's Beta Theta Pi house because of injuries related to hazing and alcohol abuse, I am convinced a new anthology is needed by students, their parents, their educators, and their coaches.

The collaborators in this volume include two researchers whose interviews with Greek hazers and hazees in African American Greek groups pulled curtains open on the topic. Among the scholars in the volume are Elizabeth Allan of the University of Maine and Norm Pollard of Alfred University, the authors of important surveys and studies on hazing in our schools. Legal experts (Chloe Neely, Douglas Fierberg, Connie McGlone, R. Brian Crow, and Susan P. Stuart) have written essays on hazing laws and Title IX. Also in these pages are leading student life and faculty practitioners Tracy Maxwell, Robert (Bob) Biggs, David Westol, Ashley Stone, Allison Swick-Duttine, Ray Begovich, Travis Apgar, Gina Lee-Olukoya, Malinda Matney, and Morgan B. Kinney. You'll read the cautionary stories about young men who have died at Cornell University, Purdue, Indiana University, and Plattsburgh State. Finally, you'll hear in their own words why a student who tried to change a hazing culture was battered mercilessly online by alumni and fellow students, as well as a firsthand account of a mother's loss by activist Debbie Smith, mother of the late Chico State pledge Matt Carrington.

In addition, Peter Lake and Michael Kimmel have consented to interviews related to their well-known books in the areas of law and human behavior.

HANK NUWER is a professor in the Franklin College Pulliam School of Journalism. He has written *The Hazing Reader* (IUP) and *Wrongs of Passage: Fraternities, Sororities, Hazing, and Binge Drinking* (IUP).

1 Dead to Rites

The Chlorine Poisoning of Henrietta Jackson

Hank Nuwer

CORNELL UNIVERSITY SPONSORED a gala inauguration for President Jacob G. Schurman on November 11, 1892. The faculty and students applauded and stomped the floor as Schurman said, "It is my desire and prayer that Cornell University may go on to evolve a more perfect type of manhood—a manhood which, shuffling off the animal core and fulfilling the divine idea of man, shall attain to a sense of honor that feels a stain like a wound, to an integrity that will not palter with the truth."[1]

Fifteen months later, a Cornell student, in collusion with other confidantes, killed an innocent woman in a hazing incident. Here is the story of that death.

The evening of February 20, 1894, brought fair weather for Cornell's Class of 1897 freshman banquet. Hazing in the form of kidnappings and battle royals between first- and second-year class members had plagued Cornell on banquet night for years, including an 1882 incident that saw five expelled and forty disciplined. First-year class officers endured hair shaving, body painting, and abandonment in the countryside. Fraternities and sororities hazed back then also, but never with the brutality and mean-spiritedness of sophomores on the prowl.

As darkness fell, sophomores from the Class of 1896 stormed the entrance to the Masonic Block building in Ithaca, New York. The Class of '97 repelled their charge with the aid of junior class bodyguards.[2] However, one member of the sophomore class had scuttled into the Masonic Block much earlier and plotted to ambush freshman attendees.

The event began on the fourth floor in the banquet hall with toasts by the freshmen officers. A kitchen adjacent to the hall was used for food preparation. The Lyceum Theater orchestra played "Yankee Doodle Dandy" and "The Freshman Battle Hymn" to the tune of "John Brown's Body." So many students packed the banquet hall that waiters had trouble scooting by with trays. A photographer's popping flashbulbs captured the event. Cornell's carnelian red and white dominated the decorations, but the occasion also saw plenty of lavender and purple crepe, the class colors.

Henrietta Jackson, a sturdy African American cook, stood shoulder-to-shoulder with a white cook in the massive kitchen adjacent to the banquet hall. They labored to prepare the menu: blue point oysters, a bouillon soup, filet of beef smothered with champignon mushrooms, potato croquets, escalloped apples, and lobster salad. The sophomore prankster huddled in an empty office on the third floor. Days earlier the conspirators had staked out the Masonic Block and calculated that this room was situated beneath the banquet hall. The plan was to pump raw chlorine into the celebration to send revelers scattering. During a rehearsal, one of the plotters had drilled two holes in the ceiling with an augur.

That afternoon the perpetrator barricaded the flat's door with a store-bought brace, a cleat, new screws, and a wooden board.

A little after 11:00 p.m., the perpetrator connected rubber and glass tubes to two empty dark-colored jars that once had stored soda-fountain syrup. The jars contained chlorine made with commercial potash and other ingredients found in any mercantile store. He pumped the chlorine into the room above. Confused shouts erupted when the vapors spread. The raider, assuming the chaos signified choking freshmen, escaped through a window, knocking puffs of snow off the sill. So little snow was knocked off, according to an investigating Ithaca police officer, that it was likely one person had committed the act. Light snow coated the alley ground. He obliterated his footprints, with or without the help of conspirators, and bolted like a thief in the night. However, the amateur criminal left behind paraphernalia that later served as evidence. The potash package, purchased from a local merchant, bore the store's name handwritten in ink. The perpetrator also had abandoned a shipping box from a New York merchant labeled with the address of "6 Cook Street," likely his own boardinghouse.

If the prankster had removed the labels, he would have left no clues.

The Pranksters' Misjudgment

The conspirators had miscalculated. Instead the tubes went into the kitchen, where waiters loaded trays with lobster salad,[3] and poked out the floorboards beneath a wood-burning stove. Had the gas entered the packed hall as intended, it would have sickened many freshmen. The toxic gas would have caused instant coughing, suffocating, and, likely, a mass panic. A reporter wrote that students would have gotten trampled at the exits.[4]

What happened was bad enough.

The menacing gas overtook the kitchen workers. Several were students from Cornell hired by the caterer for the night. Others were regular employees of the caterer. A few were moonlighting Ithaca blue-collar helpers.

A server named John from Utica, New York, gasped for air. "I have got to get out of the room," he complained, wheezing. The white cook started gasping and said, "I can't stand this." Waiter Samuel Hutchings was overcome by the gas and could not breathe. It was a sensation that continued the next day after he had passed out at home. "It felt as if I were being choked," he reported.

Quick action kept a bad situation from getting worse. Someone shut the doors leading into the banquet hall. Consequently, no freshman was gassed, although the *New York Times* reported incorrectly that some had been. Upperclassmen E. A. Ladd and Thomas McNeil III, who were serving as sentries, raced into the kitchen to render assistance but were overcome. (McNeil, once an outstanding athlete, suffered respiratory issues after the chlorine incident and died eleven years later). Someone misdiagnosed the problem as a malfunctioning stove and doused the fire with water. Two men grabbed cloth rags to avoid scalding their hands and tossed the stove reservoir out the window.

Many workers fled. One stumbled into a hallway and was helped downstairs. A drugstore adjacent to the Masonic Block was open, and some of the stricken were helped inside. Others stayed in the room to assist gasping, falling-down workers who felt disoriented and were vomiting. Workers opened the windows to inhale chilly winter air. One student worker passed out as he draped his body over the sill, but fortunately he fell onto the floor instead of pitching to the ground. A worker who recognized the scent of chlorine purchased a vial of ammonia at the open store and raced back into the kitchen prepared to revive any passed-out workers.

Pandemonium in the Kitchen

Henrietta Jackson wheezed. The cook had been working alongside the stove longer than anyone, including her daughter Mary Matilda Jackson on the opposite side of the kitchen. Mary had been minimally affected, but her mother was prone to chlorine sensitivity. The savior with the ammonia pressed some to the cook's lips with a handkerchief to revive her.

Warren Kenyon, by day a clerk at Platt & Colt's Pharmacy, was on cleanup duties in the kitchen when the gas poisoned the air. He thought that a skunk had gotten into the building. Miss Jackson shouted that her mother needed assistance. Although he himself could barely breathe, Kenyon staggered to assist Mrs. Jackson down the stairs. They fell and other rescuers took her by the arms and led her to the street. "She seemed to be very still and quiet," said Kenyon. "[Mrs. Jackson] walked right along quiet, and apparently had her eyes shut, I thought."

Once outside, the victims took heaving gasps of air, but Mrs. Jackson found it impossible to breathe. While the Cornell Class of '97 remained in the hall and toasted one another with Roman punch, Mrs. Jackson's bleached lungs failed her. The cook's daughter went back inside the Masonic building to retrieve her belongings. A rescuer took the stumbling Mrs. Jackson to Dr. Walter Lockerby's home office at 26 East Seneca Street. The physician and surgeon was an ear, nose, and throat specialist.

The time was close to midnight. Dr. Lockerby answered the doorbell and let the two inside. Mrs. Jackson collapsed in the chair nearest to the door and asked for water. He fetched a glass as the rescuer explained how the cook had come to be in this condition. Her suffering was immense, and the reddish color to her cheeks signified that her brain and heart were oxygen-deprived. Her breath emitted the distinctive odor of chlorine that the physician used to sanitize his office. Mrs. Jackson managed to take swallows of water. Dr. Lockerby snatched her arm. Her pulse was imperceptible. She clearly was asphyxiating. Her shallow breaths made it apparent that she was at the point of death, and the man who had brought her here for help now hurried to get Mrs. Jackson's daughter.

The physician assembled a teaspoon of digitalis squills, glycerin, and water in hopes of helping her heart work. When that treatment failed, he tried to force ammonia spirits into her. The doctor's wife, Edith, scrambled out of bed to offer assistance. Mrs. Jackson's body relaxed, and the victim sank back into the chair. A puddle of urine leaked onto the floor. Mrs. Jackson's death occurred a mere five minutes after she had entered the house. Dr. Lockerby and his wife dragged the cook out of the chair and placed her body flat on the floor to try to revive her. Mary Matilda Jackson arrived and saw her mother's corpse. She ran to summon her father, William.

After the gas subsided, kitchen workers returned to the scene while the banquet still reigned, there to be interviewed by Ithaca night sergeant John Edgar Clapp. Clapp was a retired professional baseball catcher. He had informed police in 1881 that a gambler had offered him a bribe to throw a game, earning his moniker "Honest John."

The next morning, Clapp and a second officer traced the tubes from the kitchen to the source. With the door's room barricaded, they had to gain entry by smashing a hole in a door panel. They found the boxes with identifying labels and some tin wires hidden in a long stove used to heat flatirons. The jugs, brace, and a bit were stashed behind a sign and covered with abandoned clothing.

Newspapers Blame the Victim

The cook was survived by Mary, William, and her elderly mother. Mrs. Jackson had been the family breadwinner. Media coverage the day after the attack embarrassed Cornell's administrators. President Schurman promised that the instigators would be punished. Editors disparaged the institution as nothing more than a trove of ruffians, murderers, and cowards. The initial newspaper coverage, edited in the wee hours, was dismal journalism. The *Ithaca Daily Journal* mistakenly reported that daughter Mary Matilda Jackson, not Henrietta Jackson, had been killed. Newspapers as far away as Missouri incorrectly announced that student worker Thomas McNeil had died.

In a day the Ithaca papers correctly identified Mrs. Henrietta Jackson as the deceased victim. An Ithaca newspaper printed a brief correction acknowledging that McNeil and the other student were alive and recovering. However, much coverage was unfavorable and disenfranchised Mrs. Jackson. Papers described her as an overweight, elderly "colored woman" with a bad heart. They printed rumors she had been in ill health. One of the most disturbing aspects about Jackson affair is that out of thousands of news stories, few, if any, reporters interviewed the cook's surviving husband and daughter. Instead of afflicting the comfortable, journalists censured the aggrieved family, rarely taking their side.

Because Mrs. Jackson's death was a homicide, a coroner's jury was empowered to find the individuals responsible. In charge was J. Watson Brown, MD, a local physician who had been elected Tompkins County coroner in 1892. The grand jury was charged with determining if murder charges could be brought against the person or persons whose "act evinced [a] depraved mind, regardless of human life."[5]

An autopsy destroyed the *Ithaca Daily Journal*'s speculations about the victim's age and health. Dr. Martin Besemer, who performed the postmortem examination, swore to the inquisition that Mrs. Jackson was extraordinarily healthy and had the internal organs of a much younger woman. She was only fifty-three years old, not elderly. He found no sign of disease, which he testified to in the inquiry conducted by the coroner's jury foreman D. F. van Vleet, Esq., a Cornell alumnus, Chi Psi fraternity alumnus, and Democratic Party leader.

The only sign of aging at all was in the left lung where the doctor found "a slight degree [an inch in diameter] of some calcareous matter."

"Was that deposit sufficient to have caused death?" asked van Vleet.

"No, not sufficient probably," said the doctor. The lungs did show evidence of congestion that "could have been" due to the chlorine, however. He went on to say that either smoke from the stove or an irritant gas caused her death. Jackson's lungs had filled with clotted blood.

"The heart was an extraordinary specimen . . . for a woman of that age?" inquired van Vleet.

"That is the conclusion we came to," Dr. Besemer said.[6]

A handful of Cornell class officers took up a collection and purchased an Ithaca City Cemetery grave marker for Mrs. Jackson. A funeral was held on February 24, 1894, at the M. E. Zion Church. Pastor J. H. Callis denounced the killing by individuals making sport at the expense of others.[7] Many Cornell students attended the funeral. Seating was standing room only.

Testimony at the Inquest

Witness Edwin Gillett, a clerk at C. J. Rumsey & Company hardware dealers, revealed an important piece of testimony at the inquisition: "A young man, clean face I should say, about seventeen to eighteen," had walked into the store to purchase an augur for boring holes. He came back and talked to another clerk, saying it was too short at about six inches, and he wanted to trade for a longer one. Gillett told the inquiry that he wasn't sure if he would be able to identify the purchaser.

The inquiry called Hiram Haskins, a druggist at 6 East State Street in Ithaca, and showed him some wrapping paper in a package bearing that address. He did not know who had purchased the package but was certain it contained a half-pound of potassium permanganate, which was an antiseptic and disinfectant used to make chlorine. He described the buyer as short, maybe five-foot tall or a little taller, and around thirty in age, a dozen years or more older than the average sophomore. Nonetheless, he had reckoned this man of mystery to be a student. The two had a conversation about making chlorine. Haskins also recalled selling customers rubber tubing in recent weeks but added that as it is a supply that is purchased every day, he could not identify who had poisoned Mrs. Jackson.

The jury interviewed Charles F. van Houten, a tailor who worked in a suite opposite the office where the gas had been released. He said several young men had been running in and out of that room for a week. Although they had made a slight commotion, he hadn't confronted them. He convinced the jury this had been no operation of a single rogue, but rather a confederation of rogues. He testified that he heard no sound in that room the day of the banquet. The perpetrator had operated with stealth. This was a planned ambush with malice aforethought, not a spontaneous act of hazing.

The jury also conducted interviews with sophomore class members, but all of that testimony went nowhere. Most testified that they were nowhere near the Masonic Block that fateful night and were questioned no longer.

The coroner summoned six students who lived at the 6 Cook Street boardinghouse. Local newspapers had named sophomore roommates Carl L. Dingens of Buffalo and Frederick L. Taylor of Plainfield, New Jersey. Suspicion arose when the coroner was unable to locate them. A Cornell probationary student who lived at the Cook Street boardinghouse testified that Dingens was absent from the house for two days. Taylor turned out to be spending time avoiding reporters at his fraternity house instead of studying in his studio.

Based on testimony and investigations by Ithaca police, a list of suspects was put together by prosecutor J. H. Jennings. All evidence was circumstantial. Not one witness admitted seeing anyone suspicious in the Masonic Block on the day in question. Prime suspect Carl Louis Dingens was the son of Joseph Dingens, a Buffalo, New York, merchant known for his marketing skills. The father published and sold his own *Cosmopolitan Cook and Recipe Book* and hawked mixed drinks sold in fancy bottles, such as Persimmon's Rye, Magnolia Rye, and a drink named after Napoleon. His company sold the finest coffees in the world, or so his brochure boasted. Together with his brother, Joseph ran the Dingens Brothers store at 333 Main Street in Buffalo, peddling wine, liquors, cigars, mineral waters, and food products.

When Joseph was a boy, he stood outside his boyhood home in Buffalo across from the Phoenix Hotel and recalled watching his Catholic father, John Dingens, founder of the family's business, drive by him in a carriage pulled by six white horses. Seated with his father was the Irish clergyman John Timon, who had been appointed the first bishop of Buffalo in 1847 after Pope Pius IX named Western New York State a diocese.[8] The wealthy Joseph Dingens owned a 2,700-square-foot, five-bedroom house with three bathrooms on Buffalo's fashionable Park Street. Dingens also owned a weekend and vacation home on nearby Grand Island. The vacation house was nicknamed Red Top. It was two-and-a-half stories tall and topped by dormers to allow for more space in the upper loft. A photo taken in 1888 shows the family and guests enjoying an outing.[9] In evidence are an old-fashioned, tall-wheeled bicycle, tennis rackets, boat oars, and a banjo. The family, including Carl and his four sisters, enjoyed weekend excursions on the steamer *Periwinkle*. The elder Dingens loved to journal and kept extensive notes about events in his life, such as walks with his son Carl. In one 1885 entry, Dingens avowed how his son and he had passed a farm and witnessed a two-headed calf, which Joseph illustrated with a doodle.[10]

Most Sunday mornings found the family seated in their pew in Buffalo's majestic St. Louis Church, founded in 1829, the oldest Catholic house of worship in Western New York. "Buffalo has always known a Dingens among its foremost citizens," a Catholic newspaper declared.[11]

Carl Louis Dingens at Cornell

Young Dingens was a member of the fledgling Cornell society Scalp and Blade, made up entirely of Western New Yorkers with Buffalo ties. He participated in Cornell athletic contests, although not in intercollegiate competition.

By February 24, 1894, reporters for the *Buffalo Evening News* had camped outside the Dingens home on Park Street. A daughter who answered the door said her brother had been in Buffalo a few hours earlier, but an uncle denied that he had been home.[12] He *had* been home, Carl Dingens confirmed in testimony at an inquest. The uncle had been misinformed or lied to a reporter.

Two days later a reporter talked to Frederick Taylor and reported that Carl Dingens was off to Syracuse, New York, by train to meet one of his four sisters. Another morning newspaper corralled Eugenia Dingens, Carl's sister, for an interview, and Miss Dingens, known locally in Buffalo for her skills in community theater, repeated the story that her brother was visiting an invalid sister. However, the Ithaca paper declared that young Carl "by his continued absence from the city is being reported as being implicated in the affair." It carried a report that Dingens's father had been in Ithaca, and that the police had searched the young man's quarters but found him absent. Eugenia Dingens vowed to a reporter that her brother "would return directly to Ithaca, explain his absence, and prove that he had no hand in the affair."[13]

The story about visiting his sister was a tale Dingens later denied under oath was true, saying he had gone to Syracuse for his own medical care.[14]

Around that time, three students were placed in custody for failing to cooperate. They were Dingens, C. H. Mitchell of New York City, and Charles B. Gorby of Pittsburgh.[15] Two other students—Frederick Taylor, a Phi Kappa Psi fraternity member and glee club singer, and Earl Stimson, an aspiring railroad engineer—had cooperated with authorities to a point. These were the five persons of interest named in the press. An additional two conspirators were described by physical appearance but not identified or known by name. This was a blue-blooded wall of silence made of brick and mortar.

Mitchell was not a Cornell student. He was enrolled at a preparatory and remedial school founded by 1891 Cornell graduate Charles A. Stiles. Mitchell had arrived from New York City on January 24, three weeks prior to the banquet. He refused to answer the jury's inquiry about whether he had been in the Masonic Block's main hall at the time of the poisoning, but he admitted acquaintanceship with Dingens, Taylor, and Gorby. He conceded to knowing the dry-goods company of New York, James McCreary & Co., whose wrapping paper was found on the abandoned clothing box (with Mitchell's name and initials and address) in the Masonic Block:

MITCHELL: I know that firm very well, but to my knowledge I never saw that paper before.

FOREMAN (*PRESSING*): Have you recently had a package from New York [that] contained a paper of that description?

MITCHELL: I refuse to answer.

FOREMAN: On what ground(s)?

MITCHELL: On the advice of counsel.

FOREMAN: Do you know who took that [McCreary] paper from your room?

MITCHELL: No, sir.

The foreman, D. F. van Vleet, reminded Mitchell that he had given *Ithaca Daily Journal* reporter William Armstrong (who also was a coroner's grand jury voting member despite the conflict of interest) a preliminary statement that he had received the package from McCreary & Co. Mitchell was on shaky grounds if he perjured himself. The foreman attacked Mitchell with a barrage of questions, but the witness answered with the same refusal to out the perpetrators and to reveal their involvement.

The Testimony of Charles B. Gorby

Charles B. Gorby stated before the coroner's jury that he was a sophomore in the Class of 1896, had studied chemistry as a mechanical engineering major, and lived at 27 William Street, less than a half mile from Dingens and Taylor. He, too, refused to answer questions about how the chlorine entered the Masonic Block kitchen. He declined to say why he refused, not wanting to claim the Fifth Amendment fully and say anything about incriminating himself. To claim self-incrimination was to tell the public you were guilty.

FOREMAN: Are you acquainted with Mr. Dingens?

GORBY: I am.

FOREMAN: Have you been frequently to his room?

GORBY: I should say so.

Pressed whether he had conferred with Dingens or Taylor the week before the banquet, Gorby refused to answer.

The *New York Times* reported on February 23 that Dingens was on the lam, and the paper convicted him in the press. "His action in remaining away from the scene of the investigation makes the finger of suspicion point toward him as one of the guilty parties."[16]

On several occasions, reporters claimed that at least one unnamed "guilty student" was ready to confess, but pressure from the other suspects had thus far kept him from coming forward.[17]

Another person of strong interest, Earl Stimson, gave his testimony to foreman van Vleet on March 1, 1894, at 2:00 p.m. He acknowledged that he was a sophomore and a neighbor of Dingens, boarding with a Mrs. Crozier at 7 Cook Street, the house where it was established that two unidentified young men (one with a sandy moustache) bearing extract jugs had shown up weeks before the chlorine incident.

Stimson refused "on advice of counsel" to share any facts that might "throw any light" on the criminal act at the freshman banquet. He refused to say whether it was on grounds that any statement might incriminate him. He said he was obeying instructions from counsel (likely paid for by Joseph Dingens or possibly his son, Carl).

Stimson said that Carl Dingens and he had known each other since each had started studies at Cornell. He had been downtown while the banquet transpired, but he swore under oath that he had not been in the Masonic Block that fatal day. He refused to answer whether he had discussed ways and means of breaking up the freshman banquet. He refused to answer the follow-up questions posed by the district attorney.

On April 24, Earl Stimson boarded a train in Ithaca that shut down for an emergency stop. Ithaca sheriff Charles S. Seaman was on the train and asked if Stimson could assist a Cornell junior named James Harry Root. After realizing he was on the wrong train, Root leaped off while the train was going thirty miles per hour. His coat caught on a car step, and he was swept under the wheels, ripping off one leg and most of another. Stimson rushed to the hospital with Root, sitting at his bedside until the victim died. After Root's mother and sister came to the hospital, Stimson comforted them as well.

False Coverage

Early newspaper coverage of the "Jackson Affair," as journalists termed the death of "the colored woman," misled readers into thinking fresh news about a confession soon would break. Armstrong reported that Coroner Brown had "informed a reporter that he had discovered what he deemed important clues, which would undoubtedly sooner or later reveal the identities of the parties mixed up in the affair."

An Ithaca newspaper paraded this snapper of a headline on February 28: "Confession Coming: One of the Cornell students will make a clean breast." In a poorly sourced article, the anonymous reporter concluded that the "public awaits with the deepest anxiety the promised disclosure of the manly student who stated it was his intention to make such a disclosure."[18]

Seeking additional sources, Armstrong quoted Professor Charles A. Collin of the Cornell Law School who had opined to his classroom of third-year students that the individual or individuals who had caused Henrietta Jackson's death showed a "depraved mind" as evidenced by the deadly ensuing actions. However, given that the chlorine death of Mrs. Jackson was an unintended consequence, Collin told his law class he thought the offense might prove eventually to be ruled an involuntary homicide, which was of lesser consequence for the perpetrators. Even so, it likely would be a felony conviction and a mandatory prison stretch.

In a related story that day coming out of the capital, the *Cornell Daily Sun* quoted New York Senator Henry J. Coggeshall of Utica as saying Cornell's administration and students appeared to want the "criminal outrage" to simply go away. He said, "I shall watch the matter closely and if such a disposition

continues and no convictions are made, I will introduce a resolution in the legislature for an investigation of a wide scope with power to engage expert detectives
and counsel. It is time these outrages termed 'fun' cease, and in any event I shall
try to amend the penal code by providing a heavy penalty for any kind of hazing."[19] (In reality, despite such bluster, New York's hazing code remained weak
until challenged by Eileen Stevens, the mother of an Alfred University hazing
victim, in 1978).

Predictably, the faculty of Cornell condemned the death of Henrietta Jackson but maintained the matter was to be investigated by officers of the law, not
by professors and deans. As is true of collegiate hazing cases to the present day,
the faculty declared that any known offenders additionally could face the institution's justice if convicted in a court of law. Cornell President Schurman attended
most hearings of the coroner's jury but had no comment for reporters.

The *Ithaca Daily Journal* noted that the disgrace had offended the sensibili-
ties of alumni who worried their Cornell degree might be cheapened by scandal.
"It is my earnest hope that the perpetrators of this stain on the good name of the
university may be brought to speedy and stern justice and that the full extent of
the law be meted out to them," wrote one alum. "To name a punishment severe
enough seems almost beyond me at the moment, but had the injured ones been
relatives, the horror felt at the affair by alumni in this city . . . is greater than
words can express. We hope that no stone will be left unturned to discover and
punish the guilty parties. The reputation of all those who are and have been connected with the institution is at stake in the matter."

The Coroner's Inquiry Stalls

On March 1 the coroner's jury played hardball. With Carl Dingens absent, the
jury tried squeezing the truth out of Frederick Taylor, his roommate. Taylor
had perplexed and perhaps angered the coroner's jury when he had refused to
acknowledge that Dingens and he shared living space. "I refuse to answer, by
advice of my counsel," Taylor had said.[20]

In the midst of questioning, counsel interrupted van Vleet's interrogation.
"At this point, gentlemen, we represent this young man, together with several
others. This is the only tribunal known to the law, where a person even suspected
of a crime can be forced to go upon the stand," challenged Myron M. Tompkins.
"You can put him upon the stand in your investigation, but you cannot compel
him to answer, and we take the responsibility of advising this gentleman to put
himself upon his privilege, which is laid (sic) down in the court of appeals, that
he has the right to . . . refuse to answer any further questions."

The coroner confronted Tompkins, together with Frank M. Leary, the local
legal representation for Taylor and several other students. Tompkins refused to

bend, telling the coroner that his client could not be compelled to testify because of his constitutional rights.

Coroner Brown demanded clarification from Taylor: "Do you refuse to answer because it will [in]criminate you?"

When Tompkins ordered his client to stay silent, van Vleet, the foreman of the jury, insisted the lawyer and the press had no right being in the room for Taylor's questioning. Brown agreed, tossing Tompkins and all reporters out of room.[21] Armstrong, doing double duty as reporter and coroner's jury member, stayed put. The impatient van Vleet, by tossing Taylor's counsel out of the hearing, may have set up the outcome for a future appeal that took all the suspects off the hook.

Dingens on the Stand

Carl Dingens returned to his boardinghouse and at last responded to his subpoena from the coroner. Foreman van Vleet began his interrogation with simple questions, to which the witness gave short responses. His major was electrical engineering, a popular one at the time as work on hydroelectric plants flourished in Buffalo, soon to be nicknamed the "City of Light." He admitted to having taking chemistry. He admitted that he had been in Buffalo on February 22 at the request of his mother. Instead of traveling to Syracuse to meet an ill sister as Taylor had told a reporter, Dingens testified that he had been seeking medical treatment from his family doctor. He said his counsel was Tompkins & Leary.

The questions from the foreman became more pointed and Dingens parried them. He refused to say whether he had made certain purchases from stores such as Platt & Colt.

Pressed, Dingens acknowledged that his father had been in Ithaca as recently as the previous day. He himself first heard "that this colored woman was dead" at about 7:00 a.m. on Wednesday, February 21.

VAN VLEET: Were you one of the parties that helped to manufacture the gas, which was forced into the banquet hall of the freshman class?

DINGENS: I refuse to answer your question.

VAN VLEET: Upon the ground that it would tend to [in]criminate you?

DINGENS: It might tend to [in]criminate me.

The foreman dismissed Dingens.

Official Cause of Death

The coroner's jury took testimony from Dr. Lockerby. He gave a long and detail-filled narrative about the night he treated Mrs. Jackson. He described how he had "wet her handkerchief and put it across her chest, with the idea of getting up some counter-irritation there [that] might relieve the spasm of the bronchial tubes. The breath didn't seem to enter her lungs at all, and it didn't seem to do any good whatever. She just simply sank away, and in fact died."

His official medical opinion was that she perished from "spasmodic contraction of the bronchial tubes" likely caused from inhaling irritant gas.

The jury also questioned Dr. John Winslow, an Ithaca physician who treated the two juniors that had passed out from fumes while trying to assist the staggering kitchen staff.

CORONER: Do you think chlorine gas would produce death under any circumstances?

WINSLOW: I think it might under some circumstances.

CORONER: Under what circumstances, Doctor?

WINSLOW: Under circumstances which would produce permanent spasm of the glottis until suffocation was complete.

CORONER: And that would be the process of death from the chlorine gas?

WINSLOW: Yes, sir.

CORONER: If [chlorine gas is] taken in a concentrated form, death would be liable to be produced by suffocation?

WINSLOW: Yes, sir. A cramping up of the glottis and the vocal cords would close together and shut off the air at the glottis; and also probably produce a spasm of the smaller bronchial tubes.

The jury empowered to look into the tragedy of the cook's death rendered its collective opinion on March 14, 1894. The jurors decided this: "The said Henrietta Jackson . . . came to her death on the night of February 20, 1894, by reason of the inhalation of chlorine or other irritant gas manufactured and introduced into a room in Masonic Block in the City of Ithaca, New York, where deceased was at work by a person or persons to this jury unknown."

In the same article, the headline proclaimed that "[Carl] Dingens of Buffalo" had an explanation for his absence, or at least his family so claimed. The reporter quoted the family's protestations that claimed Carl was innocent of all involvement. Dingens himself offered the excuse that he was "much shocked" at numerous requests he make a "speedy return to Ithaca," and unaware he had been sent a summons. He was not under oath when he spoke to a reporter. He was without question the prime suspect in the Jackson affair.

The case now went before a grand jury with Judge Gerritt A. Forbes determined to reject all refusals from those that refused to testify. Worried that at the least his son would languish in jail for contempt of court, Joseph Dingens retained renowned criminal attorney John B. Stanchfield from Elmira, a partner in the law firm of Reynolds, Stanchfield, and Collin, to help local counsel represent his son and the other defendants. Stanchfield, always impeccably dressed, was a former mayor of Elmira, New York, and a close friend of Mark Twain. Stanchfield's wife, the former Clara L. Spaulding, was Twain's wife's best friend and twice visited Europe with the Clemens family.

Stanchfield conferred with the Ithaca attorneys to keep Taylor from being compelled to offer testimony that almost certainly would have led to jail time for Dingens, Stimson, Gorby, and other defendants who had yet to be named. An Ithaca reporter claimed testimony by Frederick Taylor, if compelled, could implicate at least six persons in the cook's death.

Frederick Taylor, well coached, invoked his constitutional guarantees to "throw himself upon the privilege which the law allows me on the ground that it may tend to criminate me" on the murder one charge. This was his standard response to questions about the origin of the jugs, about the purchaser of materials used to make chlorine, and any other question where an answer might open the prosecutor's way to expanding his questions. He almost lost that privilege by opening up on rare occasions to admit he and Dingens had taken a chemistry class and knew the rudimentary steps in creating chlorine.

On March 28, 1894, Judge Forbes banished Taylor to jail for contempt for refusing to testify to what facts he knew to be true in the Mrs. Jackson case. In essence, Taylor could only stay silent if he pleaded the Fifth Amendment and admit that what he was holding back would incriminate him in a case of manslaughter in the first degree, plus a misdemeanor disruption of a lawful meeting. Subsequently Taylor, on advice of counsel, planned to say he refused because some statements might incriminate him. Newspapers in Ithaca reported that Taylor seemed to be innocent of at least some of the charges of collusion.

Taylor's lawyers ran an end around the current court and approached a judge in a neighboring county to set Taylor free and allow him to claim his constitutional rights. The judge agreed with their argument.

On April 5, Sheriff Charles S. Seaman greeted Taylor in his jail cell, presumably in the company of a reporter since the conversation appeared verbatim in the local newspaper. Fordyce A. Cobb, the managing clerk for the Ithaca law firm of Tompkins & Leary, had visited the jail and served the sheriff his client's release papers.

"Mr. Taylor, you are released from my custody and are free to leave this place at any time," said Sheriff Seaman.

With his left hand Seaman handed a subpoena as he shook hands with his right hand. Taylor learned that he had been remanded to speak to a grand jury on April 24, 1894.

Taylor expressed gratitude nonetheless for his treatment in jail. "I am very much pleased at the news you bring me and wish to express to you, Mr. Sheriff, my sincere thanks for the kind treatment you have shown me, and shall always remember you with feelings of gratefulness."

The sheriff dashed off to catch a scheduled train to Rochester and told Taylor to use his official office for a celebration. Taylor's fraternity brothers and Cornell friends came over to mob him. These fraternity fellows, glee club friends, and sophomore class members celebrated the chance to visit a pal in the pokey. They accompanied him to his cell where he held forth with them for nearly two hours until exiting the building around 6:00 p.m. "He was in no hurry to leave jail" a local paper headlined its story.

Taylor had one complaint. The faculty had suspended him while he was in jail, and he had been unable to take required exams. "I think the faculty was rather hasty and unjust," he said to the reporter. "But I think they will do right by me and reinstate me."

Conspicuously missing from the articles were any words of contrition from Taylor about Mrs. Jackson's survivors and how he felt about her painful end. Not one of the accused ever showed public remorse.

Taylor predicted rightly that the Cornell faculty had no choice but to reinstate him, and it did so. He was readmitted in good standing to Cornell.

In April, a second death occurred in the Masonic Block building. Dentist William L. Brenizer shot and killed himself in an office below the room where the chlorine jugs had been placed. He left behind a rambling note that complained he had been blamed (by teasing friends of his) for creating the deadly banquet gas mixture. His note admitted having been in the room where the gas had emanated some six months prior, but protested his innocence, stating he had never committed a crime in his life. The coroner acknowledged Brenizer's depression, declining to ask for an inquest after Brenizer's friends informed newspapers that the dentist's obsession with the chlorine case had exacerbated a previous mental condition that had forced him to abandon his dental practice. Brenizer's will donated his brain to Cornell for scientific study.

Gerritt A. Forbes on the Bench

Now the legal ball rolled into the court of Gerritt A. Forbes, a long-bearded justice of oyer and terminer in Ithaca. Frederick Taylor, in his testimony before Forbes, alternated between giving many "I don't remember" statements and otherwise refusing to testify. Taylor remained silent even when Forbes browbeat him and said he wanted Taylor to make a clean breast of matters. "The court takes the responsibility under the laws of this state of squeezing, so to speak, this evidence out," said Forbes. "Young man, you are directed to return to the grand jury room and to answer any question which is put to you in reference to anything you know about that transaction."[22]

Taylor, on advice of attorney, defied Judge Forbes and remained mum. A showdown was in the making.

No Jailhouse Confession

Ably advised by Stanchfield, Taylor triumphed in the case of *People ex rel. Frederick Luther Taylor* against Gerritt A Forbes, the justice of the New York Supreme Court. Essentially, in his quest for a guilty verdict, Justice Forbes had stripped Taylor of his civil rights.

In May of 1894, attorney Leary also argued his case with justices from the state's court of appeals on behalf of Taylor's right to invoke the Fifth Amendment privilege. On May 16, the court ruled that a stay of proceedings was proper. In other words, unless some witness came forth with evidence against Taylor, the case was over.[23] There would be no grand jury indictments. The case lingered on for a little over two months more, but all that remained was posturing, as topnotch legal counsel led by Stanchfield had represented Dingens and Taylor perfectly to keep them out of court. A grand jury and a coroner's jury had flexed their muscles and ordered Taylor to testify, but in the end, Stanchfield persuaded the New York court of appeals to issue an extremely rare "stay of proceedings," stopping all legal action in the Jackson murder investigation.

In mid-May, the humiliated Justice Forbes acknowledged that the sealed lips of Taylor meant that Mrs. Jackson's murderer or murderers would never face criminal trial. He thanked the grand jury for its service and dismissed the foreman and members. Not a single newspaper ever put in a statement from Mrs. Jackson's daughter and husband for their reaction to the disposal of their mother's case without attributing guilt to any party.

Stanchfield's Legal Move

Taylor's unremitting refusal to offer testimony effectively removed Carl L. Dingens and the other suspects from trial.

In addition to the known suspects, there had been unnamed conspirators. A clerk named Samuel McKinney testified that he sold tubing to a short, sandy-haired young man who had a moustache. A female neighbor at 7 Cook Street testified that two men (one with a light moustache) carrying jugs (resembling the homicide paraphernalia) came to her house seeking two people, one of whom she told them lived across the street at 6 Cook Street. That same young man, or a different culprit, approached a merchant tailor with an office in the Masonic Block to ask how to turn off the water in the building. That apparently was an alternate plan to disrupt the freshman banquet. Dishes could not be washed, and the banquet's servings would stall midmeal.

Based on the circumstantial evidence at hand, and no willing eyewitness to testify, the local prosecutor had no chance for a conviction. The wall of silence lasted all the way to the death of the last Ninety-Sixer. No deathbed confession came from Dingens, Taylor, Stimson, or any other.

Likewise, no one came forward voluntarily to make amends with Mrs. Jackson's descendants. William Jackson announced plans after the funeral of his wife to launch a civil suit against Carl Dingens and Frederick Taylor, but the case never was tried, perhaps because the wealthy Joseph Dingens could easily and quietly pay the $5,000 sought in damages to Jackson as an out-of-court settlement. Not one newspaper published follow-up stories reporting precisely why the civil suit failed to materialize.

Mrs. Jackson's daughter, Mary Matilda Hedgepath, wife of the late William A. Hedgepath, died in 1929 after a serious illness. She had no grave marker.

The Taylor decision by the New York court of appeals was a nineteenth-century landmark case for the protection of an individual's civil liberties. Here, in part, was the ruling by the court of appeals:

> [Taylor], though in fact he may be innocent, was so situated, with reference to it, and so related to the circumstances and results, that it is apparent that at some point and in some way it became, under all the circumstances, not only prudent, but necessary and proper, to claim the privilege of refusing to disclose the information sought to be elicited by the questions. He was a student at the college. He belonged to the sophomore class and the class in chemistry. He boarded at the house from which someone took the jugs. His roommate [Dingens], at least, seems to have been one of the persons suspected as being in some way connected with the transaction.
>
> He was so surrounded by elements of circumstantial proof that the answer to any one of the questions might form a link in the chain sufficient to subject him to the hazard of a criminal charge. Whether innocent or not, there was a combination of facts and circumstances that brought him perilously close to the charges which was the subject of investigation, and the answer which he was required to give might have completed the chain of proof. He was then placed in a position where he might lawfully claim the protection of the law and remain silent.[24]

The Jackson chlorine case over time has become one of the least remembered of many sensationally covered hazing stories, but as late as 1955, well-known divorce attorney Richard H. Wels, a 1933 alumnus, lavished praise on Taylor for his refusal to let Justice Gerritt A. Forbes bully him into naming names and cooperating with the prosecutor to turn in collaborators. The letter from Wels came out in the days of the Red Scare and hunt for past celebrity Communist members by Senator Joseph McCarthy of Wisconsin. "In these days, when the

Constitutional guaranties afforded by the Fifth Amendment are being whittled away, devisecrated [*sic*], and attacked by many elements in our community, there is much to be learned and remembered from the decision of the court of appeals sixty-one years ago," wrote Wels. He lauded "one member [Taylor] of the Cornell community in 1894 [who] did not hesitate to uphold and invoke our constitutional liberties."[25]

Epilogue

The Henrietta Jackson case ended in a cold case, all evidence from the Masonic Block office destroyed over time that might have revealed, in our own time, fingerprints and DNA samples to identify the guilty parties.

Carl Dingens and Frederick Taylor made up lost work at school, graduated from Cornell University, and found professional employment, respectively, in the fields of business and law. Dingens became manager of the New York branch of G. Hussey and Company, leaf tobacco dealers. Taylor pursued a law career in New York City and joined fellow attorney Raymond D. Thurber in a law partnership. As a pastime, the defendant who had refused to sing in court sang with other Cornell alumni all his life in a New York City glee club.

Carl Louis Dingens died April 30, 1927. He was the father of Carl H. Dingens and husband of Mabel Hobbs Dingens, daughter of a New York City meat wholesaler. Dingens's last residence was on Park Street in Buffalo, where he grew up, and at his last job he worked as an executive for a stationery company. He had one patent for a stationery binder in 1915 under his name but assigned that patent to the Bigelow Binder Company of New York. After his death, a survivor wrote the alumni association a curt note demanding that all materials relating to Cornell University cease being mailed to the Dingens house. The family had had quite enough news from Cornell, the short letter said.

Joseph A. Dingens died at age seventy-one in 1907. He kept a pleasant journal of events almost all his life. The story of Mrs. Jackson and his own involvement and lawyering up to save his son from prison escaped the pages of his journal, however.

John B. Stanchfield continued to serve Mark Twain as his personal attorney for many years but also fielded high-profile criminal cases and was written up in newspapers for his extraordinary lucrative client billings. He tried to enter public service in New York but was defeated for New York governor in 1900 and senator for that state in 1903. He died at age sixty-six in 1921.

For the Cornell University graduation celebration in 1896, the outgoing Taylor had been chosen by his classmates to be the toastmaster. The class cheer resounded at commencement for the last time. "Ninety-Six, boom-rah-rix, boom-rah-rix. We are Cornell, Ninety-Six."

Henrietta Jackson's body lies in her Ithaca grave, and the tombstone the Cornell community bought for her is yet readable. Her daughter's grave is close by, but Mary Matilda's lacks a headstone.

The death of Mrs. Jackson failed to stop the battles between Cornell first-year students and sophomores despite a pronouncement by President Schurman forbidding the practice. By 1896 hazing was back, resulting in the expulsion of several students.

HANK NUWER is a professor in the Franklin College Pulliam School of Journalism. He has written *The Hazing Reader* (IUP) and *Wrongs of Passage: Fraternities, Sororities, Hazing, and Binge Drinking* (IUP).

2   Hazing in Fraternities and Sororities

A Primer

Hank Nuwer

HAZING IN UNIVERSITY fraternal groups in the United States is a pernicious and sometimes even deadly practice that dates back to the founding of the first collegiate fraternities in the nineteenth century. In spite of growing antihazing sentiment, laws against hazing in forty-four states and campus crackdowns, hazing persists as a rite of passage and tradition in colleges and universities across the United States and Canada. This chapter examines the roots and manifestations of hazing in university-based fraternities and sororities in the United States. It includes a discussion of university policies and practices to curtail it by national fraternal organizations and antihazing activists.

Best hazing-prevention practices include the encouragement of bystander intervention to halt hazing as it happens, along with the mandating of alcohol-free fraternity houses, putting an end to the pledge period, delaying rush until a student's second semester, putting responsible live-in adults in Greek houses as supervisors, offering orientation for parents on signs of hazing and substance abuse, transferring governance of the Greek system from self-governing interfraternity councils to university control, and requiring transparency of all schools by publishing all infractions on their websites in easily accessed locations. Also needed is accountability, namely prompt and even harsh action to expel or suspend a chapter as soon as hazing acts are verified, as occurred in January 2017 when Delta Tau Delta suspended its Indiana University chapter for hazing, and in February of 2017 when Penn State shut down its Beta Theta Pi chapter after pledge Timothy Piazza died accidentally on bid day. Even as this book goes to press, comes an announcement from Louisiana State University president, F. King Alexander, that police are concluding the sudden death of Maxwell Raymond Gruver, nineteen, was an alcohol-related hazing that occurred at the Phi Delta Theta house, and that all Greek activities are suspended.

Passage of federal legislation against hazing would give prosecutors a potent weapon, but prior to 2017 all proposed legislation has been flawed in the writing and has died in committee. As this book goes to print, however, federal hazing legislation known as the Report and Educate about Campus Hazing Act of 2017, introduced by Rep. Pat Meehan (R-PA) and Rep. Marcia Fudge (D-OH) has widespread congressional interest owing to the grim details behind the death of Penn State's Piazza. Finally, universities need to revise their web and print publications, deleting or rewriting all hyperbolic accounts of Greek Life if such information gives students and their guardians a false portrait of fraternities and sororities with regard to risks and safety concerns.

On the other hand, there are a substantial number of Greek groups that provide a safe, nurturing home-away-from-home environment, stressing comradeship, philanthropy, values, scholarship, and other laudable aims of founders. Their schools and national organizations must support such chapters, but even exemplary nonhazing groups must not rest until hazers in their midst no longer are welcome at the table.

How does one know if a fraternity is responsible? Trust Aristotle, who wrote this: What are its habitual actions? In short, to know the behaviors is to know the chapter and whether or not it is responsible. We pull for the characters in a book or movie because they truly want something above all else. The chapter that wants to continue hazing will trumpet that it is hazing-free, but in reality its behavior will not end until the chapter's charter is yanked and its members are expelled.

Defining Hazing

The number of serious researchers devoted to studying and highlighting hazing is still limited, but the subject is attracting increasing study from social scientists and other academics concerned with trying to end the unabated string of deaths that have occurred every year from 1961 to 2017 in fraternal chapters, as well as in other collegiate clubs, bands, and sports teams. An updated list of all deaths on campuses from hazing can be found at HankNuwer.com. Scholarly research on hazing as late as 1978 was confined primarily to abnormal psychology and education journals and dissertations. Today, excellent research is conducted by scholars in psychology, ethics, history, education, folklore, popular culture, sociology, literature, athletics management, student affairs, and on and on.

What exactly is hazing? Researcher Aldo Cimino defines the term as "the generation of induction costs (i.e., elements of the experiences necessary to be acknowledged as a 'legitimate' group member) that appear unattributable to group-relevant assessments, preparation, or chance." He uses calisthenics being required by a fraternity as an example of hazing and cites automatic accrual theory to explain why higher-status fraternities with more and better benefits for a pledge can demand far more severe tests of hazing than a chapter with less status and fewer benefits can expect.[1]

Most higher education institutions in the United States use the definition of the practice of hazing devised by the Fraternity Executives Association and endorsed by the Fraternal Information Programming Group, the leading fraternal organization addressing risk-management issues. According to these organizations, hazing is "any action taken or situation created intentionally, whether on or off fraternity premises, to produce mental or physical discomfort, embarrassment, harassment, or ridicule." All higher education institutions and all national and international fraternities and sororities in the United States publish strict policies forbidding hazing. Umbrella groups such as the North-American Interfraternity Conference, National Panhellenic Conference and National Pan-Hellenic Council condemn hazing. Yet the practice endures.

Hazing also meets a definition of bullying if fraternal members put newcomers through tortures intended to make the pledges, neophytes, or associate members quit a chapter, as opposed to the usual hazing methods of putting newcomers through stressful and illicit conditions in order to welcome them eventually into the group. When hazing gets carried away to include elements of torture, the gap between welcoming a newcomer and bullying him or her appears wide indeed.[2]

The term hazing has been used by journalists, educators, legislators, and researchers to fit conduct such as performing silly tasks or errands on up to paddling a pledge or requiring the guzzling of alcohol alone or with other neophytes. Hazing becomes difficult to define in a legal sense, and it becomes near impossible when lawmakers attempt to define the term, especially if they are looking at a single highly publicized case, such as the Piazza tragedy, instead of a wide range of hazing cases. Additional public debate needs to address when the line gets crossed between a pledge participating willingly and being coerced, often to protect other members of a pledge class that get punished when one pledge displays defiance.

Not surprisingly, undergraduates have a simple classification all their own. They refer to "big H" hazing and "little h" hazing. As a consequence, many fraternity and sorority members view bottle exchanges, drop-offs of pledges in the country, lineups, and other events as "little h" offenses. However, even these "little h" activities have at one time or another have resulted in serious injury or death as participants cross lines and reject boundaries and civility.

Hazing: Cross-Culturally Widespread and Persistent

Early research work by Lionel Tiger of Rutgers University promoted the term "male bonding" and made a case for the evolutionary aspects of hazing from his neo-Darwinian perspective. In 1969, in his book *Men in Groups* (revised in 2004 by Tiger as "Males Courting Males" in *The Hazing Reader*), he focused on hazing in male fraternities as a means of addressing and explaining some hazing activities he witnessed firsthand at McGill University, a Canadian institution of higher learning. Tiger states that men attracted to high-status groups, actual or perceived, are attracted in part because they define their own self-image from attractive, higher status males. In groups such as fraternities that haze (and not all do haze), Tiger states in that the males staunchly try to defend the status quo by incorporating new members willing to show they are a suitable "fit" by performing and successfully participating in whatever hazing practices the group deems appropriate. These practices at the chapter level can be crude, even demeaning, and run counter to what the national or international umbrella fraternal groups may approve. Thus, all the over-the-top practices in a chapter get hidden away in hazing episodes done clandestinely, behind closed doors, and out of sight of advisors and national executive officers.[3]

Tiger stresses that the ability to consume copious amounts of alcohol, in the presence of other fraternal values, is a common bonding practice carried out by some fraternities and other high-status male groups such as athletes. In "Males Courting Males," Tiger also observes that many fraternal chapters that haze require members to participate in activities that appear homoerotic in nature, requiring pledges alone or in the pledge group to be fully or partially nude during one or more hazing sessions and occasionally assuming submissive poses in front of dominant senior members. Once initiated, the pledge is given the opportunity to buy a costly ring with the fraternity's Greek letters on the stone, and the ring is worn on the finger traditionally reserved for a wedding ring. There also are pins with the fraternal insignia reserved for females that members find attractive.

Tiger's observations on the need for new fraternal members to achieve a "clubby" bond with senior members have echoes in the well-established "Groupthink" theory of researcher Irving Janis.[4] In 1999 I adapted Janis's term to "Greekthink."[5] The basis for Groupthink and Greekthink is that the clubby nature of groups noted by Tiger reflects the overarching quest for camaraderie and a desire for harmonious relationships seen in high-status groups such as fraternities, even rising to a US president's inner circle of advisers and cabinet members, athletes, and so on. Which may not be so surprising given that *Inside Greek U* author Alan DeSantis counts seventeen US presidents since 1877 that claimed fraternity affiliations as collegians.[6]

Groupthink neatly sums up fraternal organizations and their compulsive need and appreciation for camaraderie and the approval of current members, and even much older alums, whose presence at several hazing incidents in which a pledge died I noted in *Broken Pledges*. Groupthink captures the behavior of members performing acts of hazing in a group that, prior to joining, they as individuals likely would have dismissed as deplorable. Groupthink also explains why fraternal members can display a delusional belief in their own invincibility while encouraging or ordering hazing activities in order to foster group unanimity. The Groupthink theory espoused by Janis also explains the deception, denial, and dishonesty that hazing chapters often demonstrate after a risky practice leads to serious injury or death and an associated investigation. Janis's extensive study in group dynamics further points out that the group's excessive need for solidarity colors the judgment of its members, leading them to approve and carry out activities such as hazing and alcohol overconsumption that, if exposed, can lead to that hazing chapter losing its charter. The cost of losing that charter includes the consequence that the university and its national organization order individual members to disband for anywhere from a year to forever and lose the privileges and status of membership during that ban. Yet, in spite of so much to lose, hazing continues, and also continues to attract media coverage and legislative attention.

Because actual acts of hazing are so widely different, ranging from beatings to drinking extravaganzas to nude groping and lining up to take verbal abuse, it is difficult to point to a single behavioral cause of hazing. Many hazing researchers refer to "The Effect of Severity of Initiation on Liking for a Group" by Elliott Aronson and Judson Mills as of crucial value. The two researchers established through experimentation that hazing leads to tighter group solidarity because severe initiation practices cause initiates to appreciate and like the group more than do initiates who are simply invited to join a group without hazing-like demands and sacrifices.[7]

Another observer of hazing behavior is James C. Arnold, who applied the work on cults by Margaret Thaler Singer, author with Janja Lalich of *Cults in Our Midst*, to fraternities.[8] Arnold asserts in his long essay "Hazing and Alcohol in a College Fraternity" published in Nuwer's *The Hazing Reader* that many fraternities fall under the category of "addictive organizations." Such groups quite convincingly are compared to individuals obsessed with alcohol, for example, and are similar to a dysfunctional family unit. In short, the chapters that haze use cult-like systematic manipulation and coercion to effect psychological and social influence. In particular, cults and hazing fraternities alike purposely engender enforced dependency by instituting ways and means to make potential members and new members spend the majority of waking and sleeping hours in the company of current members and their fellow newcomers. Such organizations promise the new initiates enduring abuse that if they only persist all will be well in the end, and they will experience many incentives once awarded membership when the time of trial expires.[9]

In addition to his essay in *The Hazing Reader*, Arnold undertook close participant observation as a doctoral student over a long period of time under the supervision of George Kuh, well-known Indiana University Professor of Higher Education and Director of the National Institute for Learning Outcomes

Assessment (NILOA). Arnold on many occasions observed his study chapter perform acts of hazing and alcohol abuse while he performed research for his dissertation on higher education at Indiana University.[10] He was allowed by the local fraternity chapter, its national organization, and Indiana University to have nearly complete access to such fraternity customs as rush, in which attractive newcomers get invited to the house for inspection under party conditions and then are given a "bid" if enough members agree they possess the "right stuff" for membership.

Sometimes, the bid results in a good fit, and sometimes it results in conflict when an independent thinker among the new class of pledges raises concerns about the illicit or even illegal behaviors that the newcomers must brush away. The desired outcome of hazing is to achieve 100 percent pledge-class unity—that is, the class becomes fully and wholly subservient to the wishes of the veteran members. Ironically, to get the "trust" of the pledges, the senior members may lie, deceive, and deny all responsibility, noted Arnold. What occurs during the stress and chaos of a pledgeship marked by hazing is what ethnographer John van Maanen refers to as "cultural learning" for a group.[11]

In its barest form, the pledgeship involves full indoctrination of the new members and total obeisance on the part of pledges as a socialization practice. Members justify their poor treatment of pledges and force them to endure oft-squalid living conditions for weeks under the justification that everything asked of the pledges serves some important bonding purpose, observed Arnold. The chapter he lived with even used such terms as "responsible hazing" and "responsible drinking" that were oxymoronic since from rush until initiation the chapter's behavior was flagrantly irresponsible and reckless. In the end the outward result of an entire chapter as a model of control is a hazing chapter that Arnold stresses must live with "denial, dishonesty, self-centeredness, [and] confusion." All this is done by a group that projects what Arnold says is an "illusion of control."

All hazing chapters strive to admit members who respect the status quo and work to maintain the often illicit and even criminal behaviors that mark homogenous Greek chapters. Nothing incurs the collective wrath of a hazing group's members more than a pledge that refuses to cower and reports hazing to the school or police or who quits pledging and rejects future membership in that hazing group. Arnold establishes that the group treats the unhappy quitter as a pariah with disdain, anger, and even threats. Conversely, male fraternity pledges—away from the security of family and home—who buy into the addictive chapter mentality then get rewarded by the senior members with a supply of alcohol, parties, and access to desirable women who tolerate or even support the practices of the addictive chapter. Arnold says addictive groups and members have a dualistic approach to perceiving the world. Everything is all right or all wrong, and pledges are told it is "our way or the highway." Whatever good philanthropic activities the chapter supports are, in part, an attempt to cover up the confused, addictive nature of the chapter, Arnold concludes, citing the theories on the pervasive and persistent nature of addiction noted by *The Addictive Organization* authors Anne Wilson Schaef and Diane Fassel—that the national organizations and Greek Life staffs at colleges can make a difference if "they can turn away from a model of control and continued participation in an unhealthy system and through their actions demonstrate a healthier way of being."[12]

Symbolic Interactionism Theory

Stephen Sweet uses a frame of symbolic interactionism to explain how some undergraduates attracted to hard-hazing groups will do whatever it takes to belong. Herbert Blumer's symbolic interactionist construct, cited with regard to fraternal groups by Sweet, declares that human beings react to events because the events have meaning for them based on the social interaction they have with one another, and then they interpret those events with some selectivity—perhaps even outright justification and rationalization for activities banned by society. Blumer's theory in particular fits when applied to fraternal group members whose concept of self is, at the time of pledging, being crucially shaped. Sweet notes that the fraternal rings, T-shirts, and paddles represent part of the identity pledges are accepting as they enter a crucial stage of their lives. In turn, the social relationships with those who already wear the colors and paraphernalia of the group they aspire to join can be a powerful lure to those young people who see enduring hazing as a necessary price to pay to get into an organization that has value. Conversely, says Sweet, those who quit pledging rather than endure not only suffer guilt because their pledge brothers will be asked to carry an additional burden, but they also lose a tie and part of their identity by forgoing all connection to the chapter they already may have sacrificed much for during early. hazing.[13] The research by Thomas A. Leemon, who lived with a fraternity chapter for one entire pledging period to observe it, demonstrates that fraternity chapters very deliberately in the hazing process set out to manipulate and to alter each pledge's concept of self.[14]

The work of researcher Ricky L. Jones also takes a close look at hazing in his book *Black Haze: Violence, Sacrifice, and Manhood in Black Greek-Letter Fraternities.* Jones postulates that veteran fraternity members in hazing chapters love their pledges even if they put them through beatings with canes, fists, and paddles. While not every African American Greek chapter hazes, the heaviest hazing chapters, according to Jones, demand the ability for pledges to withstand such sacrifices to demonstrate their readiness and willingness to maintain the group. Significantly, physical hazing at the chapter level is fundamentally the exact opposite of the relatively tame requirements for initiation that the national organizations put out in pledging manuals. Jones persuasively argues that hazing deaths in Asian fraternities at the University of Texas and California-Irvine, for example, demonstrate a requirement to endure physical challenges and a demonstration of sacrifice on the part of initiates. While the physical hazing may be a part of the black membership process in groups that violate their national organization's mandate to be hazing-free, it is also very much present in the rites of even some integrated chapters or mainly Caucasian chapters that have seen new members hospitalized with physical injuries.

Jones, himself a member of a black fraternity, has become a nationally known antihazing activist, particularly outspoken in his objections to hazing of a severe physical nature.[15] Psychologist Susan Lipkins, in her book *Preventing Hazing: How Parents, Teachers, and Coaches Can Stop the Violence, Harassment, and Humiliation*, maintains that even short-term hazing can lead to long-term, even lifelong, psychological and physical consequences for hazing victims. Short of death, psychological trauma due to hazing may be even more pernicious a problem than physical injuries. The latter nearly always heal, while traumatized victims report an inability to get on with their lives in normal fashion due to the afflictions of hazing, according to Lipkins who says no pledge gives informed consent.[16]

Hazing in US Universities

Hazing in fraternities and sororities in the United States involves expectations of senior members that potential new members—often called pledges or associate members—will perform stunts that demean, degrade, or endanger them. Those that endure the group's humiliation prove their willingness to conform to a perceived status quo. The members that insist newcomers endure barbaric initiations claim they are merely protecting established tradition and ensuring group solidarity. They maintain that hazing weeds out potential members that lack the wherewithal to do anything the fraternal chapter asks of those who seek membership. It also establishes a senior pecking order in which new members learn the rules of precedence and a need to respect both senior members and alumni.

Thus hazing is common, albeit forbidden, among fraternities and sororities whose reason for being at educational institutions is to instill a lifelong commitment to leadership, community service, and the worth of lasting friendships and mentoring. This general "mission" coincides with functionalist theories of rites of passage extending back to Arnold van Gennep, the first prominent researcher to note similarities in initiation rituals from society to society.[17]

Hazing in university and college fraternities and sororities is an illicit rite of passage (against the rules of the institution) that provides opportunities for veteran members to include or exclude new members on the basis of a variety of trials that involve varying degrees of physical and psychological stress. In all too many cases, the theory of social exchange put forth by psychologists Harold H. Kelley and John W. Thibaut describes the recurring reality. According to this theory, newcomers submit to whatever torture or trials are asked of them, comforted by the assurance that all abuse will cease after the organization declares them full members. During the next cycle, the new veterans get to turn the tables and haze the next set of newcomers.[18]

All new pledge classes experience much of the same brutal hazing their predecessors endured. Hazing can increase in intensity if members are inebriated or inclined toward sadism. After initiation, the hazed become the hazers and return the ordeals they experienced in equal or greater intensity and measure to the next pledge class. The rule of reciprocity in social psychology dictates that newly initiated members will keep watch over their pledge-class members to make sure they all replicate the ordeals on the new pledge class that they once had experienced. Many a fraternity and sorority member has felt the displeasure of peers for being too soft on neophytes. A rare but occasionally lethal form of hazing occurs when veteran members for shortcomings of one kind or another punish an initiated member.

Deaths of pledges in Greek organizations have occurred under bizarre circumstances as Nuwer's database of hazing deaths attests. Some have consumed lethal amounts of alcohol, being required by members to fill garbage pails with the collective vomit of new members. Some have perished after being dropped off far from campus (with victims dying in falls, in auto accidents, and by drowning). Some have endured hours of strenuous exercise in steam rooms with fatal results. Some have died after being on the receiving end of beatings with paddle, fists, or cane. Pledges Max Gruver, Tim Piazza, Gabe Higgins, Chad Meredith, Harrison Kowiak, and Gordie Bailey all died pledging fraternal chapters—in all cases veteran members delayed calling 911, and in some cases actually castigated other members who suggested calling emergency services. Many pledges like Matthew Ellis at Texas Tech die at parties.

History of University Hazing in the United States and Abroad

Rampant hazing in medieval European universities, such as the fifteenth-century practice of pennalism, developed over the following two hundred years into sometimes-savage hazing practices quite similar to the aptly named hell nights of today's hazing fraternities and sororities. In France and Germany, the hazed pledges donned a foolish cap similar to the beanies worn by pledges until nearly all national groups began outlawing them as symbols of hazing around 1979. At Cambridge and Oxford in England, physical beatings and enforced servitude among even the aristocracy was carried out in a custom known as "fagging," where new boys on campus became the manservants of older students.

Hazing deaths weren't always historically attributed mainly to fraternities, however. Rather, they were a greater problem in so-called "class hazing" that pitted first-year students against upperclassmen. (While female class hazing existed, not once did a death occur to either a first-year or second-year female, but a female cook did perish in 1894 when an undergraduate piped chlorine gas into a class party to disrupt it). Eighteen of the twenty-five hazing deaths of males that occurred on US college campuses from 1838 through 1927 were a result of freshman-sophomore class hazing excesses during battle royals, pranks, and organized fights to capture class flags, but not because of fraternity hazing. Fraternity hazing claimed the lives of seven young men 1838–1927, according to the appendix of deaths in *Broken Pledges*.[19]

During the late 1920s, thanks to more awareness on campus and an outpouring of condemnation of hazing by students themselves, hazing of first-year students included fewer battles for class flags and class pennants that had seen so much violence earlier in the century. From 1928 to March 2014, only two first-year class-hazing deaths occurred (a Cheyney State College beating and a University of Richmond accidental drowning), and the rest were committed by hazers in fraternities, sororities, athletic teams, and one band (Florida A&M University).

Fraternities and sororities often trace their origins back to literary and honor societies that flourished in 1776. The first was Kappa Alpha Society founded in 1825 at Union College in New York. The first fraternities emulated early literary societies in their educational values, and their founders were students who wanted to engage in intellectual debate as well as to socialize. In addition to establishing the solemn initiation rituals that often borrowed symbolism from Masonic initiations, the early fraternity chapters also hazed new members on occasion in ordeals known as "stunts." Some stunts included riding a real or mechanical goat or tossing a newcomer in the air on a blanket. Injuries occasionally occurred as a result of youths getting carried away. Nuwer's *Broken Pledges* documents injuries to two University of Georgia Zeta Chi pledges that jumped out a window when an older member whipped out a pistol as a prank.[20]

The first fraternity death was that of Kappa Sigma Society pledge Mortimer Leggett in 1873 at Cornell University. At least one newcomer has perished while enduring hazing every year from 1961 to 2017, which Nuwer has documented in *Wrongs of Passage* and an internet list of verifiable hazing deaths. There occurred at least fifteen collegiate hazing deaths from January 1, 2014, to partway through 2017.

Some years more than a single death have occurred in Greek organizations. Because some law enforcement officers label a hazing death an accident because of their lack of a clear understanding of what hazing actually is, it is plausible that the number of deaths on Hank Nuwer's database list of hazing fatalities is even lower than the listed total. Local school officials, police, and/or prosecutors investigating the incident wrongfully have dismissed more than one hazing death as a mere accident. Similarly, neither universities nor Greek national organizations are eager to claim a death as related to hazing lest that admission result in damages during civil litigation.

Hazing deaths are not limited to fraternities and sororities, but those two groups have experienced the majority of incidents. In the United States, the vast majority of hazing deaths from 1838 to 2017 have involved newcomers in fraternities and, to a lesser extent, in sororities. Far more males than females have perished in Greek organizations because of hazing.

According to a University of Maine national survey conducted by Elizabeth Allan and her colleagues, about half of all students acknowledge that they belong to groups that haze. While sorority hazing is oft reported, it rarely rises to the level of a crime and is more likely to be addressed by the hazers' institution as an infraction rather than by a criminal prosecution. It is important to note that deaths in local, unrecognized, or suspended fraternities have resulted in deaths at several institutions, including the University of Nevada, SUNY Plattsburgh, Chico State University, and SUNY Geneseo. Deaths by hazing also have been reported in countries such as the Philippines, India (where it is termed "ragging"), Japan, Canada, and Great Britain.[21]

Hazing and Alcohol Abuse

Alcohol was consumed by fraternal chapters in the nineteenth century through 1939, but such factors as alumni, faculty, and administration supervision of chapters resulted in far less tolerance for drunkenness or using alcohol as a litmus test of new member readiness during hazing. Significantly, fraternities likely did not experience a single reported hazing death due to alcohol until 1940. That year, Hubert L. Spake Jr. died following a mandatory drinking session at the University of Missouri while pledging Theta Nu Epsilon. Clearly, with the escalating number of hazing deaths from 1961 to 2017 (compared to 1838–1968), a case can be made that the presence of alcohol has made hazing rituals far more extreme and life-threatening than they were when many chapters banned or limited alcohol consumption. For example, from 2005 to 2008, ten of twelve hazing deaths (83 percent) were related to alcohol abuse. From 2004 to 2011, sixteen of twenty-one hazing deaths (76 percent) were alcohol-related.

My research on hazing deaths demonstrates that the majority that occurred in Greek groups from 1970 to 2017 involve an overdose of alcohol. Other victims from 1873 to 2017 died from beatings, car wrecks, pedestrian accidents, falls, burns, drowning, choking, or ingestion of water. A small number of suicides have occurred immediately following hazing activities and are listed on the list of hazing deaths with the caveat that it is difficult to prove that a suicide was the direct cause of hazing since other factors must also be considered.

Here are six examples of hazing deaths due to alcohol from my "List of Hazing Deaths" maintained on my website:

- In 1980, University of South Carolina Sigma Nu pledge L. Barry Ballou choked to death after passing out at a ritualized drinking session attended by an alumnus and members.
- In 2007, Phi Kappa Tau pledge Gary DeVercelly Jr. died of alcohol poisoning during a hazing incident at Rider University. He was a baseball player from California prior to coming to Rider. His parents subsequently became hazing activists, board members of the Clery Center for Security on Campus, and advocates for strict governance of Greek houses.
- In 2008, eighteen-year-old Theta Chi pledge Harrison Kowiak of Lenoir-Rhyne University died following a physical hazing "game" that the school and local Theta Chi chapter were reluctant to term hazing. Harrison's mother Lianne Kowiak became an antihazing advocate and winner of Hazing Prevention.Org's Hank Nuwer Anti-Hazing Hero Award.
- In 2012, Pi Kappa Alpha pledge David Bogenberger, a Northern Illinois University freshman, died after being asked to chug copious amounts of hard alcohol. Police charged twenty-two individuals with crimes.
- In 2013, members of Baruch College's Pi Delta Psi pleaded guilty to voluntary manslaughter and other serious charges after pledge Chung Hsien (Mike) Deng was beaten and died. Members refused to call 911 in a timely manner.
- In 2016, Nevada-Reno pledges were given enormous amounts of alcohol to consume as they cleaned house, watched strippers perform, and violated school and national regulations on drinking. Pledge Ryan Abele died in a fall that university officials denied was hazing-caused.

US Laws Against Hazing

Hazing may be illicit (i.e., against the rules of a collegiate institution) or forbidden by state law. As of November 2017, hazing was illegal by statute in forty-four states, but there was no federal law regulating hazing, although activists such as Lianne Kowiak and scholars such as R. Brian Crow are advocates for passage of such a sweeping federal law. In most states, hazing is a misdemeanor. Florida has the strictest possible penalty among all US states, allowing a sentence of six or more years to be imposed upon conviction for felony hazing. As this book goes to press, a former member of the Florida A&M marching band, who was serving a lengthy sentence as a participant in the death of Robert Champion, has persuaded the Florida Supreme Court to hear his appeal based on his claim that the state hazing law is too broad.

Nonetheless, outside of Florida, California, and New York, the courts have traditionally imposed light jail sentences, often requiring mere community service or fining individual hazers and/or their chapters. Hazing can be hard to establish since these illegal actions often take place behind closed doors. The fact that Tim Piazza's hazing was captured by security cameras from start to finish has added a dimension to the subsequent state's hazing inquiry seldom seen in the courtroom.

In addition, after a death or serious incident, uncooperative members refuse to share details of what took place when investigators interview them. This is why prosecutors for the state often file more easily proven charges, such as assault or serving alcohol to a minor, because hazing is a more difficult crime to prove in court. Felony convictions for repeated hazing beatings were imposed on a Florida A&M fraternity, and a Chico State fraternity member was convicted of a felony following the death of pledge Matthew Carrington who was required to drink so much water that his body chemistry was altered.

University Hazing Practices and Deaths

The increasing numbers of prospective members injured or killed by hazing reveals that prospective members stand ready to do whatever is necessary for acceptance into an organization. When a fraternity or sorority pledge fails to complete the pledge process, it can be a traumatic experience for individuals that fail to cross the liminal space, particularly if they feel less than full-fledged adults and must ask either their parents or school officials to intervene on their behalf.

Sororities have been connected to eight deaths of females and one death of a male in alleged hazing incidents. In 1970, an Eastern Illinois sorority member became the first female Greek member to die after she perished from effects of a head injury incurred in a vehicular accident after she had resisted being "kidnapped" by pledges that intended to abandon her in the country as a prank. Three female deaths have been attributed to drowning in dangerous ceremonial initiations, one at Virginia State and two at California State, Los Angeles.

A 2012 lawsuit launched by the mother of a deceased sorority pledge at East Carolina University maintained that the 2010 deaths of her daughter and a second pledge were directly caused by sleep deprivation due to hazing. According to that lawsuit, twenty-year-old Delta Sigma Theta pledges Victoria Carter and Briana Latrice Gather died in a car accident. In addition to the aforementioned two sorority deaths at Eastern Carolina University, one additional death occurred at Plymouth State University during an automobile accident while pledges allegedly were made to lie flat on the floor of an SUV that then overturned.

None of these deaths involved alcohol. However, in 2008, a total of twelve Chi Omega sorority and Sigma Nu fraternity members at Utah State University were charged with crimes following the alcohol-related hazing of eighteen-year-old Michael Starks. In addition, in March 2014, an alleged hazing incident involving Kappa Kappa Gamma sorority and Sigma Alpha Epsilon fraternity at the University of Connecticut resulted in the hospitalization of a sorority member admitted with a life-threatening blood-alcohol concentration, according to widely published media accounts and an email to Nuwer from the victim.

In addition to pledge deaths, so-called pledge "sneaks" routinely occur in which pledges haze senior members to retaliate for what they themselves have gone through and endured, and these have resulted in deaths at schools such as Eastern Illinois University, University of Texas, and University of Georgia. Such a practice of rebellion is often encouraged by the membership as a means of forging pledge solidarity. The latest example of the reverse hazing of members by pledges has been the death of Sigma Alpha Epsilon member George Desdunes who was "encouraged" by pledges to drink what proved to be a deadly amount of alcohol in a spurious question-and-answer session at his Cornell University chapter house in 2011.

As mentioned, hazing can also have serious consequences even without a death. Many male and female students have been hospitalized for acute alcohol intoxication, for example. Greek chapters have been punished for such behaviors as activities of a sexual nature, physical pummeling, verbal abuse, overwork, sleep deprivation, branding with chemicals, and bizarre pranks intended to amuse veteran members.

To be sure, hazing can also involve activities that do not qualify as deadly or particularly demeaning, such as requiring a pledge to sing a song or carry a veteran member's books. Nonetheless all national and international fraternal organizations ban these activities as well since the possibility exists that a rogue member or members might get "creative" with a relatively noninjurious act of hazing and take the activity to a potentially harmful level. In addition, what may seem like innocuous hazing to a perpetrator may be perceived as threatening to a newcomer. Fraternal leaders routinely refer to resultant psychological trauma as a type of "hidden harm." Even the most stable of new recruits can break down when subjected to night after night of verbal abuse, subjugation, and sleep deprivation, particularly when forced to sleep on a floor in confined quarters and to leap up on the instant to carry out some inane errand that a veteran member has conjured up. These latter cases are examples of cult-like systematic hazing.[22]

Prosecuting and Preventing Hazing

From the first fraternity hazing death in 1873 to deaths in 1973, there appear to have been few arrests and no convictions of any consequence for fraternity and sorority hazing deaths.[23] And while the adviser in the 1974 shooting death for a hazing at Bluefield State was convicted and served time for killing a Tau Kappa Epsilon pledge, and a North Carolina A&T University fraternity member in 1987 received a two-year sentence for pledge beatings, it was not until 1999 that tightened state laws and increasing media attention led to observable and verifiably stricter enforcement, and a small number of arrests resulting in convictions. Most notable was the 2007 sentencing of nearly two years in prison for two Florida A&M fraternity men who pleaded no contest to felony charges of beating a Kappa Alpha Psi pledge; they served jail time but on appeal had the charges expunged from their records.

By 2010 more arrests and a handful of convictions for serious hazing cases began to get the attention of the press. For example, two young men were convicted of misdemeanor hazing in the 2008 death of Cal Poly Sigma Alpha Epsilon pledge Carson Starkey and received jail sentences of thirty days each. On the other hand, in the 2010 death of a Radford University fraternity pledge, the court punishment was merely $1,000 each and no jail time for five Tau Kappa Epsilon members in a plea deal.[24]

Other efforts curtailing hazing have been attempts by international organizations, such as Sigma Alpha Epsilon, to ban or shorten the pledge period. By March 2014, according to the website of the parent SAE organization, all pledging has ceased due to the deaths of ten SAE pledges. Another effective best practice was the dry house movement followed most conspicuously by all chapters of the large national fraternity Phi Delta Theta, which in 2000 removed alcohol from the premises of chapter houses, thereby eliminating the substance that has been linked to the most hazing deaths after 1970.

Civil lawsuits in the aftermath of an injury or death blamed on hazing have become quite common. The parents of Chad Meredith, a University of Miami pledge who drowned when forced to swim across a lake by older Kappa Sigma members, resulted in a $14 million judgment against those young men. The highest settlement ever paid by a university in a fraternity hazing death was $6 million in 2002 by Massachusetts Institute of Technology to the parents of Scott Krueger, who died of alcohol intoxication following a Phi Gamma Delta pledge party. The largest settlement in a hazing band death was $1.1 million by Florida A&M in 2015 to the parents of Robert Champion.

Prevention of Hazing

As might be expected, since deaths by hazing largely occur in fraternities and to a lesser extent in sororities, the main antihazing activists are parents of dead or injured pledges, undergraduate members, alumni, and national officers of fraternities and sororities. The two most influential organizations are the web-based

StopHazing.org, created by University of Maine hazing researcher Elizabeth Allan, and the national group HazingPrevention.Org, inspired and founded by Tracy Maxwell, a nationally known antihazing activist from Colorado.

StopHazing's Allan is a professor at the University of Maine in Higher Education Leadership, one of the few academic programs offering a hazing studies concentration. She and former Maine colleague Mary Madden completed in 2011 a three-year research project on hazing with responses from 11,482 college students enrolled in fifty-four colleges. The survey response rate was 12 percent.

Slightly more than half of all respondents acknowledged participating in acts of hazing as members of student groups such as fraternities and sororities. In her essay for *The Hazing Reader* titled "Hazing and Gender: Analyzing the Obvious," Allan notes that empirical research on gender differences is scant, but while a national survey distributed to Greek professionals found that 44 percent had to deal with reported hazing cases, the number of violent and otherwise physical hazings were far fewer than those committed by male students.[25]

HazingPrevention.Org is dedicated to empowering people to prevent hazing in college and university student groups. HPO's board of directors and numerous volunteers and small staff provide antihazing education through conferences, webinars, and training sessions. HPO sponsors its annual Hank Nuwer Anti-Hazing Hero Award that to date has honored mainly fraternity and sorority undergraduates who effected positive changes in their own chapters to curb hazing practices, but also it has honored the likes of former National Football League quarterback Peyton Manning and Lianne Kowiak, an antihazing activist and mother of a pledge killed in a Theta Chi hazing incident.

In addition to these two antihazing groups, there is a college archive that attempts to put all hazing scholarship under a single collection. Buffalo State College's Butler Library has since 2006 sponsored an extensive Hazing Collection available without charge to hazing researchers and undergraduate students alike. Under the direction of archivist Daniel DiLandro, the Hazing Collection has set an eventual goal to house every hazing-related scholarly article, doctoral dissertation, master's thesis, book, and miscellaneous research item for free use by researchers. Before the collection was established, one difficulty for researchers was that the literature related to hazing was scattered at widely separated libraries and institutions, making research an expensive, time-consuming challenge for researchers.

While a number of best practices to curtail hazing have been championed by a number of educators, no single solution has been found to stamp out hazing. Allan, Maxwell, myself, and other authors have argued that bystander intervention might have prevented specific hazing incidents from leading to serious injuries and deaths in a number of fraternity tragedies. Bystander intervention refs to the practice of emboldening those who witness crimes or potential criminal behavior to step in and take action to halt the behavior before it escalates. The writings and seminars by hazing intervention expert Alan Berkowitz and National Federation of State High School Associations spokesperson Elliot Hopkins target bystander intervention as an important means of stopping a hazing activity before it reaches the point of no return. In addition, a great many US educational institutions use social norms data in an attempt to discourage binge drinking and hazing by stressing to undergraduates that such unacceptable practices are anything but normal. In an attempt to sway behavior changes, there have been marketing campaigns such as posters in college classroom buildings and residence halls.

Other education experts, including Christopher Bollinger, coauthor of *Violence Goes to College*, have argued for the value of substituting useful, benign group-building activities in place of hazing practices.[26] HazingPrevention.Org offers Greek Life professionals and administrators hands-on, scientifically sound strategies to make campuses safer. (Disclosure: I have worked with both).

In 2013, the VTV Family Outreach Foundation, founded by the surviving families of a 2007 Virginia Tech (Virginia Polytechnic Institute and State University) school shooting massacre, brought together nine experts (including me) to create "32 NCSI" (the 32 National Campus Safety Initiative), which has identified best practices for schools to counter campus behaviors such as hazing and sexual assault. A pilot program was initiated with a number of institutions to provide a voluntary rating system so that an institution not only can judge how it measures up in terms of combatting hazing and other behavioral maladies, but also to shore up areas where deficiencies appear to occur. In 2017, 32 NCSI partnered with the National Association of Student Personnel Administrators. The union's value, if any, remains to be seen.

As the number of deaths associated with hazing continues to climb, a trend of late has been the zero tolerance toward the practice by a number of institutions. In addition to the expulsion of chapters caught hazing, a number of universities also have created hazing task forces composed of faculty, staff, and, in some cases, outside experts. Some schools have pressured fraternity councils to curtail activities.

For example, following the hazing death of George Desdunes, then Cornell University President David Skorton issued a clear warning to fraternal groups that the new hazing policy was zero tolerance. The new no-nonsense policy resulted in nine fraternities cited and/or punished by Cornell for hazing from 2012 to March 2014, according to that institution's website, and additional fraternities were reprimanded from March 2014 to August 1, 2017. In addition, Cornell established the Recruitment, Acceptance, Retention, and Education (RARE) Task Force (I was an unpaid consultant) to find and research best practices for curtailing hazing in fraternities and other student groups.[27]

In California, following the alcohol-related birthday death of a Chico State University pledge that institution president Paul Zingg (now retired and a member of the AHA! Movement Board) termed hazing-related, all campus fraternities and sororities were suspended in November 2012. The unprecedented step was taken because of a rash of nonhazing-related deaths at the same time, as well as the fact that this was the fourth hazing death at Chico State. Likewise, Central Florida University, which had a near fatality during pledging for Kappa Alpha Psi, put an end to all pledging and fraternal social activities in 2013, concerned by reports that pledging activities had in some cases escalated into hazing, The University of Virginia ordered all pledging to cease immediately in 2013 or the offending chapters would be shut down.

Other schools emulated in 2017. If these hardline steps fail to work, no doubt some universities will follow the example of Alfred University. In 2002, following a number of hazing deaths in local and national fraternities, the Alfred board of trustees decided regulation of Greek groups was not working. Consequently, the board moved to shut down all Greek houses permanently. However, it is unlikely the majority of colleges will risk alumni outrage by banning fraternities and sororities. National fraternities and sororities vociferously defend the right of public universities to maintain a freedom of association, making it unlikely that any educational institutions (besides the occasional private college) will ever ban the entire Greek system. At present, besides Alfred, the handful of private colleges in the historic past to close their Greek systems included Middlebury College (1990), Williams College (1962), and Colby College (1983). A few private colleges, such as Bates College in Maine, never have permitted fraternities. One public university to ban pledging for a semester was the University of Alabama in November 2012. A committee at the University of South Carolina in 2016 recommended a permanent ban on pledging, but the matter was tabled for one year by the veto of the USC president. In July of 2017, Harvard University debated a measure that, if passed, would phase out fraternities and sororities because of faculty objections to serious issues perceived to be associated with Greeks.

In the end, however, in spite of all these well-intended and laudable hazing prevention strategies, the demeaning and sometimes deadly rites of hazing clearly will continue until undergraduates and high school students themselves universally condemn, counter, and shame peers who haze. Such a needed change demands nothing less than a paradigm shift.

HANK NUWER is a professor in the Franklin College Pulliam School of Journalism. He has written *The Hazing Reader* (IUP) and *Wrongs of Passage: Fraternities, Sororities, Hazing, and Binge Drinking* (IUP).

3 A Need for Transparency

Parents, Students Must Make Informed Decisions About Greek-Life Risks

Douglas Fierberg and Chloe Neely

THE PUBLIC AWARENESS about the prevalence of fraternity hazing violence and campus sexual assaults has grown exponentially in recent years. In March 2014, the *Atlantic* published a lengthy exposé on the hidden dangers of fraternity life following a yearlong investigation into the perils of Greek life on college campuses.[1] However, the risks posed by fraternities are not a new phenomenon. By the 1980s, fraternities were ranked the sixth worst risk for insurance companies by the National Association of Insurance Commissioners, just behind hazardous waste disposal and asbestos.[2] Fraternity or sorority membership has been cited as the strongest predictor of binge drinking by college-aged students,[3] and members are significantly more likely to both drink and binge drink than nonmembers.[4] Among reported campus sexual assaults, 78 percent involve alcohol.[5] Fraternity men are three times more likely than other college men to commit sexual assault,[6] while sorority women are 74 percent more likely than other college women to experience rape and three times more likely if they live in sorority housing.[7] Hazing violence occurs regularly, resulting in serious injuries and at least one death in U.S. college groups and secondary schools per year since 1961).[8] James R. Favor & Company, an insurance broker for the fraternity industry, reports handling more than six thousand claims against fraternities involving more than $60 million in payouts.[9]

The confirmed dangers of fraternities are a pervasive, nationwide problem that universities and colleges have purportedly spent years trying to address, without significant success. Yet, despite the growing public cognizance of the horrors of fraternity life, universities rarely, if ever, disclose the truth behind their own Greek systems, choosing instead to shamelessly promote an infrastructure that has caused decades of harm to their students. This chapter addresses the failure of universities and fraternities to provide timely, accurate information about incidents of violence and misconduct occurring on campus, specifically at fraternity houses and events, and in doing so, stripping students of the fundamental right to know about risks on campus so they can protect themselves.

The first and most crucial step toward universal fraternity reform begins with honest, accurate information about the real dangers associated with fraternities. To achieve meaningful change in the fraternity industry, all of the relevant parties—students, parents, university administrators, fraternity members and leadership, lawyers, legislators, and public health experts—must come to the table with the same set of accurate and specific information about the true nature of the problem. Without a full understanding of issues at play, the conversation simply cannot move forward and future generations of students will suffer.

Following the deadly shooting at Virginia Tech in April 2007, the governor of Virginia convened a panel of experts to undertake an independent, comprehensive review of the events leading up to and on the day of the massacre, as well as the subsequent response.[10] Among its various findings, the panel concluded that the university had made a "questionable decision" when it waited nearly two hours after receiving reports of a double murder in a residence hall to notify the campus community.[11] Even once the alert was finally disseminated, at a time when many students were already in or headed to class, university officials failed to disclose the true nature of the situation, referring only to a "shooting incident" and urging students and faculty "to be cautious."[12] The panel ultimately concluded that the campus community was entitled to timely, accurate information about the true nature of the risk, stating: "Nearly everyone at Virginia Tech is adult and capable of making decisions about potentially dangerous situations to safeguard themselves. So the earlier and clearer the warning, the more chance an individual had of surviving."[13]

Precisely the same logic applies to the risks of fraternity hazing and sexual violence, yet time and time again universities and fraternities fail to provide clear and timely information to allow adult students to make educated decisions and protect themselves. Virtually every university that allows Greek organizations to operate on campus enables those very groups to benefit from university resources, staff, and institutional affiliation, especially through on-campus recruitment and heavy promotion on university websites. The available information, however, is largely limited to promotion only, with little to no information about the actual risks and precise misconduct occurring in fraternity houses or at fraternity events. Almost every university in this country refuses to provide specific information about incidents of hazing, sexual violence, and other injury-causing misconduct associated with fraternities. Those universities that do provide some information often sanitize their treatment of hazing, stating merely that hazing is against university policy and the law and without any indication of the frequency or magnitude of hazing incidents occurring on campus.[14] Some universities will even discourage parents and students from considering the risks associated with Greek life. Penn State, for example, the school in which Beta Theta Pi pledge Timothy Piazza perished in a hazing incident, provides answers to frequently asked questions in its *Parent's Guide to Fraternity and Sorority Life*:

Q. How will my student benefit from joining a fraternity or sorority?

Sororities and fraternities have a rich history at Penn State dating back to the 1870s. These organizations are rooted in founding principles that foster academic achievement, student involvement, community service, and life-long friendships. Fraternities and sororities are groups of men and women who come together to form a personal network of individuals with similar ideas, interests, and a mutual pursuit of a well-rounded college education. Advantages include:

- A support group to help make the adjustment to college easier
- Scholastic resources to help student achieve their academic goals
- Leadership skills acquired through hands-on experience
- Encouragement to get involved and maximize their potential on campus
- Opportunities for active participation in community service projects[15]

Nonetheless, the Penn State fraternity system has been plagued by allegations of extreme hazing,[16] sexual assault,[17] suicide,[18] and other fraternity scandals;[19] and in January 2017, Penn State failed to provide this type of information on its Greek website or in any of its public disclosures to students and campus community. The last time Penn State admitted a serious incident had transpired was in February 2017 when State College police said in a release that alcohol and hazing led to the death of Tim Piazza from fatal injuries.

Only a few universities in the country have begun to disclose misconduct by fraternities, but rarely in a clear or satisfactory manner. Cornell University, for example, touts its fraternities and sororities as "values-based social organizations"[20] that are "among the best in the nation."[21] This information is consistent with the vast majority of university websites nationwide. Yet such information, despite recent improvements in the Cornell Greek community, remains misleading and wrong, both generally and specifically. For example, a few years ago Cornell actively promoted its fraternity system. Yet far behind the front pages of its promotion of its Greek system, deep within its annual report on fraternities and sororities, Cornell documented fifty-one incidents of social misconduct, thirty-three incidents of hazing, thirteen incidents regarding "expectations for membership," seven "recruitment violations," and four "bias report[s]" in a single year.[22]

Such information is presented only as raw data, without any indication of what specifically any given incident entailed. Now Cornell has chosen to go even further with its disclosures, moving them to the front of its publicly available information and becoming one of the few universities prominently disclosing violations and sanctions for misconduct by fraternities.[23] Cornell hosts a separate website dedicated to hazing within student groups, which documents the actual details of hazing incidents since 2004.[24] While the more complete disclosure is commendable, unfortunately the website itself is not easily accessible from Cornell's Greek Life website. Rather, the link to the hazing prevention website is buried at the bottom of the web page used for reporting incidents of misconduct, part of the Office of the Dean of Students, where one would have to be actively looking to find it.[25]

The handful of other universities or fraternities that began to disclose incidents of misconduct similarly provide only the most opaque descriptions, leaving students without any reasonable way to discern the true nature of the risks they face.[26] These universities publish reports of misconduct without disclosing any detail, relying instead on euphemistic phrases like "harm to person," "injury on property," or "dangerous environment [for] guests."[27] Without any specific information, "injury on property" could just as easily mean intentionally inflicted injury resulting from severe hazing, as it could a fraternity member stubbing his toe on a loose floorboard.

The University of Virginia's abysmal disclosures concerning the "Chapter Conduct History" of its fraternity system demonstrates this point clearly.[28] The university publishes a history of the sanctions imposed on its various fraternity chapters in the self-proclaimed "spirit of transparency and accountability."[29] Ironically, the supposed "transparency" of the university's disclosures could hardly be less transparent. In its "issue summaries," UVA describes violations such as failing "to comply with university standards regarding new member activities," failing "to comply with IFC standards regarding alcohol, physical abuse, and personal conduct," and failing "to comply with national fraternity standards regarding personal safety." The true nature of these violations, however, is anyone's guess.[30]

The university has made a very specific choice to hide the true nature of these incidents from its students and the public, particularly since clear, accurate disclosure of the incidents would violate no law or privacy right. Instead one must engage in a web-based search to try and learn some of the truth, which reveals incidents at the university ranging from threats of violence and sodomy[31] to forced consumption of alcohol, beverages, live fish,[32] or excessive amounts of soy sauce, which landed one fraternity pledge in a coma.[33]

There is no basis for an educational institution to manipulate information in this manner. If those who possess the specific information about the type and magnitude of these problems (i.e., universities and fraternities) refuse to disclose them fully and accurately, there is little hope of beginning to truly address and solve the rampant problems of fraternity violence and misconduct. Similarly, in the context of sexual assault, schools that refer to instances of "sexual misconduct" similarly fail to provide students, primarily female students, with the requisite information to fully and appropriately protect themselves.[34]

Any publication of information about fraternity misconduct is the result of a choice made by university administration, including what, if any, specific information to include. Thus, the choice to refer vaguely to "sexual misconduct" rather than "rape" or "sexual assault" is intentional, compounding the failure to adequately disclose. Schools' failure to provide any details of the circumstances (e.g., particular fraternities with histories of sexual assault[35] or perhaps a pattern of assaults involving date-rape drugs) creates an environment in which female students are particularly vulnerable to sexual violence. While the problem of campus sexual assault has been front and center in the news for the past several years, much of any potential solution depends on a shared understanding of the facts and true nature of the problem.

The Clery Act[36] attempts to ensure that campus communities are informed about safety and risks by requiring institutions of higher education to report campus crimes.[37] Such reports, however, require only aggregate numbers of incidents and contain only rudimentary information, such as the date of the report, the date of the crime, and the general location of the incident.[38] Without specific information, particularly in situations involving known fraternity houses with repeated violations, students are incapable of assessing the true risks and taking steps to make informed decisions to reasonably protect themselves. Moreover, universities create a particularly treacherous risk when they fail to disclose risks unique to one gender. Both the high risk of fraternity-based hazing violence for college men and sexual assault for college women create environments that perpetuate discrimination on the basis of sex in an educational context, which is in violation of Title IX.[39]

In failing to disclose information known to universities and fraternities about the nature of these risks, and in some contexts actively providing materially false information, schools or fraternities arguably engage in forms of fraud. To date there are few lawsuits against universities and fraternities based upon such legal theories, but that is likely to change soon. Concepts of fraud and actionable misrepresentations are based in state law and as such can vary widely from state to state while sharing core concepts. In general, liability can stem from intentional[40] or negligent[41] misrepresentation, involving risk of physical harm, and fraudulent misrepresentation causing physical harm, where there is a duty to disclose.[42] Misrepresentations can include "not only words spoken or written but also any other conduct that amounts to an assertion not in accordance with the truth."[43] Telling only part of the truth, and leaving out information that would advise students about real risks, could subject the school or fraternity to liability when a student relies on such misinformation and suffers subsequent harm from hazing, sexual violence, or other misconduct.[44] That student was, in fact, denied the opportunity to understand the risks and protect herself.[45]

Beyond explicit statements vouching for the safety and quality of a university's Greek system, "other incomplete statements or partial truths" can constitute a misrepresentation, according to the American Law Institute (ALI).[46] ALI also states that "a representation stating the truth so far as it goes but which the maker knows or believes to be materially misleading because of his failure to state additional or qualifying matter is a fraudulent misrepresentation"[47] and "a statement containing a half-truth may be as misleading as a statement wholly false. Thus, a statement that contains only favorable matters and omits all reference to unfavorable matters is as much a false representation as if all the facts stated were untrue."[48] Fraudulent concealment can also arise when a seller of a product—here, educational services and experiences—has no duty to speak but chooses to voluntarily.[49] Once a university voluntarily speaks to the quality and value of its fraternity system, it accepts the duty to make a "full and fair disclosure as to the matters discussed."[50] Thus, by exclusively promoting Greek life and its myriad benefits without any mention of the well-documented and rampant risks, schools commit fraud of a severe and potentially deadly type.

Under theories of consumer protection, students act as consumers when they pay tuition to colleges and universities in exchange for the receipt of educational services. In such circumstances, nondisclosure or concealment can be fraudulent in situations where there is a duty to disclose. For example, the Pennsylvania Unfair Trade Practices and Consumer Protection Law defines "unfair or deceptive acts or practices" to include "[e]ngaging in any other fraudulent or deceptive conduct which creates a likelihood of confusion or of misunderstanding."[51] Undoubtedly, refusal to disclose the risks of fraternities or disclosure of only the partial truth creates a strong likelihood of confusion or misunderstanding that these risks either do not exist or those that do are insignificant.

Full disclosure of the true risks of fraternity life will convert students and families into well-informed consumers, rather than those who blindly accept the marketing put forth by the university or fraternity. Without all of the relevant information, students are actively prevented from engaging in a truly free market, informed choice. In this way, fraternities can be compelled to change through pressure from market forces. Individual fraternities strive to distinguish themselves from one another and attract membership. By fully disclosing the conduct and risks of each chapter, students as consumers can assess for themselves whether any given fraternity succeeds in self-management and stays within its purported ideals. As new generations of students continue to fight for change in their educational communities, they can speak volumes through the choices they make—to join, which fraternity to join, or not to join at all—but those choices mean little if they are not well informed. Fraternities that meet their ideals safely should push for transparent reporting since it will enable them to thrive and rise to the top.

Universities and fraternities have exclusive knowledge of the details and circumstances—the material facts—of reports of sexual violence in particular and owe a duty to students to alert them to known patterns of risk or danger that develop at particular fraternities. For any genuine effort to reform American fraternities to succeed, those who have the information must be compelled to disclose what they know. Compelled disclosure will ensure the greatest chance of success, as any meaningful change addressing the deeper roots of the problem of fraternity misconduct must begin with a comprehensive understanding of the issues shared by everyone. Universities and fraternities that continue to unequivocally promote fraternity and sorority membership, untempered by disclosures of the reality of misconduct and violence, must shoulder the blame when students are unable to take reasonable precautions. The point of this is clear: The judicial system might be called upon and used to justly compel universities and fraternities to do what is expected of everyone: tell the truth. Unfortunately such intervention is necessary because schools are not doing it voluntarily, and no state or federal legislature has required them to do so. Numerous social problems have been resolved in this manner, including, for example, desegregation of schools as a result of the historic decision by the US Supreme Court in 1954 in *Brown v. Board of Education.*[52]

College has long been considered the training ground for adulthood in the United States. Most fraternity systems themselves extensively promote the importance of self-governance and responsibility.[53] The refusal of universities to fully and accurately inform their students of the risks and dangers posted to them by Greek organizations undermines the maturity and responsibility of all students. In order to begin to truly address the hazards of fraternities, students must be equipped with the necessary information to protect themselves and make fully informed decisions. The need for full disclosure goes even further than simply the ability for students to protect themselves, which is a purely reactive response, and is required for broader reform in the fraternity industry—a proactive approach to preventing misconduct, rather than simply minimizing its harm. The mission of higher education and the law demand that universities and fraternities alike end the longstanding practice of obscuring, concealing, and denying the whole truth about the risks of Greek membership and its activities.

DOUGLAS FIERBERG established a legal practice specializing in the representation of victims of school violence, now operating as the Fierberg National Law Group. Fierberg also founded the national litigation group

Schools: Violence, Misconduct, and Safety, which operates within and under the authority of the American Association for Justice. He is a past president of the National Advisory Board of the National Crime Victim Bar Association.

CHLOE NEELY is in law school at New York University and is clerking for the Fierberg National Law Group. Neely secured a federal clerkship and plans to represent survivors of sexual assault.

ıame

ιne Hidden Harm of Hazing for Victims and Hazers

Tracy Maxwell

"Hidden harm" is a phrase coined to describe the effect a previous trauma—usually psychological, but sometimes physical—can have in exacerbating the impact of hazing on an individual. It can manifest from a variety of sources, including childhood abuse or neglect, sexual assault, violence, wartime military service, loss of a loved one, depression or other emotional issues, coming from a family with a history of alcoholism or drug abuse, and having been hazed or bullied before.

All of the above backgrounds—as well as countless others we can't even imagine, much less know about—could put someone at higher risk of being retraumatized through hazing. The autobiographical book *Goat* by Brad Land describes the carjacking in which the author was tied up, put in the trunk of his car, beaten, and driven around in fear of his life, only to have his attackers dump him in a ditch in the middle of nowhere several terrifying hours later. A short time after this incident, Land joined a Clemson college fraternity where he was brutally hazed. One of his pledge brothers committed suicide because of the experience, and Land suffered post-traumatic stress symptoms in which the faces of his "brothers" and those of his carjackers became interchangeable.[1]

Hazers often believe that by "breaking people down and building them back up" they are providing some kind of benefit to their victims, toughening them up to face the rigors of life. This is a perspective I've heard many times throughout my career. Michael Colfield, a hazing victim himself, shared with me a different view: "Life itself is a hazing process, so it should not take another human being to do what life is already going to/has done to an individual."

Others see hazing as a loyalty test and believe that how well you perform in their ridiculous tasks is a measure of how much you will contribute as a member. Further, arguments are often made that hazing bonds people together, and to some extent that is true, but mostly just within small groups of the hazed and not the larger organization or team. Researcher Judy van Raalte showed that "hazing exposes athletes to physical and psychological risks, and is associated with reduced rather than greater team cohesiveness."[2]

In her book *Daring Greatly*, Brené Brown, a shame researcher, explains why this approach doesn't work: "In an organizational culture where respect and the dignity of individuals are held as the highest values, shame and blame don't work as management styles. There is no leading by fear. Empathy is a valued asset, accountability is an expectation rather than an exception, and the primal human need for belonging is not used as leverage and social control."[3] She goes on to suggest that "we can't control the behavior of individuals; however, we can cultivate organizational cultures where behaviors are not tolerated and people are held accountable for protecting what matters most: human beings."

Her words, of course, have meaning in so many areas of modern life where it seems intolerable behavior is present in our presidential candidates, social-media cyberbullying, and hate speech, as well as in today's rampant hazing.

The Public Perception of Hazing

Part of the dissonance that comes with hazing is the fact that most people hear about it only when it reaches physical extremes to be reported in the press, sometimes when someone is seriously injured or killed. Because of the shame and self-blame that many victims of hazing feel, we rarely find out about the psychological trauma that can be felt for decades afterward from either physical or emotional hazing. In the case of psychological hazing, the shame is so great that the hazing itself is almost never revealed, much less the long-lasting individual impacts.

Travis Apgar, Dean of Students at Rensselaer Polytechnic Institute, is a notable exception with his own story that he has taken to dozens of colleges to talk about hazing. The antihazing activist tells the story of being a child witness to his father's suicide with a gun, and the triggering hazing event involving Russian roulette in his college fraternity that caused him to experience a severe psychological response years later. Apgar left school over the incident and has told me that he believes he would have been diagnosed with depression had he gone to see a medical or mental health professional. Instead, being able to tell his story has been as beneficial for him as it is for his audiences.

Because shame and self-blame prevents individuals from sharing these types of stories, the perception of hazing by the public is often that it only includes serious physical harm. Therefore, acts of humiliation, degradation, embarrassment, harassment, and ridicule mostly escape the hazing label and aren't taken as seriously. Until more of these stories come to light, it is difficult for the public to truly understand and recognize the devastating and long-term emotional impact hazing can have. "If we can share our story with someone who responds with empathy and understanding, shame can't survive," advises Brown.[4]

Band Hazing

After I asked a well-known figure in higher education and fraternity life about his passion for hazing prevention, he listed a litany of experiences and involvements over the years before finally divulging the real reason. "I have never shared this with anyone before," he said to preface his confession, "but I was seriously hazed in the eighth grade." He proceeded to tell the story of being proud to be selected for a prestigious band program that took him to another city with students from across the state.

Because he was from a small rural school, he didn't know anyone else, and he shared that some participants from a larger city school saw him as weak and decided to haze him. They stripped him naked and left him in a public place at the state fair for nearly an hour as people streamed past pointing and laughing at him, and no one helped or stepped in to stop the abuse. His voice full of emotion, he said, "That happened over fifty years ago, and I have nightmares about it to this day."

I asked permission to tell his story since it contains several important lessons. My vision was to videotape an interview or write about it as I have here. He gave me permission to tell the story as widely as I like as long as I didn't ever share his name. Though he is a widely respected PhD hazing researcher and pillar of the community, his shame is still so deep that he can't bring himself to be associated with this painful episode from his past. There is a lesson here. If he can't come out with all of his knowledge and training, it demonstrates how difficult it is to find and share these stories when the shame causes younger victims to suppress or deny their experiences.

Colfield was also hazed as a band member at Grambling State University in Louisiana. His story has been featured in *Ebony* magazine and on HBO's *Real Sports with Bryant Gumbel*. He shared the following in an interview with Hazing Prevention.Org for the 2012 edition of the National Hazing Prevention Week resource guide.[5] "I was ashamed and afraid to allow anyone in my family to know what was happening to me," he said. "I almost got put out of school due to my hazing. During the process, I risked not going to class, losing sleep, and had a great loss in my personal finances. Almost everything was lost, but my academics suffered the most." He advises: "Hazing comes with a price . . . scarring physically, mentally, and spiritually, and a possible breakdown in all aspects."

Camp Hazing

At the thirty-year reunion of the Girl Scout camp I attended as a kid and then returned to as a staff member after college, someone who came a few years after me said to another woman at the dinner table one night, "I have this memory from camp of you crying at the shower house one night. What was that about?"

That question triggered the worst fear of this former staff member—that she would only be remembered for her reaction to a camp activity that had happened fifteen years before. She had been nervous to attend the event because of the impact of this one incident that involved the hazing of new staff members. The incident itself was fairly innocuous, and one I participated in myself with little thought. But the way staff members were treated in the holding area prior to be taken in one by one for the activity, which took place in the lodge in front of the entire camp, was militaristic, involving yelling and other mild forms of abuse. It simply was not in keeping with what this woman had come to expect at this camp she had attended since childhood and where she had always felt safe. She shared that she had been hazed again later, in college, but it didn't affect her as the camp event had because she anticipated it. She never would have expected to be talked to or treated in an abusive or harmful way at camp, which had always been such an uplifting and special place filled with supportive and caring people, so in that setting it was a complete shock. It illustrates all too well that it only takes one or a small handful of individuals to drastically change the tenor of an activity or experience, and also that each individual reacts differently. I was completely unaffected, while this woman was still ashamed about the event.

Other staffers said that they were also negatively impacted, and one former director of the camp discussed how she led efforts to eliminate all forms of hazing from traditional camp activities. "I am thankful the hazing I went through did not escalate and never caused anyone physical harm," she said. "It did cause emotional scarring for a number of young women, though. I know because I was one of them."

Both of these stories illustrate the damage that can ensue when victims internalize their humiliating experiences. While they may have held some animosity for their abusers, they also blamed themselves for not being able to take what fellow staffers seemed to take. They were more upset by their reaction to the event than to the experience itself. Both were ashamed and traumatized, and both have carried those feelings around with them for years, decades even! This is an aspect of hazing that is rarely discussed, and research into the detrimental effects of shame are showing us that we need to be much more aware of this phenomenon.

The Impact of Shame

Leslie Shelton wrote her doctoral dissertation on the impact of shame in relation to childhood literacy and learning.[6] The following quote comes from another unpublished paper titled "Transforming the Shame of Early School Difficulties" and is relevant to the hazing discussion as well: "As I studied the psychological research on shame, I began to see how the persistent shame of failure in school at an early age causes enormous harm to the entire self system—not only to self-esteem (how one feels about oneself), but also to a person's self-image (identity), feelings of competence (or incompetence), and sense of belonging (or lack of belonging)."

The definition of shame, in its simplest form, is the exposure of a weakness or failure to measure up to any family or cultural norm.

Shame research explains how persistent failure overtakes identity and leads a person to think that one is flawed as a human being. The feeling of shame is so uncomfortable and disturbing that children develop coping mechanisms to avoid or deflect the ongoing torment, including hiding, running away from school, giving up, or attacking themselves or others. The harm caused in childhood persists into adulthood and continues to eat at the soul, undermining learning and well-being.

Research has long correlated a link between shame and depression.[7] Feeling ashamed influences self-esteem, which is a measure of our sense of belonging.[8] Therefore, the literature demonstrates that shame can be a particularly strong indicator of the fear of social rejection because it involves a negative evaluation of the self.

Shame as a Trigger for Perpetrators

Shame doesn't just impact victims of hazing or bullying. It is now believed by many shame researchers that bullying and other acts of violence all have shame as the underlying trigger as well.[9] Perpetrators experience shame too, particularly when they have some insight into the hurt they have caused their victims. Think about the amends made years later by school bullies as a result of participation in a twelve-step program, or just on their own initiative.

Eddie Banks-Crosson, Director of Fraternity and Sorority Life at the University of Pennsylvania, shared an experienced with me that changed his life forever, and he admits it could have been much worse. He slapped a membership candidate for his fraternity when the newbie dared to make eye contact, and the impact caused the younger member's eardrum to burst. Seeing him the next day bandaged and fighting back tears "rocked my inner soul to the core," Banks-Crosson admits. "I felt like the worst person in the world at that moment," especially when the other man said, "All I wanted was to be like you."

After initially distancing himself from the fraternity for a time, Banks-Crosson made the decision to try to change things, and he started by reading the fraternity's history and to understand the true purpose behind his and all fraternal organizations. Following graduation, he worked in corporate life for a time before returning to higher education and fraternity and sorority life as a career. Ten years after the incident that changed his life, he ran into the person he had injured at the bank and began an awkward apology for his actions a decade before. The man stopped him and said, "It's OK. I forgave you long ago, and from the look on your face, you need to forgive yourself."

Often before taking responsibility for their actions, either internally or through actual contact with victims, perpetrators have a need to protect themselves and their own self-worth. This can happen in a variety of ways: denying that their behavior is a problem, blaming the victim or viewing them as weak, rationalizing behavior as legitimate, and justifying it as providing some perceived value. An Australian study showed that this displacement of shame increased the likelihood of bullying behavior. Other factors increasing the prospect of bullying include a student's dislike of the school and the perception that bullying was condoned by those in authority.[10]

Students often have the sense that hazing is ignored or even condoned by the actions of coaches and teachers or administrators.[11] When statements about hazing include the sentiment, "Just don't let me see it," students can read into that, that the behavior itself might be tolerated as long as it is kept secret. If hazing is widespread and known about by students but not investigated, taken seriously when reported, or severely punished, perception continues that it's "not a big deal" or even can be a valuable "tradition."

The Role of Individual Healing

David Hawkins, in his numerous volumes about the nature of human consciousness, as measured through the science of kinesiology, ranks shame at the very lowest level on the scale of energetic vibrations. He says, "Shame is used as a tool of cruelty, and its victims often become cruel. Shamed children are cruel to animals and to each other. The behavior of people whose consciousness is only in the twenties is dangerous."[12]

Hawkins developed a numeric scale of consciousness from 1 to 1,000 with shame at the lowest end—20 and below—and 500 and above signifying unconditional love to enlightenment. His work is important to this conversation for two reasons. First, it demonstrates that consciousness levels below a certain level (200 as a baseline) indicate people prone to using force as a means of getting their way, while those above 200 (the level of courage) exert power in a more benevolent manner. Second, his work proves that there is a counterbalancing effect from higher consciousness levels to lower ones because the scale itself is logarithmic.

For example: One individual at 400 counterbalances 400,000 individuals below level 200, and one individual at 300 counterbalances 90,000 individuals below level 200. This pattern continues up the scale with more and more lower vibrations being balanced by fewer and fewer higher energetic vibrations. In other words, if just a few individuals rise in consciousness within a group or within society, they bring up the level of the whole on average, making conditions less favorable for violence to occur. I find this a significant factor in possible hazing intervention and prevention among groups such as fraternities, sororities, athletic teams, and bands.

It is certainly a tragedy that dozens of people have been killed in hazing incidents over the years, but I believe the tragedy of so many of the hazed and bullied feeling ashamed, often for years afterward, is also a significant public health issue. The walking wounded among us are more likely to suffer from depression or other emotional issues and to become perpetrators themselves. Because it is hidden from our view, we don't know how far-reaching it is, nor do we consider the negative impact it has on our society. We should. More studies in this area can and must be completed.

TRACY MAXWELL is the founder of HazingPrevention.Org. She has been working in and around higher education for more than twenty-five years. She currently speaks about hazing for CAMPUSPEAK. Her work as a healing coach assists survivors of hazing and their families.

5 Sexual Hazing

A Wrongful Passage

Norm Pollard

WHAT MAKES ATHLETES allow themselves to be put in dangerous and vulnerable situations? Why do athletes allow themselves to be degraded, humiliated, or hurt, all in the name of so-called tradition? Why would any person work so hard to be humbled for acceptance into a group that treats them in a way more reminiscent to Abu Ghraib than team building? These questions over the years have baffled educators.

About fifteen years ago my university, Alfred University in New York State, had such an incident when veteran football-team players were caught hazing the rookie players. In this situation, a group of freshmen were bound together and made to consume alcohol until they vomited.

The question once again arose: what would make such talented student athletes allow themselves to engage in such a dangerous rite of passage, especially when the group that was forcing them to engage in this dangerous and possibly deadly hazing act was the very group they wanted to be a part of? This cannot be explained as simply being a matter of "boys will be boys" or just a few students who were not aware of the possible consequences of their actions. The situation actually is much more complex, including the need to prove their worthiness to become part of the group and the need to demonstrate their readiness to move into adulthood. To understand hazing, it is necessary to understand the connectivity of these things.

Initiation, or rite of passage, is a coming-of-age process. It has typically been the central form of education and guidance for adolescents in their ascension into adulthood. It is a ritualistic process that clarifies and affirms their new status or role in the adult community. The process is an intentional one. The traditional ritual cycle has three phases: (1) willingness of the chosen initiate to assert that they are "worthy" of membership (2) the period of time that includes specific and traditional rites that signify the transition from adolescent to adult, and (3) the successful completion of the initiation and the ceremonial reincorporation as a full member back in to the group. The elders (really pseudo elders), or those initiating the new members, have specific goals. The goals usually are not evident or understood by the new member and only the so-called elders have the "wisdom" to understand the complexity of the initiation. The initiates' knowledge and comprehension come gradually. Usually they do not know what is happening to them or what it means. The initiation process establishes a hierarchy between those with power versus those without power (rookies/pledge/newbie vs. the team/club/group).

By asking each generation to participate in a process of initiation, traditional rites reappear and the entire community is reinvigorated. To know that every generation of one's culture (team/club/group) went through the exact same process creates a "connectedness" to something greater than the individual. Anthony Cohen stated that "adolescent initiation rites weaken a youth's emotional identification with members of his nuclear family, and, at the same time, define his social identity." Participants feel part of the community and the community knows it has been renewed. The process is profoundly personal and communal and could possibly help explain why so many hazed individuals view their experience as positive. The larger group has helped the individual to become an adult and full participant in the group.[1]

Unlike some cultures that have very clear rites of passage regarding transitioning into adulthood, the United States has very mixed messages. There is no one clear ritual that signifies that a person is no longer viewed as a child. The age of majority is eighteen and so would seem that all above the age of eighteen would be considered an adult, but that age does not automatically allow them to participate in all adult activities. For many things, such as buying and consuming alcohol and often renting vehicles, the age is higher. This sends mixed messages to a group with insecure feelings about becoming an adult. They often do not know what it means or entails since few have been taught or mentored.

As a result of my involvement as a researcher on hazing, I've concluded that our society has abdicated its responsibility for initiating the young and no longer provides challenging, rigorous, and meaningful rites of passage.[2] In previous generations, families would work side by side in the fields, eat every meal together, sometimes build adjacent homes next to their parents, and transition directly from adolescence into adulthood. As our culture progressed from agrarian to industrial to informational, it seems there are few "elders" in our society willing to teach the values and knowledge adolescents need to become adult members of our society. As a result the developmental process has been elongated to include another life stage labeled as "emerging adulthood." Even though hazing typically occurs during this new life stage, the research has yet to fully take into account the manifestation of emerging adulthood as a factor in participation.[3]

This lack of knowledge creates a situation where the adolescent turns to the sources around them to find some answers. Rather than seeking knowledge and direction from adults or mentors, however, adolescents are garnering knowledge through peers, YouTube, online chat rooms, Google, and Wikipedia. It's not the fault of parents, teachers, or society; it is the lack of confidence our culture has to teach values. Our society has "evolved" to value tangible cognitive abilities and skills, rather than intangible cultural values and norms.

For many emerging adults, popular media is a source that can give false narrative of what it means to be an adult, especially for males. Popular media often has equated the hypermasculine superhero as the icon of male adulthood. As a result, boys equate being "macho" with being an adult, and those activities associated with being macho as their "rite of passage" toward adulthood. One of the major macho icons would be that of the high-status athlete, and the rite of passage into that category would be through involvement in a team, club, or group.

A Sense of Belonging and Hazing

Humans are social beings and the need to belong is a fundamental human motivation. They have a strong desire and need to be part of a group. As quoted in Hank Nuwer's *Broken Pledges: The Deadly Rite of Hazing,* Irving L. Janis, a Yale psychology professor emeritus and author of *Groupthink,* explained that membership is "a basic aspect of group psychology" and that a new member "has the enormous fear . . . that to refuse puts one in danger of begin a deviant by violating a group norm."[4]

Emerging adults are especially driven toward social and group acceptance. Initiation rites are frequently used to create such a feeling. They are used to enhance the cohesiveness among group members and to increase this sense of belonging. The initiation process allows entry into a select group so sustained personal contact can be assured and the newfound relationships can provide a stable force in their lives.

Initiation rites are often harmless and might even be fun or educational, but at times they cross the line into involving activities that are humiliating, dangerous, or illegal. Hazing also typically requires potential members to engage in actions that under normal circumstances would be automatically refused and dismissed. Some recent examples of these include five St. Louis–area high-school athletes at summer sports camp accused of sodomizing four rookies, four Ootlewah (Tennessee) High School basketball players being sexually assaulted by fellow teammates while out of town for a holiday basketball tournament, and five Spotsylvania (Virginia) High School football players that were criminally charged by police after at least one other player alleged that he had been penetrated with a broomstick. In January 2017, a judge convicted a Philomath (Oregon) High School volunteer assistant coach of criminal mistreatment for failing to stop a sexual hazing. The aforementioned behaviors are humiliating, dangerous, and illegal, but they are also considered hazing.

Hazing has been recognized as a problem in America since the founding of Harvard College, but people often mistakenly associate only activities done by fraternities and sororities to be hazing. This is a major misconception and the scope of hazing is nowhere near that narrow. As seen by the surveys done by Alfred University and the comprehensive national survey done by Elizabeth Allen and Mary Madden, hazing can be found in any organization—especially organizations for adolescents and young adults, including religious groups, honor societies, scouts, bands, all types of athletics teams. Thus this misconception has been definitively corrected.

Hazing from a Developmental Perspective

Hazing typically occurs during particular developmental periods. The Alfred University studies found a steady increase in endorsed hazing behaviors from middle school to high school and peaking in college. The phenomena of hazing rarely occur once an individual reaches their midtwenties, with the exception of newcomers assaulted as part of initiation into occupations such as firefighters, chefs, and professional athletes. Hazing, called a tradition, also is imposed upon new legislators, although it never gets to the point of being a criminal act. Similar patterns involving emerging adults have also been found in alcohol use, crime rates, and many other socially unacceptable behaviors.

Hazing more typically occurs when adolescents are transitioning into their adulthood. Developmental psychologist Erik Erikson posited that the teen years were a period of time where a person is trying to figure out who she or he is and to learn the roles to be occupied as an adult.[5] College-aged students would then begin to enter a phase in which a person begins to look for long-term commitments and relationships outside of his or her family. These stages help to provide a possible explanation as to where the haze is developmental. Emerging adults wholeheartedly believe that their core identity is profoundly changed by participating in this pseudo–rite of passage. The sense of identity and belonging appear to be cemented by the activity. But, as explained by researcher Jeffery Arnett, there is a developmental stage—emerging adulthood—that is the most frequent age of those hazed.

Researching the Problem

In an effort of better understand this dangerous phenomena, Alfred University conducted the landmark study "Initiation Rites and Athletics: A National Survey of NCAA Sports Teams." The first task of the researchers, including me, in trying to understand this behavior was to define it. For the study, a fairly generic and now widely used definition was developed. This definition was an all-encompassing definition stating that "any activity expected of someone joining a group that humiliates, degrades, abuses, or endangers, regardless of the person's willingness to participate" was considered to be hazing. Respondents were then asked to provide demographic information and answer a team-initiation questionnaire.

Several interesting, even surprising, items soon emerged. One was that only a few of the respondents were acknowledging the existence of hazing, even those that clearly *had* experienced it. This was not just true of a number of respondents but interestingly even included the students who were directly exposed to it. A mere 12 percent of student-athlete respondents reported being hazed to join an athletic team. However, a full 80 percent reported participating in one of the activities that are considered hazing activities. The discrepancy between these two figures suggests that even when given a straightforward definition of it, students did not really know what constituted hazing. It also indicated a general lack of concern about hazing practices. Students knew that the idea of hazing had negative connotations; therefore, to label their experiences as hazing implies that they have done something wrong or been a victim. So it is no surprise that so few were willing to report that they'd been hazed.

Those who did acknowledge hazing practices defended them strongly, claiming that they build "team chemistry" and are "traditional." As one student wrote on his survey, "If no one is hurt to the point where they need medical attention, just leave it alone." Many respondents appeared to have had very little concept of how harmful hazing could be, or how easily it could get out of their control.

This incongruence appears to be more widespread than just this initial survey. Often times those who are reporting or describing hazing fail to fully appreciate that the act of hazing is more of a process than a one-time occurrence—that those involved are participating in a rite of passage, an initiation. That the hazing occurs over an extended period of time, in private, and gradually escalates from silly, to nonsensical, to humiliating, to dangerous. Since they endured some of the hazing and feel that it must end soon, those hazed adopt the philosophy of "in for a penny, in for a pound." Additionally, since our society values perseverance and belittles quitters, those individuals enduring the hazing often will tough it out, with the hope that it'll end soon.

Another interesting result of the studies was that one of the reason students appear to be so reluctant to see the harmful aspect of hazing is that hazing is very much a part of their lives. As Laura Robinson chronicled in a hard-hitting investigation of Canadian hockey titled *Crossing the Line*, players often endured hazing from peewee to junior to pros.[6]

Not only has hazing been going on so long in the university atmosphere that it is considered tradition, and is often glorified in movies about college life, but it is also present and, in some areas of the United States, even rampant at the high school level. Of the athletes who reported being hazed in the Alfred study,

42 percent of them reported being first hazed in high school. Another 5 percent said that they were hazed first in middle school. If hazing is something that students have been exposed to from the beginning of their athletic career, it is understandable that they think it is acceptable. As substantiated in Alfred University's follow-up study of high-school hazing, students are coming to college campuses from a culture of hazing. For these students, the hazing is as much a part of being the team as eating meals together or having team mascots.[7]

Through the various research, the scope of the problem was becoming more apparent; however, there became a strong need to more fully understand the motivation for participation. Some researchers and educators have speculated that the purpose of hazing is to create "dependence," and thereby the hazee increases his or her liking of the abusers.[8] Respondents to the first Alfred University survey frequently indicated that abusive behaviors were seen as a very positive experience and was not defined in their perception as hazing. They saw it as an initiation that contributed to the bonding of the group and created a sense of group solidarity. There was a sense of cognitive dissonance between their two beliefs and thoughts: the positive being a sense of belonging and the negative being the danger and humiliation experienced. As cited in Hank Nuwer's book *Broken Pledges*, Elliott Aronson and Judson Mills explained in their article on hazing and cognitive dissonance, "the initiate who endures a severe ordeal is likely to find membership in a group all the more appealing."[9]

A Tradition in Name Only

Hazing is an unsanctioned, organizational self-governance by individuals, who themselves were most likely hazed a few months or years earlier and have a warped perception that such illicit activities are a "tradition" or unofficial requirement of joining the group. Since the hazers are attempting to create an initiation without the benefit of true elders or wisdom, they often default to acts of humiliation, degradation, and/or dangerousness. Paradoxically, rather than creating a cohesive group of equal participants, hazing promotes a dysfunctional sense of loyalty and the appearance of "team" bonding perpetuates the code of silence over hazing incidents. Additionally, they may become aware of an additional hazing activity to add to what was previously done to them as a way of adding their own unique touches to this and trying to "enhance" the experience so it becomes the new "tradition." When alcohol is present, anything goes and often has. It is also possible that the acts of sexual hazing can be learned from students from other schools via the internet.

It is worth noting that hazing is a group activity that does not usually take place under the supervision of "adults" or in the public eye; rather, the activities are done in private, in secret, and in a location that is unknown to anyone outside the group. This creates the reality that if the hazee should attempt to resist the hazing activities, no one knows where they are or what is occurring so there is also a sense of needing to participate. If the new members perceive an advisor or coach is aware of the conduct and has not stopped the activity, then they could assume it is in fact sanctioned by the person or the school and would therefore not be considered harmful.

Hazing is often tolerated by new members because of a misguided assumption that this process is necessary in order to be accepted and that doing so demonstrates the new member's allegiance to the group. As stated earlier in the chapter, if this had been true about their previous participation in group activities, then future instances would be the norm to them.

Like rape, hazing also is about power. While many involved would point out all the positives of the initiation process, few would mention the role that desire for power plays in it. Specifically, those often bigger, stronger athletes that intend to dominate those who wish to join the group are the ones that wield the power. It is common that hazers will use a variety of humiliating, and often times dangerous, acts to control and pacify the new initiates. In fact, the hazee's personality or identity is stripped away and the victim is usually viewed as a number, nickname, or object. The acts aren't "personal," but collective. We know from the Philip Zimbardo "Stanford Prison Experiment" that once people get into certain roles they often perform differently than their normal behavior. The Stanford professor researched how readily people would conform to the roles of guard and prisoner in a role-playing exercise that simulated prison life. The investigators concluded that people will readily conform to the social roles they are expected to play, especially if the roles are strongly stereotyped.[10]

Associating Quitting with Losing

"Quitters never win and winners never quit" according to legendary coach Vince Lombardi, who tolerated hazing in the mild form of buffoonery and singing of college songs by rookies. This quote has appeared in numerous locker rooms and been repeated many times to most athletes over the course of their athletic careers. Quitting is not considered honorable, not during the big game, not during practice, and not when being hazed. This belief also contributes to the acceptance of hazing. Contrary to many other types of assaults, the initiation process is perpetrated by the group's established members onto a group of potential members and takes place over time. It is not normally a one-time act, but rather the "initiation" often progresses from being welcoming to being very dangerous. The incremental progression of activities seduces the participants to tolerate more than they normally might. Additionally, many rationalize that they've endured so much, that they don't want to quit, thereby forfeiting the opportunity to become part of the group. Besides, they see hazing on ESPN by professional athletes as another form of entertainment.

Initiation Rite or Sexual Assault?

Depending on the audience, when talking about hazing many people still associate it with eating goldfish, wearing silly outfits, shaving one's head, or even drinking excessively. Often times groups will have new members conduct the silly or nonsensical behavior in public, and engage in the dangerous, often abusive acts in private. There was an incident in New England where all the rookie female gymnasts had to dress up in bibs, sleepers, bonnets, and pacifiers while parading through the local grocery store singing "I'm a Little Tea Pot." While the adults watching were amused, what they didn't see was the procession going out to the back parking lot. Those spectators failed to watch each girl walk through a ring of packed cars with their lights shining to the center, and see them get on their knees and eat a banana protruding out of a football player's pants. What is often missed is the increasingly more sexual and sexually violent behavior that is being done in hazing.

While the students in the surveys revealed the depth and scope of hazing, the results did not fully expose the vast continuum of hazing behaviors. Even when researchers followed up with the subsequent survey "Initiation Rites in American High Schools: A National Survey," stories began to emerge about "sexual hazing." As a condition of securing the database of names, the questions for the high-school survey had to be modified to exclude any questions specific to sexual acts. Even with this restriction, participants provided their own accounts of being hazed sexually.

The hazer and hazee frame the pseudoinitiation, which is often unsanctioned and not required for actual membership, as an opportunity to prove their unwavering commitment to the group. Participants often feel that the more extreme the initiation, the greater the sacrifice and loyalty generated. The test is one of sacrifice and subordination—to show that one is worthy to be part of the group. Since the hazers typically experienced the same or similar ritual a few months earlier, and they have no maturity or wisdom, they will resort to their own pseudoinitiation activities. As seen too often, this can evolve into what is commonly called "sexual hazing."

Typically, sexual hazing is between same-sex initiates and the literature has most frequently studied the phenomena in men's groups. According to research, it is designed to emasculate new members to establish and reaffirm their "position at the bottom of the team's hetero-masculine hierarchy."[11] The sexually exploitive acts often contain an element of "misogyny and homoeroticism to demonize homosexuals in an attempt to ensure the initiates are heterosexual or at least propagate a well-defined heterosexual identity."[12]

As previously mentioned, hazing is on a continuum, with a wide variety of activities that can fall under our definition. Since individuals rarely come forward to disclose their initiation activities, accounts of the different sexual hazing practices have been typically exposed through surveys, police reports, and lawsuits. Reports have described a gamut of sexually related male-on-male hazing, including same-sex kissing, nakedness, consuming alcohol off of other men's bodies, "elephant walks" or grabbing genitals, simulated sex acts, genital shaving, sexualized games, cross-dressing, masturbation, fellatio, and sodomy. To the extreme, there have been several reports of anal rape, as well as members having to masturbate and ejaculate on a cracker, with the last member to ejaculate being made to eat it.

The year 2016 concluded with the shocking allegations in *Sports Illustration* and many other publications that Dominica Republic police said that eight prospects from the Texas Rangers had held down and sexually dominated a teammate. If true, and police investigation bears the charge out, it will be the first time professional baseball players serve time for hazing. Also, in December 2016, pressure from activists and the fear of an inevitable Title IX lawsuit pressured Major League Baseball to outlaw, at long last, the hazing rituals of many teams where rookies are portrayed as caricatures of women. Nonetheless, other forms of costume and types of hazing continue.

While this tends to be a male hazing phenomena, there have been reports of female members requiring female rookies to disrobe and have their bodies "rated" for physical imperfections, as well as simulating fellatio on bananas. Additionally, other female college sports teams have had strippers brought to "rookie night" to embarrass the new members. Other incidents have included blindfolding new players and having demeaning and graphic words written on their bodies or T-shirts.

Also, with the advancement of Title IX and barriers for girls and women collapsing, over the last two decades there have been challenges to traditional male and female stereotypes. As researcher Jay Johnson has cited, the "more traditional 'male sporting domains' such as hockey, wrestling, and rugby, has also increased court cases and media reports suggesting that the masculinity of the hazing culture is now coursing rapidly and uncritically into the world of organized women's sports." It is a likely hypothesis that over the next decade there will be an escalation of hazing, and specifically sexual hazing, within all women groups.[13]

Sexual hazing is a form of sexual harassment, and depending on the affiliation of the group, a probable Title IX violation. As noted in *Doe v. Rutherford County*, sexual hazing as a Title IX issue is coming forward through the courts.[14] This form of exploitation is a viable tool for maintaining the power structure through humiliation of the less powerful members of the group. It also serves to perpetuate the power structure by "subjecting rookies to acts that are too degrading and humiliating to report."[15]

To the outsider, hazing may make no sense, but to the emerging adult contemplating participation in a team, club, or group, the noble idea of making sacrifices for the group, striving for uniqueness, engaging in an arduous process, and refusing to quit in the pursuit of belonging can be a very seductive proposition. Additionally, according to those surveyed, hazing does achieve that powerful and idealistic sense of belonging among initiates who experience it together. The initiation process, albeit painful, demonstrates that the hazee will "take one for the team, that he is dedicated to the team, and that he is worthy of membership in the team community"[16] As stated by researcher Eric Anderson, participants assume that the riskier the hazing is the greater level of commitment and sense of "brotherhood" will be generated.[17]

Initiation rites and rituals are particularly important for men in sex-segregated environments, such as athletic teams, fraternities, and certain clubs. In the anthropological literature, Michael A. Messner and Donald F. Sabo suggested that male rites serve as a means for older players to persuade younger members, often through pain infliction, to conform to the social roles and appreciate behaviors of the team. Rituals also help create and maintain the hierarchical authority and power structure of the team where the veterans of the team are superior to the rookies, even if the rookies show themselves to be better performers on the field.[18]

Contrary to bullying, where those in power have little to no interest in maintaining a relationship with their target, both the hazer and hazee are part of the same team, club, or group. The relationship between the two factions is erroneously thought to be enhanced through their misguided initiations. The group dynamic is a significant aspect of the induction experience. The rituals themselves present the opportunity for new members to prove their commitment to the team, group, or club.[19] The hazing process distinguishes members from nonmembers and without the "team's" acceptance, the initiate can never be completely accepted by the group.

By its very purpose, hazing is a process of initiating new members into a group that is typically gender specific. The all-male or all-female group is a critical factor, as is the overwhelming need to belong. It is also most typical during adolescence into early adulthood. It is suggested that intensity of the hazing has a direct correlation to the participant's desire to be part of the group.

As demonstrated by Philip Zimbardo in the Stanford Prison Experiment, this almost blind willingness to do whatever it takes to belong is a form of deviant overconformity. It occurs when participants engage in uncritical and unquestioning acceptance of the norms of the group. The power of the group and the role that the members take on can result in individuals doing things that they normally would not believe themselves to be capable of doing. When added to

Stanley Milgram's Teacher-Learner Experiment, which demonstrated that good people were willing to inflict harm on innocent people if told to do so by someone who they viewed as being in authority, it becomes easy to see how this type of deviant behavior can occur.[20]

Deviant overconformity is common among many male-dominated clubs, teams, and groups because it allows the participants to do whatever it takes, regardless of the consequences, to gain status, respect, and privileges associated with belonging.[21] Overconformity to this tenet results in a complicit "code of silence" of everyone associated with the group. Even if the participants are able to recognize the behaviors as hazing and do not agree with it, many of them will not report the often-times abusive acts to officials, administrators, or authorities. It is a common assumption among experts that hazers participate and minimize the abuse as no big deal because to admit it is wrong would be to have to admit that they were victimized in some way and that paradigm does not fit in their image of being a man. To report sexual hazing would mean that upon conviction, one's teammates would serve prison time and be placed on a sex-offender registry. Even if the hazed are victimized, they may not be willing to see the hazers so vilified.

Even with defined prevention strategies and tactics, the allure of hazing can be extremely seductive and appealing. As stated in a recent article about hazing in athletics by Susan P. Stuart, "the sport ethic, or tradition, has four distinct values: making sacrifices for the game, striving for distinction, playing through pain, and refusing to accept limitation in pursuit of winning."[22] For a young athlete just joining a team, those "values" can be easily manipulated and misrepresented by older players to become the motivation for hazing. Additionally, it is not a huge leap to assume that individuals joining nonathletic groups would have the same or similar four distinct values.

Macho Men

As stated earlier, society often gives conflicting messages about what it takes to be a man and males often turn to the media and peers to understand their emerging identity. A way of trying to make sense of this behavior is looking through the lens of "macho theory" espoused by Aldo Cimino.[23] The theory postulates three factors involved in sexual hazing: (a) hazing generates group solidarity, (b) hazing is an expression of dominance, and (c) hazing allows for the selection of committed group members. Macho theory is grounded in social psychology's concept of cognitive dissonance, that participants justify their high levels of effort by increasing their liking for the hazing group and believing that even an uncomfortable process is worth membership. Additionally, "members establish or reaffirm a dominant position with respect to initiates is very common and the humiliating nature of many hazing practices and the humble, passive behavior expected of hazees."[24]

As mentioned, since most hazing occurs in single-gender organizations, a male-defined and male-dominated organization provides a ripe environment for uninhibited hegemonic masculinity to flourish. Johnson, a longtime expert on hazing in sport, defined hegemonic masculinity as a "culturally identified form of the masculine character that emphasizes the connection between masculinity, toughness, and orientation toward competition and subservience of women."[25] The combination of hypermasculine postadolescent males charged with facilitating a secret rite of passage creates a process where new members are often initiated using degrading sexual acts. There seems to be a consistent theme of the hazers dominating the initiates by the use of homoerotic acts and feminization. This behavior exploits the vulnerability and insecurity that most young males have about their sexual identity.

While hypermasculine tendencies lead to extreme male hazing, Johnson also found that this "genderization" of the hazing activities is a common theme in both male and female teams, as is the "heterosexualization" of the rites of passage. The use of humiliating, embarrassing, provocative, "slut-like" attire required by female newcomers, as well as cross-dressing by males, is purposeful as a mechanism to shame and degrade the inductees by exaggerating a female sexual stereotype. This stereotypical misogynistic practice would not serve its intended purpose if a woman in our society received the same respect, dignity, and equality as men. Since gay men are also often disregarded in our society, many hazing activities involve homoerotic activities or demeaning exercises simulating gay-male sexual activities.[26]

This homophobic behavior is often used as a "weapon to stratify men in deference to a dominant hegemonic force."[27] This rather powerful and confusing, but seemingly "acceptable," closeness and intimacy they receive with other new members through a common, albeit sexual, hazing experience may at times eclipse its negative aspects and may be an important facet why initiations that include sexual hazing are difficult to detect.[28]

Part of the allure of participating in a secret rite of passage is the ability to join an exclusive group that is seeking your membership. An initiate has very little understanding of all the different required hazing activities, the duration of the process, or the consequences if they decide to opt out. They believe and trust that the process is a defined tradition, required for acceptance and the attainment of indisputable masculinity. Their unwavering commitment to "tradition," even though the specific initiation activities may vary significantly year to year, helps "perpetuate hegemonic masculinity and new members rationalize the acts as a requirement in this rite of passage."[29]

The study by Anderson, McCormack, and Lee examined the use of a specific homophobic and sexist masculinity in the hazing rituals. The content and sequence of the initiation activities is firmly linked with "stratification of masculinities" and the "determination of valued characteristics of men in Anglo-American societies."[30] Hazing activities have therefore given insight into the developmental issues of young men as they transition from adolescence into adulthood.

In our society, young men, as part of their developmental evolution into adulthood, are insecure about their masculinity and sexuality. Since masculinity is often perceived as being only binary, there is a fear—or "homohysteria"—of being publicly accused of being anything but a traditional heterosexual male and deviating from the rigid perception of what it means to be a man. For these young men, there often is a cultural and societal belief that masculinity and homosexuality are seen as contradictory and opposing. Therefore, it is hypothesized by Anderson that "homoerotic hazing has traditionally served the purpose of closing down future same sex behaviors." That this group experience that is conducted in secret, at the direction of individuals who will determine your eligibility to become a member, and often alcohol-infused serves "to dismiss the possibility of same sex desires." This form of sexual hazing is often "marked at the end of the sexual exploration of adolescence and solidified a form of heterosexual adult masculinity."[31]

Consequences of Hazing

There are significant social and psychological consequences for participants—both the hazers and hazees. The Alfred University study of NCAA athletes found three quarters of those who acknowledged being hazed reported one or more negative consequences such as anxiety, depression, and suicidal ideation. Furthermore, 13 percent left the group because of being hazed and an equal number wanted revenge. Even though an initiate refusing to be hazed may still be able to participate in the organization, their refusal will have an adverse effect. They most likely will be seen as "less than" a full member, be seen as not as "tough" or "manly" (i.e., heterosexual) as those who survived the initiation, and they will therefore be shunned, humiliated, and isolated by the group. Additionally, refusal is perceived as a threat to the "cultural order" and the in-group will viciously protect their "traditions." This may, in part, explain why many students perceive positive consequences of being hazed and would not report it.

Those that haze typically were hazed the previous year. Often times they are motivated to justify their own experience by perpetuating the "tradition." Unfortunately, they may also incrementally ratchet it up a notch and make the hazing rituals a little more humiliating or dangerous than what they experienced. This explains why former members of the same group can report vastly different initiation experiences.

By transitioning from the hazee to the hazer, the members are able to have their own "sacrifice and subordination," vindicated by witnessing the new member's willingness to endure the same or similar humiliating or dangerous process.[32] Even though that member was victim to the exploitive sexually hazing just a few months earlier, he or she now has the power and seem willing to perpetuate the cycle of abuse by emasculating and humiliating the new initiates.

It also reinforces the accepted roles of group: "the hazed, the hazer, and quiet witness who doesn't rock the boat."[33] The sexual-hazing process not only tests the new member's masculinity, but also their acknowledgment of "the power structures of team leadership."[34] Hazing is about power, control, and dominance. The hazee is willing to endure the ordeal in order to gain membership into an exclusive organization that will satisfy his or her need to "belong," fulfill the desire for a rite of passage, and prove their willingness to sacrifice for acceptance. Presumably, a number of young males will quit a team rather than permit hazers to have their perverse way with them. Therefore, in addition to having strict vigilance in locker rooms, sports camps, and team buses, it is imperative that athletic directors talk to athletes that suddenly quit a team. If hazing is the reason the athlete quits, he or she has far less reason to keep silent, and an ugly practice may be halted before it is repeated or spreads to other teams.

Concluding Thoughts

Since there is nothing remotely team-building or educational in such abusive activities, and they will only stop when faced with the intentional intervention of school authorities rather than the benign neglect that currently prevails, we must redouble our efforts to deliberate the poignant question posed by Hank Nuwer: "What compels young men and women to accept degrading and dangerous rituals in order to belong to a social club, sport team, sorority, or fraternity?"[35]

As mentioned previously, very few emerging adults have secure feelings about their own sexuality, much less about becoming an adult. They do not know what it means or entails since few have been taught or mentored. Almost every culture has a defined process for adolescents to pass into adulthood, and while our culture has few opportunities for our youth to participate in a process of initiation, it does not mean they don't yearn for the opportunity. It's important to recognize that adolescents will grow up to become an adult with or without a rite of passage. The question becomes what type of adult does society want? As college students emerge into their adulthood, they strive for inclusion and belonging. They will find something; it's up to us (society, parents, coaches, teachers, etc.) to give them a healthy and powerful option.

The sad truth will soon reemerge and we ask again: what would make such talented student athletes allow themselves to engage in such a dangerous activity, especially when it was being done by the very group that was forcing them to engage in this dangerous and possibly deadly hazing act? As detailed in this chapter, it cannot be explained as simply being a matter of "boys will be boys" or "girls will be girls," or just a few students who were not aware of the possible consequences of their actions. Hazing, especially sexual hazing, is much more complex; hazing victims demonstrate the need to prove their worthiness to become part of the group and the need to demonstrate their readiness to move into adulthood. In closing, I'd like to nudge along the next compelling question. Since hazing research and surveys have provided a sense of the scope of the problem, and there are viable, research-based prevention strategies emerging, the next task is this: How do we develop effective rites of passages that are compelling enough to replace hazing—especially sexual hazing?

NORM POLLARD is Dean of Students at Alfred University, a licensed mental health counselor, and a certified Title IX investigator. Pollard was coauthor with Nadine Hoover on a seminal study of hazing among athletes and hazing in high schools in the United States.

6 Ill Met by Moonlight

The First Fraternity Hazing Death

Hank Nuwer

MORTIMER MARCELLUS LEGGETT was born on June 5, 1855, to Marilla and Mortimer D. Leggett. He entered Cornell University on September 11, 1873. Young Leggett's dream after graduation was to join his father in the practice of patent law.

Following its founding not long after the end of the Civil War, Cornell had attained the reputation of being an exhilarating place to learn. The school catalog, *Cornell University Register of 1873–74*, dedicated a page to an illustrated medallion of Ezra Cornell in profile. His motto circled his profile: "I would found a university where any person can find instruction in any study." The school recruited scholars who delivered the spirited lectures favored by its cofounder over the stand-by-your-desk rote learning of lesser educational institutions.

Leggett minded his studies but was no "grind," the term for academic overachievers in the nineteenth century. The university invited men and women of all races to apply, but enrollment in 1873 overwhelmingly was white and male. Earlier that September, Leggett had traveled by train from Washington to Ithaca with his muscular, bushy-bearded father. They engaged a well-appointed house owned by a Mrs. Girard at 16 South Aurora Street. Students whose parents had means chose comfortable, furnished studios with board in Ithaca's abundant Greek Revival houses as an alternative to rigid dormitory life.

Leggett's father was familiar with Ithaca, having grown up in the village before moving in his teens to a family farm in Ohio. Although he was Quaker, the elder Leggett was no pacifist, but true to his sect he did refrain from alcohol and tobacco. He also was a celebrated Civil War warrior. As the vaunted leader of the 75th Regiment of the Ohio Volunteer Infantry at war's beginning, he became famed for locating fresh horses to mount after his own steeds were killed. Mr. Leggett distinguished himself at the battles of Shiloh, Corinth, and Atlanta.

Upon disembarking in Ithaca at the train station, the father entertained his son with family reminiscences and visits to kin. They strolled the city and fished Cayuga Lake for trout.

Young Leggett selected Charles F. Clark, also an abstainer from alcohol and tobacco, to be his roommate. Reassured that his son was safe at a school that prided itself on religious education, Mr. Leggett returned to Washington, DC, to his post as commissioner of the US Patent Office. As September moved into October, Leggett kept his ties to home through daily letter writing. Hazing by upperclassmen was on the minds of all freshmen in those days. Many a new college student had his head shaved, buttocks paddled, and head ducked under a water pump. He mailed his father a letter that said Cornell was hazing-free, and that all upperclassmen had shown him great kindness. That, however, wasn't entirely true. The faculty had banned the class rush in the fall of 1873 because of injuries, and when a sophomore tried to instigate a rush, he was expelled. His boisterous classmates escorted him in carriages with a band to the train station and toasted him as he boarded.[1] The 1873 Cornell yearbook published a long, humorous ditty that upperclassmen sang to serenade the first-year students: "'Tis September's golden myth when the opening is at hand. There is stumpy Fresh, and seedy Fresh, and Freshies short and tall. The Freshman with the goggles, and the Fresh who wears a shawl."

These were some trying times already for the former general. Postwar economic speculation in America and Europe sank the country on September 18, 1873, into a depression to linger six years. The Panic of 1873, caused in part by loan-greedy banks and railroad speculation, led to widespread unemployment. Particularly hurt was Ezra Cornell who had transferred much of his fortune in telegraph holdings to Cornell University. This great depression took most of what fortune Old Ezra had left.

Kappa Alpha Society's Influence

Cornell President Andrew Dickson White encouraged the formation of fraternities at his institution. As a Yale undergraduate, White had been a member of Alpha Sigma Phi and Skull and Bones. At the beginning of October, Kappa Alpha Society (KAS) began to recruit Leggett.

KAS was the first social fraternity, founded at Union College in New York in 1825. Members of the Cornell chapter assured Mort Leggett that the society was known for oratory brilliance, academic excellence, and stunning success later in life. The roll of loyal alumni included statesmen, authors, military geniuses, and judges.

Leggett wrote his parents to tell them about this development. "He spoke in the highest terms of the character of the young men at Cornell who belonged to [KAS], and said that its rules prohibited its members from using strong drink in any form, and from the use of profane and obscene language, and had in view only social and literary culture. We gave him our full consent to become a member," the elder Leggett later would state.[2]

As was often the case, whether a fraternity hazed or not depended upon a definition of that elusive term "hazing." The Cornell chapter of Kappa Alpha Society, although in its infancy, already had instituted a series of preliminary challenges for prospective members. The first was scheduled for October 10, 1873, and its members justified Leggett's first challenge to be nothing more than a long walk in the country that was anything but hazing in their estimation. True, they bound a blindfold over the eyes of young Leggett. True, they marched him in the dark on a narrow trail through the vacant, shrub-dotted countryside along ravines and Ice Age drop-offs to a hidden hill where they were safe from prying eyes and meddling school administrators. *But that couldn't be dubbed hazing now, could it?* Especially if Leggett, eager for acceptance by these sophisticated sophomores who had taken that forced march themselves, came along of his own free will.

Undergraduate Charles Wason was the initial member of Cornell's Kappa Alpha Society to befriend Leggett, after the second-year transfer student's enrollment (although the Cornell chapter listed him as a first-year student in the 1873 yearbook entry.) He made several visits to Mrs. Girard's boardinghouse to get to know Leggett. Wason was a sturdy man of twenty-three whose side-whiskers made others take him for older than he was.

On the evening young Leggett began pledging, Kappa Alpha Society member Henry Northrup called on him at Mrs. Girard's. Mort was alone; his roommate had departed for a Presbyterian service. Getting an invitation to join a prestigious fraternal organization was a heady, butterflies-in-the-belly opportunity, as it still is now for many young men.[3]

Northrup and Leggett walked to the large white boardinghouse on 113 East Green Street that housed several other KAS members. Leggett changed out of the better clothing he was wearing into rougher attire because he was informed that he had to endure some challenging "preliminaries" to initiation. KAS brothers expected him to "earn" his membership by accomplishing certain physical feats that all Cornell Kappas had undergone.

After Leggett dressed in knockabout wear, he and Northrup went on a tiring walkabout on Ithaca's hilly streets. They went along Green Street to Cayuga, to Clinton Street, and to Aurora, Hudson, and Giles—the latter at the edge of town where Cornell's famous gorges drew tourists. On Giles Street they passed the impressive Greek Revival house built by stock dealer Rufus Bates, a former president of Ithaca village. They marched onto a trail above an old icehouse and the waters of Six Mile Creek. Leggett passed impressive gorges and spectacular waterfalls that had been formed by glaciers.

Around 9:00 p.m. or shortly after, while Leggett was marching with Northrup, about nine Kappas and one pledge headed from Ithaca toward the rough country near Giles Street with plans to meet the duo. Lee was the first to catch up with Northrup and Leggett. Three weeks earlier, Lee himself had passed all preliminaries and been initiated into the society. The three paused at a fence, and the next preliminary ritual commenced. Northrup, with Lee's approval, blindfolded Leggett and then helped him get over the fence into a field appointed for additional rituals.

Not long after the blindfold went on, KAS members Wason and William Sturges, both Cleveland residents, vaulted the same fence and approached Leggett, Lee, and Northrup at the rendezvous point. Wason and Sturges had been here in this appointed field several times previously with pledges that now were initiated members. Thus, this was a planned chapter event, albeit mild hazing in the eyes of outsiders. Cornell KAS men who cherished fraternity membership all their lives regarded it as nothing less than a dignified ceremony with gravity and merit they would reminisce about as old men.

Usually, at this point, two Kappas were supposed to link arms with the pledge so that he didn't trip or fall over potholes and rocky dodges. Wason, one of the strongest members, alone linked Leggett's arm in his, although Lee was close at hand.

There was time for the trio to relax as they waited for others to show. Northrup and Sturges walked about the field and shared light conversation. Wason saw a hemlock tree and decided he'd take Leggett over to rest up against it for the grueling preliminaries that remained. Lee followed.

The Hemlock above a Gorge

The lone hemlock's roots dug like claws into uncultivated earth at the edge of a gorge. Its roots were misshapen, bulging, and ready to trip all interlopers. The tree's leafy lower limbs resembled small bushes that blanketed the roots. Blindfolded pledge Mortimer Leggett leaned against the tree with the two society members at his side. The two would continue the preliminaries as soon as the second blindfolded pledge arrived in the escort of additional KAS members. Had these other men come a few minutes earlier, the trio would have never approached the tree.

As with most hazing incidents, when a death occurs, both reckless disregard and the absence of common sense are to blame. Neither of the two brothers with Leggett had carried a lantern to the dangerous gorge area; it was lit only by moonlight. Had Wason and Lee brought an oil lamp, they would have spotted the yawning gorge hidden behind the hemlock and backed away.

Leggett did not know where he was or precisely what the brothers expected of him. He assumed that he was in good hands. The blindfold was part of a trust-building exercise.

Lee, later described by a New York reporter as a beardless and handsome lad of twenty years old, observed that the pledge appeared tired after the long pledging walk.

Wason also saw Leggett slump from fatigue. He sprang to give the pledge a helping shoulder. Leggett, unable to see through the blindfold, took a step toward the sound of tree limbs cracking under Wason's footgear.

Lee watched his companions begin to sink through the leaves. He threw out his arms to save them, concluding that a ledge must lie beneath the canopy of leaves and roots. Lee dropped through the tree leaves and over the hidden cliff wall, the bodies of his friends flailing in the air beneath him.

The trio plunged more than forty feet to the hard ground. Wason later described the sensation in testimony as feeling as if he were coasting on a swing.

Wason's body was the first to slam into the earth. He heard "two distinct thuds" as Lee and Leggett landed almost atop him. Wason tried to scream but the air in his lungs had been knocked out. Leggett landed headfirst on the stony clay. The impact created an indentation the size and shape of his head that someone unknown later marked with stakes to preserve the impression.

The pledge managed a few words. "Oh, don't," he murmured.

Initial Reaction

Seconds before the three men fell into the chasm, KAS brothers George Halsey and J. Harvey Pierce, a Chicago native and mainstay of Cornell's golf squad, helped the second blindfolded pledge, Joseph G. Ebersole, over the fence. At that moment, William H. Flint, Northrup, and Sturges looked up and saw Leggett, Wason, and Lee in front of the hemlock. Then they looked away at Ebersole. Another moment passed. When they looked once more, the trio standing on the shaky tree roots had vanished. None of the KAS brothers witnessed the actual catastrophe.

Flint ran to the hemlock with Northrup, Sturges, and the others. In hindsight, given the relative darkness and how well hidden by foliage the brink of the cliff was, it was fortunate even more students did not plunge to the rocky gorge bottom.

Despite the anxiety of the moment, Northrup, Pierce, and Sturges formed an action plan to assist the three fallen chaps. Northrup agreed to race back to Ithaca to seek rescue help; Pierce insisted that Northrup engage a carriage to transport the injured three men from the creek bottom. The others searched for trails that ended on the floor of the gorge and descended in safety. They dreaded what they might find.

Getting Help in Town

Born and reared in Ithaca, Northrup knew the city well. By the light of a streetlamp on the corner of State and Tioga Streets, he located Theodore F. Crane, twenty-nine years old and a popular Cornell professor of folklore and languages.

Crane was not only a professor, however, but also a fully initiated member of Kappa Alpha Society from his own not-too-distant undergraduate days at Cornell. Tongues wagged in Ithaca all the next week, saying it was too much of a coincidence to believe that the first person Northrup met on his errand was another Kappa brother. Crane tried to calm the distraught Northrup. "He was breathless and excited," Crane recalled when asked to testify.

Northrup spat out the grim details. Crane and Northrup hailed a carriage-for-hire being driven by Ithaca hostler William Hoose. The professor knocked hastily on the door of Charles W. Carrier, MD, and the physician grabbed a bag and climbed aboard the carriage.

Aftermath of the Accident

Back at the site of tragedy, Kappa brothers Flint, Sturges, and Pierce bolted down the steep embankment trails with bushes tearing at their trousers. Some light from the rising moon illuminated the path.

Flint was first to reach the three victims, each murmuring incoherently. He found Leggett in a position on his left side with his blindfolded face pointed upward. Leggett could move his arms and legs, but his neck and head seemed unnaturally fixed in place.

Flint unstrapped Leggett's blindfold and took it off (contrary to published reports that wrongly asserted that Leggett had the blindfold removed *before* he fell).[4] He then poured water from the nearby creek over the moaning victims in hopes of reviving them.

Pierce and the other Kappa rescuers joined Flint. Leggett seemed past hope. He had a fractured skull, broken nose, and dislocated neck. Seeing Leggett shiver in shock, one youth covered him with his own coat. Leggett said with a moan, "Take it off! Take it off!"

Many newspapers of the day published his plea. Sturges thought the dying Leggett imagined he had a heavy weight on his body. However, one paper speculated that young Leggett must have been referring to the blindfold.[5] Perhaps the pledge referred to the coat meant to warm him. The exact meaning of the cry for help would soon die with Leggett.

Kappas to the Rescue

The hostler cracked the reins over his carriage horse and drove Professor Crane, Dr. Carrier, and Northrup to the accident site. Dr. Carrier examined the three accident victims on the bank leading to the creek.

He found that Wason had struck land with his feet first and bounced, smashing a collarbone. Lee had landed on his side, severely bruising a hip and possibly incurring internal injuries. Had he dropped any farther and faster he would have shattered his hipbone. Leggett's traumatic brain injury was apparent, and he likely had ruptured blood vessels beneath the scalp. All three young men had traveled at similar velocity, but Leggett's body had assumed the cruelest, most punishing angle of trajectory. The inches-deep indentation where his head had struck the packed earth displayed the deadly effect of sudden deceleration and trauma.

Dr. Carrier reassured Crane that Wason and Lee eventually would recover. Poor Leggett was another story. The physician ordered Pierce to put Wason on the carriage first and then Lee (assisted by Pierce) second in order to transport them to the Kappa chapter quarters on the third floor of the Finch Block (a building named for businessman and Cornell University executive committee member Francis M. Finch who built it). The carriage hostler asked to retain his vehicle because he had a waiting fare, but Pierce convinced the stableman that the injured men had a greater need for transport. The hostler left on foot for Ithaca, and Pierce drove the commandeered carriage.

The carriage traveled over bumpy ground into Ithaca with Lee and Wason. Pierce helped the other two into their rooming house, and then he returned for Leggett. Using a torn-off fence gate from private property as a stretcher, the Kappa Alpha Society men set Leggett down on the cart. Moving him in such a condition may have been an unsatisfactory choice, but Dr. Carrier saw no other option.

The rescuers transferred Leggett to the fraternity's formal chapter headquarters. Dr. Carrier, aided by his medical partner, John Winslow, MD, could do little more than ease Leggett's agonies.

Professor Crane tried to comfort the youth. The now unconscious Leggett tried to answer, but failed to utter an intelligible word. "His moans were indistinguishable," Crane would later recall.

Within thirty minutes of arrival at the Kappa headquarters, Leggett's moans ceased. The doctors closed Leggett's eyes around 11:00 p.m. and pulled a sheet over him. The *Cornell Era* student newspaper of October 17, 1873, would term the incident "the saddest accident that the *Era* has ever been called upon to chronicle." The *Era* also reported euphemistically that Leggett died while fulfilling "society purposes."

A writer for the *Era* added that Leggett died without pain, but that may have been either a consoling fabrication or wishful thinking. Prior to passing out, Leggett had incurred injuries to his skull, nose, and neck that were quite serious. He also had injured his hand, possibly upon smashing against a hemlock root when he first fell, according to Carrier's recollection at the inquest.

Ithaca undertaker Harrison Howard was summoned to embalm Leggett and to prepare the corpse for viewing by the family in Washington. Howard, the co-owner of a mercantile and furniture store that peddled caskets, chose one, and the body was shuttled to the north-wing parlor of the Clinton House for a

Christian ceremony the next morning. The irony of the choice of Clinton House, a posh establishment that had been renovated and expanded in 1871 after a ruinous fire, could not have been missed by the Kappas; they had placed reservations to dine at the Clinton that evening when the preliminaries were over.

Early Deaths By Hazing

Leggett's was the first fraternity hazing death. The first American death linked to hazing in a secret society resulted from a perverse joke in 1737 played upon Philadelphia apothecary apprentice Daniel Reese who was eager to undergo any indignity to gain acceptance into the Society of Freemasons. The joke-turned-tragedy was first reported in the June 9–16, 1737, issue of the *Pennsylvania Gazette*, published by Benjamin Franklin, and later discussed in great detail by *The Franklin Bi-Centenary, 1706–1906*, published independently by Franklin's Grand Lodge. What happened was that cruel jokesters not associated with the Masons arranged a hoax initiation to which the "credulous and unsophisticated apprentice" Reese was invited to partake with no knowledge that the initiation ceremony was bogus. The perpetrators were lawyer John Remington, the apothecary Evan Jones, and others; these men hazed Reese unmercifully, including having him kiss the buttocks of one of them. Not content with humiliating the gullible Reese once, the hazers invited him to a second ceremony to which he supposedly would receive admission at last to a higher Freemason order. After getting Reese to utter blasphemies and to pledge allegiance to the devil, one of the hazers, dressed as a devil, tossed boiling liquid on Reese, who died the next day from the scalding. Franklin was later publicly condemned in the *American Mercury* by rival publisher Andrew Bradford; the latter opined that Franklin had known in advance about the joke to be played but had not put a stop to the nonsense, and thus he was as much responsible for Reese's hazing death as the outright hazers were.[6]

Leggett's was the fourth death overall attributed to hazing at a US educational institution. The first, claimed in a family history, was John Butler Groves (1819–1838) at Franklin Seminary in Simpson County, Kentucky, although details were erased in a disastrous fire.

The second was first-year Amherst College (Massachusetts) student Jonathan D. Torrance whose 1847 death after an illness was attributed to older hazers soaking his bed sheets, according to allegations made by the institution's president Edward Hitchcock in his 1863 book *Reminiscences of Amherst College*.[7]

The third occurred at Delaware College, a precursor of the University of Delaware, when horseplay and hazing associated with class rivalries (between seniors and sophomores and juniors) in 1858 erupted in a wild brawl in which seventeen-year-old student John Edward Roach had his throat slit in a residence hall. A jury acquitted Roach's Delta Chi fraternity brother Isaac H. Weaver because witnesses failed to see who made the fatal thrust. Weaver denied doing the killing but admitted the blade used to pierce Roach's neck was his. Roach and Weaver had had a previous falling out.[8] The fact that they were fraternity members seems not to be connected to the class hazing that led to the tragedy.

Bad News Travels Even Faster Than Good News

The horrific news of a pledge's death spread across Ithaca at first light on October 11, 1873. Gawkers trampled the hill and perpendicular drop along the stream where Leggett had perished. At least one photographer snapped the imprints of where three human bodies had struck the ground.

A telegram informing General Leggett of his son's death reached the US Patent Office where he held command. The staff members were stunned, having sent the popular Mort off to Cornell with cheers and well-wishes one month previously. A reporter approached the grieving father to get any sparse details he cared to share. The elder Leggett acknowledged that his namesake voluntarily had chosen this society and did all things asked by his own choice.[9]

It would always be this way with a fraternity hazing death. A family that lost a son in a hazing became fodder for front-page news coverage from Maine to California. Editorials on the evils of secret societies always accompanied a death. So it was with the death of Mortimer Leggett. No war exploits of his vaunted father ever drew as many headlines. Following young Leggett's death, newspapers cobbled together a fanciful and lurid false account of what must have happened. One story, reprinted by other papers, imagined that members dressed as devils made a blindfolded pledge teeter on the edge of a yawning gorge that had been made to resemble hell with lanterns and lights. As the story of the cliff fall spread, many gossipy individuals embellished it. One stretched tale had it that chapter members had dangled the victim above the gorge and accidentally dropped him. Over the years, some version of the bogus claim became the stuff of Cornell urban legend with no basis in fact.[10]

Delivering His Body Home

Roommate Charles Clark awoke the next morning and saw he was alone. The flame in the oil lamp he had lit still burned. But Leggett was not in his bed. Before long, a visitor informed Clark that Leggett had perished and that the roommate was needed immediately as a pallbearer.

The additional pallbearers were Kappa members Flint, later a respected physician known for his many works of charity in his adopted California; Northrup, later a civil engineer; and Kappa member Frank H. Hiscock, a future judge and Cornell chairman of the board.

A large number of students and faculty attended Mortimer Leggett's service. Alford Stebbins, MA, Cornell assistant professor of South European languages, said prayers over the casket. Afterward, in a solemn procession, the attendees accompanied the casket to the train station.

Clark, Sturges, and Pierce departed on the train to Washington. They had volunteered to deliver the body to the Leggett family. Young Leggett was interred in Oak Hill Cemetery in Washington, DC, on October 14, 1873.

Many were surprised that Leggett's family had failed to claim the body in Ithaca. In an exchange of telegrams between the senior Leggett and President White, the Cornell authorities learned that General Leggett had no intention of visiting the campus. He had some relatives still residing in Tompkins County, and they promised to uncover whatever facts they could. Rightly or wrongly, a couple city newspaper editors reported that President Andrew White's initial telegram to the parents failed to disclose that their son's death was a result of a fraternity stunt. The papers claimed that Cornell's president had portrayed the event as a sort of game of hide-and-seek in the country. The telegram was never presented at the official coroner's inquest, and so there is no primary source available to verify or discredit the claim unless it is preserved in archives somewhere unseen by the author of this essay.

Parents of Cornell's student body read the newspaper articles and wrote their sons and the Cornell administration for answers as to how this tragedy could have transpired. One with parental concerns was suffragist Elizabeth Cady Stanton, who wrote a comforting reflection on death to her son, Cornell senior Theodore Stanton.

The Coroner's Inquest

A coroner's inquest convened immediately after the funeral to determine manner of death and to rule on whether any group or individuals possibly bore criminal responsibility. Leggett's death could not have come at a worst time for Cornell in terms of bad publicity. Over the next year, Ezra Cornell and President White found themselves facing allegations of fraud over the sale of lands to Cornell University, according to numerous articles in Rochester, New York, newspapers in 1874. A committee appointed by then New York Governor John Adams Dix never sustained the charges, but neither the founder nor the president needed more tinder placed on the flames of public opinion at the time the Leggett inquiry took place.

Over time, a number of individuals have recused themselves from hazing cases due to a possible or perceived conflict of interest. However, no member of the Leggett inquiry stepped down to avoid public condemnation for a possible conflict of interest. Three members of the Leggett inquest could not have been more connected to Cornell University if Ezra Cornell and President White had appointed them.

Jury foreman Samuel D. Halliday entered Cornell University in 1868, the year it opened, as a transfer student. A former student at Hamilton College, he graduated from Cornell in 1870 and was elected, as a Democrat, the local district attorney in 1873. A few months after the Leggett inquest, alumni of Cornell voted to honor him as a trustee of the college. He later passed the New York bar as an attorney and was named a Cornell University trustee by vote of other trustees. Halliday's son Morris later played football for Cornell.

Jury member George W. Schuyler was even more invested in Cornell. He had served as unpaid treasurer of the university since its founding, and he too was a trustee of Cornell at the time of the inquest. In addition, he served with President White and Ezra Cornell on the Cornell executive council.

A third juror was local justice of the peace James Tichenor. His mentor, Ezra Cornell, had recommended his early training.

Others on the inquest committee included attorney and future Republican candidate William Nelson Noble; Allen Gray, co-owner of Gray & Willets mercantile and grocery store; prosperous bakery and mercantile operator David B. Stewart, the former mayor of Ithaca; Charles S. Seaman, a local livery stable proprietor and a member of several secret societies; and firefighter Henry M. Durphy, who had celebrated his fortieth birthday on October 11, 1873.

Dr. Erastus C. Moe headed the inquiry. A graduate of Buffalo Medical College, Dr. Moe had moved to Ithaca in 1872 and established a practice in town while in his late sixties. He was also a Baptist deacon.

For all or part of the inquiry, also present were members of the press, the Kappa Alpha Society members, Cornell Vice President and Professor William Channing Russel, Professor Burt G. Wilder (an expert on brain injuries who exhibited human brains in glass jars at Cornell), the undertaker Harrison Howard, and citizen S. H. Wilcox.

The three individuals with the most to contribute to the inquiry were Professor Crane and eyewitnesses Wason and Lee. Although Crane, as a KAS member, had direct knowledge of the society's rituals, his testimony was short of any important revelations.

Was Crane fully aware or in ignorance of the blindfolded walk by moonlight? Could testimony conclude that Brother Crane, pledged as faculty to watch over Cornell students in the absence of their parents, had turned a blind eye to the repeated risky hikes in treacherous gorge country?

No one asked those questions.

Instead, Professor Crane fielded puffball questions from the committee. He denied that there had occurred the sort of orgies many newspapers had described.

"I have never known of any cruel, violent, or outrageous treatment of students in the university," Crane testified. "I am well acquainted with all the party and believe them to be true gentlemen. They were personal friends of the deceased and for some time had treated him with great kindness."

The Kappa Alpha Society members were careful to stick to the facts of the tragedy. They exercised care not to expose any rituals of their secret society. Northrup did note that the Kappa members present at Leggett's preliminaries planned to renew their collective pledge to the society at the Clinton House when his exertions were over.

Sturges testified that there was nothing malevolent about the night's journey. "Deceased was taken there by invitation, not forcibly," Sturges declared. "There was nothing of an illegal or marauding nature intended."

Northrup also defended the chapter's actions. "We were not on the bank for any unlawful purpose," he declared. "There was nothing in the way of hazing or quarreling or violent usage. No one of the party had been drinking to my knowledge. We were all on the most friendly terms with each other and the deceased [and] did not go there to abuse or frighten him in any way." That Northrup failed to see how blindfolding a pledge and putting him through paces could be an act of hazing was not surprising. Surveys of undergraduates over the years have clearly established that men and women who have endured all kinds of illicit and even illegal stunts fail to label their experience as fitting their personal definition of hazing.

Testimony left no doubt that Leggett had been blindfolded before being helped over the fence and blindfolded as he leaned against the hemlock. However, his hands and feet were never tied with rope as rumormongers in the press shrilled. Northrup admitted to placing and adjusting the blindfold on Leggett. Lee was present, and Lee had worn a blindfold for his own initiation.

"Leggett was not bound or pinioned in any way. His eyes were bandaged. They were blindfolded before we climbed over the fence. I bound them principally, assisted by Lee. [I] believe I did it wholly myself," testified Northrup. "I did it because it is customary to blindfold all new candidates for admission to the society."

Northrup said Leggett made no protest before or after the black cloth was secured with a buckle clipped to the back. Had the tragic episode not occurred, Leggett would have retained the blindfold all evening, Lee acknowledged.

The coroner's jury pushed Northrup on the question of whether anyone had been drinking. He acknowledged that whiskey was present at first, although apparently the bottle never had been opened because it had fallen out of his pocket when he responded to the falls of his chums. Thus, technically no chapter member had consumed a drink, although the injured Wason had cried out for one to ease his agony.

"Yes, it is customary to take a bottle along on the initiations to have it on hand in case of accident," Northrup told the committee. "It is our habit to lead candidates all the time, so they may not be in danger of being hurt. I never knew of any accident before."

Northrup's testimony took the form of denial, perhaps in deference to reporters from the *Ithaca Daily Journal* and the *New York Sun* (present in the rooms at the inquest) that had speculated about what might have occurred to Leggett and assumed the worst. "There is no precipice where the blindfold has to be removed; it is no part of the ceremony to take the subject to a cliff to intimidate or frighten him, or to suspend him or put him in bodily fear anywhere," Northrup declared. "A rocky precipice has no part in the initiation."

The committee tried to reconstruct Leggett's last hours. Lee revealed what had been the society's overall plan for that fatal Friday night. "The initiation with Leggett had not yet commenced," he swore under oath. He said that some or all of the KAS group had reservations in town for a late repast at the Clinton House. Given the formality of fraternity affairs in the nineteenth century, it is possible, perhaps even probable, that Leggett would have been brought to the hotel for initiation and congratulations. The coroner's inquest should have uncovered all of this, grumbled the editors of numerous newspapers across the country. But the coroner focused on the facts of what happened that night, and not on what was supposed to happen.

The committee interviewed Lee and Wason in their boardinghouses in separate rooms on the second day of the inquest. Lee had been insensible much of the day after the accident, and Wason had been in agony as well. Their physician ruled they were in no condition to face a grilling on the opening day of questioning.

Dr. Carrier pronounced the two fit enough to testify on October 16, 1873, at 5:00 p.m. No doubt stung by newspaper criticism leveled against an absence of tough questions at the coroner's inquest on October 11, questioners this second day grilled the Kappas.

Lee's testimony and his crude illustrations of the accident site shed some light for the jury on the last seconds of the deceased that previous interviewees had not shared. "I was entirely ignorant that there was a precipice there. [I] was greatly surprised to see them disappear, and imagined they must have slid down a bank. The idea of a precipice never struck me. My natural impulse was to help them, and acting upon it I ran or moved diagonally off the cliff."

Lee acknowledged to the committee that he himself had been initiated just three weeks before his testimony. "When I was initiated I was held all the time under the arms of two strong fellows, and I felt perfectly safe. They took me over rough places, but did not stumble."

Wason testified next. He had recruited Leggett and knew him as a friend. He was put in charge of Leggett's safety for that reason. He guided Leggett by touch occasionally but not for every second they walked to the tree.

"I stood him against the tree, or rather he leaned against it. He was leaning against the tree and I stood about a foot from him, or within reaching distance. In about three or four minutes I saw his body inclining to one side, as though his feet were slipping and he was going to fall. He was on the right side of the tree, or rather on the south side. I thought he was merely falling to the ground, not down the precipice. I moved forward to steady him, and in so doing stepped on what I thought was the root of the tree. It caused me to slip, and I fell over the brink. In attempting to save him I fell myself."

The closest the committee came to any sort of revelation about the content of Kappa preliminaries was from Wason's testimony.

"I was blindfolded when I was initiated," testified Wason. "[I] have assisted at three initiations. A man on each side locks arms with the candidate and holds him from falling. They probably thought I was strong enough to hold Leggett, and did not put two or three more to guard him. The ceremonies of initiating into our society are very impressive; at least they were in my case. I was very tired and quite hungry after going through."

Wason, the son of a banker from Cleveland whose family had traveled to Cornell to oversee his recuperation, would graduate from Cornell and enjoy a career as president of a railroad line. His generous gift to Cornell University upon his death at age sixty-three was his valuable personal collection of holdings on Asia, known today as the Charles W. Wason Collection.

The coroner's inquest ended with the conclusion that this had been an accident and in no way a homicide.

General Leggett as Media Figure

In the two weeks following his son's death, General Leggett found himself thrust into one major newspaper story after another. Reporters parsed the details of the general's life to readers. He had been born in 1821 to Isaac and Mary Leggett. In his late thirties, as the nation teetered on the brink of war, Leggett, a graduate of teaching and law colleges, had made a comfortable living as a school superintendent and lawyer. Even before the American Civil War began in 1861, Leggett and his wife, though members of the pacifist Society of Friends, had become passionate supporters of the Union and critics of the secession movement. Their household evolved into a salon for political discussions.

After a distinguished war record in his forties, he became the entrepreneurial cofounder of a pioneer electric company eventually acquired by the General Electric Company.

However, as successful as the father was in life, he endured considerable pain. General Leggett and his wife bore four sons. He was to outlive all four and his wife. Marilla died November 14, 1876. She was a prolific journal writer and somewhat of an adventurer, traveling as far south as Tennessee and Mississippi during the Civil War for visitations to her husband's military headquarters.

The grieving father spoke and wrote about his son's demise to newspapers in New York and Washington, DC. "There was no 'hazing,' and the young men who were with and near my son at the time of the fatal fall were his friends, and actuated only by feelings of kindness and friendship," Leggett wrote to the editor of the *New York Times*.[11] "It was while joining this society that he lost his life. It seems that the ceremonies of initiation include the foolish mummery of being blindfolded and led around between two members of the society through some grove or forest in the night season. While making this ramble, and in ignorance of the immediate proximity of danger, the three were precipitated from an abrupt cliff—my son was killed—and the other two, who were sophomores, and members of the Society, very seriously injured."

General Leggett made an assumption that many others, including school administrators and prosecutors continue to make. Namely, that a group's action cannot be hazing if the neophyte shows himself willing to be hazed. His letter to the editor continued, "Mortimer was there of his own free will, and with his own chosen friends, and by very careful inquiry, I am satisfied those friends were young men of unexceptionally good character, among the best in Cornell University, and no institution in the country embraces a more promising class of young men. In the ceremonies of that awful night, those students had in view Mortimer's pleasure and profit, and had no more expectation of danger or accident than he had. He was there from his own choice, and when he submitted to be blindfolded, he did only what he was informed every member had before done—and probably what every person does who joins a secret society. Such mummeries are foolish and heathenish and belong to a darker age, but they are common in nearly all the colleges of the world, and are part, probably, of every secret society. I cannot, therefore, find it in my heart to specially blame these young men, nor Cornell University."[12]

Knowing that his son had so valued membership in Kappa Alpha Society, General Leggett accepted induction into the society after the Cornell chapter offered it to him in a letter dated January 12, 1874.

"I have no doubt the sad catastrophe will serve to some extent as a warning against the continuance of such needless exposure, and may save other hearts from the crushing bereavement that has fallen on ours," Leggett informed the *New York Times* in its October 1873 issue titled, "Result of Inquiry into the death of [Mortimer] Leggett." Leggett also resigned his position as Commissioner of Patents in April 1874 to pursue his private law career and passion for developing electrical lights.

Leggett's death led to stern Cornell-faculty pronouncements on the dangers of hazing and also some temporary restrictions on pledging, but in no way did the practice cease at Cornell. In 1899, the Cornell Kappa Alpha Society conducted another version of its sojourn in the countryside. Eight pledges were made to get off a train near Geneva, New York. The brothers ordered Edward Fairchild Berkeley of St. Louis, Missouri, and the others to carry out some pointless errands, including a long journey through the countryside precisely as Leggett had done. Senior KAS member Philip Dickinson, an athlete from Denver, ordered Berkeley to carry out a task written on a scrap of paper over what turned out to be dangerous terrain. Berkeley came to the bank of a canal and forged past a mucky bank into deep water and drowned. The first responders failed to find him immediately, but the St. Louis Post Dispatch reported on October 30, 1899, that the Samaritans had found Berkeley's hat floating on the water.

Once again, the nation's newspapers all railed, particularly after Berkeley's father bitterly denounced the Cornell chapter members.

Young Leggett, forgotten those twenty-six years, was back in news headlines once again as newspapers compared his death to Berkeley's and found the two hazing walkabouts to resemble one another in format and ritual. Another coroner's jury convened. KAS members were judged blameless.

HANK NUWER is a professor in the Franklin College Pulliam School of Journalism. He has written *The Hazing Reader* (IUP) and *Wrongs of Passage: Fraternities, Sororities, Hazing, and Binge Drinking* (IUP).

7 Eliminating Band Hazing

What Must Be Done

Malinda Matney

COLLEGE AND HIGH school bands are part of what makes a campus feel like *your* campus. When someone walks down a hallway and hears a part of a rehearsal, it is clear that music is the focus of the class, something different from any other subject area. When attending a game, the sound and spirit of the band make this environment feel like home, and different from a professional sporting event. When major events happen in a campus community, one of the school's bands is usually asked to play appropriate music, whether the occasion is a presidential inauguration, a pep rally, a somber day of memorial, or a cultural festival.

Within this chapter, we are going to explore the intersection of hazing and band activities. What we will not do is speak at depth about specific band programs that have been in the news as a result of death, injuries, investigations, or scandal. There are others who have written in depth about investigations and the outcomes for specific programs. We will instead focus on what makes the band context different from many other contexts in which hazing arises, what conditions make a band program more or less likely to have hazing behavior within it, and what different people who intersect with a band program can do to be part of the solution.

What Is Band? What Makes It Different?

These two questions seem obvious to those both highly involved on the inside of a band or looking in from the outside. In assuming one knows what a band is, however, one misses so many of the essential elements of why a band context cannot be treated in the same way as fraternities, sororities, or student organizations. It is easy for those unfamiliar with band programs to assume, for example, that a high school or college band is a student organization, so some distinctions need to be made.

Bands are curricular: Band is a class in most settings, at both college and high school levels (and the levels below that). Band is actually a curricular offering. For music majors, it is usually part of the ensemble participation requirements of their degrees. For nonmajors, it is a course that allows them to continue honing skills that they have developed for years. For all students, learning outcomes, lesson plans, and grades are involved. Faculty lead the activity. There are exams in the form of auditions. There are quizzes in the form of performances. Whether the band is a concert band, a marching band, or a pep band, many observers watch the quiz in action. Imagine taking a math quiz in front of one hundred thousand people in person and millions of viewers on television. Saturday football is the equivalent.

Bands have many forms: Some people refer to "band" as only a marching band. Certainly the marching band is the front porch of many total band programs. However, there are a variety of concert and symphonic bands, pep bands (smaller bands that perform at sports other than football), chamber ensembles, and winter guards (a performing ensemble of color guard members, such as flags and rifles). While winter guards are fairly new, most band programs include most of these aspects. Likewise, most students are performing in multiple types of ensembles during the year—for example being involved in marching band, concert band, and pep band in the course of a single year—and often perfecting a different instrumental specialty in each one.

Bands have auditions: While student organizations usually accept most people who ask for membership, and fraternities and sororities have more subjective membership selection processes (i.e., "is this person a fit for us"), bands have auditions for membership and for chair placement. These may be led by faculty, graduate student assistants, or section leaders, but they are almost always connected back to the faculty leadership of the ensemble who are reinforcing learning objectives for participating students. Audition outcomes are based on musical ability, prior preparation, and the number of spaces available in the ensemble.

Bands are a multi-year involvement: In most college ensembles, new members are expected to have already performed on their instruments for several years before setting foot on campus. It is more common than not for members to have spent five to seven years (or more) performing in secondary schools prior to college. This is an important feature to consider; members already have experience in several settings and have been acclimated to a band lifestyle of multiple performances. They've had the best tans in fall from outdoor rehearsals, the pastiest skin in winter from indoor rehearsals, and hours of practicing one's own part before coming to rehearsal.

Overall, band involvement and training start early, and problems can creep into the lifestyle early as well. These elements are true at multiple levels, from the beginning ensembles through the highly selective collegiate ensembles. That said, there is also rich cultural learning that both student members and the broader community receive from having bands as part of their campus experience. As we discuss signs of potential problems and ways to encourage healthier participation, the goal is to maintain an enthusiastic, highly enriching cultural experience, whether it is on stage or leading a football game on a Friday or Saturday night.

What Sets the Stage for Hazing in a Band Program?

Whether one is examining high school or college band programs, several key factors can create the conditions in which hazing practices may take root. These are conditions that can be examined by prospective members, parents, administrators, band directors, or graduate students considering affiliation with a program. Most of these points distill into two concepts: (1) the reduction of outside influences and contact, and (2) insufficient supervision by band directors.

An important note about all of these conditions is that strong performers do not do most hazing. The students who excel at musicianship, or at marching, are not typically the ones leading hazing activity. The volunteers and staff who take pride in their specialty, and take seriously the work of teaching and learning, are not the ones encouraging hazing. The directors who care greatly about their students' educational experience (and their own careers) generally do not turn a blind eye. Hazing is not correlated to a pride in outstanding performance.

Isolation, or Limited External Influences

Most college band programs include staff who have many previous academic and band experiences. Among the staff, graduate students, and key volunteers, one might see a dozen or more college and university band experiences represented. At the high school level, the families themselves may come from a variety of previous high school and college experiences. The variety of experiences is important as they help set the stage for continual examination of the practices of the program. There should be people around who routinely ask, "Why do we do that?" In the absence of that level of questioning, necessary conversations do not happen. These clearly go beyond risk reduction to other best practices for teaching and learning, new artistic ideas for shows, and new ways to promote the activity. Questioning the status quo is an important part of the academic activity and health level of the band.

High school and college bands may differ in key ways regarding how isolation takes root. For parents in locations where they may have been involved in the same band as their children, they may feel invested in promoting behaviors that have long since outlived anyone's idea of a good practice. This can happen if all the parents come from a similar social class as well. This is not simply an issue of isolated neighborhoods or small towns, and it can affect any income level of parents. Volunteers with a high school program may themselves be recent alumni of the same program and not necessarily consider that they have new and different leadership roles as volunteers than they had as students. A special challenge exists with high school bands in terms of often having far fewer professional staff available to coach and observe volunteer performance. Unfortunately, many parents and volunteers make decisions based on their memories as students rather than drawing from a leadership perspective when working with their own alma mater. This can even happen among parents and volunteers who are otherwise accomplished in their professional lives.

It's important to note, too, that most matriculating high school seniors have encountered hazing before arriving on a college campus, often administered or condoned by parents or other volunteers throughout their high school or middle school years. As a result, the protective element of victim pushback may be dimmed. This is not exclusive to bands; other high school organizations and even church-related camps can demonstrate hazing behaviors as well. For this reason, it is especially vital to support antihazing efforts and healthy teaching practices at the high school level.

In the case of college bands, a band at risk is one that has most of its faculty, staff, and volunteers coming from its own program. In the worst cases, these individuals may not have any experience at another institution (for example, as a graduate student or a previous staff role). As is the case with high school insularity, when few outside perspectives exist, serious conversations about best practices do not happen. On the contrary, there is substantial peer pressure to not "make waves" or introduce large-scale changes.

Across both of these settings, the key element is that questions are discouraged and change of any kind is considered "not our way." In any band program, change is hard. Most bands have particular stress at the moment of director transition, and a wave of "that's not how we do it" might take root, even in a healthy program. Making sure there is the space to ask questions and examine various practices is essential to creating a healthy program.

Isolation from the Rest of the Campus

Creating an insular idea of the band not being integrated into the life of the campus gives students, volunteers, and others the idea that bad practices can go unchecked. In the worst of situations, these players may assume that the director will protect them from questions from the dean of students or involvement by the local police. On the contrary, greater isolation will set the stage for problems that are too large for a director to survive.

Some campuses have even decided that band should be a cocurricular activity, and at times have taken a program's faculty and staff. By not supporting regular professional supervision these campuses have opted to promote risk-related behaviors. These campuses have no serious training for student leadership, and at the worst actively promote a climate of "this is where we blow off steam." These are unsteady organizations that can create risky moments at any time, no matter how small, large, or prestigious the school.

Insufficient Faculty Supervision of Challenges and Discipline

Band programs at all levels, even at the early years of a student's career, involve countless auditions. Throughout the year, a series of miniauditions, known as "challenges," are common. The basic concept is that a student may try to advance another chair in a concert ensemble, or into the top performance group of a marching band, by performing music (and marching, if applicable) against another student. This is not unlike the athletic context in which a student may work hard to attain a starter role midseason. Challenges are intended to keep every member sharp and motivated throughout the season.

Students and volunteers can play a role in assisting with challenges but must be carefully supervised and trained. Just as we do not assume that students know how to grade an essay without coaching and rubrics, it is not appropriate to have students adjudicate challenges without appropriate training and ongoing supervision. In the absence of supervision, members may find themselves "challenged" for reasons having nothing to do with their actual performance, such as interpersonal grudges or issues of social identity.

Likewise, some band programs leave to section, rank, or squad leaders the enforcement of disciplinary measures for the ensemble (such as attendance or sectional participation). The role of section leaders (students selected as the top performers in each section) needs to be clearly outlined, with adequate training and supervision. This may be a first leadership role for many students. Most are eager to perform their roles well and will seek guidance wherever it is given. If band directors are silent, other students or alumni may fill the void with the wrong information or a best guess.

Insufficient Supervision of Sections

Bands rely on sections for several good purposes. Each instrumental grouping of the ensemble has its own work to do to prepare for rehearsals, concerts, and performances. These tend to be social groups as well as functional groups; a student will spend most of his or her time in the band with one section, and deep allegiances form. This can provide a great sense of belonging in a large organization. However, when sections devise their own forms of initiation, these can create the worst conditions for a member of the band. Ensuring knowledge of what sections are doing is essential. There are many positive ways to welcome new members into the section, such as dinners, buddy systems, and other positive forms of welcome. Band directors should actively seek information about what sections are doing.

Insufficient Musical Rigor

Students want a challenging experience. There are positive ways to accomplish this, starting with the rigor of performance standards. In my various roles working with college band programs where hazing practices had taken root, almost every time I would hear from students that the program was not as musically demanding as their high school programs had been. Students want to feel that they have earned something. Band directors can ensure that they earn something of value, such as the accomplishment of great literature, a difficult and complicated marching show, and a semester of health. Directors should not be afraid to test the musical limits of their students, and parents and students should not be afraid to ask for the higher musical standard.

Insufficient Screening and Training of Staff and Volunteers

Band programs rely heavily on staff, graduate students, and volunteers. The size of most programs requires the use of volunteers in order to ensure that basic elements of the program happen. For example, at the largest college levels, band programs may have about half the students of the entire athletic program, but with only a small fraction of the staffing.

Unfortunately, there are many volunteers who are only too happy to hang on to the program, and who are there primarily because they were previous members, and not because they have expertise in working with any particular specialty. In the largest band programs, specialties can include medical staff, instrumental specialists, public relations staff, refreshment teams, and coaching for student organizations. The smallest programs may lean even more heavily on volunteers to deliver basic instructional elements. In all cases, not only volunteers but also graduate students and paid staff should be screened to ensure that they understand and are compliant with a culture of health, and at a base level present no other issues. All of these people should receive training and regular supervision to ensure that they understand the expectations for their performance in ensuring that hazing behaviors do not happen.

Turning a Blind Eye

Faculty for decades have been coached by those coming before them that if they do not get involved in the lives of students outside of their classroom then they are not liable for students' activities. This is both a common trope and a false sense of security. Not even attempting a basic understanding of who volunteers are, what attitudes graduate students bring, and what sections are doing when a director is not present will not protect any band director. These are basics in any organization. Instead, working to understand the student experience while connecting with colleagues across campus will provide a greater foundation for preventing problems, addressing problems that do happen, and having appropriate legal safeguards.

Bands, in general, are typically conservative institutions. This statement is not a political position but rather a way of being that preserves traditions and ways of working. This is not itself a bad thing. Many bands convey healthy campus traditions; many ways of working with hundreds of students in an efficient manner have evolved over years; the very idea of conveying cultural ideas in the concert realm requires a respect for and knowledge of history. These are not reasons to not continuously seek the best ways to teach, learn, and promote health within ensembles. Just as in other academic components of the campus, teaching and learning continuously improves even as the notion of education in its current form is hundreds of years old.

Creating a Culture of Health in the Band

After understanding these elements that can lead to a hazing risk, one might ask if there is anything to be done to save a band from health or legal dangers. The fact that bands are conservative institutions, while at times frustrating, can also boost positive behaviors and support healthier organizational habits.

The very things that make band participation attractive to students are the protective elements that can be essential in a culture of health. With the exception of music majors, no students are required to participate in band. Even music majors are driven by a passion for their majors, as well as the elements that are attractive to nonmajors, such as musical growth, social environments, emotional expression, and a leadership role in the school or campus culture. Faculty and staff, volunteers, parents, and students can use these elements to turn away from unnecessary risk-related behaviors and toward positive risk, such as elevating one's musical goals or striving to achieve a leadership role.

What Can Directors and Faculty Do?

The role of the band director is key. The band director sets the direction of the program. This could be an expectation of an involved, exciting musical experience. On the contrary, this direction could be a benign neglect of what is happening in an ensemble. At worst, the direction is an active encouragement of abusive behaviors. While no person has the ability to be in all corners of every room at all times, investing reasonable effort to understand and shape the student experience makes considerable difference between a healthy band program and a destructive one.

Set a clear syllabus, and follow it: As basic as this step is, many programs of any type that have problems stem from having one set of expectations in writing, a different one spoken, and perhaps yet a third actually happening from student to student. Enforce grading and disciplinary standards. Creating conflicting standards empowers those in the band program who would want to drive a wedge between the director and students to carry out hazing practices.

Be clear about what is happening on the schedule at all times: Particularly when the band is working in different sections, be clear about where and what work is being done. When student leaders are taking on part of the instruction or social components, be clear about how these parts are being implemented as well. Student leaders should also have clarity about the expectations and learning outcomes on which they will be evaluated.

Know who is being hired as staff or accepted as volunteers: Proper vetting of all who work with the band, including volunteers, is essential. Not only should these people be screened for their backgrounds and their current attitudes toward hazing, they should also be trained in risk-reduction behavior and given clear standards about what is expected of their role with students. Volunteers can be particularly challenging if they are motivated by hanging onto a band experience from their past rather than supporting the educational standards of the present. Regular meetings and ongoing professional development are essential.

Build diversity into the leadership: Being an alumnus or alumna of a program is not a qualification for leading it. If that is the only screening question for staff or volunteers, problems will arise from staff and volunteers not asking challenging questions or trying to improve current practices. Rather, seek diversity in all forms, including an array of university experiences, instrumental specialties, social identities (such as gender and race, among many), and leadership styles. Through these means, a greater variety of questions about current practice will emerge, and improvement can take root.

Do not overpromise the role of supervisor of all activities: It is particularly tempting for a director to assure external parties that he or she has total knowledge of all aspects of the program at all times, that certain activities never happen, and that no further questions need be asked. Be clear when communicating with parents, administrators, and students that this is a team effort. This is not about excusing a director's role as the leader of the ensemble. Rather, an effective director conveys the standards of the ensemble, the staff working with the ensemble, the processes in place when problems arise, and ways for anyone wanting to report problems to do so. The effective director is clear about using the words "I don't know, but I'll find out." These words alone make the difference between inferring all knowledge and opening the door to honest questions. Ultimately, those words help prevent a director from appearing to endorse a hazing activity about which the director is unaware. This multipronged effort provides both transparency and clear direction, and it assures those who worry about how to raise concerns that their voices will be heard.

Build strong ties with campus administrators: Whether a high school principal or a college dean of students, these campus administrators want the student experience to be excellent. They also are required by a variety of federal and state mandates to ensure that campus leaders (which include student leaders) go through key workshops or other educational initiatives. By working closely with these administrators, what could seem like a collision of expectations can actually become a supportive foundation that eases the director's workload. Students learn essentials about bystander behavior, risk reduction, and leadership, and the director gets to focus even more on musicianship and performance. Administrators such as deans of students and principals go into those specialties because of their care for student welfare; these administrators are key allies.

What Can Parents Do?

While parents have less of a role in the college band program than in the high school band program, the key role for parents at either level is to understand the role of the director as outlined as well as get clarity about the background of the band program and the supporting structures of the college or school. Reading along with the director's component above will help parents with their checklist of things to learn.

Support students in forming the right questions to ask: Encouraging student voice is essential. A parent learning about the organizational structure, for example, can help a college student understand where to take concerns or questions about activities. At the high school level, the parents obviously have a lead role in asking these questions themselves.

Do not relive past school experiences through students: No matter how excellent, or terrible, a past school experience was, current student experience will be different. Maintain the focus on the student getting the experience that is relevant today. No amount of musing about "students weren't as soft back in the day" or "we had it much harder" improves a student experience. As well, not allowing students to build their own relationships gets in the way of the basic experience of band for the student.

Be open to new experiences: Setting a tone for students in terms of learning new things and asking appropriate questions allows students to have "their day" while keeping a band program from becoming insular.

What Can Student Leaders Do?

Student leaders of the band have a special role of trust and also often feel caught between peer pressure and articulated director expectations. Student leadership often is a first teaching or leadership role for a student, and it can be a particularly stressful transition as fellow students test their limits with the student leader. So what is a student leader to do to get started?

Understand the director's expectations: Meet with the director and define the expectations of this position. With the expectations should come the identification of skills and knowledge that are needed and how to acquire them. Also get clarity on any available training to be received. Seek out additional leadership training across campus or suggest to the director additional topics where further instruction and education is needed to best fulfill the student leadership role.

Understand responsibilities for risk: Student leaders can be held accountable for hazing activities within a program and, as such, could be legally charged in a hazing incident. How a student leader sets a tone for risk management makes a difference. Make sure discussions about hazing occur within sections. Encourage members to speak up without fear of retribution.

Be clear about what hazing is: Simply defined, hazing is any act committed against a student who is trying to join a new group that is humiliating or demeaning, or endangers the student's health and safety. Hazing can occur as a new member, as a student trying for student leadership (itself a new group to the student), or a student who subsequently chooses not to continue in the group. Hazing can occur regardless of consent or willingness to participate. If a student leader chooses not to take part but knows what was happening, that leader is part of the problem and is culpable for any damage. Become familiar with the myths and truths of hazing and utilize these concepts in group discussions with directors and band members.

Do not try to pursue leadership alone: Discuss with other student leaders strategies to welcome new members. Set a climate and environment that insists that everyone—from new members to seniors—be treated with dignity and respect. Create "meaningful" traditions, ones that develop pride among the members and in which everyone's dignity is respected. Should incidents or suspicious activities happen, do not try to handle them alone. Report these to the directors.

Emphasize that respect comes from performance and attitude, not from hazing: New members, and members in new roles, should understand that complying with hazing is not what will win them the respect of the director or advancement to leadership roles. Hazing does not build better musicians or performers. Hazing is, at best, a time waster; at worst, it is the end of a membership, college career, or life.

What Can Every Band Member Do?

Every single member of a band can do much to eradicate hazing.

Say something. If any member sees or hears something that looks or sounds questionable in a band, ask questions and speak out with fellow band members. Even something as simple as "why in the world would we do *that*?" is effective in reducing so many actions. Hazing thrives in secrecy. Talk about it. Challenge it!

Get peers on the same page. Ensure that fellow members are fully aware of calendars of events and are active participants. Sometimes hazing thrives when some events become "optional"—with a wink and nod—to allow those who don't like hazing to leave and look the other way. Be active everywhere.

Build knowledge. Become fully aware of every possible resource for hazing prevention and make that information widely available to fellow band members, band alumni, and even parents of band members.

Challenge stories. When people talk about how great/valuable/funny hazing is, challenge that position. Do not shrug and laugh at a "back in the day" story. This can be a moment to educate the person telling the story and to remind today's band members that we are not back in *that* day.

These steps do not make anyone an "unfun" person, or a weak one. Opposing hazing, and supporting the true values of college bands, takes a strong person who wants everyone around him or her to enjoy music and grow to be excellent in every way.

Conclusion

Band work is about values, accomplishment, and relationships. In most areas of society, it is not the strong performers who haze, but the weak ones. Hazers actively seek to reduce the quality of an ensemble (or an athletic team's performance, or a fraternity or sorority's academic and social engagement). Hazers fear real work and quality.

In my various roles across my career, I have been actively a part of the college band community and a part of university administration. I have done research on hazing activities in many arenas as part of my studies of student behavior at the University of Michigan. I have led Kappa Kappa Psi (the national honorary band fraternity) as its national president, and at this writing as a member of its board of trustees. In some of my roles with Kappa Kappa Psi, I have done hazing investigations. I have been a part of college bands at two universities, and currently volunteer time with the University of Michigan. I am not neutral about the value of bands. This makes me both someone who advocates strongly for the band experience, and someone who is especially critical of band programs that do not promote a healthy environment. In short, I want students to have the advantages in life that I feel I gained from band. Many of my colleagues writing other chapters in this volume have similar passion for organizations they hold dear. We write about and focus on hazing because it gets in the way of what we hold dear: the best in educational experiences and lifetime relationships for the next generation.

This work will not be easy. Those who threaten the true values of college bands will try every method to silence those who oppose hazing. However, living up to our work calls us to be strong. Keeping high school and college bands vital into the future requires our strength. Now is the challenge—and the opportunity.

MALINDA MATNEY is Senior Research Associate for the Division of Student Affairs at the University of Michigan and the former national president of Kappa Kappa Psi National Honorary Band Fraternity.

8 Hazing and Gender

Lenses for Prevention

Elizabeth J. Allan and Morgan B. Kinney

In a culture that immerses us in a gendered track from a pink or blue baby blanket to superhero or princess costumes, to the type of shampoo we use as adults, gender differences are often seen as natural and inevitable. We all know that many behaviors are learned, yet environmental influences tend to be minimized when it comes to explaining differences between women and men. Prevailing assumptions about the biological nature of sex/gender differences provides fertile ground for reinforcing gender stereotypes.

This leads to an important caveat for the terminology in this chapter: In using the terms "girls" or "women" and "boys" or "men," we do not intend to reinforce the gender binary. Rather we seek to acknowledge its existence as a dominant way of thinking within Western culture. Our intention is to disrupt the gender binary by bringing it to light and discussing the numerous ways in which this schema (a socially constructed understanding) can impact behavior and perceptions of behavior. We will explore this both on a broad scale, through an overview of gender theory, and then with its application to hazing behavior. Finally, we conclude with a discussion of implications for prevention.

Background and Context: Gender Stereotypes and Differences

A stereotype is a belief about a group that is applied to all individuals perceived to be a part of that group. Stereotypes are often based on misinformation and they are often tied to firmly held beliefs. This is not to say that we cannot draw any generalizations about women as a group or men as a group, but generalizations based on research (called empirical generalizations) are different from stereotypes. Empirical generalizations are based on research that takes differences within a group into account (typically through statistical tests of significance) and can be revised when new data emerges that differs from previously drawn conclusions.

To what extent do biological differences (anatomical, hormonal, or chromosomal) between women and men shape behavioral differences? It is exceedingly difficult to know for sure. In fact, there are few scientific studies that currently support a biological basis for substantial differences between the way women and men think.[1] Rather, research indicates there is more variation among women (or men) on cognitive, emotional, and psychological variables than between the two groups.[2] Despite this, the idea persists in the dominant culture that women and men are vastly different in their thinking and hardwired to assume different social roles. This speaks to the power of gender-role expectations that have become so familiar they are simply assumed to be normal. It is this assumption that often prevents individuals from acknowledging the powerful influence of implicit and explicit gender-role expectations.

Sex and Gender Differences in Hazing

National news accounts of hazing and anecdotal evidence point toward gender differences in hazing activities. A common conclusion is that hazing among men is more likely to be violent in nature and hazing among women is more likely to be psychological or emotional in nature. Such perspectives align with and also reinforce predominant understandings of differences between women and men. A study analyzing media accounts of high school hazing incidents found hazing was described in ways that presumed and reinforced gender differences with female hazing needing to be "explained and contextualized" while male hazing was considered "par for the course."[3]

Gender differences were seen also in results of the National Study of Student Hazing, in which participants were asked about specific hazing behaviors that they experienced while gaining membership to various student groups.[4] While the top two behaviors—participating in drinking games and singing or chanting by oneself or in a select group—were the same across male and female groups, some of the lower-ranked, but still frequent, activities reflect the tendency of women to engage in more psychological hazing than men.[5] For example, being asked to "associate with specific people and not others" ranked third for women as opposed to fifth for men, and wearing "clothing that is embarrassing and not part of a uniform" was tenth for women as well as in the top ten hazing behaviors for men.[6] Physically taxing experiences that were more widely experienced by men than by women included having to "drink large amounts of alcohol to the point of getting sick or passing out" and "endure harsh weather conditions without appropriate clothing."[7]

Research that focuses specifically on gender differences and hazing is limited, however. In a 1999 study sponsored by Alfred University and the NCAA, differences in hazing practices among male and female athletes were documented but not the focus of the study.[8] In another study aimed to create an instrument for measuring attitudes toward hazing, hazing and counseling psychology expert

Kevin Cokley and colleagues found that women were more likely than men to believe that pledging a Greek organization should be a positive experience, though gender differences were not the focus of the study.[9] The vast majority of research on hazing, and media attention to particular incidents, has focused on male groups. In the few studies with a focus on women, hazing has been found to be prevalent, however. For example, in a survey distributed nationally to professionals who advise fraternities and sororities on college campuses, 44 percent said hazing incidents among sororities were reported to them. "Of the incidents reported, 20 percent considered them psychological, 2 percent considered them physical, and 28 percent considered them both."[10]

We have also seen this general trend in the National Study of Student Hazing wherein 55 percent of respondents reported experiencing some form of hazing behavior while in college. Of these 55 percent, 61 percent were male and 52 percent female.[11] Hank Nuwer details accounts of hazing in college sororities in 1999, and on athletic teams and cheerleading squads in high schools in 2000.[12] According to his accounts, far more hazing incidents among sorority women have been reported in the decade from 1988 to 1998 than in the previous ten-year period. It is possible, however, that these numbers may reflect an increase in reporting rather than an increase in incidents.[13] "Although some violent hazing, alcohol misuse, and even branding have occurred in college sororities, it may have been far less a problem in female clubs than in male fraternities," according to Nuwer.[14]

Many scholars have examined male group behavior and hazing from various disciplinary and interdisciplinary perspectives.[15] Of these, the studies of fraternity culture draw on theories of gender, sexism, and homophobia to explain aspects of fraternity life that increase the probability of men's violence against women who come into contact with these groups. University of Pennsylvania anthropologist Peggy Reeves Sanday describes how "pulling train," or gang rape, becomes a normative part of the fraternity's behavior and group identity. She also identifies the pledging process as an important means of socializing men to endorse such attitudes and behaviors.[16]

Applying a Gender Lens

Analyzing hazing through the lens of gender can provide insights that may strengthen approaches to prevention. Since gender norms are often taken for granted, they can be easily overlooked. A gender lens works against this omission because it makes gender the focus of analysis. Here we draw upon gender theory as a lens to illuminate ways in which rigid gender norms can influence hazing behavior and support hazing cultures.

We use the term "gender lens" to refer to frameworks that explore cultural expectations of femininity and masculinity and how these expectations shape understandings of women and men as gendered selves. Gender lenses proceed from an understanding that versions of masculinity and femininity are largely learned and performed, and therefore open to change. In other words, femininity refers to the aggregate of qualities associated with being feminine, and masculinity refers to the aggregate of qualities associated with being masculine.[17] That said, we continue to recognize and challenge the gender dichotomy implied by the use of these two terms. Michael Kimmel explains the necessary challenge to this concept when he states, "Gender must be seen as an ever-changing fluid assemblage of meanings and behaviors." With this point in mind, Kimmel uses the plural terms "masculinities" and "femininities" to distinguish between the dominant discourse of biologically determined masculine and feminine traits, and we will use the more-fluid understanding in this chapter.[18]

The use of the term "gender," then, refers to the cultural and learned aspects of the gender spectrum that are also shaped by class, race, ethnicity, age, sexuality, disability, and other differences. As sociologist Kimmel notes, "each of these axes modifies the others."[19]

Researchers Elisa S. Abes, Susan R. Jones, and MaryLu K. McEwen explain this concept in their paper "Reconceptualizing the Model of Multiple Dimensions of Identity." This model includes not only a person's intersecting social identities, as described above, but also a meaning-making filter and contextual influences. Contextual influences, such as sociopolitical conditions, peers, and family views, combined with one's cognitive abilities, contribute to how an individual perceives his/her/hir identities.[20] Despite this seemingly infinite variation, particular versions of femininity and masculinity rise to ascendancy during different social periods.

As early as 1971, sex-role inventory expert Sandra Lipsitz Bem pointed out that even while the predominant versions of masculinity and femininity may shift periodically, they generally operate as two poles of a binary where the masculine is positioned as active and the feminine is positioned as passive.[21] In other words, whatever traits are understood to characterize the feminine, also connote the antithesis of masculine and vice versa (see table 8.1).

Active, strong, aggressive, independent and invincible are examples of gender binaries that depict masculinity. Depicting femininity are terms such as passive, fragile, submissive, dependent, and vulnerable. These are polar opposites of a vast gender divide. While this particular construction of femininity is rooted in perceptions of ideal womanhood for white women specifically, it remains a powerful and pervasive image or standard against which all women are compared.

Another perspective gained from gender theory, one that is important to an understanding of gender dynamics and hazing, is the analysis that gender norms are typically cast in ways that privilege masculinity over femininity. In other words, the dominant culture tends to value masculine traits more than

Table 8.1. Traditional Attributes of Femininity and Masculinity

Feminine	Masculine
Passive	Aggressive
Nurturing	Analytical
Gentle	Strong
Submissive	Dominant
Yielding	In Control
Tender	Tough
Dependent	Independent
Collaborative	Competitive
Emotional	Logical
Supportive	Self-reliant
Fragile	Brave

feminine traits. An exception to this occurs when women behave in ways that are perceived to be too masculine. Consequently, women find themselves in a lose-lose situation where the performance of femininity is often devalued (and is disempowering to them), yet the alternative performance of masculinity can result as well in negative consequences. The dominant culture of heterosexuality also supports this dynamic. For example, a woman whose behavior is interpreted as "overly aggressive" (i.e., masculine) will likely be labeled in ways that are perceived negatively (i.e., "bitch," "dyke") in the context of heterosexist/homophobic culture. Thus, women are in a double bind—they are disadvantaged when they act in gender appropriate ways *and* when they don't.[22]

While individuals are active in defining themselves as masculine and/or feminine, alternatives to dominant cultural expectations are often overshadowed by the power of the ascendant image pervasive in popular culture. While the United States has seen more acceptance of gender fluidity in recent years, those who wish to stretch beyond the narrow confines of normative gender roles risk being labeled as somehow deviant.

Social Construction of Gender

A social-constructionist view of gender posits that masculine and feminine behaviors are largely a result of learning what is expected in a particular culture (rather than what is imprinted on one's genetic material). Thus, gendered behavior is historically and contextually situated and can change over time or differ among cultures. Within the Western culture of the United States, a multidimensional shift has occurred over the past couple of decades that has troubling repercussions for our young people all along the gender continuum. In his book *Guyland: The Perilous World Where Boys Become Men*, Michael Kimmel captures the economic and biological aspects of this shift. Because Kimmel's main focus is on men, we will turn our attention first to how this shift is affecting the cultural conceptions of masculinity.[23]

Largely due to adolescence beginning earlier and the economy in the United States, there is an extended period of time in which boys are going through the process of becoming men.[24] For much of the society, this period of time is taking place now not in high school, where there is adult supervision, but in college where adult supervision is minimal and the societal laws for men are governed by their (slightly) older peers.[25] Kimmel points out this major difference when initiation or rites of passage in the United States are compared to most other cultures where adults are overseeing the process of initiation into manhood.[26] The result is a place called "Guyland" where winning is crucial and concepts of kindness and compassion are strictly prohibited.

As Kimmel describes it, Guyland is ruled by four components of the "guy code" as well as three overarching cultures. Researchers Deborah Sarah David and Robert Brannon originally described guy code in 1976 as four metaphors: "no sissy stuff," "be a big wheel," "be a sturdy oak," and "give 'em hell."[27] These essentially translate to avoid anything feminine, be financially successful, do not show emotion, and take risks.[28] The three cultures defining Guyland are entitlement, protection, and silence.[29] Each of these cultures undoubtedly contributes to the continuation of hazing practices in many male-dominated organizations.

The pressures of Guyland, however, are not isolated to the male experience. "Girls today are unlike any generation in our nation's history," Kimmel claims, acknowledging the undeniable wins of the feminist movement, but their experiences are not universally liberating and empowering.[30] Rather, Kimmel maintains, "Girls live in Guyland, not the other way around. . . . As second-class inhabitants, they are relegated to being party buddies, sex objects, or a means of access [for males] to other girls."[31] As surely as Guyland suppresses young men, it privileges them in comparison to their young-women counterparts.

Working in tandem with (or perhaps helping to create) the rules of Guyland is the onslaught of media images teaching girls, from a disturbingly young age, that their worth is a direct result of physical appearance. The messages coming from popular culture and the media are influencing girls to become obsessed with any perceived imperfection.[32]

In the 2011 documentary *Miss Representation*, psychologists, feminist activists, politicians, and actresses speak out about the startling inequities in media portrayal across genders. Furthermore, the makers of the documentary draw many pointed lines between these inequities and feminine issues from the epidemic of eating disorders to underrepresentation in politics. Once inoculated with the expectations of the American media, it is no surprise that hazing involving young women often capitalizes on the anxieties associated with becoming a desirable sex object within Guyland. Many hazing activities put women's bodies on display to be sexualized, criticized, and demeaned by peers of both genders.

Related Dynamics

It is impossible to provide an analysis of gender without also attending to the role of homophobia and heterosexism in reinforcing rigid expectations of masculine and feminine behavior. This dynamic is clearly indicated when a group of high school students is asked to consider what happens if a man is a little bit *too* nurturing or a bit *too* emotional. They are quick to respond, "he's a pussy," or "he's a fag." Women who cross the line of normative expectations for femininity may face similar social consequences of being called "butch" or "manly." Of course these terms are unlikely to serve as deterrents unless they are perceived negatively. Homophobia—the fear of same-sex attraction in oneself or others—serves as just such a deterrent for many. Working alongside homophobia is heterosexism—the system of attitudes, biases, and discrimination that places opposite-sex relationships in a position of privilege. These attitudes are so powerful and pervasive that they reinforce what has been termed a "gender straitjacket," ensuring that boys and girls do not deviate substantially from culturally proscribed beliefs about appropriate behavior for men and women.[33]

It is essential for any gender analysis to delineate how these social constructions reinforce rigid (and sometimes harmful) expectations of acceptable behavior for females and males. This can be seen in hazing with the presence of both same-sex and hypermasculine behavior. For example, the hazing practice of "performing sex acts with opposite gender" was the ninth most common hazing activity experienced by male respondents in Allan and Madden's National Hazing Study and was not listed in the top ten experiences for female students. On the other end of the spectrum, hazing that involves forced or coerced same-sex behavior can serve as a deterrent for reporting due to the shame associated with these acts, whether consensual or not.[34]

In sum, the predominant social construction of gender as well as cultural dynamics of homophobia and heterosexism create a climate in which violent and demeaning hazing practices are more likely to be tolerated and even considered beneficial for young men. Gender theory provides an important lens for deepening understanding about the prevalence and persistence of hazing and this understanding is vital for strengthening hazing prevention initiatives.

Masculinity and Hazing

The connection between masculinity and hazing is not a difficult one to make. Nonetheless, it is a connection that is not often thoroughly addressed or even articulated. One need not look very far to find examples of how hazing behaviors in male groups often serve as a test of masculinity or as an opportunity to prove one's masculinity. When hazing occurs among men, regardless of the type of group, it is often framed as a test of "strength," "courage," and "determination." For instance, accounts of hazing incidents among high school boys and college men frequently include tests of physical endurance, forced/coerced alcohol consumption, paddling, and other forms of physical assault/beatings.[35] In Martin and Hummer's research on fraternity cultures, they found that fraternities emphasize "toughness, withstanding pain and humiliation, obedience to superiors, and using physical force to obtain compliance."[36] Even at the US Naval Academy where men and women were found equally likely to experience hazing, men were still more likely to condone some of the more physical activities such as "being tied up, taped, or restrained."[37]

In support of hazing, men will often say that such "traditions" are necessary to "weed out" those unworthy of membership. Some men who have hazed are believers in the process of hazing and insist that they "enjoy the challenge." But it is not just the hazers who hold this belief. In fact, a common response to the question, in the National Hazing Study, of why one did not report hazing activities was that it "made me a better man."[38] Such arguments are firmly embedded in cultural expectations around masculinity and what we are taught to expect of stereotypical, so-called "real men."

A gender lens helps to illuminate why it can be so difficult to eradicate hazing practices. For instance, in a fraternity, "'becoming a brother' is a rite of passage that follows the consistent and often lengthy display by pledges of appropriately masculine qualities and behaviors."[39] Since hazing can serve as an opportunity for men to prove their masculinity (and heterosexuality), the elimination of hazing traditions can be quite threatening on multiple fronts. Stephen Sweet points out that the pledging process forces many students to terminate or sharply curtail social interactions outside the fraternity, ensuring that sense of self for pledges, and eventual brothers, becomes closely tied with the organization itself. This increases the "exit costs" of leaving a hazing organization; fraternity members can "literally lose a major part of themselves by withdrawing," notes Sweet.[40] In fact, the fifth most common hazing behavior experienced by male students according to the National Hazing Study was associating with specific people and not others.

Social anxieties around masculinity are central to the continuation of hazing practices. The more the boys or men are fearful of being labeled as weak, the more likely they may be to participate in hazing practices that are dangerous and even life-threatening. For example, in her examination of violence in Canadian hockey, Laura Robinson interviewed a sixteen-year-old boy subject to hazing as a junior hockey player. His comment is illustrative of the way in which hazing preys upon anxieties around proving one's masculinity: "They were persistent and giving us alcohol. Lots of beer. We might look like a wimp if we turned it down."[41] Alternatively, Aldo Cimino's experiments in evolutionary psychology suggest that hazing is an "evolved response to preventing the exploitation of automatic group membership." That is, in addition to gender influences, motivation for hazing may be fueled by human desire to reduce "freeloaders" in group membership.[42]

Some researchers have considered how the learning of gender may affect patterns of health and well-being. For instance, an argument has been made that we can understand the phenomenon of longer life expectancy among women through a social learning lens (rather than simply as a consequence of biology). Research indicates that higher mortality rates for men are attributable to higher accident rates for younger men and to heart disease for men at older age.[43] However, as Krieger and Fee point out, "the higher accident rates of younger men are not accidental" but are due to hazards related to gender-role expectations, including more hazardous occupations, higher rates of illegal drug use and alcohol abuse, and injuries related to firearms and in motor vehicle accidents. While heart disease is a leading cause of death for both men and women, many of the risk factors may be associated more with gender than with biology; higher rates of cigarette smoking and fewer sources of social-emotional support among men, for example. A similar connection can be made between gender and deaths due to hazing. Nuwer's chronology of hazing fatalities reveals that men are far more likely to die from hazing activities than are women. Of the more than two hundred documented US hazing deaths, fewer than ten have been female according to Nuwer's documentation, and the majority since 1961 involved pledge deaths or the deaths of brothers from reverse hazing by pledges.

Femininity and Hazing

Femininity serves as a powerful cultural force for defining womanhood. In brief, a gender lens helps to illuminate how dominant understandings of femininity shape women's desire to appeal to men in ways that limit their power and reinforce male power. Table 8.1 presents the list of attributes associated with the traditional and predominant version of femininity. When placed beside the list of masculine attributes, gender polarization is evident. Further, as we have described, homophobia serves to reinforce compliance with these narrowly defined versions of gender.

When considering the social construction of gender, it is also important to acknowledge race, ethnicity, and other cultural forces that also shape what is deemed acceptable behavior for men and women. The list of masculine and feminine attributes is based primarily on a white middle-class dominant ideal that has dominated much of popular culture. Alternatives to the dominant conceptualizations of masculinity and femininity do exist. However, they are often eclipsed, devalued, or labeled deviant. Such labeling can be seen in a study of two high schools in suburban areas of the Southeast United States wherein girls who were observed fighting were categorized differently based largely on appearance. The popular term for girls who deviated from the norm of femininity and heterosexuality were consistently deemed "tomboys" or "tough girls," while the terms "ghetto girl" and "homie G" were used to describe low-income girls of color.[44]

Objectification

The objectification of women is sometimes implicated in hazing behaviors. We draw on the term sexual objectification here to refer to the ways in which women's bodies are commodified—made into objects of heterosexual male desire. This can be seen daily in the popular media, where women's bodies or particular parts of women's bodies are used to sell products. In a society where heterosexual men hold more fiscal, political, and institutional power than women (on the whole), the objectification of women's bodies occurs with a far greater frequency and intensity than objectification of male bodies.

In her analysis of fraternity little-sister groups, sociologist Mindy Stombler uses theories of gender, sexism, and sexual objectification, describing sexual objectification as a "fundamental process in maintaining male dominance."[45]As discussed earlier in this chapter, the ways in which women's bodies are objectified in the media tends to have a dehumanizing effect; women may come to be seen as objects rather than human beings. Some contend that the sheer volume, the cumulative and often unconscious effects of seeing women's bodies as "things," may contribute to a greater cultural tolerance for violence against women.[46] An analysis of a fraternity culture by Robert A. Rhoads supports this contention: "Women were frequently characterized in ways that depicted them as something less than human beings. . . . They were discussed as 'tools' or 'whores' and were frequently seen as targets of sexual manipulation."[47]

Instances of sexually charged hazing behaviors range from objectification to harassment, and in some cases assault, which we will discuss further in the following section. Some hazing activities that objectify women occur behind closed doors. One example of this is photos of naked female peers on a group Facebook page, which led to the suspension of a fraternity at Florida International University. Other techniques, however, cross the line from objectification to sexual harassment. Such was the case in the 2016 incident at Ole Miss where fraternity brothers asked sorority sisters sexually suggestive questions, including which brother they would have oral sex with, over a speaker system to a crowd of hundreds of peers.

Similarly, an example of hazing called "The Circle of Fat" demonstrates how women themselves also partake in the planning of degrading events wherein their sisters, teammates, and fellow group members will be sexually harassed. In her 2005 book *Pledged*, investigative reporter Alexandra Robbins recounted her personal experience of being blindfolded in her underwear at a sorority house that was then filled with fraternity brothers, armed with Sharpies to circle the unsatisfactory areas of the women's bodies. After the men leave, the women are instructed to remove their blindfolds, look in the mirror, and remember that the boys were only there to help the girls "become better sisters."[48] Here lies one of the paradoxes of sexism: women themselves actively participate in sustaining the "object" status of other women. This dynamic works especially well in the context of hazing, a practice that is designed to humiliate, degrade, and disempower.

Sexual Assault and Hazing

Simply put, sexual assault refers to sexual contact that is not consensual. Consent is a choice that is made without coercion and without impaired judgment (i.e., induced by alcohol, other drugs, or other conditions). Since hazing activities are generally predicated upon an abuse of power involving intense peer pressure, coercion, and alcohol and/or other drugs, any hazing activities that are sexual in nature are likely to fall into the category of sexual assault and victimization.

Sexual victimization in hazing is a deeply disturbing trend. Among males, the frequency of same-sex assaults, particularly penetration performed with broomstick handles or other objects, appears to have increased dramatically over the past twenty years, particularly among male high school athletic teams.[49] One highly publicized example of such hazing occurred at Sayreville War Memorial High School in New Jersey, where the allegedly traditional abuse and sexual assault of freshmen football players was eventually reported. Through the haze of eyewitness accounts from peer-pressured teenagers, reports ranged from pushing and shoving to kicking, groping, and digital penetration while pinned upon the locker-room floor. Ultimately, six upper-class students from Sayreville were sentenced to probation, but none were listed as registered sex offenders. Other recent accounts of sexually abusive behavior among boy teammates have arisen in St. Louis, at a football camp hosted by Principia Upper School, at La Puente High School in California among soccer teammates, and at high school varsity wrestling meet in Denver, Colorado, to name just a few.

Other documented examples of demeaning and sexually violating hazing behaviors include forced nudity and smearing of initiates' bodies with food products; using duct tape or athletic tape to immobilize nude recruits; "butting"— where the rookie player is held down while a veteran puts his naked buttocks in the player's face; connecting a string weighted with a heavy object to a new recruit's penis; immobilizing initiates in a chair while strippers perform in their laps; or expecting other sexual acts or simulated sex with strippers as was reported in the 2015 case of fraternity pledges and members at Indiana University.

Power Dynamics, Identity, and Hazing

Girls and women can also gain credibility and status by proving they are tough, rugged, and strong. Consequently, hazing activities among women's groups sometimes mirror hazing typically associated with men and masculinity. For instance, excessive consumption of alcohol (especially in predominantly white organizations and teams), forced sleep deprivation, ingestion of vile substances, branding, paddling, and beatings have all been documented among groups of women. A study from two major suburban areas in the United States found that some girls see fighting as an empowering way to gain attention and agency within the social context of their high schools.[50]

Conversely, it is less likely for male groups to mimic hazing activities typically associated with female groups. Given the cultural context, it is not surprising that some hazing activities among women's groups valorize masculine attributes or prey on gendered vulnerabilities associated with femininity. Nevertheless, the social stigma that was once attached to those who challenged the expected passive and fragile role of "true femininity" (as black women and working-class women have done for many years) has been substantially eroded. This is not always the case; the classic double bind remains a common experience for women.

Consent is a key factor in determining the ways in which any sexual activity is experienced and interpreted by others. Just as hazing differs for male and female groups and reflects gendered (and heterosexist) power dynamics in the larger culture, hazing practices are also shaped in relation to other aspects of identity. For example, scholars John Williams and Paula Giddings describe their own experiences and reflections on how pledging and hazing in black Greek-letter organizations (BGLOs) was specific to conditions resulting from centuries of racial oppression in the United States. For instance, in her book on the history of Delta Sigma Theta, Giddings writes, "Hazing had always been a part of the initiation period . . . but may have a particular meaning and character among Blacks."[51] She cites the "stripping away of individuality" and the emphasis on unity and unconditional respect for sisters as having "a particular resonance in terms of the black experience." Patricia Hill Collins provides a detailed account of how black women's experiences of sexism are in some ways paralleled and also markedly different from the experiences of white middle-class women.[52] Clearly, cultural differences among women of different racial and ethnic backgrounds, economic statuses, and sexual identities must be taken into account when considering how gender influences hazing. Much more research needs to be done in this area in order to broaden and enhance understanding of these dynamics.

According to Gregory Parks and his research team, black Greek-letter fraternities place a particularly strong emphasis on proving masculinity through the pledging process.[53] In the 1990s a rise in violent hazing acts resulting in multiple deaths of young men pledging BGLOs led to their national organization banning all pledging activities. Regardless, subsequent research showed that hazing within BGLOs only increased in severity and frequency following the ban. Among many reasons cited for black Greek hazing, proof of commitment and "separating masculine men from feminine men" provide an overarching understanding of motives based on the current literature.[54]

Types of hazing practices also reflect cultural differences among groups of men in fraternities. According to Nuwer's research spanning from 1978 to the present, and a number of experts cited by Paul Ruffins in 2007, beatings, paddling, and other forms of violent pledging practices are the primary cause of injury and death within historically black fraternities, while pledging deaths among predominantly white fraternal groups are more likely to involve alcohol poisoning and other substance abuse as well as violence.[55] (That is not to say that the opposite doesn't happen. White pledges have been savagely beaten by fellow members, and black pledges have been coerced into drinking, including the 1983 alcohol-related hazing death of Vann Watts at Tennessee State University.)

Sociologist Michael A. Messner points out that "within a social context that is stratified by social class and by race, the choice to pursue—or not pursue—an athletic career is explicable as an individual's rational assessment of the available means to achieve a respected masculine identity."[56] He draws on the work of sociologist Maxine Baca Zinn to explain the particular salience of athleticism for men who have been oppressed by racism or poverty: "When institutional resources that signify masculine status and control are absent, physical presence, personal style, and expressiveness take on increased importance." Understanding the complexity of cultural forces that operate in the shaping of gender is exceedingly important. While many white, economically privileged boys and young men wrestle with fulfilling dominant expectations around masculinity, the available options for achieving "real man" status are increased by access to education and well-paying occupations. In contrast, males from disadvantaged backgrounds may have much more at stake when it comes to developing their gender identity. As Messner asserts, "For lower status young men . . . success in sports was not an added proof of masculinity; it was often their only hope of achieving public masculine status."[57]

Implications and Recommendations

Broadening and deepening one's awareness of the cultural constructions of gender and homophobia, as well as the historical influences of race, social class, and other aspects of identity, can help to strengthen hazing-prevention efforts. Speaking specifically about masculinity, antiviolence educator Jackson Katz points out, "It is rare to find any in-depth discussion about the culture that's producing these violent men. It's almost like the perpetrators are strange aliens who landed here from another planet. It is rare still to hear thoughtful discussions about the ways that our culture defines 'manhood,' and how that definition might be linked to [violent acts]." Understanding and confronting problematic masculinities, Katz argues, is an essential first step to violence prevention efforts. Likewise, making femininity visible will also help draw attention to ways in which females, as well as males, are more or less likely to engage in particular types of hazing practices.[58]

More research is needed to help sort out ways in which hazing may be shaped by gender and other identity differences. The vast majority of studies have examined hazing among groups of white men. While there are similarities in hazing practices across all groups, there are also differences. For example, in her research on sorority hazing, Heather Wishart Holmes found that many women defined hazing as "a fraternity issue involving physical activities including drinking, running, and calisthenics."[59] So while these women describe their own participation in activities that constitute hazing (i.e., pledge drops, servitude, not allowing friendships outside the chapter, and verbal abuse), they did not define it as such.

In this chapter we have described how rigid and narrow versions of gender work in tandem with homophobia to create environments that are more likely to tolerate and perpetuate hazing practices, particularly forms of hazing among different types of groups. If we are committed to circumventing the harm that is often produced through hazing, we need to become more cognizant of how gender, race, social class, and other social hierarchies shape our understanding and tolerance of the role of hazing—even in light of the emotional and physical damage and sometimes lethal consequences that can result. Working to expand narrow and confining gender norms and eliminating homophobia is not only important for understanding and preventing hazing, it is an important step toward providing children (and adults) with opportunities for lives that are more fully human.

Research in prevention science reminds us that human behavior is exceedingly complex, and in the context of different types of colleges and universities with varied histories and traditions there is no one-size-fits-all solution. Effective prevention is comprehensive, strategic, and targeted with an understanding of the social ecology in which the behavior occurs.[60] In the case of hazing, this guidance can help campus professionals engage with stakeholders to analyze the problem of hazing on multiple levels, including individual, group, institutional/campus, and broader community (e.g., alumni, family members of students, popular culture/media, state laws). Adding a gender lens to this process can help campus professionals become more strategic and targeted by tailoring trainings, workshops, and social-norms campaigns to particular target populations within the larger student body.

Understanding gender schemas can help campus professionals become better communicators with students. In particular, acquiring a gender lens can help individuals avoid the likelihood they will unintentionally reinforce rigid and confining gender roles and stereotypes. At the same time, a sharpened gender lens can help individuals understand how different communication styles are more likely to resonate with particular groups of students.

Since there is no "magic bullet" or one-size-fits-all solution to prevent hazing, a gender lens combined with assessment data can help us design alternatives to hazing that will meet the needs of particular target audiences. For example, if proving "toughness" is a key goal for hazing, then nonhazing activities can be designed that incorporate safe and professionally supervised approaches for achieving this goal. While research on the efficacy of such alternatives is limited, one study of several college sports teams in Canada shows promise for outdoor adventure-based activities. Following an orientation involving team-building challenges such as rock climbing and ropes courses, student athletes reported more inclusive and egalitarian team dynamics and less reliance on traditional hazing practices as initiation.[61]

In light of this backdrop, we offer the following recommendations for practice:

- Design hazing prevention trainings to include time for discussion about actual gender differences and perceived gender differences and the implications for hazing.
- Draw upon campus resources and experts to assist with designing workshops, trainings, and other prevention materials that take into account an analysis of gender as well as other identity-based differences.
- Use individual and group advising sessions as opportunities to catalyze student thinking about taken-for-granted gender schemas and the implications for leadership and group dynamics.
- Include trainings about gender schemas in leadership training programs for students.

- Evaluate trainings and other prevention initiatives to determine effectiveness and whether responses differ on the basis of gender.
- Provide hazing alternatives that disrupt harmful gender norms (i.e., build self-confidence and positive body image among women and emotional competency among men).

Summary

Hazing prevention is vital for promoting campus and school safety. Analyzing the problem of hazing within the larger social context is a first step in effective prevention. In this chapter we described how prevalent assumptions about gender can shape hazing behavior in ways that exacerbate the emotional and physical risks of both gender stereotyping and hazing activities. Considering how gender and other aspects of identity are implicated in hazing can provide an important, but often overlooked, opportunity for understanding the abusive power dynamics inherent in hazing. This understanding can strengthen the resonance of hazing prevention by helping educators tailor efforts to the target audience. A gender lens can also help educators capitalize on teachable moments to help students disrupt harmful stereotypes that may support hazing.

ELIZABETH J. ALLAN is Professor of Higher Educational Leadership at the University of Maine. She is the principal investigator for the National Study of Student Hazing.

MORGAN B. KINNEY is a graduate advisor at University of Maine, Student Life. She has a University of Maine master's degree in Student Development in Higher Education.

9 Listening to the Voices of the Hazed

An Examination of Race, Violence, and Black Fraternity Membership

Ashley Stone

THE NEGOTIATION BETWEEN both race and gender has had specific implications for black men in the United States. In *The Slave Community*, John W. Blassingame states, "After marriage, the slave faced almost insurmountable odds in his efforts to build a strong, stable family. First, and most important of all, his authority was restricted by his master. . . . When the slave lived on the same plantation with his mate, he could rarely escape frequent demonstrations of his powerlessness."[1]

One institution that arguably and historically has pursued the development of black men is the black Greek fraternity (BGF). The purpose of this essay is to understand how masculinity is constructed and achieved in BGFs by closely examining race, violence, and bodily performance. The origin of Black Greek Organizations (BGOs) dates back to 1903. Determined to "strengthen the negro voice," black undergrads at Indiana University founded Alpha Kappa Nu in 1903. The organization folded due to low membership.

Created in response to racial segregation, black Greek organizations (BGOs) maintain that they have played a crucial role not only in higher education, but also in the black community. Recognizing the social and historical contributions of these organizations, author and black fraternity member Ricky L. Jones states in his book *Black Haze*, "We must acknowledge that black Greeks have built a great historical legacy of placing powerful black men and women at the forefront of the black freedom struggle."[2]

While some black fraternities and sororities are perceived in the media today as problematic because of behavioral issues, particularly from pledging abuses, they continue to attract prospective members and retain the allegiance of alumni. BGOs are also noted for having an impact on individual members, imparting leadership and life skills, and serving as a basis for racial uplift for blacks. Further, historically black fraternities have been credited with providing opportunities for young black college men to develop their masculine identity.

Black fraternities were developed to combat racial oppression on college campuses in the twentieth century. Years after the civil rights movement they continue to grow in the United States and abroad. The growth of these organizations indicates that they still serve a purpose for many young black men.

Historical Background of BGOs

At the start of the twentieth century, blacks in the United States faced racial discrimination and violent acts in private and public venues. Black students on college campuses also experienced discrimination. Jones notes, "African Americans apparently made considerable efforts initially to participate in the larger campus community of predominantly white institutions through athletic teams, literary societies, musical groups, and fraternities and sororities. But, like many things in the United States at the same time, participation in these groups on most campuses was continually restricted according to race."[3]

Racial discrimination in higher education generated feelings of isolation among black students on college campuses. Over time, black college students took organizational action to create their own safe spaces. In *Black Greek 101*, Walter Kimbrough sheds light on others that were founded throughout the remainder of the twentieth century. As their numbers grew, rival fraternal organizations were formed amid claims that prior organizations had deviated from their original purposes and missions. Some of these organizations even defied the mainstream fraternal structure and turned strictly to African culture for inspiration.[4]

Black male students at Cornell University decided to take action toward change on their campus. Alpha Phi Alpha, founded in 1906, began as a study group for black students at Cornell and later developed into a fraternal organization. With an emphasis on "manly" deeds, scholarship, and love for all mankind, Alpha Phi Alpha quickly spread to other universities, satisfying the need for solidarity among black students in higher education nationally. By the 1980s, Alpha Phi Alpha had grown to an international membership of over 175,000 males with more than six hundred chapters.

Kappa Alpha Psi started at Indiana University in 1903. Elder Watson Diggs and Byron Kenneth Armstrong, along with eight other men, founded Alpha Omega, the forerunner to Kappa Alpha Psi. The ten founders finalized the new organization, renaming it Kappa Alpha Nu, on January 5, 1911. The organization was renamed a final time to Kappa Alpha Psi, in response to a racist reference, "Kappa Alpha Nig," coined by antagonistic white students. The fraternity developed into a major support system for black students at the university and throughout Indiana at a time when the Ku Klux Klan openly operated in the state and an occasional public lynching occurred.

Students Edgar Love, Frank Coleman, Oscar Cooper, and Ernest Just founded Omega Psi Phi at Howard University in 1911, a historically black college/university (HBCU). Omega Psi Phi was grounded in four principles: scholarship, manhood, perseverance, and uplift. Like other BGOs, Omega Psi Phi has trumpeted its efforts in community outreach.

With Leonard Morse and Charles I. Brown, A. Langston Taylor created another fraternity at Howard University named Phi Beta Sigma. In November 1913 the fraternity received recognition as an official school organization. As the organization grew, it focused on business, particularly in the aftermath of the 1929 Great Depression, in order to provide financial empowerment to the black community.

In 1963, Iota Phi Theta came into existence at Morgan State University (formerly College) with one of its purposes being to recruit the nontraditional student. While contributing to the community at large, Iota Phi Theta was not officially entered as a member of the National Pan-Hellenic Council until thirty-three years after its founding. Iota Phi Theta brands itself as innovative, in line with its motto "Building a Tradition, Not Resting on One."

The five aforementioned fraternities belong to the National Pan-Hellenic Council (NPHC), which was established in 1929. NPHC was founded as an umbrella organization to serve and address the needs of BGOs. The legacies and contributions of each of these were constructed with a great vision "for the sake of the race," advancing not only fellow members, but also the black community.

In *Black Haze*, Jones argues that many predominantly white fraternities continue to be exclusionary organizations, stating that concerns about racial acceptance can exacerbate the normal stresses for new students wondering if white peers accept them. For example, University of Oklahoma students in 2015 chanted and sang a widely circulated offensive internet message on a party bus that vowed, in crude, racist language, that there would never be a black man given a bid to join Sigma Alpha Epsilon, an integrated international fraternity. Thus, understanding the role that black fraternities play in the lives of young black men first involves understanding the impact that these organizations have on black students overall.

BGO Research

The founders of BGOs have stated aims of their respective fraternities and sororities, saying they have operated in hopes of creating solidarity among themselves and more opportunities for future generations of black students. However, while black students today seemingly have more educational opportunities, they continue to report feelings of isolation from other students, with black males reporting these feelings more often than black females. Moreover, racial discrimination on college campuses can cause psychological distress, particularly for black male students, causing feelings of isolation counterproductive to classroom success. Stephanie McClure found that BGOs play a significant role for both members and nonmembers on campus, as these organizations attempt to integrate *all* black students on campus, combating the reported feelings of isolation.

Research shows that undergraduate students who are both academically and socially integrated are more likely to succeed in college. According to McClure's study on voluntary association membership, BGOs not only connect black students socially, but they also connect their members to black history. Respondents to McClure's study discussed how their membership made them feel more connected to the founders of their fraternities, imparting them with a sense of pride. This connection to the founders was not taken lightly but instead viewed as a serious responsibility to uphold their vision of the organization, as well as the visions of other illustrious alumni. McClure also found that membership to a BGO can also provide opportunities for individual success, affording job-market networking after college graduation. McClure's study concluded that members of these fraternal groups can develop a deeper and more positive racial identity.[5]

Development of Masculinity in BGOs

In *Masculinities*, Raewyn W. Connell conceptualizes masculinity as "simultaneously a place in gender relations, the practices through which men and women engage that place in gender, and the effects of these practices in bodily experience, personality, and culture."[6] Masculinity, then, is created and reinforced through personal interactions. Connell also asserts, however, that masculinity cannot be defined solely by one's gender, stating that "because gender is a way of structuring social practice in general, not a special type of practice, it is unavoidably involved with other social structures, specifically race and class."[7]

Michael Kimmel asserts in *Manhood in America* that men and women of all races feel an uncomfortable paradox because of a tendency for stereotyping of black males to occur in society. According to Kimmel, the stereotyping caused "a noteworthy confusion . . . a confusion that has remained to this day. Black men . . . were seen simultaneously as less manly than native-born whites and as *more* manly, especially as more sexually, voracious, and potent."[8]

Patricia Hill Collins expounds on this point in *Black Feminist Thought*, commenting on the implications of the black male physique and how this dictates the lives of black men: "Historically, African American men were depicted primarily as bodies ruled by brute strength and natural instincts, characteristics that allegedly fostered deviant behaviors of promiscuity and violence. The buck, brute, the rapist, and similar controlling images routinely applied to African American men all worked to deny black men the work of the mind that routinely translates into wealth and power. Instead, relegating black men to the work of the body was designed to keep them poor and powerless. Once embodied, black men were seen as being limited by their racialized bodies."[9]

In her study on the impact of membership in black fraternities on black men who attend predominantly white universities, McClure found that membership assisted the respondents in creating a new model of masculinity. The Afrocentric model of masculinity, emphasizing community collectivity among men and also *with* women, was found to befit the experiences of the study's respondents. While the Afrocentric model of masculinity can vary based upon economic class differences among black men, McClure found that a combination of elements from both the hegemonic and Afrocentric models of masculinity create an "amalgamation" of masculinity that is more conducive to the experiences of black men.[10]

Based upon interviews with members from the southeastern chapter of one black fraternity, McClure concluded that membership was a mechanism to counter the negative images of black men in the media. In line with the dominant model of masculinity, the respondents expressed the desire to graduate from college, pursue professional careers, and become successful. While respondents sought success on an individual level, they also expressed their desire to be successful collectively for the sake of the fraternity and their community, accomplishing more as a group than they could alone. Respondents also expressed the satisfaction of being in an environment where they can express their emotions openly without ridicule. All of these components align with the Afrocentric model of masculinity. Based upon the findings of this study, it is clear that the black fraternity serves as a space for black men to further develop their unique identity and gain a supportive network of other black men to reinforce it.

Violence and Pain: The Impact of Gender Performance in BGOs

According to Connell, "many members of the privileged group use violence to sustain their dominance."[11] Hazing is a common practice of many organizations perceived to possess status and power, including fraternities, sororities, and marching bands, according to Hank Nuwer in his book *Wrongs of Passage*. By definition, hazing refers to "an activity that a high-status member orders other members to engage in or suggests that they engage in that in some way humbles a newcomer who lacks the power to resist because he or she wants to gain admission into the group."[12]

Hazing practices have specific implications for men. Connell states, "The constitution of masculinity through bodily performance means that gender is vulnerable when the performance cannot be sustained." She continues, "Violence becomes important in gender politics among men. Most episodes of major violence . . . are transactions among men." Violence serves an added purpose for black men. In *Tough Guise*, Jackson Katz explains, "Men of color need to adopt a hyper masculine posture in order to get the respect they have been stripped of."[13]

While it is postulated by a number of authors that pledging and hazing are synonymous with many Greek-letter organizations, Jones argues strongly to the contrary: "The modern pledge process is an operation of historical social import as well as a powerful aspect of black fraternity legend and lore. We must understand that, contrary to the beliefs of many black fraternity members, at its heart, this process is a sacrificial rite that these fraternities did not create. Therefore, the pledge process is not unique in and of itself." Jones also asserts that the sacrificial rituals performed by black groups such as the Mysteries had also been adopted by other institutions in modernity, including the Freemasons and the military, and were then introduced into collegiate Greek-letter organizations.

Aside from the symbolism involved, Jones lists two specific reasons for the use of such rituals. First, he elaborates on the significance of the ritual for the individual who experiences it: "Completing this ordeal symbolically represents the replacing of a life of hopelessness, selfishness, and solitude with one full of hope, light, and fraternal love. All of these aspects, along with the desire to attain and affirm manhood, serve as the carrots [that] secret orders dangle to attract men. . . . These rituals established not only a fraternal identity, but also forged a vision of a complete Self to help men take their place in society." Additionally, Jones says that having a symbolic journey serves a purpose for the larger organization: "If successful, this common experience gives the organization continuity and structure. . . . This is central to fraternities' notion of brotherhood. Consequently, rituals that achieve such an attachment are strongly functional. Fraternity initiation rituals (of which the pledge process is only a part) are meant to bring about solid, concrete results."[14]

Modern Greek-fraternity pledging and hazing practices serve as great a purpose as the ancient rituals from which they are borrowed; that is, to provide stability for the organizations, as well as an opportunity for initiates to obtain a new identity. Further, some BGO members feel that the pledge process is pivotal to being a part of the organization and thus as integral as other fraternal ceremonies, writes Jones: "Most supporters of the ritualized pledge process defend it as central to fraternities' purposes. . . . Taken together, ritual and tradition form almost impenetrable barriers that determine whether a person is accepted into the bond or denied access. Bonding rests on the supposition that every member participates in the same ceremony, hears the same words, and lives the same experience."[15]

Thus, a question arises. If these practices are akin to other rituals found in society and history, why are the hazing practices of black fraternities seemingly controversial? Jones issues this warning: "If the functional nature of this operation is not realized, the moorings of this historic phenomenon will remain misunderstood and the particular type of violence that has become part of it will never be resolved."[16]

In a study examining violence and aggression in fraternities, Tyra Black, Joanne Belknap, and Jennifer Ginsburg found that violence was prevalent in both white and black fraternities. Where black and white fraternities differ is upon *whom* they perform violence. Black and her team found that members of white fraternities tend to display sexual violence toward women, but that members of black fraternities display violence toward other men.[17] This study confirms Jones's point that "modern hazing . . . is the phenomenon of members taking tests out of the realm of symbolism and catapulting them into reality. Instead of the initiate being threatened with [ritualistic] torture to prove his fraternal worth and manliness, he is actually tortured."[18]

This violence is further exacerbated by the fact that some Greeks view pledging (a vow of membership) and hazing (physical and/or mental assault) as identical. Further, hazing is justified because obtaining membership itself is not as important as *how* one is initiated. Jones states, "Just as accepted avenues to achievement in the larger society exist—attending the 'right' schools, obtaining the 'right' degrees, and living in the 'right' neighborhood—[there are] avenues of entrance into black fraternities that are considered more legitimate and respectable than others."[19]

If modern hazing is so brutal, why has there been no official cessation of it by BGO leaders? Speaking to the maintenance and continuity of hazing practices, Gregory S. Parks and Tamara L. Brown state, "Intuitively, another likely explanation is that a significant number of BGLOs condone the practice, either actively or passively, and that group officials have yet to propose a suitable alternative."[20] However, an alternative process has been created, called a membership intake process, which has been instituted by BGOs in an effort to replace the pledge process, as well as diminish and (eventually) eliminate incidences of hazing. Supporters of this new process proposed that it would become an educational tool for prospective members to learn more about the organization from which they sought membership.

Why do young black men continue to engage in hazing? One possible piece of the answer is to look to who were America's black heroes during the twentieth century as fraternity membership grew, and even as American universities, such as the University of Mississippi, one by one grudgingly accepted a federal mandate to accept integration. The heroes included hard-knuckled boxers such as Jack Johnson, who roundly defeated his white opponent James J. Jeffries in the so-called "Fight of the Century" and was married to three white women in his lifetime. But while Johnson's victory led to the resentment of white bigots in the United States and retaliatory violence against blacks and him personally, the victory of Joe Louis in 1938 over Germany's Max Schmeling prior to World War II made Louis a celebrated hero among all races. Johnson and Louis demonstrated time after time that they could not only throw a lethal punch but also take whatever punishment was inflicted to earn their championship rings.

Jones, again, succinctly provides that same explanation for why black males not only haze others but stand tall and take all punishment thrown their way in order to become members of an organization prized by them and their role models (e.g., Michael Jordan of the Chicago Bulls proudly wear Greek tattoos openly):

> The dependence on the physical often occurs because many black men feel (rightfully or wrongfully) that they are not privy to the same opportunities to define themselves as their white counterparts in U.S. society . . . that social and political marginalization helps to promote the black man's search for alternate arenas in which he can be regarded as a man. One way to define manhood that has emerged, particularly in black interracial interactions, is to be physically dominant or able to withstand physical abuse. In this manner, physical toughness eventually can be equated with manliness and this phenomenon carries over into black fraternities. This reality helps to explain why many individuals continue to submit to hazing—they feel that it affirms their toughness and manhood."[21]

Parks and Brown add that "because of the emphasis on pledging among some BGLO members, in many circles, members who pledge but are not initiated (ghost members) are often more respected than members who are initiated but do not pledge."[22] Hank Nuwer and other authors long have written about the term "paper members," a pejorative expression reserved for members of BGOs that have full membership rights but escaped all the sacrificial pummeling associated with acts of illicit pledging. It would appear that black men are bartering their social standing to gain a masculine identity by engaging in traditional methods of gender performance, or what political sociologist Anthony Chen famously calls the "hegemonic bargain," the predominance of one social group over other social groups.

Traditions, bonding, and the search for identity aside, Brown and Parks argue that what needs to be taken into consideration are the risks involved in hazing: "In addition to civil action, criminal litigation is the new front on which hazing is fought. Hazers can be charged with simple assault, battery, kidnapping, false imprisonment, manslaughter, or murder. Criminal liability can even be extended to individuals who assist or encourage hazing or who aid and abet or assist in the crime."[23]

Hazing has become a point of conversation and contention for Greeks and non-Greeks alike. While these practices are seemingly contradictory to the mission and values of black fraternities, Parks and Brown pose that "because there is such a strong need for this rite of passage—providing a transition from adolescence to adulthood and from prospective membership to full-fledged membership—banning pledging outright is likely counterproductive."[24]

Methods

Respondents for my original thesis, titled "Building Brotherhood" were invited to participate through sampling. A recruitment script was e-mailed to the members of the principal investigator's social network, who then forwarded the message to BGO members. Members of BGFs who were interested in participating in the study then contacted me, the principal investigator, express interest. Data was collected from interviews conducted with nine members from three black fraternities governed by the NPHC.

Of the nine respondents interviewed for my small study, six of them became members of black fraternities during their undergraduate tenure. The other three joined after they completed undergraduate studies. Seven interviewees attended undergraduate institutions located in the Midwest, one attended an institution on the East coast, and one attended an institution in the Southeast. One respondent completed his undergraduate education at a HBCU.

Face-to-face interviews were conducted with seven of the respondents. Phone interviews were conducted with two of the respondents due to geographic distance. Respondents were not compensated for their participation.

Negotiating Identity: Race, Gender, and Higher Education

Respondents who attended predominantly white institutions (PWIs) were asked about their decision to attend their undergraduate institution. One interviewee said, "I wanted to go to a predominantly white institution because it was more realistic of what the real world is. Nothing against historically black colleges, but I didn't feel like it was a good representation of what you were going to come across when you graduated and [were] in corporate America . . . so I wanted a different experience."

A graduate of a Midwest university spoke positively about a social experience he had with a white male: "One of my good friends was white and I was the first black dude he had ever met. . . . We hung out . . . I really didn't notice [racial difference] that much. . . . There was white people, I would hang out with them, like obviously, it's gonna be different conversations and stuff like that but I didn't really notice it. Maybe that's why I'm one of the few people that went to [the school that I went to] and didn't mind going and actually enjoyed the experience."

Another student discussed his experiences in the classroom:

> Well, to understand my personality, I'm a very confident person, but some people may consider it to be overconfident, but its actually me being comfortable . . . so I walked in with the same sense of entitlement that a lot of people, specifically nonblack people, have and don't realize that they do.

And since mine is pronounced as theirs is, it's actually perceived as me being overconfident or arrogant. So when it came to the classroom, it was a "you're a know-it-all" situation. I learned a lot from them and the experiences that they brought to the table, but it was a situation where I walked in wanting to learn from everybody around the table and got the feeling that some people believed that I didn't have anything to share. Or that I should just be happy to have actually even been in that environment.

Three respondents discussed the impact of race on their academic experiences. The first said, "I thought we had to prove ourselves against the racism on campus, because we were such a small minority there, particularly in [our academic field], we had a bad retention rate for blacks, really bad. . . . The way you feel, somebody else can give 80 percent, you feel like you have to give 130 percent." Another said, "It wasn't [sic] many black people in there, so, considering my background, I still wasn't comfortable associating with whites all that well. It would probably be me and maybe one or two more black people in the classes, so we kind of connected, which probably wasn't the smartest thing because we didn't do that well [laughter]. We need [whites and Asians] on our team too." And the third said, "The relationship with other black men . . . that basically became strong because there were so few of us and there wasn't that many of us, especially in the departments we decided to major in . . . there weren't a lot of black representation in those areas, so naturally, when we saw each other in the building or saw each other in different classrooms, we would naturally migrate toward each other instead of push each other away because it was very few of us in class . . . we weren't expected to get as high as we got."

Irrespective of their experiences with white students, respondents who attended predominantly white institutions expressed their need to seek out other black students on campus:

> Socially, outside of class it was great. . . . When I first got to [college], in my mind I said, how am I gon' [sic] meet other black people? How am I going to interact with whoever out here? So I started playing basketball every day. I figured if I'm gonna meet some black folks, they gotta be on the court (laughter). . . . [One guy] introduced me to everybody else. We were cool. We were tight. Outside of school, they came to my neighborhood from time to time and I went to theirs. We were instant family. It was great.
>
> What happens is, you go into a survival you didn't even know you had, and that is meeting with folks that you normally wouldn't might even attempt to. . . . I didn't go to college to . . . only hang out with black people. That never was my intent, but based upon everything that happens around you . . . I felt like I didn't have a choice. . . . [They were] people going through similar social issues as I was and that I could relate to . . . regardless of class or where we came from in the country or any other type of segregation that you would look at.

One respondent discussed being grounded in his racial identity while making conscious efforts to engage with students who were not black:

Being a black man on campus, I actually felt very secure and very strong because I knew my worth, and I grew in worth throughout my college years. I was a bit more "militant" in terms of my worth and the places that I was involved in and was active. But my position was to never be a black student on campus; I wanted to be a student on campus who was black. And that means to be involved with as many different people as possible. I regularly went to Asian American Association meetings and the organization for Latino American students. I went to different programs and salsa lessons and hip hop lessons, I wanted to be as involved as possible, but as a black man I felt very secure in who I was and wanted to be sure that everyone knew that being black was in any way not a hindrance or in any way an advantage, it's a part of who I am. Arguably the largest part because . . . I feel black first.

Negotiating racial identity among students of other races on campus was not the only challenge faced by respondents. They also spoke of the challenge of negotiating race among other black students:

[I]t was rough at first because other black men didn't see me as black enough. That happened a lot. . . . I just wasn't black enough, particularly when it came down to music. I listened to everything and as a performer I am classically trained, so my voice . . . at that time was much more classically oriented. A lot more "legit" . . . like opera. So I had to . . . make my voice more R&B, more soulful . . . and because of that . . . it was difficult to connect to other black men.

The one respondent who attended a HBCU discussed how skin color and class became a source of contention among black students on his campus:

At first . . . it was kind of strange. Being from [a major city], and growing up . . . going to diverse schools, I was used to being around different types of people and when you go away to a school like that, where [people from my hometown] are in the minority, you know, you have very few people that can relate to you. I was kind of lucky because one guy I went to elementary school with went [to school with me] so I kind of stayed in touch with him. . . . I knew the stereotype of the school I went to about [bourgeois], upper-crust black people and stuff like that and a lot of that was prevalent, like light-skinned versus dark-skinned, and they would butt heads on where they were from or people would make assumptions about someone by how someone was dressed.

The majority of respondents reported isolation based upon race in institutions of higher education. Despite the varied experiences with students of numerous racial backgrounds, respondents indicated they had sought fulfilling relationships with other black students to create an environment of inclusion. This included memberships in black student unions, as well as choice of seating areas in cafeterias, classrooms, and auditoriums. In some cases, relationships with other black students became tense, based upon the "legitimacy" of one's blackness, issues of skin color, or class.

Being "In the Cut" [Paddling]

During the interviews I always asked why they personally had gone through hazing. In the view of one respondent, hazing was essential to developing men: "As you become a man, when you think about it, what really disciplines you? . . . There's only one way to do that and that's through physical pain." Respondents provided insight on the rationale behind hazing in black fraternities and, beyond that, developing a black-male identity. One respondent in particular eloquently expressed the historical and cultural nature of hazing in black fraternities:

> The older brothers who were going to pledge us sat us down and said, "Look, what is going to come up next is going to be very difficult—physically, emotionally, mentally, spiritually, it's going to be very difficult. You have primary responsibilities in this order: God, family, school, [the organization]. Those are your priorities in that order. The reason you will be going through this is we have a strong adherence and desire to enforce a historical knowledge and identity within our members. A large part, if not the largest part of African-American historical identity comes from slavery, so you will, of course, not be a slave, but some of the things you will endure will have [be] slavesque or be in the realm of slave life, physically, mentally, so its very easy for one to lose one's identity, which slaves did. They did not have much of an identity except among themselves.' [The brothers] also made it a point . . . that our well-being was of top priority. We had to submit medical reports before any of this took place, so they take the greatest precaution if we had any type of medical concern or condition that would prevent us from doing any activity, we would not do that activity.

Another respondent also discussed the parallel between the oppression faced by the founders and modern forms of hazing in developing a strong morale: "That physical and even mental humiliation far trumps getting hit with a wooden paddle. You're trying to mimic what they really did, what they went through. But the difference is today we need mental strengthening, just like they did."

Another respondent spoke to the difficulties of pledging but also maintained that the practice had a long-term, positive impact on him:

> I said myself before I joined that I wouldn't get beat on, so when I realized what it was for and the symbolism in it, the symbolism is a strong part in any fraternity. But I realized [what] that symbolism represented. And it does work. . . . It works for the rest of your life (laughter) from being humble to respecting your elders, valuing your time, perseverance, to being an example. . . . It's like being made [hazed] means that you're really being born again, you're broken down . . . you brought down to your most humble state like a boy, and then you develop from that into a better man.

One respondent spoke about developing male identity as also being central to the hazing he had experienced:

[You learn] very basic things to some more elaborate ones. The way you walk, you need to walk with confidence, people should be able to look at you and say, "He's proud. He's a man." You know, shoulders back, chest out, head up, as well as more elaborate things like the family dynamic, definitely are proponents that the man should be the head of the household within a partnership with his wife, but should . . . be able to take care of and provide for his family. There is not a large emphasis on any type of vulnerability or sensitivity of any sort. I will say that there was never any chastising or punishment for showing vulnerability or crying. A lot of times, it was encouraged to promote strong emotional health, but those were in emotional situations. If it was in a physical, if it was a reaction to a physical situation . . . [crying] was definitely shot down immediately.

Another respondent echoed these sentiments about hazing:

This is the most valuable reason . . . for instance someone says, "What color is the sky?" and I say blue, somebody else says "Naw, it's green" and they keep sayin' "Naw, it's green" for hours, and [finally] I say, "Naw, it's green." Well, I'm [going to] get hit while I'm sayin' blue and *especially* because I said green, because I changed my answer. In a man, it teaches you that you have to be stable, and that's one thing that men, especially black men, do not have in our families today. There is no stability. . . . You need to be consistent in your answer. That's the bottom line.

Additionally, respondents suggested that physical hazing facilitates a process that allows pledges to learn the history of the organization that they are going to join. In that respect, it may remind observers how important oral traditions were to the ancestors of today's students when education, reading, and writing were forbidden or at the least discouraged. One respondent said, "[You get hit] for a lot of reasons, one I say the org[anization] is an oral tradition. Nothing is written down. When you have that kind of pressure on you to memorize something that's not written down, exactly word for word, you develop a pride in it, so you don't want anybody messing it up."

Along with having a sense of black-history and black-male identity, some respondents mentioned hazing as a means to facilitate a bond with members of a new pledge class:

Basically the reason for hazing, and a lot of people ask . . . well, I never got it myself at first, but [people] ask, "Why do you have somebody abuse you or hit on you" and stuff like that. Basically, the whole entire process of hazing is . . . you don't know those people you're pledging with, the hazing process is supposed to get you to where you'll lay your life on the line for those people that you initially don't know. So the closer you become with your comrades who you're pledging with and the more you guys look out for each other, the closer you'll get to understanding what hazing is, and that's when the process is sped up. . . . A lot of people come in and think you just get paddled . . . and then you're in. No, it's to get you to the point where you have to develop a bond with these . . . individuals to the point you have a tight knit with them as you would with your regular friends.

How specific hazing tactics were utilized to generate brotherhood was also discussed:

This is the thing, they wouldn't hit you . . . if you got [something] wrong . . . they would tell your brother, "Get in the cut," [endure paddling] if you're wrong. So what that makes you do is learn or be more efficient for the sake of your brother. So we didn't want to walk in session getting something wrong, because you didn't want anybody else to get hit on. And another thing that developed brotherhood is usually when men get into fights, a lot of times, that kind of bonds you a little bit because, if my line brother got hit on for me, something I did, of course after sessions you're riding on each other because you messed up and somehow in that, you develop a really close bond, just like real brothers. Somehow in that there's a bond. You can't describe it. So that's another reason why it happened.

One respondent stressed the necessity of hazing in order to create a universal experience for all members that crossed after him. He said, "When you come across a brother that didn't go through [hazing], or didn't go through anything, they're still [a member] at the end of the day, but you don't connect on the same type of level because you don't have the same commonalities about what you did to get your letters versus what he had to do. . . . I look at it as part of the process."

While hazing is used as a method to facilitate fraternal relationships and construct manhood ideals, these practices cannot simply remain romanticized. Respondents spoke to the physical and mental impact of hazing that created challenges for them:

The physical aspect was the most difficult. Pledging is not a fun experience, to say the least. You go through a lot of physical strain, whether that be . . . standing for long periods of time, paddling, or just certain physical trials and tribulations that you have to go through. [It] can be very hectic and can run a very large strain on your mental capacity too, because it's not just the physical portion, it's very difficult in that it can wear on you too, to where your morale and your spirit gets drained. Not to mention you also have to be a student, and I find that's where most people who pledge where they take the largest brunt of their burden is on their academics, which is unfortunate.

Another respondent (identified as "R" here) discussed how his chapter felt it had gained status by its reputation for hazing:

> R: I think there's a large Greek presence in the school and the city where I
> went to school, so it was kind of known what Greeks did and how we
> got down and that we did not, as we call it, skate [when aspirants sign a
> piece of paper to gain membership to a Greek organization as opposed to
> pledging], so dudes just kind of recognized that, oh, he went through that,
> so . . . you may get less respect, but you don't have to pledge.
>
> AS: But you all were known for not skating?
>
> R: Yeah.
>
> AS: So there was a level of respect given to you because [you did not skate] by
> men outside of the organization?
>
> R: By men outside of the organization and by other Greeks too because they
> knew how we got down, and we knew how they got down, so there's a
> mutual respect there. There's, of course, healthy rivalries, but there was
> never "we do this, and y'all don't do that," because we're friends, we go to
> the same schools and have the same classes and know each other, so there's
> an acknowledgement of you got down and we got down.

Respondents were also asked about their experiences hazing other men. Upon being asked about how active his hazing participation was, one respondent said, "I just did it enough to keep you honest because I know, for us, people who weren't hazing wasn't [going to] get no respect [*sic*]." Another respondent, however, expressed a vastly different opinion:

> I mean . . . with people getting hurt, I'm not sure if you really need that. If you
> do it, it needs to be controlled, because you have people who are on differ-
> ent ends of the spectrum, you have people who just like to hurt other people.
> That's just a reality. I knew some people like that, they just really like hit-
> ting people. . . . I don't know if there is a way to completely eliminate it . . .
> because that's what made [being in an organization] exclusive. . . . I'm exclu-
> sive because I was able to go through this rigorous process. And now that
> we've gone through this process we're like brothers. I think if you take that
> completely out, I think the story kind of isn't as compelling for other people
> to join. But it probably should be a way to . . . because I know if I had a son, I
> wouldn't want him to go on line personally. I don't know these people that's
> hazing him.

One respondent expressed his view for the necessity of hazing with the caveat that caution was also needed:

> R: I felt that it was necessary for him in this particular situation, because it
> didn't happen often, it was only with, if my memory serves me correctly,
> members of my chapter. I would never touch anyone else's boys. And that's

because I felt it was my responsibility to play a role in the formulation of that identity, that African-American, historical, slavery-based knowledge identity. I definitely did less than [other members] because I was never comfortable stroking [paddling] anyone.

AS: Why not?

R: I *hated* strokes and I never wanted to do that to anybody because my idea was like, if I didn't like it, I know you don't like it, so why would I do that to you? But I think I've taken maybe five total on another dude that was younger than me, one because they really did something wrong and he needed some type of deterrent from doing it next time, like things from skipping class to lying about where they were or what they got on a test, things that were really detrimental to them, that's when I was like, okay, you need to not do this again, so I'll do something to make you not do this again.

In speaking of what they took away from hazing, respondents spoke to implications of racial identity being paralleled with hardship, and further, with a masculine identity. One interviewee explained, "I think it's the machismo in the black community . . . the masculinity taking over. For years black men have had to overcompensate with being overly masculine, whether it's sexually or physically or whatever. I think that just comes from years of oppression and dealing with stuff and that's one thing you can control . . . being physically imposing and stuff like that."

Another respondent discussed the negotiation of racial and gendered identities for black men as it pertains to hazing. He referred to the concept of reciprocity, so well known among advisors who work with Greeks, which, in its simplest manifestation, often finds pledges who were mentored to go on to mentor neophytes, while those who were beaten or vilified during pledging find themselves dishing out similar treatment. His comment echoes the condemnation of hazing uttered by well-known black fraternity alumni such as Jones, Kimbrough, and former NPHC head Michael Gordon:

It's like something that should be so celebrated and joyful becomes terrifying and stressful and frustrating and painful in multiple senses of the word simply because it happened to people before and we feel like we have to do it to other people because it happened to us. And that's . . . that's so, so stupid. Even saying the words makes me irritated because of the level of stupidity. Hazing someone doesn't make me stronger. Beating somebody with a wooden plank doesn't make them more of a man and doesn't make you more of a man.

He further discussed his perspective on the crisis of identity among black men in relation to hazing. He refers to the type of brutality that has led to numerous close calls, pledges with kidney failure, and hazing deaths of black pledges at Tennessee State University, Morehouse College, and Southeast Missouri State University:

> I think [hazing is out of hand now] because . . . black men really don't know what they're supposed to be doing any more. Yeah, we have [had] a black president [Obama], but he is an extraordinarily unique individual—an exception to the rule. . . . The one thing we know is pain. We know that beyond a shadow of a doubt and how to inflict it and how to deal with it. Any time you can justify beating someone to the point where they are bloody and bruised and you have their blood on your body, you have to think about the mental aspect of that. And it used to be back in the day, in the '6os and '7os, there was still structure to the hazing, like it never reached disproportionate levels, but now we got into an era where men are trying to make men harder than they were made. And when I stop to think about how . . . it's now [a matter of] "I went through this and they have to go through three times this much."

Other respondents decided to become a source of support and encouragement for the pledges aspiring to membership, point out that it may well be that even in a hazing fraternity, the fact that one or more members prefer mentoring to punishing may lead to some pledges enduring the pledge period instead of quitting. One of them explained:

> My thing was I wanted to build people up. A lot of brothers say we have to break you down and build you back up. I'm like, can we just build on top of what they already have, like, that just seemed better to me. I was always trying to instill confidence because brothers play different roles in the chapters, some bros will be the go hard, stroke, stroke, stroke, and other brothers will be the encouraging one, so I'm like, I'm gonna be the encouraging brother. Like, *good job, well done, do you need anything? How are you doing in school?* That type of thing. That's the type of role I like to play. There was enough of the negative dynamic or the physical, deterrent dynamic. I'm gonna do something else.

The implementation and endurance of hazing are the archetype of male gender performance in black fraternities. Hazing, in this instance, is not necessarily arbitrary, but the results of this survey may indicate that hazing is used to facilitate learning and instill discipline in pledges as they balance all aspects of their lives. Significantly, Hank Nuwer in *Broken Pledges* has quoted educator Martin Luther who offered a similar justification for allowing young boys to be hazed when he was in charge at Wittenberg in 1539. Luther said, "You'll be subjected to hazing all your life. When you hold important offices in the future, burghers, peasants, nobles and your wives will harass you with various vexations. When this happens, don't go to pieces. Bear your cross with equanimity and your troubles without murmuring. . . . Say that you first began to be hazed in Wittenberg when you were a young man, that now that you have become a weightier person you have heavier vexations to bear. So this test is only a symbol of human life in its misfortunes and castigation."[25]

While there is clear acknowledgement and comprehension of the history and purpose of hazing practices specific to BGFs, and the unified experience it creates for pledges to facilitate personal bonds, it appears to survey respondents that without hazing, masculine identity cannot be validated or that the expected gendered personality is not being fully realized. Further, in the extreme instances, the survey indicates that hazing may be used to temporarily acquire dominance and control over an individual or individuals. This endurance is intricately tied not only to a man's gendered identity, but also to racial identity, perhaps in an attempt to find stability amid social incapacity.

Talk Is (Not) Cheap: Using Dialogue to Build Brotherhood

Through the course of numerous interviews with these members of BGFs, it became apparent that interviewees tended to believe that the bonds of brotherhood are built not only through the act of hazing, but also through time spent with pledges before the process begins:

> R: We never had a large problem with the hazing; we knew it would never go past a certain point . . . because so much happens before that such as building relationships and that trust and getting to know one another before that part of the process takes place, and I think that a lot of organizations, primarily white fraternities, they don't do that.
>
> AS: So there is a dialogue before and after and relationship building?
>
> R: I started [in one semester], [but] I didn't go on line until [the next semester]. So [during that interim period], that's all that building of that relationship and that African-American history and that familial feel and that trust— all that takes place before.

Respondents reported being engaged in this "prepledging"—the opportunity for current members to get to know pledges before underground pledging or nationally sanctioned practices begin. By engaging in dialogue, pledges and members are able to facilitate bonding and mutual understanding in a safe space that does not condemn men for being vulnerable. Dialogue also continues during sessions where pledges are being hazed. However, one interviewee points out that sometimes there is a "teaching moment" as a justification for the hitting, but sometimes it appeared to him to be a show of force without any bonding purpose:

> Now, what's not being made right is I would say when the people that are "making" you, so to speak, are not being conscious of teaching you the [principles of the organization]. . . . When you have a line that you makin' right, at

the end of session, it ain't like you say "go home, leave me alone." You sit people down. You sit 'em down and let them know, this is what we learned today. This is what we were taught. You progress. It's like the army, you teachin' somebody, but you also discipline them. Like you're learning both ends of the stick every night. The difference is . . . when you are hit, you are learning from the hits. The other end, you just gettin' hit. I've seen that happen, where people just want to see how hard they can hit somebody. And that's not being made.

Black Fraternities and Intake Process

Regarding hazing, one respondent to this study stated that hazing is "a tradition that needs to die, but I'm not going to be the one to break it." Some respondents alluded to the membership intake process, and two of them admitted becoming members through this alternative process. One outlined his experience going through the intake process as follows:

> Well, I knew they were having a line pretty soon, so I reached out to the people who were in charge of that and told them I was interested. . . . I went to an informational session. They explained to me what the fraternity is about and . . . they have basic qualifications they want you to meet, no criminal record, stuff like that. . . . You have to have at least three letters from someone who is a financial member, things of that nature. . . . It's an interview and they ask you questions. . . . Then you have someone contact you via phone or e-mail telling you that you made the next step . . . you meet other people who got the call to move forward. And at that point the line is formed. . . . We quiz each other in different ways about what we are supposed to know, the bylaws and the rules of the frat, getting to know, like, the history of the particular chapter as well as the fraternity. . . . A lot of studying and homework involved . . . sometimes you're up at night learning this stuff. . . . For me, it wasn't any type of physical harm or physical damage. It was more of a mental thing. . . . It was a lot of information. . . . You have to know it and memorize it. The thing is . . . you're also waiting on the other people on your line to know this information, so we're constantly quizzing each other. . . . It's a process. . . . We got a test to see where our knowledge is at, and once I passed that, we were initiated. . . . It was a ceremony . . . to become official members of the fraternity.

This respondent was asked whether he feels that he was or is perceived differently by other fraternity members because he was not hazed physically. He said, "No, no one has come to me and said, 'You're not a member because you didn't go through what I went through,' so . . . they call [the intake process] 'skating' or 'paper.' Personally, no one has directed that toward me . . . but honestly, I'm just as much of a brother or member as they are."

One respondent who went through both sanctioned and unsanctioned processes for BGF membership believes that the intake process can work, but he was critical of how it is being implemented: "The program that is in place, the membership intake process, is there. It just needs to be strengthened. Because all the organizations are taking a zero-tolerance policy on hazing, but that's really on the front . . . because you know behind closed doors everybody's talking about how they were hazed and everything that they went through. . . . Like, you can't denounce it on a podium and then backstage applaud it. And that's what's happening. So if it's going to be the intake process then it has to be strengthened."

One respondent discussed a potential drawback of the intake process as the impression that it does not facilitate a bonding experience with other members who have been hazed. He said hazing is "not even linked to being a man, it's just . . . they didn't go through the same process or the same lengths you went through to get these letters. . . . If you just signed your name on a piece of paper and took a test 'cause you studied a book, that don't [*sic*] go over well."

In speaking to respondents, it is clear to me that the membership intake process has been enacted in some chapters of some organizations, though not universally accepted. For the members who go through this approved process, it may become difficult to develop bonds with members who gained entry into an organization while undergoing hazing. Further, for some, there seems to be conflicting ideas about whether this alternative process is the most effective way of "making" members, considering that it has not been made universal. Based upon the comments of the two respondents interviewed who gained membership through the intake process, they said they had as much knowledge of their fraternities as did the other seven respondents, which is an essential piece of membership into a black fraternity. In either case, membership intake seems to have compelled these black fraternity members to rethink the methods of how to "make" men.

Discussion and Conclusions

In negotiating race and gender in higher education, respondents reported feelings of estrangement and distress, particularly in the classroom. While some respondents experienced challenges engaging socially with students of other races, they actively sought other black students, especially other black men, with whom to relate. Tensions did arise, however, as they developed relationships with other black students (outside their chosen fraternities), based upon other social structures, particularly socioeconomic class.

Gender performance as it pertains to hazing became a prominent topic in this study. Respondents revealed the nature of hazing in the black fraternity, its ties to specific representation, and, further, its use as a tool to facilitate bonds among current and new members through a universal experience. The ability to withstand hazing, as evidenced by respondents cited in this study, may be an unsanctioned means to develop and validate a pledge's racial and gendered identities. Respondents spoke to the use of hazing as a means to connect pledges to their racial identity and the struggles historically endured by blacks. Hazing was noted as a disciplinary tool for pledges that interviewees felt interfered with their balancing responsibilities as a pledge and as a student.

Based upon the findings of this study, it could be argued that BGFs covertly highlight aggressive behavior to strengthen black men in preparation for navigating their way through systems of discrimination. Despite efforts of respondents to reiterate the importance of academics as essential to the success desired by pledges in line with hegemonic models of masculinity, through hazing, it is still maintained that "masculinity is associated with the use of the body, not the mind."[26]

While respondents stated that there was some secrecy surrounding hazing practices in regard to knowing what would occur at various sessions, there was a great level of transparency between pledges and fraternity brothers particularly after sessions where hazing took place. Respondents discussed the ability to openly dialogue with their big brothers about their thoughts and feelings without fear of criticism. Additionally, respondents expressed their desire to provide this opportunity to new pledges. Dialogue became a major component in pledges endorsing elements of Afrocentric models of masculinity. This may counter the notion of members "masking" their true feelings and beliefs to conceal any vulnerability to pledges technically still outside the chapter.

The approved membership intake process that BGO administrators validate was given much attention in the interviews. Those initiated through the intake process said they did not experience any consequences of being viewed as less masculine for doing so, though becoming a member that way might not grant them the same respect as other members who endured and then valued physical and mental hazing. Even those who became members of a hazing chapter said in retrospect they viewed as questionable some aspects of "traditional" hazing, such as calisthenics until pledges dropped. Of interest, most respondents said they would not engage in hazing again due to the personal risks and potential consequences.

This research contributes a greater understanding of hazing in black fraternities. Some scholars suppose that all fraternal organizations are nearly identical, and more so, that their activities also are identical. Male violence is a central problem in our society. Black violence mirrors the styles and habits of white-male violence. It is not unique. What is unique to black-male experience is the way in which acting violently often gets attention and praise from the dominant culture. Even as it is being condemned, black-male violence is often deified. As Harvard University Professor Orlando Patterson suggests, as long as white males can deflect attention from their own brutal violence onto black males, black boys and men will receive contradictory messages about what is manly and about what is acceptable.[27]

However, the findings of this present study provide an additional premise that must be considered. Can it be that modern hazing has ties to a larger historical significance that instills a sense of positive racial and gendered identities in those who participate? For this reason, it may be beneficial for scholars to probe for answers regarding the intent behind hazing practices. Surveys like the present one remove the secrecy from rituals, and the secrecy may have exacerbated preconceived notions of some that black fraternities are no more than educated gangs on campus.

There are certainly limitations to this study. First, it included only nine respondents, and the hope is that other researchers will execute much larger surveys and scholarship that further academic understanding about the practice of hazing. While respondents provided a lot of insight into masculine identity development in black fraternities, having more respondents in future studies can and will provide needed information to confirm or refute this survey's findings.

Given the alarming dropout rate among black teens in high school, the opportunity to experience black membership is available to the relatively few black males who attend college. Future opportunities for BGF membership may be limited as well if extreme hazing practices persist. Kimbrough warns that "the courts will soon abolish black fraternal organizations altogether."[28] The findings of this study are essential to continuing a dialogue, not only in the black Greek community about transforming ideas about masculinity, but also in the black community and all educational institutions that sanction black fraternities.

ASHLEY STONE is an academic counselor in the African American Academic Network at the University of Illinois at Chicago. Stone has used her background in nonviolence education and sociology to create identity-conscious programming for various audiences.

10 Unspoken Sisterhood

Women in African American Sororities and Their Physical and Mental Ordeals— "Weeding the Good from the Bad"

Gina Lee-Olukoya

Introduction

On most college campuses during the fall and spring semesters, women prepare to attend informational sessions to learn what is required to become a member of a sorority. Some of these women seek to join a historically African American sorority to continue their family legacy, and others seek to join to be part of a social community that gives them entrance into a highly selective and privileged society. There are many reasons why these bright and gifted women seek to become members; chief among those reasons is the need to belong. Belonging is a powerful motivator and is one of the prevailing reasons why women joining African American sororities eagerly submit their applications, complete with letters of recommendation and transcripts, and often willingly participate in hazing practices in order to join.

Hazing in African American Greek life is not a new phenomenon, but it is a practice that can be viewed among women as elusive, or "deep undercover." There are far more published stories, incidents, or legal cases that involve men's groups, but women can and do haze their members. By nature of being a "woman" doesn't negate the ability for women to engage in the oppressive practice of hazing. On the contrary, women are engaging in hazing rites like their male counterparts and counterparts of all races in other student clubs and activities. Reflecting back in history, it was 2002 when the black Greek world was jolted with another fatal incident. An event involving Alpha Kappa Alpha Sorority left two young women dead on a beach in California. By all measures this could have been a seminal event in the evolution of hazing in women's organizations.

When dangerous or demeaning hazing acts occur, these organizations, designed to empower young women to inspire their communities, evolve into oppressive societies. "Little hazing took place in the black sororities before the

1960s; however, by the early 1970s, hazing had become severe," says Hank Nuwer in *Wrongs of Passage*.[1] At the same time, black women in these societies have benefited greatly from their association. Referencing the calling card of privilege that membership in a historically black sorority offers, Roxanne Roberts argues, "Membership means getting African American women into positions of power: political, business, and economic."[2] Arguably it is this contrast between the cultural purpose of African American sororities and the violent nature of hazing as a tool to transmit culture that is worth the exploration to determine a resolution in ending hazing traditions.

African American women have found membership in black sororities as a means to address issues of race and gender for over a hundred years. As black women have emerged from roles of "mammies" and domestic workers to the ranks of the college-educated citizenry, the role of the historically black sorority has aided in the transformation of the African American community. Discussing the evolution of the club movement for black women, Paula Giddings explains, "Their job was to help by word and by deed—to create that opportunity and environment for all black women."[3] Traditionally, membership in a historically black sorority represented the opportunity for women to change the racial, social, and economic dynamic of African Americans, particularly the unequal state of affairs for black women. Though African American sororities would not necessarily define themselves as "black feminist" organizations, the espoused values of these organizations, and their continued involvement with black communities to address issues of race, childcare, economic empowerment, and health-care disparities, give credibility to the notion that these organizations are predicated on feminist thought.

Thus, it seems contradictory that these organizations with membership that have significantly contributed to the empowerment of African American women have engaged in violent hazing rituals that have caused an enormous amount of psychological and physical harm. The evolution of the historically African American fraternity and sorority is marked by multiple dynamics that include the expansion to predominantly white institutions, the development of critical social-action agendas, and the dramatic increase in hazing violence. It is the hazing violence within the African American sorority that presents concern, as it is a subject that continues to be a problem for members, potential members, and the institutions that host these organizations.

Focused Problem

By all accounts, hazing among students at colleges and universities is a familiar practice by upperclassman to indoctrinate newly matriculated students.[4] Hazing emerged in the pledging practices of historically black fraternities and sororities, and increased in severity as well as being unchecked until 1989, when the death of a Morehouse College student, who was pledging Alpha Phi Alpha, caused a major paradigm shift among these organizations. Pledging and the harshness of the process, including hell week, became viewed as a critical problem even though hazing had existed in these groups since at least the 1920s.

In 1990 the nine historically black Greek fraternities and sororities eliminated "pledging" as a design to remove hazing from many chapters. However, "since then, hazing has grown more violent as the activities have become hidden in the underground culture of the chapter."[5] The decision to eliminate pledging in 1990 promised to eradicate hazing from chapters; however, since then widespread hazing incidents still have been reported.

Hazing, as depicted in movies such as *School Daze* or popular books such as *Pledged* or *Be My Sorority Sister—Under Pressure*, has been a part of higher education in some form or another in the United States since the 1700s. The prankster qualities of this process eventually evolved into initiation rites of passage that have sometimes fatally injured young people and have cost organizations millions of dollars in liability claims. Thomas Leemon defines "rites of passage as the recurring social mechanism that a society provides for the orderly transition in its social relations and that serve its revitalization, comprise a series of events that include rituals and ceremonies."[6]

For many in fraternities and sororities the practice of hazing is a rite of passage deemed necessary to be worthy of initiation into the organization. "This process enables the Greek chapters to establish unity among the pledges, and hence reinforce and ensure the future of the fraternity."[7] Black Greek organizations have historically been viewed as a viable resource for African American communities, an avenue for student involvement and activism, and finally a community that appears to be mysterious and aloof. Through the involvement in black Greek organizations, African American students have the opportunity to develop their identity and learn valuable skills for the future. These organizations have impacted African American students significantly. However, rising concern over deadly hazing activities have caused many educators and media observers to question the validity of the "black Greek experience."

To understand the problem of hazing in African American sororities, it is essential to reflect back in time to establish the benchmark for the evolution of these rites of passages. As noted, the 1990s marked the prescribed end of pledging as a rite of passage within historically black Greek lettered organizations. These pledging activities, marked by a series of tasks, were outward displays that signified to the general public that one was participating in the process to become a member of a fraternity or sorority. Despite this landmark policy shift, "continued media reports of hazing suggest that pledging and hazing activities continue underground."[8]

Walter Kimbrough in 2000 replicated the 1992 dissertation of John Williams by examining undergraduates' perceptions of the no-pledging policy of the historically black Greek organizations. This study discovered that of the two hundred participants, more than 53 percent reported that they had engaged in pledging activities, such as sessions and paddling.[9] The problem of hazing in black Greek-letter organizations was and is at a critical juncture; more importantly, the hazing crisis brewing within historically black sororities has risen on occasion to the level of more publicized brutal fraternity hazing. In 1991, for example, the Alpha Kappa Alpha chapter at Jacksonville State University was found guilty of physically and mentally mistreating pledges during "underground" activities.

The experiences of the women belonging to historically black sororities and the hazing activities that they perpetuate are a subject with limited studies. Shaw and Morgan postulated that there is little literature on hazing in sororities because much of the focus remains on men's groups.[10] While there have been studies about black Greek life (primarily fraternities) and the educational outcomes of membership, few studies evaluate historically black sororities and the evolution of hazing.

In *Wrongs of Passage*, Hank Nuwer details hazing events involving two historically black sororities at Kent State and Jacksonville State engaging in "paddling, pushing, and slapping pledges."[11] Additionally, Nuwer describes a particularly violent incident at Western Illinois University where undergraduate and graduate members hazed a pledge. The student was forced to "grind her elbows in cornflakes until she bled, and then to eat the red flakes."[12] Thus, the contradictions within the black sorority experience are the clear commitment to public service by which members shall "uplift" their communities versus the horrific and sometimes deadly acts of violence, which degrade the community. Mary Geraghty details hazing incidents involving physical abuse by members of Alpha Kappa Alpha sorority and Delta Sigma Theta sorority. She notes the following from a woman active in Delta Sigma Theta: "Despite Greek organizations' official positions against hazing, it is a pervasive problem, especially among the nine traditionally black fraternities and sororities. It still happens, and it happens a lot."[13]

The list of sorority hazing is extensive. In 1998 at Bennett College, Alpha Kappa Alpha was suspended for physical hazing, and two members were barred from participating in commencement. In 1999 at Western Illinois University and at Norfolk State University, Delta Sigma Theta was suspended for hazing aspirants, which led to aspirants being hospitalized and members expelled from school. In 2000 at Ball State University, Zeta Phi Beta was suspended for mental abuse and mild physical hazing.[14] Finally, in 2002, the deaths of two women pledging Alpha Kappa Alpha sorority in California confirms that sororities are capable on rare occasions of executing hazing practices that have been as violent and deadly as activities conducted by their male counterparts.

Unpacking Hazing

In the literature on Greek life, the voice of the African American sorority member too often is silent. There are many assumptions about the impact of membership in a historically black sorority and how the women who belong are socialized. The literature suggests that as organizations with feminist traits, the experiences of women in historically black sororities and the oppressive violent nature of hazing stand in contradiction. Additionally, the phenomenon known as hazing, which is a part of the pledging process and includes both mental and physical abuse, appears to be more of a significant problem for men's groups, as demonstrated by this focus in the scholarly literature.[15] However, what is known is that "membership intake has mutated the pledge culture into an underground event predicated on quasi-secrecy and loyalty to a chapter versus the national organization."[16]

As women's clubs, the black community knows the black sorority among its members and society as a strong opportunity for growth, social development, and connection. "Black female clubs and organizations were potentially more feminist and radical in nature than white women's clubs because of the difference in their circumstances created by racist oppression."[17] For African American students, involvement in organizations such as sororities supports their socialization, particularly on predominantly white campuses. "Affiliation with Greek-lettered organizations plays a significant role in the student's ability to counter social isolation," contended Colette Taylor and Mary Howard-Hamilton.[18]

Hazing as a phenomenon within college and university student cultures is a phenomenon that has roots in the early colonial era of higher education. The process to indoctrinate members into a society, club, or organization ranges from the intimidation of young college freshman by their upper-class peers, to marching bands inflicting tremendous physical abuse to the new initiates of the drum line. Hazing within military institutions is well documented as a means to train and indoctrinate soldiers for the harshness of war. Understanding the phenomenon of hazing is complex, and it is likely that one may never understand the cultural complexities driving the perpetrators engaging in hazing activities. Hazing within organizations is a cultural artifact, meaning that it becomes a repeated and replicated custom of the organization and, for members, has value and relevance within organizational dynamics. Central in the literature explored is the commitment to hazing practices for the purpose of preserving the culture, status quo, and traditions of the organization.

It is difficult to process a logical theory to explain the occurrences of hazing practices in Greek-letter organizations. The reality that can be suggested is that hazing is a part of the culture of Greek societies that permeated organizations on some level after the founding of the first fraternity in 1825. As a phenomenon, hazing operates as a cultural level of an organization. A culture of a phenomenon gives meaning to the organization's philosophies, is affirmed through artifacts, and influences beliefs and assumptions about the organization.[19]

As addressed previously, students' need to identify with a group motivates their engagement in hazing practices within the pledging process. "To obtain the social acceptance, students had a strong need to assimilate into these cultures, and through this, the power of the student culture influenced student behavior," claim Dawn Person and Monica Christensen. They further point out that student members are taught cultural traditions and customs, such as dress and language and chapter secrets, to gain entry into their community.[20]

The idea that hazing continues as part of the fabric of fraternity and sorority life is often attributed to the fact that with these societies, cultures and traditions are passed down from one generation of members to another, and alumni pressures can be intense and influential. Cultural levels are the properties that exist to transmit traditions and customs, such as beliefs, values, and artifacts. As organizations, Greek-letter societies are unique in their articulation of their value and culture system. The culture of the Greek societies allows for the development of shared beliefs, a common language, artifacts of the system, and a means to transmit the culture of the system. Fraternities and sororities require their members to be committed to the cultural and value system of the organization that often appreciates extremes and certainly identify with a high need to become part of a community. In this environment, hazing practices thrive as part of the system to support and maintain the tenets of the culture of the secret society.

Students seek to join Greek societies to belong and develop a social network. These seekers will tolerate hazing because of their need and interdependence on fraternities and sororities to provide them with a support family, academic support, or simply friends. For African American students, membership in a historically black Greek-letter society provides them with support to combat isolation and hostility, particularly on predominantly white campuses.[21] Traditionally, black Greek fraternities and sororities provide their members with peer connections, social activity, and connections to black faculty. Joining a black fraternity or sorority is a gateway into an elite campus structure. However, to gain a key, students seeking to belong often allow themselves to be part of pledging activities that can be described as submission to physical and psychological abuse. Like their white counterparts, submitting to hazing practices is the key to full and credible membership into the organization. In the era since the creation of membership intake, to be accepted as a legitimate associate suggests that one submit to pledge abuses, otherwise known as hazing.

Students place such a value on pledging, even though the rules prohibit, that they punish students who actually follow the rules to not engage in pledging. While they say they are about scholarship, leadership, and service, they really value how a person comes into the organization. This means they value lying, deception, and breaking the rules—all to avoid being labeled "paper."[22]

Gaining acceptance through hazing is the defining characteristic of the hazing phenomenon in historically black Greek-letter societies. Constructing an complete understanding of this fact is difficult; however, it is necessary to understand that hazing, as it is constructed today, emerged in the pledging activities, which were designed to build camaraderie and commitment to fraternal values. Hazing for many black Greek organizations has become a part of the culture and adds emphasis to the Greek legend and lore. For many organizations the need to legitimize members through hazing acts will continue to prevail over reason and logic.

A Newer Paradigm

Eliminating hazing rituals from pledging and membership activities is the goal of student affairs practitioners, national fraternal and band organizations, family members, and other stakeholders. Eliminating hazing is a goal that is complex and must begin with understanding how these practices live in our organizations, and more specifically, how they live and perpetuate in the fabric of African American sororities. Hazing rituals are rites of passage that some women in historically African American sororities have embraced and engaged. Understanding and uncovering the position that hazing purports is a fascinating challenge that requires unique research capacities. To this challenge, a contribution to our understanding of hazing rites among women is explored in the results of a multigenerational study of women who belong to African American sororities.

To begin, seventeen multigenerational women, each given a pseudonym for their identities and organizations with which they are affiliated, were invited to participate in a study on hazing within African American sororities. More specifically, I wanted to learn how hazing operationalized in the membership process and became part of the culture of the organization. One of the questions asked in the study was, how do members understand the role of hazing activities in maintaining the integrity of the organization? This study relied on the participants' stories, descriptions and assessment of their entire membership experience, including their reflections of hazing as a practice within their organizations.

The question itself was complex and posed challenges. While women certainly were willing to discuss their experiences in sorority life, there was initial concern that they might not be as willing to discuss activities such as intimidation, harassment, physical assault, and verbal abuse that they either inflicted or received (or both). Through descriptive stories and analysis, the hazing experiences of women formulated into themes that describe how these women rationalized and supported hazing practices within their organizations. The study served as a means to provide an understanding of hazing experiences from the perspective of women who choose to affiliate. The study provided a descriptive assessment, along with analysis of the experiences of women in African American sororities and the role that hazing plays in the culture of these organizations. What is learned from the analysis is that hazing in African American sororities represents a unique paradigm of the hazing ideology that is wrapped around a complex reflection of sisterhood and sisterly relationships.

Membership in a historically black sorority provides a unique standpoint by which to view, live, and understand the complexity of the "black American experience." As Clarenda Phillips suggests, "African American women have been central to sustaining their families and their communities, the sisterhood network of African American sororities has provided avenues for self-improvement, racial uplift, and leadership development."[23] With this in mind, we learned from this qualitative analysis of themes from interviews with seventeen multigenerational women that a hazing ideology is shaped by a variety of unique experiences that are rites of passage believed to build traditions, cultivate power, and ensure integrity.

The purpose of qualitative interviews is to uncover knowledge from a participant by exploring through questions the meaning of their experiences: "Interviewing is necessary when we cannot observe behavior, feelings, or how people interpret the world around them. It is also necessary to interview when we are interested in past events that are impossible to replicate."[24] Furthermore, Michael Quinn Patton argues: "We interview people to find out from them those things we cannot directly observe. . . . The fact is that we cannot observe everything. We cannot observe our feelings, thoughts, and intentions. We cannot observe our behaviors that took place at some previous point in time. We cannot observe situations that preclude the presence of the observer. We cannot observe how people have organized the world and the meaning they attach to what goes on in the world. We have to ask people questions about these things."[25]

This qualitative study utilized participant interviews to collect data to support the objectives of this study. Open-ended questions were developed to probe and engage the participants in the process of defining their world and unique life. Each interview was semistructured in nature, which allowed for the greatest conversational opportunity. The in-depth nature of the interview design was guided by an interview protocol that also explored topics that I determined were critical to the objectives of the study. The semi-structured nature of the interviews allowed for me to explore topical areas that were presented by the women in this study.

Traditions, Power, Commitment

When examining the conversations of women in African American sororities, an important notation, developed around a concept that I referred to as the "hazing ideology," emerged as a significant theme. Hazing ideology in this case refers to the shaping of how women processed hazing based on their unique experiences. In their own voices, the women in the study articulated characteristics of hazing, the psychology of hazing, the outcomes of hazing rites, the level of commitment to hazing by members, and how hazing evolved through generations among sorority women. From running errands to paddling to eating foods that one wouldn't necessarily eat voluntarily, hazing for some of the women was characterized and demonstrated by physical and nonphysical intimidation, chiefly a repeat cycle of traditions, influenced by peers, and used to support the development of pride and respect.

Historically women have not been in the forefront of hazing tragedies as much as their male counterparts. Additionally, it has been a misnomer that women engage in simple mental harassment, taunting, and mentally tasking their aspirants. From the stories of the women in this study, this general claim is not supported. The women in the study suggest that both physical and mental hazing were and still remain part of the black sorority experience and, as one claimed, "weeded the good from the bad." Some of the women in the study argued that hazing ensured that the women joining their organizations would be disciplined and that hazing would correct unwanted behavior. In many ways, hazing demonstrated the power the organization held over its potential members. Nineteen-year-old Jamece defines this philosophy in terms of the tools of parenting:

> The physical things . . . in the process it's sort of a connection to, like, when my mother, you know, if I didn't do something she beat me, and I made sure I did it right the next time. I can see if you're not doing something to the point you should be then, you know, there is a form of punishment to get you to where you're supposed to be. To everybody else it seems like an improvement from the person they started out to be, to the person that they are now after the process. It's just, like, you wind up being a greater person.

Within the black Greek community is a large population of women who believe that physical hazing is an appropriate means for those seeking to become part of an organization. Jones argues, "To many black Greeks, physical hardships speak much more thunderously than intellectual challenge, for these hardships are thought to instill fraternal love and also serve as mechanisms, which supposedly afford the pledge an opportunity to prove his worth."[26]

As illustrated by a few of the women in this study, it is not an uncommon practice for sororities to engage in physical assault to indoctrinate members. Though physical hazing is a reality for some seeking to belong to a historically black sorority, verbal, nonphysical violence and intimidation occurs more frequently. The majority of the women in this study would describe their pledging experiences in terms of physical hazing; others expressed significant verbal, nonphysical intimidation. As one of the women stated, "They played so many mind games with us. We had a lot of mind games going on." These minds games consisted of mental games that tested the women's values and self-perception. Another woman noted, "They had us doing crazy stuff like kicking down the wall, acting like we were having sex with the wall, [and] we had to eat a whole onion."

As many women in this study discussed their views of hazing and their direct experiences with such activities, the idea that hazing is a repeat cycle of tradition was repetitive through many of the interviews. The tradition of hazing is part of the historically black sorority experience. As many of the women pointed out, hazing is a tradition that is passed on from member to member, and it is still today a very real element of the black sorority experience. One of the women called "Catherine" summarized this concept: "Because of the tradition. Because of what they've been taught by their members and they know in order for you to be a member of this chapter, in order for you to come in the right way, you have to follow this tradition."

From the stories told by the women in the study, hazing as a traditional practice of the black sorority experience is a widely held belief. Many of the women in this study identified that hazing is a tradition that continues through the generations. Here are the words of one: "We were suspended in 1993 and came back in 1997. Then the grad chapter had a line in 1999 and then in 2001, 2002, and 2004. They were going to have a line in 2005, but they have been kicked off the yard for illegal activities."

Antihazing activists maintain there are no meaningful outcomes from hazing. However, women interviewed clearly continued to engage in the practice. Some were more passive, merely going along with the abuse, never attempting to interfere with so-called tradition. As Rebecca noted, "It [hazing] really doesn't bring you together. The only way I can justify doing it is because it's tradition. Because I really don't know what the purpose of it is. But I don't know how I could tell others they're wrong, because I'm not doing what's right either."

The peer influence to haze is a characteristic of hazing practices discussed by the women in this study. The women expressed the need to be the "other," or to not be those who were not part of the inner circle of hazers within their community. In fact, the women detailed that the need to haze brought creditability to them among their peers and added value to the black Greek experience. "People treated us different because they knew what we had been through," claimed one. A woman we'll call Mercedes elaborated on this idea, saying, "On campus, you kind of tell who hasn't been pledging. You have [sorority members] running around here who don't know each other's names; they don't get any respect." The influence of the peer group is unquestionable. Peer culture influences how members of the community act, what they believe, and what they value. Cynthia points out, "I think it has a lot to do with peers. With our peers, we want to look good for our peers. Back in college, I could say with myself, I would not have gotten involved with some of things that I did if I didn't want to look good with my peers—be in the 'in crowd.'"

Being in the "in crowd" prompted many of the women in these sororities to engage in hazing behaviors. Many of the women in this study articulated how important it was for them to not be outsiders when it came to hazing. More specifically, they did not want to be those who were ridiculed for not engaging in hazing acts. There is a distinctive level of pride and respect by hazers for those who have been hazed. Additionally, there are contradictions revealed by the women who discuss that they were willing do what was necessary to be a member, even if it was wrong, violated their values and standards, or was grossly inappropriate. As one of the participants firmly stated, "When I was going through it, it was really fine. I was, like, whatever; I'll do whatever I got to do to be [a member]." Another clearly responded to the idea of being torn between doing what was right and doing what was acceptable to her peers: "You know when we would have our meetings, we had to eat things that might not have been tasty. It could have been tasty, but when it is mixed with something else, it isn't. Why are we doing that? That was something that I didn't understand. It was all part of seeing how bad you really wanted it."

A few of the women in this study discussed how they were part of a select group of women, the chosen few who were part of hazing activities. These selected few garnished the respect of their sisterhood and their peers more so than the women who did not participate. As Sophia said, "Some got hazed. But you are always in their eyes an elite group, the chosen ones. You were basically getting more respect than a person who didn't go through with anything. We all get respect, but you would just get more respect. And after that they were cool. Once it was all over, those were some of the best sorors because of what you went through."

Allison, who was separated out from the larger group and became part of the elite group of those being hazed, described it this way: "I think we had a high level of respect from the sorority members. But as far as our group, we didn't look down on the other women who did not get selected to be hazed; we just didn't really know them. We didn't socialize with the other members of our line as we did with each other or the big sisters."

Through these hazing rituals, these women articulated in interviews the power of a subculture that actively selects and singles out those who can be part of an even more selective and elitist group.

As researchers explore further ways to understand how women maintain hazing rites in their organizations, it is important to note that, fundamentally, women rationalize the negative behaviors of those who are hazing them. It is clear that hazing rites, either physical or verbal, do impact their self-esteem and their concept of a loving sisterly bond. It is also evident that through the hazing culture, women can rationalize and accept hazing as a legitimate practice. "Big sisters" in the sorority utilized their power to rationalize hazing and to entice their aspirants into believing that engaging in hazing would be value added to their overall membership experience. The majority of the women detailed the level of influence that their big sisters had over them. "I felt degraded and humiliated and, like, why the hell did I do this," recalled one interviewee. Though this is a strong statement from this participant on her feelings at the time, she later followed up on this idea by stating, "But what I did go through was meaningful to me. I didn't regret anything; I didn't feel they beat us to death."

Allison also commented in like fashion: "There were times I did wonder why I was putting up with the stuff I was doing. I was never physically touched or things like that, but even those little stupid games that were played with me, sometimes I would wonder, 'Why am I doing this?'"

The concept of power and status is brought up repeatedly throughout the many discussions with the women in the study. Power is viewed as a status symbol within the dynamics of the black sorority culture. As the women engaged in hazing rites, there was an underlying message that those initiating the hazing rites were the wiser individuals shepherding the aspirants through the process.

The pledging process for the participants, which often involved hazing activities, was an unforgettable moment in the lives of these sorority women. Commonalities for the participants who experienced hazing activities during the pledging process included self-doubt, a poor self-image, and a negligent concept of love. Rebecca rationalized, "Even though it's not necessarily right, it may hurt at the time, they're not going to do anything to you that is serious. They obviously love you for a reason; you are one of their pledges. They're not going to let anything serious happen to you."

Many of the women rationalized their negative hazing experiences by clinging to the belief that the perpetrators held a high level of affection for them and would not harm or mortally damage them. Jamece said, "There was never a point in time that I ever feared of my life being in danger. It's just different things to bring out the person that you are. Its things that will help you, like, build your communication skills. It's part of the process that helps you, like if you are a shy person like I was, to speak up. We're able to look at this person and see that she might be weak in the area of communication, so we will bring this person out."

One woman in the study named "Rose" articulated a similar belief: "You know, I never did feel like I was in danger. I never did feel like they could do anything to hurt me. I felt secure with them. They would kidnap one of us and we would all have to get [her] back, [like] a grown-up game of hide and seek."

Another woman recalled, "I think there is a deeper appreciation for the organization. I'm thinking about what I'm saying and it just sounds crazy but it could just be conditioning. I said that, now I'm thinking, is it a deeper appreciation for the organization as a whole or is it a deeper appreciation for my undergrad chapter. I think it is both. I'm glad I did pledge and [did the] things I was a part of. It wasn't anything that was totally out of the box."

The discussion of hazing is complex and incorporates many levels of understanding or disciplines. It is clear that the majority that engaged in hazing, in retrospect questioned the process. Not only did they question the process as to whether it was right or wrong, but also processed what they could do differently when in control of pledges themselves. For example, Jamece explained, "We have to say, 'Are we going to do this to our girls?' It's weird because at first I was, like, I really don't understand it. I don't think I'm going to do it. And here we are, doing the same thing we did to the next set of people. As dumb as it is, does it ever really stop? I do it, but I can't justify why I'm doing it. I'm just doing it because I did it. So I'm going to make them do it."

Jamece's comments speak to the cycle of maintaining hazing within sororities. The level by which women will continue to engage in hazing is demonstrated by their rationalization of the process and then their perpetuation of hazing once they ascend to full membership within their organizations. Allison, however, noted her dissenting opinion from the ranks: "I don't think groups maintain it. I think its individuals within the groups who maintain it. I think it's just individuals who don't understand the true purpose of Greek organizations. They get a little power and authority and they take advantage of the little power they may have."

Many of the women who were hazed firmly stated that they would "do things differently." More importantly, for many of them it was unclear as to why they were engaging in these acts. One participant noted, "My first thought is why. What does that get us? People already know we're strong, already know we're hard, already know we have what it takes in order to survive. Why do we need to prove that?"

The majority of the women articulated that commitment to maintaining hazing is about (a) creating a strong appreciation for the organization, and (b) the influence of tradition. Those who haze persistently articulate the value of hazing as ensuring that those seeking membership have a deep commitment and appreciation for the tenets of the organization. Tonya noted, "When you work for something and you go through a process to get it, it makes you appreciate it more than if you just go through membership intake—you interview, you go through the pledge process where you learn the information, and you're there with a lot of other people and you never get to really know each other. I would probably say that one who went through membership intake would not appreciate the role that they actually play, or appreciate the sorority."

Clear from the words of the women presented here, there are extreme hazing cases, but some activities, in their estimation, did manage to create camaraderie and solidarity among women in the sorority. However, in the light of reflection, some sorority women admitted they were disillusioned. A few claimed, in the end, that hazing didn't have a long-lasting effect on the overall sisterhood experience and bonds.

Reflections on Study Outcomes

I argue that, generally, women in African American sororities believe that hazing practices are not helpful to the chapter or a productive means to maintain the integrity of the organization, but paradoxically they agree that hazing is practiced in order to bond individual members of the organization. From my lens, women in sororities place greater significance on hazing that is physical and particularly violent versus the pledging activities that were described as embarrassing buffoonery, psychological gaming, or mentally stressing. They described concerns or were distressed with hazing that was physical, while justifying the type of hazing that was not. For example, Rose said, "It wasn't too bad; they just had us with those mind games that are expected. It was not like they beat us daily, like some others on the yard."

The diverse women that were part of the study each had unique backgrounds and became members during various years (ranging from 1969 to 2005). They discussed hazing and reflected on the importance of it to their peer community and to the strength of their chapters. For these women, hazing was a part of their organizational culture and, more specifically, provided them credibility within and among their peer fraternity and sorority chapters. The women in this study, over multiple generations, also noted that while hazing was not supposed to be a legitimate part of the membership process, it created trusting bonds between the participants as well as loyalty and trust for the organizations and those women who brought them into their sisterhood.

The majority of the women in this study risked the integrity of their organization in order to pursue the implementation of hazing rituals. This would seem to be supported by the claims of Jones in his 2004 study of violence in black fraternities documented in *Black Haze*. He suggested that there is a belief among members that changing the dynamics of pledging or eliminating it would destroy the organization.[27] Likewise, the women in this study viewed their hazing practices as sacrifices in order to be a good member and to better the organization. The women who became sorority members as undergraduates all expressed their experience with hazing rituals, and they each to some degree agreed that it was wrong; however, they repeated the rituals and for some found value in them. Those who did said hazing rites allowed them to create a greater sense of organizational unity and commitment to the organization's values.

It is interesting to note that the women in this study spoke about their hazing experiences in clear terms. They engaged in hazing; they claimed they didn't feel that it was wrong or dangerous; and those who were part of the hazing activities were perceived as "winners" because they had endured the hazing practices and had become part of an elite group of women within their chapter. Clearly, being part of hazing rituals validated membership experiences for many of the women. They did not view their involvement as risky enough to outweigh any perceived rewards. The rewards included credibility among peers, bonding between those initiated through hazing, and commitment to the values of the organization. My conclusion is that women haze because they seek roles of power. Those who submit to hazing do so to fit in and show their love and endurance for the organization by being compliant.

There are many lessons to learn from the voices of this relatively small study of seventeen women who chose to be part of a select group to enlighten the hazing-prevention movement. However, I will focus on one clear implication from the study and the resulting understanding of hazing. It is fundamental to accept that there exists a belief, validated by the women discussed previously, that hazing is necessary to maintain the order and integrity of sorority organizations. This is not a new concept in the literature on hazing.[28] However, it suggests that women's groups are committed to the practice, including even the more violent and oppressive side of hazing. For the women presented in this text, who entered into their sorority experiences in the new millennium, their hazing practices appear to be aggressive, violent, and, if all goes wrong, potentially fatal. There seem to be few limits to the potential hazing acts that provoke members to be dangerously violent or "mean-spirited." The women who subjected themselves to these hazing rituals argue that it's important in order to value the organization, be committed and faithful members with group identification, and ensure that the organization's mission is fulfilled.

Is there a path forward that allows women to join an African American sorority that is free from hazing rituals? From the voices of these women, it is not likely. For that kind of future there would need to be the creation of new rites that take into consideration the uniqueness of the black sorority and the need for women to participate in an initiation that is meaningful. Any innovative vision would need to include, too, a willingness to accept the current articulated truths about hazing.

Women belonging to African American sororities are engaging in hazing practices that are not only psychologically damaging but also are violent and aggressive. These women find rewards in their membership that gain them entry into a privileged and elite society. There are common themes that have been articulated in the body of knowledge about hazing of women's motivations to continue hazing practices. These women appear to be motivated by the idea that hazing rites are critical to the continuation of the values and mission of their organizations. To them, without hazing, the organization would not be able to truly have members who believe in the organization's core values. The women presented here make the case that absent of hazing rituals there can be no "Greater Service, Greater Progress," which is the motto for the Sigma Gamma Rho sorority, nor could women be committed to the idea of the motto of Delta Sigma Theta, "Intelligence is the Torch of Wisdom."

The analysis of the themes presented suggests that hazing in African American sororities is a rite of passage that has evolved in its characteristics by becoming an underground and coded process that is demonstrated as a repeat cycle of traditions, influenced by peers, and used to create members' respect and commitment to the core organizational ideals. The study presented here reveals that those who are engaging in hazing practices, either as perpetrator or victim, rationalize their behaviors. While each participant had a unique story, the hazing reflections demonstrated how the practice of hazing is perceived as a form of discipline used to shape those soon to join their elders and alumnae as sorors.

GINA LEE-OLUKOYA is Associate Dean of Students at the University of Illinois at Urbana-Champaign. She is a member of Delta Sigma Theta and serves on the foundation of Hope Street Youth Development. She formerly served as a board member for HazingPrevention.Org.

All names in the study have been changed.

11 Sexually Exploitive Athletic Hazing and Title IX in the Public School Locker Room

Warriors, Machismo, and Jockstraps

Susan P. Stuart

I ONCE WROTE A law review article on litigating a peer sexual harassment case in the public schools. Among my unspoken observations was that boys had greater success than girls in cases under Title IX. The reason for boys' continued success under Title IX is because so many involved physical or sexual assault. A number of times male-on-male sexual harassment occurred in conjunction with sports. I concluded that sexual harassment might play a significant role in male athletic hazing and vise versa.[1]

Part of the underlying pathology of sexually exploitative athletic hazing is directly connected with the dominance of sports in United States culture. To the extent that we grant cultural authority and leadership to public-school sports, athletes are the standard for a hegemonic masculinity, not just for the team, but also for the community. Hazing's part in maintaining that hegemonic masculinity is often an outgrowth of "tradition" and is therefore "rationally" perceived as a rite of passage to this admired masculinity. Like sociocultural rites of passage, new members are "initiated" to the team, and the tradition is handed down to keep the hegemonic masculinity in place. In cultural traditions, sexualized acts or feats of sexuality are required to meet a society's expectations of taking the next step to manhood. So in that respect, perhaps sexually abusive behavior in athletic hazing is not an unexpected trend.[2]

Athletic hazing is not rational. It is not an initiation rite such as pledging because rookies have already become members of the team and were appointed by an adult coach, not by teammates. Nascent research suggests, instead, that athletic hazing is explicitly about team self-governance, primarily through humiliation. Thus, sexually exploitative hazing has more to do with an extension of physically abusive hazing designed to humiliate younger, and often smaller, team members and to keep them in their place. The way to do that, in the framework of the hegemonic masculinity, is to treat those younger team members as if they are not fully masculinized, but rather feminized. The younger team members are thus treated as if they do not conform to gender stereotypes and cannot conform until they become either peripheral to the hazing or perpetrators themselves. Given that foundation, any kind of abusive hazing in a male homosocial sports organization could be sexual harassment under Title IX.[3]

Title IX sexual harassment claims could become a potent weapon in cleaning up a lot of athletic-hazing problems for boys. The same systemic solutions to stop sexual harassment in the locker room will have an impact on all abusive hazing: if a coach has to supervise all locker room activities, all activities in the locker room will be supervised. And the "ick" (disgust) factor invoked by sexually exploitative hazing may be just enough to draw attention to public-school athletic hazing in particular, and perhaps to sexual harassment in an institution generally. But the onus will have to be on adults as supervisors. Disciplinary actions against individual students will not clean up this sordid trend. Pervasive systems of self-governance will always have some new adolescent willing to step into the breach and to take up the mantle of the tradition. That, of course, begs the question of how adolescents came to be in charge of team governance to begin with. Public school athletic teams are an educational function of the school district, run by and paid for by the school district, so under what circumstances did adults abdicate to teenagers their own leadership and supervisory responsibilities over team governance and their athletes' masculinity?

Hazing has thoroughly invaded high schools. A 2000 national study reported that an astounding 48 percent of students surveyed had been hazed in high school, with 43 percent reporting humiliation, 29 percent reporting illegal hazing, and 22 percent reporting dangerous hazing. The extrapolated results of the study estimated that more than eight hundred thousand high school athletes are hazed each year. The 2008 "National Study of Student Hazing" surveyed more than eleven thousand postsecondary students' high-school hazing experiences with comparable results of 47 percent having been hazed in high school, with boys more likely to be hazed than girls. Furthermore, male students are more at risk for *dangerous* hazing, particularly from athletic teams.[4]

Researchers such as Jennifer Jo Waldron are alarmed at the recent uptick in both the physical and sexual abuse that is invading high-school sports teams and are starting to focus on the characteristics and causes of the phenomenon. But it does not take too many keystrokes to retrieve an alarming number of news articles detailing hazing activities gone the way of criminal sexual abuse. One of the more horrific incidents occurred at football training camp for W.C. Mepham High School on Long Island, New York, when varsity football players sodomized three freshman players with broomsticks, pinecones, and golf balls, "allegedly rubbed [with] heat-producing mineral ice. . . . The assailants allegedly brought the broomsticks used in the attacks to the camp with them, as well as stereos that some have reported were used to muffle the sound of the attacks."[5]

The pattern of upperclassmen abusing younger players has played out in similar reports in the media: a plastic bottle was shoved up an athlete's rectum to initiate him onto the junior-varsity team; older athletes forced a sophomore teammate to shove his finger into another sophomore's rectum; a fifteen-year-old wrestler was sodomized by teammates with a broom handle; another young athlete—with a learning disability—was "welcomed" to the team by being sodomized with a plastic knife.[6]

The emerging social-science literature is developing theories of causation and motivation for sexually and physically abusive hazing on male high-school athletic teams. Sexually exploitative hazing may be just one part of the entirety of the abuse endured by high-school boys, but the increase in sexual assaults has particularly grabbed the attention of the theorists, just as it has the public imagination and outrage. Therefore, the place of sexually exploitative hazing within the general schema of athletic hazing for boys is crucial. Two theories of rational behavior have been identified: athletic hazing builds team cohesion and/or is an initiation ritual. The participants themselves, however, use athletic hazing to maintain the power hierarchy on the team whereby the older members keep the younger members in line. Unpacking the real dynamic is the only way to figure out how to find solutions for sexually exploitative hazing and requires an examination into the more specific sociological and psychological explanations for athletic hazing in the first place.[7]

As a starting point, one must first examine the "locus" of athletic hazing—that is, the mechanics of team membership. First, one must remember that the individuals who are hazed are already members of the team, selected on an equal basis by parties—usually the coaches—in positions superior to even the senior members themselves.[8] Confusing matters further is that athletic hazing does not always confine itself to one team. Rather, interteam hazing occurs when the varsity team hazes the junior varsity or the junior-varsity team hazes the freshmen. Last, within any athletic-program regime—intrateam, interteam, or simply between specific individuals—is the tension inherently created when the new members are the internal competition against the older members. Talented freshmen can be promoted to the varsity ranks, displacing older members; talented sophomores and juniors can take team positions from seniors; and talented rookies may supplant an older teammate from competing at all in a particular individual event. These decisions, too, are generally out of the hands of the older members of the team. Instead coaches make them for the good of the team record, and they are contingent on the talent of the players. Rather than a "family" of like-minded individuals, teams are about "antagonistic cooperation," according to sociologist David Riesman.[9]

Given those innate understandings, one must grapple with the role of athletic hazing as either having rational importance to the team or being an irrational form of team governance.[10] One common—and rational—justification for hazing is that it builds team unity, or team cohesion, and thereby improves team performance. However, a recent study determined that hazing has no positive correlation to team cohesion. When researchers administered a series of questionnaires to 167 male and female college athletes, they discovered that the athletes' self-identified "negative" hazing (e.g., abuse, self-abuse, degradation, abuse of others) did not create team cohesion. Instead, it "was negatively correlated with task attraction and integration, and [was] unrelated to social attraction and integration. . . . Furthermore, hazing was associated with lower levels of task cohesiveness, and was unrelated to social cohesiveness." Even self-reported "acceptable" hazing activities—which rated higher for social cohesiveness—had no correlation with team building.[11]

If any cohesion is achieved, it is within smaller team units: (1) the hazees as victims and (2) the hazers as perpetrators. In addition, the hazees—who are already members of the team—see less benefit and attraction to the activity and feel anger and frustration with the hazers. These smaller cohesive groups tend to change the *team* dynamic because now there are different groups with different loyalties and smaller spheres of social cohesion. Furthermore, hazing tends to create mistrust of team leadership "because you feel the hostility and the grudges that build with being forced to do something." A team community cannot be formed "when individuals feel violated, harassed, or disparate to other members of the group."[12]

Instead of team community, hazing promotes uniformity, which is not the same thing as unity. These rites are quite successful at breeding conformity, subservience, and discipline that, while defeating the "community" intent of initiation, perpetuate the myth of cohesion. Further, excessive physical or mental demands on a new member cause fractured units within the larger group and sabotage the development of a truly unified membership.[13] The only appearance of "team" bonding is the code of silence over hazing incidents, especially when they are dangerous. However, that "bonding" is illusory because team members are closing ranks out of fear of detection or of retaliation within each of the disparate groups: perpetrators, victims, and bystanders who did not intervene. The code of silence is not team bonding and not a substitute for hazing's negative impact on group unity and team performance.[14]

The other common—and rational—justification for athletic hazing is its function as an initiation or as "a rite of passage wherein youths, neophytes, or rookies are taken through traditional practices by more senior members in order to initiate them into the next stage of their cultural, religious, academic, or athletic lives." As a general function of male initiatory rites, males "court" other males so as to be seen in the company of "high-status males defined by their community as attractive rather than with the contrary."[15]

One of the functions of the initiation ceremonies is, in these terms, the insurance of "fit," or consonance, between the members already in a group and the newcomers to it. A group of veterans is pleased with itself and with its status and quality. To affirm to its members and to outsiders that recruits are worthy of membership, a process of initiation is contrived that involves stringent ordeals to test the courage and endurance of initiates. This proves or disproves their suitability and keenness to join.[16]

Thus, initiation is entry-level admission to the group based on qualifications that the group has determined. However, young members have already qualified for the group, making a "different" initiation seem somewhat redundant, unless the initiatory function is to a subgroup on the team.

Similarly, a rite of passage is intended to be a "transformative" experience.[17] It is intended to signify full membership into society, often entailing abusive and barbaric rituals. Modern male rites of passage have the central theme of changing the subject's identity in a "destruction/creation" cycle that constitutes the death of one identity with the rebirth into another, typically characterized as transforming from childhood to adulthood.[18]

Such rites of passage may have three stages: "separation, transition (liminality), and incorporation." In athletic hazing, these "three phases can be thought of as pre-initiation anxiety, and initiation/hazing experience, and (temporary) membership."[19]

But because rookies are already members of the team—and at the collegiate level, may have been recruited in an exchange for scholarship money—the intentional "tradition" of systemic hazing begs the question of "initiation" or "rite of passage" to what?

There is a more reductive legal analysis of the evidence that reduces the explanation for hazing as much less rational than team cohesion and initiation. This reductive analysis is particularly salient when one recalls that athletic hazing in the public schools is administered by children, some as young as sixth grade.[20] Rational and theoretical underpinnings for an initiation or ritual function in hazing, even if valid, arise from what we know about the history of hazing in the military, in fraternal organizations, and in secret societies. The individuals who impose hazing or rites of passage in these activities may be mature enough to articulate an abstract reason for what they are doing, whether we like that reason or not. Athletic hazing at any level, but particularly at the high-school level, does not have that maturity of articulation. Indeed, what we know of athletic hazing and its harms sounds more like novelist William Golding's *Lord of the Flies* than a military boot camp. Although adults may rationalize athletic hazing on a more abstract level, the participants have a messier and perhaps more "social" view.

At the high-school level, in particular, hazing resembles an immature effort at self-governance. Perhaps the most apt characterization is that hazing is "an entry ritual by the rookie contingency to mark their membership and identity within the team structure"—maybe even a type of group bullying—to coerce rookies to become part of the team family and thereby part of the team's tradition and legacy.[21]

Hazing's social function is to create a "community" or "family" in order to build team solidarity. "Athletes often describe their 'need' to have an initiation ceremony as a team bonding experience that marks the group as a 'team' and its members as 'teammates' for the first time."[22] But unlike the prospects of promoting team performance, athletes are more likely to articulate the social aspects of team membership. Athletes articulate that hazing is endured in order for them to be accepted or respected and that doing so shows an athlete's dedication to the team as well as to the other members. Hence, the more primal motivation for undergoing hazing is the need to belong to a group: "all organizations need new members to continue, and new members need a sense of belonging."[23] In sports, the athlete wants to distinguish himself as a member of a particular team and the more popular, the better.[24]

Thus, athletes view their own identity as part and parcel of the team's tradition and being identified with a particular team becomes a competition in and of itself: "You need to be able to come together and say that we are united around this experience. It is what makes us unique from everyone else. You have to differentiate your team." The sadder plaint for undergoing hazing is the need to belong as an individual, that hazing makes friends: "Usually the people that did the hazing were the hot shots of the team—you know, the big players, the star players, or whatnot. And since they don't really know you as a freshman, once you get hazed, then you could hang out with them. . . . After being hazed, then they're your friends."[25]

Even if an athlete's "need" for hazing is social, its implementation has a hierarchical paradigm, a form of team self-governance rather than of social cohesion. Maintaining the hierarchy of veterans versus rookies is important in order to establish superiority or a pecking order.[26] Seniors and varsity players are the hazers while the freshman or junior-varsity players are the hazees, author Susan Lipkins, Waldron, Norm Pollard and others have written. Hazing will keep the rookies in their place. "Quite often, first year players come into the team community with an aggrandized sense of their worth and place within the team, an attitude that can rankle the senior players."[27] The hierarchical implementation of the team "bonding" experience establishes clear-cut outlines so that "the activities are not consensual among peers but, rather, are between the rookies who have no positional power and the veterans who have positional power," note Kirby and Winthrop. Thus, the hierarchical paradigm for hazing is about power:

Through sport, males learn that power is well defined. For example, coaches have it and players do not; athletes have it and nonathletes do not; seniors have it and others do not; males have it and females do not. Power gives people the right to do as they please, to expect privileges that are not readily available to others. It is important to exert this power over others so those others, too, may learn the chain of command and learn how to assume the power when their turn comes.

Hazing helps maintain the power balance in the team hierarchy by emphasizing the superior position of the veterans compared to the projected inferior position of the rookies. However, "this hierarchy creates resentment between the rookies . . . and the veterans," and only one thing keeps this power structure in place—the desire to attain a sense of masculinity. The final result is hazing perpetuated as a lasting team "tradition."[28]

The problem is that the construct of masculinity imposed in public-school athletic hazing comes from other adolescents. Team leaders are seventeen and eighteen years old and too often have the "responsibility" of the hierarchy in and self-governance of the team. In the absence of any articulable masculine role model or rules of governance, they rely on tradition and the whim of alums to inform their leadership duties and responsibilities.[29] But the tradition did not arise on its own; it has its source in the social expectation and acceptance of the sport ethic that makes sports culturally distinct.

The sport ethic, or tradition, has four distinct "values: making sacrifices for the game, striving for distinction, playing through pain, and refusing to accept limitation in pursuit of winning."[30] Contemporary culture and social adulation imbue male sports teams with nearly the same ethic as military boot camps. "Athletes are expected to pay the price thought necessary for victory; playing with pain, taking risks, challenging limits; over conforming to rigid and sometimes exploitative team norms; obeying orders; and sacrificing other social and academic endeavors."[31] In general, hazing is an integral part of this sport ethic as a way to distinguish team members from outsiders.[32] And, insofar as sports are tantamount to war, rookies must endure the rituals that pertain thereto.[33] Individually, the hazed rookie demonstrates that he will take one for the team, that he is dedicated to the team, and that he is worthy of membership in the team community. But underneath it all, the sport ethic is a proxy for a hegemonic masculinity.[34] "Dominant expectations of heterosexual masculinity have long dictated that 'real men' should be tough, aggressive, courageous, and able to withstand pain."[35] A hegemonic masculinity may not be the most common pattern in any particular region or community, but it is an aspirational masculinity that has social or cultural authority at any particular time and place.[36]

A traditional hegemonic masculinity has been described as a social construct—touted by media, corporate culture, and political power—that defines "real men" by metaphor: "no sissy stuff," "be a big wheel," "be a sturdy oak," and "give 'em hell."[37] Local masculinities can be "constructed in the arenas of face-to-face interaction of families, organizations, and immediate communities." In the context of sport, "successful participation . . . often is a salient hegemonic masculine practice in this particular local setting," especially as proof of men's superiority over women.[38] And in schools, sport is one of the primary vortices for the development of masculinity, particularly when the broader cultural authority reveres sports.[39]

Hazing itself is a construct of and "often is grounded in [this] hegemonic masculinity. . . . Within sport a very narrow conception of masculinity is privileged—one that marginalizes being feminine or gay and that reveres muscularity and strength. Surviving hazing reinforces that one is tough as well as confirms athletes' heterosexuality."[40] And "the presence of an admired, dominant pattern puts pressure on all boys, whether or not they match the pattern—and most, of course, do not."[41] For athletes, submission to hazing is conformity to a hegemonic masculinity that emphasizes winning as a precondition to acceptance, and "in order to be winners, they must construct relationships with others . . . that are consistent with the competitive and hierarchical values and structure of the sports world."[42]

Sexual exploitation is a natural consequence of athletic hazing because it is both a means of establishing one's masculine bona fides and a successful tool for maintaining the power structure through the humiliation of the less-powerful members of the team. Hazing as a construct of proving one's masculinity is based on the notion that "sport is a strong representation of patriarchy, where males dominate in every meaningful aspect."[43] Furthermore, the hegemonic masculinity of sport has traditionally decreed "a particular kind of homophobic and sexist masculinity."[44] As a consequence, "heterosexual men go to great lengths to avoid being perceived as gay" or feminine.[45] Thus, in a homosocial organization like an athletic team, the rituals to prove one's masculinity are necessarily same-gendered and are designed to "allay any of the team's concerns about some rookies' masculinity or sexuality."[46]

"Homoerotic hazing [also] has traditionally served the purpose of closing down future same-sex sexual behaviors."[47] The sexually exploitative rituals themselves have the reckless quality inherently prized in the sport ethic, making them *ipso facto* expressions of that masculine standard.[48] And insofar as the recognition of a hegemonic masculinity presupposes a hierarchy with other masculinities, then those who have not yet been hazed have not reached the standard exemplified by the hazers.[49] Rookies can only prove their "manhood" by passing the tests of sexually exploitative hazing and transforming into hazers themselves as the new veterans.

Perhaps more important is sexually exploitative hazing's role in ensuring the team's hierarchy and power structure.[50] The threat of violence is part of any dominant-subordinate power structure: "Techniques of subordination, which convey a message that violence can take a variety of forms, are employed to secure existing power structures."[51] Indeed, "some form of pain and/or violence usually accompanies initiation rituals and has a robust but poorly understood effect of creating a sense of belonging among initiates who experience it together."[52]

Societal rites of passage often involve gendered physical ordeals, such as scarification or genital mutilation, including circumcision. Sexually exploitative hazing is the logical extension of physically abusive hazing run amok.[53] Athletic hazing usually stops short of genital mutilation, but it still often involves the public exposure of genitalia as a condition of membership to the team. "Genital shaving, sexualized games, and sodomy are . . . common hazing practices invoked by teams as dramatic displays that mark the movement of initiates from the status of nonmember to member."[54] Thus, sexually exploitative hazing overlaps with the agenda of violence of team hazing through sexual degradation, sexual assault, and physical humiliation with sexual overtones. "In showing 'who's the boss,' team leaders [exhibit] characteristics of . . . masculinity and feminize and dominate less powerful team members."[55]

Sexually exploitative hazing is the abuse of the power wielded by the older members to emasculate and humiliate the rookies to keep them in their place.[56] "Humiliation plays an important part in obedience training and may be manifested through physical, sexual, or psychological denigration." Sexually exploitative hazing targets rookies who are in no position to resist, sexualizes them, and then diminishes their masculinity and their sexual identity simply because they are rookies.[57]

Thus, "same-sex sexual activities serve the purpose of feminizing and homosexualizing recruits to establish and reaffirm their position at the bottom of the team's heteromasculine hierarchy," note Eric Anderson and colleagues Mark McCormack and Harry Lee. "At its most extreme, several episodes of anal rape (usually with objects but sometimes with fingers) have been reported in hazing episodes . . . Recruits are sometimes required to masturbate and ejaculate on a cracker, with the last member to ejaculate being made to eat it. However, the most frequent types of sexually related hazing practices come through mock sexual behaviors: same-sex kissing, nakedness, and consuming alcohol off of other men's bodies."[58]

Sexually exploitative hazing also serves to perpetuate the power structure by subjecting rookies to acts that are too degrading and humiliating to report.[59] Acceptance of their place in the power structure and of the inevitability of the hazing creates a deviant overconformity to the sport ethic, especially "to continually endorse their athletic identity and garner the respect and acceptance of their teammates."[60] And hence is a tradition born, not of masculinity but of humiliation.

Journalist Cyd Ziegler notes: "Hazing is largely about sexuality . . . [by] making someone submissive to prove your own masculinity. . . . Forcing players into sexually submissive roles feminizes and emasculates rookies while also marginalizing gay males."[61] But there are also the characteristics of gang rape inherent in males watching other males involved in sexual activity, wherein the primary characteristics are a "manifestation of status, hostility, control, and dominance."[62] There is nothing remotely related to team building or educational in such activities. They persist because team self-governance is left to adolescents without any sense of proportion or even appropriate masculine norms. They will only stop when faced with the intentional intervention of school authorities rather than the benign neglect that currently prevails. If the adults do not become more intentional about halting these abusive acts, Title IX will become an increasingly frequent and potent remedy to stop the tradition.

Sexually Exploitive Hazing, Public Schools and Title IX

School employees typically have no duty to protect students; the extent of their duty is to supervise.[63] The duty to supervise only requires the direct attention of a reasonably prudent person.[64] Tort liability will inure only "where there is a causal connection between the lack of supervision and the accident that could have been avoided by the exercise of the required degree of supervision."[65] An educational supervisor cannot be expected to be prepared for every eventuality that might take place in the classroom (or playing field), particularly when the act is unexpected or when a student breaks the chain of causation.[66] The acts of other students may break the chain of causation, but only if those acts are unforeseeable.[67]

Similar constraints govern coaches. A coach must exercise the duty to supervise "with the level of care of an ordinary prudent person under the same or similar circumstances."[68] That duty extends to the locker room in preparation for or after practice.[69] Because establishing tort liability against a school district can be problematic, recognizing that a duty exists is crucial, linking what coaches and officials fundamentally know about hazing and the direct connection between an absence of supervision and harm to their players.[70] Knowing what is common knowledge about athletic hazing—that is, its foreseeability—transforms coaches' failure to supervise from benign neglect to an active ingredient in enabling hazing to occur. Hazing is a team activity that does not usually take place on the field or in the arena; instead it breeds and grows when areas of team activities are "private" or unsupervised, such as team buses, locker rooms, overnight accommodations, and parents' or coaches' homes.[71] A wink and a nod are enough for hazing to grow and perhaps ordain its inevitability. Thus, the failure to take action to ensure against such a foreseeable harm is arguably an institutional indifference that Title IX prohibits, in both its litigation and systemic remedies.

Title IX as Litigation Strategy

A student's private right of action against a public school for peer-on-peer sexual harassment under Title IX is governed by *Davis v. Monroe County Board of Education*.[72] In that case, the Supreme Court provided that public school districts will be liable to students sexually harassed by other students "where they are deliberately indifferent to sexual harassment, of which they have actual knowledge, that is so severe, pervasive, and objectively offensive that it can be said to deprive the victims of access to the educational opportunities or benefits provided by the school."[73] Actionable harassment is determined by the constellation of circumstances that surround the gender-oriented conduct, including the students' expectations, relationships, and ages, and the number of students involved.[74] Mere "age-appropriate" student behavior—teasing, pushing, shoving, and the like—will not rise to the level of proof required by the objective standard imposed by the court in the landmark *Davis v. Monroe County Board of Education* ruling.[75] In addition, under Title IX, a student must show that the harassment was on the "basis of sex." [76] The aforementioned court case demonstrates that behavior with sexual overtones is not absolutely necessary to prove sexual harassment under Title IX, but such behavior crosses the obvious objective hurdles and includes "rape, fondling, other forms of molestation, lewd remarks and acts, sexually oriented touching, and even challenges to gender roles of masculinity"; the student must then show that the behavior denied him access to educational benefits, which may include either exclusion from an activity or an adverse psychological reaction.[77]

To be liable for damages, a school district must have actual knowledge of the harassment, which is often attributable to the knowledge of a school employee who has the power to stop the abuse.[78] After gaining that knowledge, the school district is liable under Title IX if it acts with deliberate indifference, or if its response or failure to respond "is clearly unreasonable in light of the known circumstances."[79]

For this article, eleven Title IX cases from the public schools were examined in the intersection of sexual harassment and athletics, all involving males. Although a couple of the cases involved a hostile environment perpetrated by both genders, they also included male-on-male harassment. The analysis of same-sex sexual harassment under Title IX is driven in part by *Oncale v. Sundowner Offshore Services, Inc.*[80] In *Oncale*, the court outlined three basic scenarios in which same-sex sexual harassment under Title VII might be proved: sexual desire, hostility to that gender, and discrimination between genders. Cases under

Title IX have also adopted gender stereotyping as evidence of harassment on the basis of sex.[81]

In the following cases, the connection with athletic hazing is more apparent than in others, but the importance of sports and their significance in light of sexual harassment are striking in nearly all the cases.[82] They factually demonstrate several things: (a) the severity and pervasiveness of the sexually abusive behavior, (b) the explicit "motivation" for the abuse based on gender-stereotyping, (c) the significance of the sport ethic, or masculine hegemony, in both the perpetrators' behavior and the school districts' indifference to student complaints, and (d) the actual knowledge, and even participation, of coaches.

One must also review these cases with the added knowledge that sexually exploitative behavior is rife in athletic hazing. It is not "boys will be boys" but a deliberate effort to humiliate younger players to maintain a team hierarchy. As noted elsewhere, the adoption of such team hierarchy in boys' athletics has everything to do with establishing a masculine identity for the older players and an either feminine or effeminate identity for the younger players, or gender stereotyping. Athletic hazing is therefore truly on the basis of sex. It is a power dynamic based on the "tradition" of masculinity that inherently is sexual and can only play out with boys.

Hazing as Team "Sport": Marginalized Boys

The first published case of male-on-male student sexual harassment under Title IX was an athletic hazing case. Brian Seamons was a member of the Sky View High School football team in Utah.[83] At the time of the incident, he was leaving the shower naked when five of his upper- class teammates grabbed him and used adhesive tape to bind him to a towel bar and to bind up his genitals. One teammate then brought a girl whom Brian had dated into the locker room to join the spectacle. Brian reported the incident to the school administration and the football coach, with the ultimate result that the school district cancelled the season's final game in the state playoffs. In an incident of "second" hazing, the football coach characterized the attack as a rite of passage for membership on the team—"boys will be boys"—and accused Brian of betraying the team. As a consequence, the five teammates who had committed the assault were allowed to play in the game following the attack while Brian was kicked off the team for refusing to apologize. Thereafter, the poisonous atmosphere at the school forced Brian to transfer to another school. Brian's Title IX complaint alleged that this hostile environment signaled that he had to conform to a "macho male stereotype" after being criticized for not taking the abuse "like a man," but he did not complain of the actual attack. The trial court granted and the appellate court affirmed the dismissal of Brian's complaint because he had failed "to allege any facts that would suggest he was subject to unwelcome sexual advances or requests for sexual favors, or that sex was used to contribute to a hostile environment for him." Given that his case predated the Supreme Court's decision in *Davis*, Brian's complaint was probably doomed from the start. Equally problematic was his failure to plead the act of hazing as actionable sexual harassment. Nearly as disturbing, however, was the court's tolerance of the hazing incident as an "accepted" method of promoting team loyalty and toughness. Rather than suffering "based on sex," Brian had suffered because in the coaching staff's eyes he had "betrayed" the team.

If there are hurdles to a private right of action, they might be the athletes themselves, their acceptance of the hazing as some kind of "macho" ritual, and their concomitant refusal to report hazing under the code of silence and to incur the inherent risks of a second hazing.[84] Surely such humiliation denies athletes wholehearted participation in an educational opportunity. Instead, athletes are held hostage to an adolescent vision and version of masculinity and an unbridled system of hierarchical abuse, sometimes with the cooperation and collaboration of the adults. And that is just sad.

Title IX as Systemic Remedy

Title IX offers not just a reactive litigation solution to athletic hazing, but also offers proactive systemic remedies.[85] These systemic remedies are injunctive relief and administrative enforcement by the Office of Civil Rights (OCR) in the US Department of Education, whereby federal funding may be withdrawn or the matter may be referred to the Department of Justice. Such remedies have a different framework of proof that makes it easier for a victim to get relief. "If a school knows or reasonably should know about student-on-student harassment that creates a hostile environment, Title IX requires the school to take immediate action to eliminate the harassment, prevent its recurrence, and address its effects." A school need not have actual knowledge nor must it act with deliberate indifference.[86]

As a preventive measure, Title IX and its regulations require that schools establish some basic administrative procedures to deal with peer sexual harassment: they must "disseminate a notice of nondiscrimination"; they must appoint a Title IX coordinator; and they must establish grievance procedures to handle student harassment complaints.[87] For purposes of boys' athletic hazing, school-district grievance procedures must be better attuned to the sexual deviancy that occurs in the locker room. First, the Title IX officer needs a complete education on the laws of sexual assault and sexual deviancy when males are the victims in that jurisdiction. These are crimes, not mere boyhood pranks—forcing a finger up a boy's rectum is sodomy, and even a "wedgie" is likely nonconsensual touching.[88] And long gone should be the notion that boys should have to suffer greater harms than girls.

Second, the Title IX officer needs a thorough grounding on sexual harassment as it relates to boys. The notion that "sexual desire" must be the motivation for sexual harassment of boys must be rooted out. Just as sexual abuse of power motivates some rapes, so too are the acts perpetrated on young boys.[89] In addition, the gender stereotyping that motivates this hazing for purposes of humiliating male athletes is sexual harassment under the law.

Third, and related to the first two, is the responsibility for the receipt of evidence from a male victim. Once the victim has reported the sexual abuse, it is not a mere matter of trying to find out the "whole" story by asking team members and the coach for corroboration or contradiction. Instead, the first question is whether adults were present at the location. The absence of supervision creates a rebuttable presumption of the truth of the victim's story, corroborated by other victims. Insofar as rapes can be tried based only on the victim's testimony, the Title IX officer must understand the profound import of a male victim's coming forward about what has happened to him.

Last, in those school districts where a particular sport has a particular hegemony, the impartiality of the Title IX officer might be questioned. As a consequence, athletic conferences might want to consider pooling their Title IX officers to parcel them out to member school districts.

In addition to the administrative process for victim complaints, the OCR recommends preventive education programs as follows: "(1) orientation programs for new students, faculty, staff, and employees; (2) training for students who serve as advisors in residence halls; (3) training for student athletes and coaches; and (4) school assemblies and 'back to school nights.'" These education programs should be designed to inform of both the school's policies and the very nature of sexual harassment and violence. The programs should also include educational resources for administrators, faculty, coaches, and students. Specially designed materials should be disseminated to employee handbooks and student activity handbooks, including those for sports. All school employees must report sexual harassment, but the OCR stresses that students must be educated that sexual violence is a matter of safety and encouraged to report themselves to the appropriate authorities.[90]

Therein lies the rub with athletic hazing. An educational program that relies on students reporting athletic hazing flies in the very face of the dynamic. The code of silence forbids reporting, and it is the rare young adolescent who can or will ignore that code, regardless of the humiliation. Second, breaking the code of silence will often precipitate ancillary hazing after the report; a school district that cannot control athletic hazing will not be trusted by a young athlete to control the fallout from other students and parents. Third, athletes believe that hazing is not sexual harassment, especially when their "friends" and "family" are doing it. Last, and a recursive analysis of hazing itself, the smaller group—the team—will protect itself to the detriment of the whole school where loyalty is everything, according to sociologist Donna Winslow.[91]

To break the "tradition" of hazing, we cannot rely on athletes to do it themselves. That asks a lot of young adolescents, especially in communities where sports are the primary mode of entertainment and star athletes are too often looked upon as gods. As a consequence, the adults must be responsible and must be held accountable for not supervising and for explicitly or implicitly allowing hazing to continue. Athletic hazing succeeds because adolescents have been delegated the responsibility of team self-governance and establishing a masculine identity. Understanding that dynamic reveals that adolescents are ill equipped for those responsibilities and that adults are irresponsible for thinking otherwise. William Golding described the theme of his novel *Lord of the Flies* as "an attempt to trace the defects of society back to the defects of human nature. The moral is that the shape of a society must depend on the ethical nature of the individual and not on any political system however apparently logical or respectable."[92]

Although not as grim in the outcome as *Lord of the Flies*, athletic hazing—reliant as it is on establishing a team self-governance by adolescent boys—is not unlike the tribal organizations of Ralph, Piggy, and Jack. Regardless of how one attempts to ascribe some rational basis for the roots of athletic hazing, the perpetrators themselves are the ones who actually define what is going on: humiliation and hierarchy. Organized school sports are the natural breeding ground for these problems insofar as schools are a prominent site of masculinity formation: as agency and as setting. A school athletic program for boys has been described as a "vortex" of masculinity by blending "power, symbolization, and emotion in a particularly potent combination."[93] Although the hierarchy may be explicit in hazing practices for athletic teams, implicit is that the hierarchy must also fulfill and sustain a masculine identity. Today, the dynamics of sports, misbehavior, and masculine identity are difficult for adults to uncouple, given their admiration for sports stars. Imagine how hard that is for adolescent boys, especially unsupervised adolescent boys who are left to their own devices, to establish a hierarchy that, to them, has come to be imbued with a test of masculinity. Without adult supervision and more responsible masculine role models, adolescent self-governance on a team has more of the characteristics of a street gang than of "organized" sports in an educational setting.

A Lack of Coaching Supervision

Any default of adult supervision is apparent to the athletes. This is especially true for any athletes who have been sexually abused. Rightly or wrongly, they perceive that others knew or suspected the abuse but did nothing to stop it. A recent study of college athletes indicated that a majority believed their coaches allowed hazing. Some athletes recounted that their coaches not only probably encouraged hazing, but also singled out those athletes to haze. Coaches with a hands-off leadership style might have actually been unaware of the hazing, but athletes still felt less willing to complain about hazing to such coaches.[94] Despite statutes, increased awareness, and educational programs to prevent hazing, it is clear, once again, that targeting the athletes is not the solution.

The literature is replete with suggestions for coaches and schools to implement student training programs and alternative "positive" team-building experiences.[95] In particular, "athletic administrators and coaches should help athletes to create team identities centered on pro-social behaviors and productive achievement strategies." These are a start, but not enough in isolation. Coaches and school administrators must also be intentional about breaking up the groups within the team itself through small and targeted norming interventions to change the behavior and intentionally involving the athletes' parents in those discussions. "Teachable" moments about the vulnerability of their own children can help parents understand their own role in breaking the tradition and the code of silence. Indeed, parents need to be assured that if they report hazing, their child will be protected. Targeted and intentional interventions may also destroy the street-gang dynamic that otherwise pervades athletic teams. Yet hazing also persists because it is a tradition.

Breaking the "tradition" of hazing must focus more on school officials, especially the coaches. First of all are the objective trappings of a coach's authority. For example, formal policies must be drawn up for coaches and made conditions of continued employment under their extracurricular coaching contracts. Those policies must hold coaches responsible for failing to supervise, especially when all the evidence points to lack of supervision as a breeding ground for hazing. Football camps and other off-campus collective activities must have appropriate adult supervision so that no athletes are required to fend for themselves.

The supervision of the team raises the question of the responsibility for team activities that occur outside of the "formal" auspices of the sport sometimes for the express purpose of hazing. From the perspective of the athletes who are being hazed at these events, they see no distinction between locations of hazing. To them the function is the same, the establishment of team hierarchy. So long as hazing is the natural consequence of the delegation of "authority" to team leaders to maintain the team hierarchy, then it suggests that coaches and school districts remain responsible for that delegation. The acquiescence to that continued delegation of self-governance then is not "tradition" but ratification of that delegation. All activities of the team *qua* team are the direct responsibility of the coach as team leader. The coach is at the head of the hierarchy, and he has the innate authority to dictate what activities the team will engage in.

School officials in general and coaches in particular have to take direct responsibility for the behavior of their athletes as part of the educational program of the school district. Assuming an attitude of helplessness toward hazing is an inappropriate response to a directed activity funded by the school district and governed by the school board.[96] Rather than skepticism about the efficacy of training programs for their athletes, they need to find strategies and alternatives that work, including direct discipline. Coaches were hired to undertake the responsibility of supervising their players. They therefore have the power and the duty to undo the self-governance of older team members and affect their responsibilities for supervision. Team captains must lose their positions, if not team membership, when hazing is reported. Trust in older team members is earned, not the prize at the end of a rite of passage. The pervasiveness of team hazing requires discipline that has an impact on the team, not just on individual perpetrators.

Then there are the subjective trappings by which coaches must better equip themselves for their responsibility to their athletes. Coaches should be required to do something more than attend training seminars on athletic hazing. They must learn to improve their own communication skills and to improve their coaching techniques, to "become critically reflective practitioners who examine their own behaviors." Coaches must restructure their programs when ineffective and focus on their responsibilities to the young athletes themselves, not just the sport. They must be aware of the duties that accompany their leadership position and their role in establishing an appropriate masculinity for individuals, not some hegemonic ideal that none of their players can attain. But they must also understand that their cultural authority in the community cannot be abused for the "good" of the team or of the sport at the expense of any individual child. Concern about increasing their workload is a self-indulgence, not a reason.

Last, coaches—and many school administrators—need to face their own hazing experiences and/or attitudes to hazing. Hazing is humiliating. Humiliation is harmful. Many, if not all, coaches were athletes themselves. Consequently, odds are high that a large number themselves were involved in hazing: in the absence of any evidence that they themselves refused to be hazed, then they experienced humiliation; even if not a perpetrator, they were a victim or bystander. If they themselves did not rebel, then they hardly have the moral authority or the moral fiber to suggest that a young athlete should stand up for himself against the team. That is not a healthy emotional experience under any circumstances, but reaching back to their "survival" days to suggest that "boys will be boys" and that hazing is necessary for team unity is deviant overconformity of the worst kind. When this occurs under the supervision of a coach or school administrator, he is allowing it to happen to children half his age or younger. When did these rites of passage involve human sacrifice?

Their own experience should also inform them—intelligently—that a young athlete will not stand up for himself because he cannot. An adult allowing an adolescent tradition so that everybody can have the opportunity to do so—simply because that adult "survived it"—is a pretty aberrant pathology. That makes hazing not a "tradition" but a cycle of abuse. That cycle only ends when all coaches, but especially those who have been hazed, see "training films" of interviews of these young survivors or receive counseling from a sports psychologist. And the coach who protects the program on "behalf" of the community in the face of hazing accusations is not brave.

Until the "tradition" of hazing is broken at the source, the tradition continues. Title IX's systemic remedies and the potential loss of federal funds must be an aggressive approach to making the adults in the building responsible. Handing out pamphlets and showing videos to teenage athletes assumes a masculinity and moral responsibility they do not have. That is why they haze! If the adults in the building assume that masculine role and are held accountable for their legal duty to supervise, then athletes might actually have real role models to follow instead of the deviant masculinity that is the inevitable result of continued hazing.

SUSAN P. STUART is Professor Emerita of Law at Valparaiso University School of Law. She credits her research assistants who assisted her: Colleen Clemons, Emily Calwell France, Adam Miller, William Horvath, and Shay Hughes. The original published essay was edited to reduce its length.

12 A Mother's Story

I Lost My Child to Fraternity Hazing

Debbie Smith with Stacey Kennelly

As you will learn, Wednesday, February 2, 2005, was the most horrific day of my life.

But first some back story.

I was at work the morning of Wednesday, March 2, 2005, when my phone rang. It was Detective Greg Keeney of the Chico, California, police. He was calling to tell me that eight warrants were being issued for arrests in the hazing death of our son Matthew, my firstborn. Matt had transferred to Cal State Chico after getting his AA at Diablo Valley College in our hometown of Pleasant Hill, California.

Det. Keeney told me there was a press conference scheduled in Chico the following morning and asked that we come to the police station early to meet with District Attorney Mike Ramsey beforehand. After a month of speculations we were finally going to find out what had happened to our son the last three days of his life, which ultimately ended in his death.

The Early Morning Phone Call

It was 6:10 a.m. on February 2, 2005, when my husband, Greg—Matt's stepfather—received a call that something terrible had happened and that Matt was in a hospital in Chico. Greg in turn phoned me, and when he said Matt's name I felt the blood rush from my head, as I realized I was experiencing every parent's worst nightmare.

I immediately hung up and called Enloe Medical Center in Chico. A nurse confirmed that Matt was there and asked if I was alone. I told her that my younger son, Matt's fourteen-year-old brother, Travis, was with me. Concerned by the question I immediately screamed to Travis, who had freshman finals that day and was getting ready for school, and told him to call Greg and tell him to come home. Then the doctor treating Matt came on the line. He told me that Matt had been found in the basement of a fraternity house. He was not breathing. When the paramedics got him to the hospital he was in full cardiac arrest. The doctor said I needed to get to the hospital right away and not to drive myself. I begged him to please save my son.

My mind was spinning with so many questions and no answers. I called my sister Frankie to let her know what I knew and what I speculated—that I wasn't sure if Matt was going to make it—and we prayed we would make it in time to see my son alive. She said she was leaving work and going to get our other sister, Angie. The two would meet us in Chico.

A Second Phone Call

My phone rang again; it was a social worker by the name of Stephanie. She was so kind and genuinely concerned, but again alarms . . . *why is a social worker calling me?* She wanted to know when I thought we would be on our way. It seemed like forever—time was standing still for me. When Greg finally got home from his San Francisco job, Travis and I raced to the truck, hoping we had remembered everything we might need for our three-hour drive to Matt's side in northern California.

The hospital social worker kept calling to check on us, but she could only release just so much information. I just couldn't take it anymore. I knew something was terribly wrong. When Stephanie called yet again, I begged her to tell me what was going on with my son. "Are we going to make it on time?" She then asked me what I knew, and I told her what the doctor had told me.

She paused, then said, "We don't like to do this over the phone." I gasped, knowing what was coming next. "I'm sorry, Debbie, Matt didn't make . . ."

The phone slipped through my fingers. A gut-wrenching scream came from the depths of my soul. I felt like my insides had come pouring out all over the truck.

Time went into slow motion. I turned my head toward Greg, who was visibly shaken and fighting to keep his attention on the road. Travis cried uncontrollably in the back seat. Tears streamed down all of our faces. In the distance I could hear Stephanie's faint voice, "Debbie, are you okay? Debbie, is everyone okay?"

All of a sudden we were in real time again. I told Greg to get off the freeway, that we needed to be together as a family. To this day I don't recall answering Stephanie or even hanging up the phone.

We pulled into a truck stop and jumped out of the truck for a family hug. Our first taste of reality . . . our family hug would never be the same without Matt.

Our second taste of reality . . . our family of four was now a family of three. Heartbroken, devastated, shocked, and dismayed, we wondered what could have possibly happened to Matt. The pain was so great.

All I could think of was not wanting another parent to ever have to feel this most devastating anguish. *How have other parents lived through the death of a child?* I wondered. Such loss is so excruciating that there is nothing to compare it to—my heart literally quivered in pain, something I had never felt before. *How do you possibly go on without your child? How?*

The Horrific Day Unfolds

We drove mainly in silence now, except our phones kept ringing with our friends and my sisters wanting to know what was going on. We couldn't answer them. If we did, we would have to say the grim truth out loud, and we were not ready for that. If we said it out loud, it made it true. Even though we knew it was real, we didn't want it to be.

About a half hour went by. With an hour left in our drive to the hospital, we decided we had to start letting people know what had happened. But what *had* happened? All we knew was Matt was dead. He was found in the basement of a fraternity, he wasn't breathing, and now he was . . . is . . . DEAD! *He didn't do drugs, he didn't really drink that much, what did they do to him, why is our precious son dead?*

On January 26, Matt had written that pledging was nearly over, and he should be initiated the next week. It was more imperative than ever that we get to Matt. He was alone and had been alone too long. He needed his family, he needed his mother, and I needed to be with him. I needed to hold my baby . . .

We finally got to the hospital, and after preparing us for what we were going to see, Stephanie took us to Matt. We entered the room, but before letting us see him, she told us that we would not be able to touch him. He had died under "suspicious circumstances" and there was going to be a criminal investigation. *Oh, HELL NO! I am going to touch my child, I need to hold him, and he needs his mother.*

I didn't know my heart could break any more than it had already but now it broke into more fragments. My baby was bloodied and bruised. I viewed pink foam and tubes coming out of him, and I agonized—*now you won't let me hold his fragile body.*

What had I done to deserve this cruel, unusual punishment? More importantly what had Matt, the sweetest, kindest person on the planet, done? Why was this happening? What was happening?

Learning Matt's Death Was a Homicide

We went again and again to the hospital's grieving room. Lt. Rob Merrifield and Det. Keeney introduced themselves. They said what they had learned from their interrogation of several fraternity brothers of Chi Tau, an independent local Chico chapter previously known as the national Delta Sigma Phi. This was the chapter Matt had pledged.

The fire chief who was on the scene with paramedics had called law enforcement to the fraternity house. Something suspicious surrounded Matt's death. What he was being told by the fraternity brothers did not add up with what he was seeing. And the law officers agreed his gut feeling was right.

The authorities were puzzled by what they were learning and also believed they were not getting the whole story from at least twelve young men they had questioned that morning. They told us as strange as it sounded, Matt somehow had died from drinking too much water. Chapter members all said he hadn't had any alcohol or drugs, but the autopsy would be able to tell us more. Again, my heart crumbled at just the mention of the word "autopsy."

Lt. Merrifield and Det. Keeney said they would know more once they could go through all the notes of these interviews. They were still trying to get ahold of more members, and then they would go over all evidence piece by piece to put together the events of Matt's final night. They would meet with us the next day when they had something more concrete to tell us. They gave us their condolences and their business cards with their contact information, and then Det. Keeney went a step further and added his personal contact information. He said to call him anytime. I hugged and thanked them both.

We went through a lifetime of events and emotions until we saw them both again the following afternoon. We met some of the fraternity brothers at the frat house. They were visibly shaken by Matt's death. I felt sorry for them. My motherly instinct took over and I comforted them. I worried about them having seen their friend die.

At that point, Greg and I still had no idea what had happened to Matt. We drove to the police department and sat down with Lt. Merrifield and Det. Keeney. They proceeded to tell us that it looked like a hazing incident.

My Introduction to the Word "Hazing"

Naively, we asked what hazing was.

The lawmen explained, to the best of their knowledge, that it was an initiation process that "pledges" go through to be accepted into a fraternity.

"What do you mean?" we asked. Matt had confided that the Chi Taus had made him dress like a hooker one night, but the law officers explained they had learned Matt still had to endure a physical ordeal known as Hell Week. "Hell Week was when it gets serious," they said.

They still didn't have all the facts as to what the brothers had put Matt through, but they had determined that it was a hazing and they were going to try and bring charges. However, with the way the law was written, there was a good chance that *no one* would be held accountable for killing Matt.

"What? Matt was killed, and it's possible that no one will be held accountable?"

The questions from me came fast and furious. *How can you kill someone and there not be a law for that? What is this "hazing"? And why isn't there a law that protects people from being killed by it?*

Well, it didn't take long for me to know what my mission in life suddenly had become, and it was a *big* one!

First, justice for Matt. Second, get a law passed, and I vowed it would be called Matt's Law. Third, while I'm doing one and two, learn as much as I can about hazing so that I can bring awareness to the public in hopes of saving the lives of our young people and sparing other parents the devastation of losing a child.

March 3, 2005

Greg and I left for Chico right after work on March 2 and booked a room downtown so we wouldn't have to make the long drive the next morning. We drove by the frat house; it had gotten pretty ugly there since the vigil we held there for Matt on Friday, February 4. People had been throwing bricks through the windows, and the fraternity had pretty much disassembled, with the last of the members moving out. We went by Matt's house and saw his roommates, Molly and Sara, who were both so sweet to us. We tried to prepare ourselves for the next day but had no idea what we were going to learn or how brutal the details were going to be.

We got to the police station early as Det. Keeney had requested. I was shaking, struggling to keep my composure, eager and terrified to hear what they had uncovered. It had been a month now and the fraternity had been doing its best to destroy any incriminating evidence, which I found strange. *If you haven't done anything wrong, what are you destroying and why? Secret meetings, burning documents, stories changing, lies, and cover-ups.* It made our family wonder what they could possibly be hiding. What did they do to Matt?

We were sitting in a small conference room with Det. Keeney and Lt. Merrifield waiting when in walked District Attorney Ramsey, a tall, slender, distinguished gentleman with brownish-blond hair, blue eyes, and a pleasant smile. He introduced himself to us in a kind and compassionate voice, giving us his condolences. He then told us that what he was going to share with us was going to be very difficult to hear, but he didn't want the first time we heard it to be at the press conference in front of all the media waiting in another room of the precinct.

Ramsey proceeded to lay out in graphic detail how Matt had been tortured the last three days of his life. The pledges were told they would be spending the next five nights in the basement, where etched on the wall was "In the basement, no one can hear you scream." They would be forced to sleep in a concrete hole cut into the wall and open to the outside elements, so cold they could see their breath. They would be the property of the Junior Actives (JAs), the fraternity's newest members, and the last to go through the previous Hell Week. They would only be allowed to go to school and work, if they had a job, which Matt did, and they were not allowed to talk to family or friends until Hell Week was over. The only things they were allowed to eat while in the basement were an onion and garlic.

At Long Last, the Truth

After surviving the first two hellacious nights of Hell Week, Matt entered the basement for the last time the night of February 1. All of the nights had a theme; this night was "movie night," and the members either watched a movie or played poker. Matt and a second pledge, named Mike Quintana, were forced to undress down to their jeans, stand on one foot on a narrow bench, and stare at a boot hanging from the rafters. Not permitted to make eye contact with anyone, they were then made to take drinks from a five-gallon jug of water that they continually passed back and forth. It was determined later that other members filled the jug over five times.

The two pledges were asked trivia questions about the house and senior members. When someone would get one wrong they would both have to get down on the concrete basement floor, where sewage had backed up because of broken pipes, and do push-ups. If someone yelled out "take one for the homies," they would be forced to douse themselves with water to remain wet while giant fans blew cold air on them. To further humiliate themselves, they had to ask permission to urinate on themselves; with hypothermia setting in, this was a welcome release. Matt vomited several times and as the night wore on he began to get fatigued and struggled to do his many forced push-ups. This exhaustion did not stop the process since one of the brothers grabbed his belt loop and pulled him up and down. He finally suffered from a seizure, something he had never done, and while one of those in the basement had the frame of mind to call 911, the call was stopped by other participants before it was sent.

The fraternity brothers put Matt on the couch in the cold basement. An hour later he stopped breathing. He had chugged so much water that his electrolytes were diluted, his liver and kidneys had shut down, his heart and brain were swollen, and his lungs had filled with water. He died of hyponatremia (water intoxication) and hypothermia. An autopsy determined that had the hazers made the call when Matt first went down, they could have saved his life. But for whatever reason known only to them, they didn't.

Our Ordeal As a Family

Tears streamed down our faces as we heard the terrorizing tale of Matt's last days on this earth. Then I wiped my tears and prepared myself to walk into a room the likes of which I had only seen on TV. The doors opened and with cameras rolling and flashes going off in our faces, we looked up to see a giant picture of the basement where Matt was killed, pictures of the defendants, Matt, and an actual empty five-gallon water bottle. After showing us to our seats, Ramsey, with poise and confidence, introduced himself and began to tell the story that he had just told us, but with even more details. I don't know how we made it through that day. But it would not be the last hard day. Now we had a criminal case . . .

I would cry every day for the next three years, but it did not hinder what I knew was my mission. Going back and forth to court was draining to say the least. Because we lived so far away we would have to take the entire day off from work, even if we were only there for five minutes because of a continuance, and there were plenty of those with so many defendants. But we were relentless; I never missed a court date. And because of that, and the fact the defendants were guilt-ridden and scared, we were able to get the first-ever felony verdict for hazing in the United States, even on a flawed law. Ramsey allowed me to play a part in working out the details of the plea bargains. On Friday, October 28, 2005, four defendants changed their pleas to guilty. On Wednesday, November 23, the day before Thanksgiving, I visited them in jail.

I think it is important that the vast number of victims be recognized in a hazing, especially a hazing death. As his parents and his brother, there was no greater loss than ours, but everyone who loved Matt, everyone who was touched by him, had suffered a great loss. And yet the victims go beyond us even: all the young men in that basement and their families, the brothers that weren't there that night but were a part of the fraternity . . . the list goes on and on. So many affected, so many lives changed forever that night. So many victims . . .

The Work of the Matt Committee

In December 2005, our Matt Committee was assembled and we were able to focus on getting Matt's Law passed, all the while doing documentaries and interviews bringing awareness to hazing. Matt's Law (a California state law) was written by one of my civil attorneys, Alex Grab. In the summer of 2005, we started looking for a sponsor to introduce it in September. Senator Tom Torlakson, a Democrat, agreed to sponsor it in January 2006. Suffice to say to get a law passed it takes a lot of hard work, dedication, and commitment by a lot of people. Matt's Law SB 1454 was signed into law by then Governor Arnold Schwarzenegger on September 29, 2006, and went into effect on January 1, 2007.

Birth of the AHA! Movement

Arts & Entertainment Network re-created Matt's story in a one-hour documentary with raw footage and reenactments of the horrifying events in the basement.

It aired in August 2014 and was the catalyst to the birth of the Anti-Hazing Awareness (AHA!) Movement, a 501c3 nonprofit foundation we created in Matt's memory. We launched at Chico State University on February 2, 2015, the tenth anniversary of when Matt was killed.

AHA! has instituted amazing programs, our proudest being our Be Aware Program: "What You Don't Know CAN Kill You!" We take it into high schools, colleges, and universities. It's engaging, educational, and empowering. We initiate productive conversations surrounding the dangers of hazing and how to recognize it. I share Matt's true hazing story, we show video, we have a Q&A session, and we explore alternatives to hazing. We also discuss peer pressure, the difference between hazing and bullying, mind-set, group mentality, and making better choices. Parents, as well as faculty members, are encouraged to participate in our program.[1]

Additional Insights into Matt's Death

In August 2015, *Diablo*, a regional California magazine, published a lengthy investigation into Matt's death titled "In the Basement, No One Can Hear You Scream" that was written by Stacey Kennelly. Excerpts from that article give more details about the bizarre hazing ritual that was nothing less than torture and killed my son.[2] Kennelly wrote: "Debbie's son, Matthew Carrington, hadn't planned to rush Chi Tau fraternity when he moved to Chico . . . but the somewhat shy Matt had made a friend, Mike Quintana, who had his heart set on the *Animal House* college experience . . . Most young people in Chico hear rumors about what happens during the pledge process, but only those who live it know each chapter's traditions."

Matt and Mike had made it through water torture, torturous sleeping conditions, and forced sleep deprivation. They thought they were in as members "when a senior member of the frat, who had been bar hopping earlier, insisted they continue under his reign . . . The brothers changed Matt out of his wet clothes, wrapped him in a blanket, and placed him on a couch. He appeared to start snoring, so everyone went to bed." Kennelly continued:

> But an hour later, someone noticed Matt was not breathing and started to adminiser CPR. Blood came out of Matt's mouth. What the boys had thought was the sound of Matt's snoring was actually the sound of his lungs filling with water, and by the time first responders arrived, Matt's heart had stopped. . . .
>
> In the fall of 2005, seven fraternity members were sentenced for their role in Matt's death, many of whom apologized to Matt's family in court. Only one—the man who insisted the hazing continue—was convicted of felony involuntary manslaughter. The other six were handed misdemeanor sentences. "I would ask for Matt's family's forgiveness," he told the court, "but I cannot because I don't deserve it. I can only say I am truly sorry."

DEBBIE SMITH is the founder and CEO of the AHA! Movement, a nonprofit organization created in memory of her son, college student Matt Carrington. Matt died in 2005 after enduring a horrific water hazing while pledging at a fraternity in Chico, California.

STACEY KENNELLY is a California freelance journalist and former associate editor at *Diablo* magazine.

13 How Alfred University Ended the Greek System to Become a Hazing Research Institution

Norm Pollard

THE ALFRED UNIVERSITY football team experienced a hazing incident in 1998 that became a redefining moment for the institution. At the end of preseason camp, the rookie football players were required to attend an off-campus "celebration" and "initiation." Little did they know that they would be handcuffed together with strapping tape, placed in a room devoid of furniture except for a barrel in the middle of the tarp-lined floor, and told to consume alcohol until they vomited. Fortunately staff noticed the drunken players making their way back onto campus and intervened to ensure medical care was provided. As a result of this incident, Alfred University immediately suspended six players from the team for the remainder of the season and forfeited the first game of the season against Susquehanna University. The game was to have been the season openers for both schools, which were both celebrating their 100th football seasons.

A Plan of Action

Alfred's president, Edward G. Coll, was determined not to replicate the same institutional mistakes that accompanied Chuck Stenzel's fraternity hazing death in 1978. Coll forfeited the game "as an expression of the seriousness of this incident," he said in a September 1, 1998 press release. He added, "I wanted our football team to know that we will not tolerate this kind of behavior." His initial actions were the standard institutional response—holding individuals accountable, sending letters to parents and alums pledging change, and holding on-campus forums to reflect on the problematic campus culture.

A Hazing Task Force

More importantly, President Coll created an investigatory commission. The Presidential Commission on Athletics was charged with "reviewing all aspects of the Alfred University athletic program and recommending how best to prevent alcohol and hazing abuse." Among other things, the commission recommended better integrating varsity athletes into the fabric of student life, creating alternative forms of bonding experiences, and assigning more responsibility to student and staff leaders. From the athletic director and coaches down to team captains, specific guidelines were established, noted an Alfred University press release of November 23, 1998.

While the Presidential Commission created a series of institutional recommendations, the study team also suspected that hazing to join athletic teams was not only pervasive at Alfred, but also at a significant number of the nation's campuses. Since no empirical data had been established to validate their theory, the commission recommended that Alfred form a research team and undertake a national baseline study of this issue.

As an indication of Alfred's commitment to a thorough examination of hazing in college athletics, the research team, headed by Nadine C. Hoover and myself, relied on assistance and encouragement from not only the staff of the NCAA, but also from external contributors Hank Nuwer, author of *Wrongs of Passage: Fraternities, Sororities, Hazing, and Binge Drinking*, and national anti-hazing advocate Eileen Stevens, the mother of Chuck Stenzel. The results of the landmark study, "Initiation Rites and Athletics: A National Survey of NCAA Sports Teams," were shared with all institutions expressing a concern for student health and safety. The Alfred report reached its objective to raise awareness about the prevalence and nature of hazing in college athletics.

The survey was groundbreaking for several reasons. Fundamentally, since the legal definition of hazing was extremely varied, the research team created a simple definition—"any activity expected of someone joining a group that humiliates, degrades, abuses, or endangers, regardless of the person's willingness to participate"—that has served as the foundational definition used in dozens of programs and research projects. Under this definition, 80 percent of survey respondents reported being subjected to one or more typical hazing behaviors as part of their team initiations, but only 12 percent recognized their behaviors as hazing. This means that while students acknowledged experiencing a wide range of hazing-type behaviors, they most often were reluctant to label them as "hazing."

Additionally, of those athletes who reported they were hazed in college, 42 percent reported that they had also been hazed in high school and 5 percent said they were hazed in middle school. It is interesting to note that the Alfred study found 13 percent left a group because of being hazed and an equal percentage wanted revenge as a result of being hazed. Equally as troubling was the response of 60 percent who said they would not report hazing. When asked why they would not report it, the respondents said the primary reasons were "there is no one to tell" and they did not feel as though adults would "know how to handle it." A perplexing phenomenon was that a third of the students who felt hazed reported positive consequences—namely, they felt "part of the group." These statistics helped shape our conceptual understanding of hazing and continue to shape national prevention strategies and tactics.[1]

The reaction to the results of the survey provoked coverage from news media, such as ABC World News Tonight, CBS Early Show, the Associated Press, the *Washington Post*, and the *Los Angeles Times*, that it prompted a second AU study a year later to explore the prevalence of hazing in high schools. The researchers wanted to shift the conversation from the horrors of a hazing tragedy to helping adults understand the dynamics of this misguided rite of passage, with the intention that increased awareness will decrease the incidents of hazing.

Since the release of the results in 2000, the original survey has been cited in dozens of peer-reviewed journal articles, used in multiple dissertations, and replicated in surveying other populations. Additionally, the "Alfred study" has been presented at dozens of national conferences, workshops, and webinars. The journey from Chuck Stenzel's tragic death to academic and cultural awareness has not been easy or smooth.

As chronicled in Hank Nuwer's seminal work *Broken Pledges: The Deadly Rite of Hazing*, Alfred University failed to respond to the hazing death of our student, a fraternity pledge, in a manner reflective of institutional values. Stenzel, a Klan Alpine pledge died of an alcohol overdose in February, 1978, when his "brothers" locked him, and a couple of other pledges, in the trunk of a car with copious amounts of alcohol, with the directive to finish it before they arrived at the fraternity house, then engaged in "rigged" drinking games (members with water, pledges with alcohol) afterward when pledges were already intoxicated. Stenzel's mother, Eileen Stevens, became a national activist for the passage of antihazing laws, and she carried her son's story to campuses and legislatures across the United States. Eventually, Nuwer's book and an NBC TV (partially fictionalized) docudrama were based on the tragedy, and Alfred has lived with the stigma of his death ever since. Even so, this was not the last episode involving hazing. As chronicled below, our journey with this horrible "tradition" continued even after Stenzel's death.

Social fraternities and sororities were first established at Alfred University about the time of World War I. This was significantly later than their origins in 1825 at Union College because Alfred's founding fathers and mothers were firmly opposed to secret societies. The founders maintained that the concept of exclusive and discriminatory organizations was contrary to Alfred's rich history of inclusion and equality.

Nonetheless, Greek membership went on to prosper at Alfred and peaked in the early 1930s, when about 50 percent of its students had Greek affiliation. The bonds of close, durable friendship and opportunities for leadership, as well as the social life and semi-independent living, were very meaningful to generations of Alfred students. Their importance in the history of the university is exemplified by the high percentage of Alfred trustees and other distinguished alumni who joined a fraternity or sorority, valued the experience, and cherished both friendships and memories.

Sometime during the 1970s, however, Greek membership underwent a prolonged, persistent decline from 40–45 percent of the student population to the 2002 level of 10 percent (14 percent of men, 7 percent of women) when Greek life was dissolved at Alfred University. In their prime, some Greek houses had as many as fifty or sixty members, and one had nearly a hundred. But as of Fall 2001, every house had fewer than twenty-five active members, and eight of twelve had fewer than twenty. In absolute terms, house occupancy was well below historical levels, and in relative terms, most houses were less than 50 percent occupied.

The ramifications of Stenzel's death, however, did little to halt the dangerous behavior, and neither did any disciplinary actions by Alfred University. During the decade after Stenzel's death, several other students were hospitalized for treatment of alcohol overdoses as result of parties at Greek houses. Because social fraternal groups are founded on secrecy, with rituals and initiations intrinsic to defining and solidifying each group, attempts by administrators to curtail these abuses were consistently thwarted by peer pressure to deny any violations. Changes in federal and state laws impacted Greek life during this period too when the drinking age was raised and hazing became illegal. The drinking age changed from eighteen to nineteen in 1982, then to twenty-one in 1985. This had an enormous impact on campus social life, burdening colleges with the role of policing underage drinking in addition to teaching moderation with alcohol. College administrations also had to police hazing, which became illegal in New York.

As mentioned, even after the senseless death of Stenzel and the resulting repercussions, there were other tragedies of near-tragedies as well. Some of the most widely reported incidents included:

- On October 11, 1985, several little sisters of Zeta Beta Tau (ZBT) at AU were struck by a car during a pledge activity. According to official reports, the students were blindfolded and left alongside a country road while cars sped by them. The activity was designed to engender trust, but the event was reckless at best. One pledge was seriously injured.
- In January 1986, another AU student was partially paralyzed after a "stair diving" (participants threw themselves down a flight of stairs) accident at Delta Sigma Phi.
- Lambda Chi Alpha lost its charter for seven years after a member died at the house in the fall of 1991.

During those troubling times for fraternities and sororities, the Alfred administration tried to help the Greek system in a variety of ways. It encouraged the founding of several new chapters of nationals. Alpha Kappa Alpha opened in 1988 but eventually closed, as did Kappa Alpha Psi (1989). Sigma Alpha Mu (1989), Kappa Sigma (1992) and Delta Zeta (1994) stayed open.

Despite these and other efforts by the Alfred administration, during the 1990s the problems continued and the violations escalated. As a result, some of the national fraternal organizations with Alfred chapters rated them "very risky," and two of the nationals revoked charters: Lambda Chi Alpha in 1992 (recolonized in 2001), and ZBT in 1989 (recolonized in 1990, and suspended again in 2002). These assessments and revocations from national organizations indicated genuine concerns in the external Greek community, as well as at the university. Given this track record, it was no surprise that attempts by the administration to attract new chapters met with reluctance from national organizations.

Contrary to an often-heard complaint from undergraduate Greeks, Alfred University took numerous steps to reform and otherwise support and strengthen Greek life. In the 1970s and 1980s the Dean of Students/Vice President for Student Affairs served as Greek adviser and met regularly with the Inter-Greek Council and individual house officers to discuss standards and expectations. A minimum grade point average for pledging was established and rush was delayed to second semester of the freshman year, in line with trends and recommendations of the time. Consultants were brought in to assess the system and in the early 1990s a new position, Assistant Dean of Students for Greek Affairs, was created even as membership took yet another precipitous decline from about 40 percent to about 20–25 percent of the student body.

Much of this happened under former President Coll, who campaigned tirelessly for a Greek Row on university property. He hoped to create safe, modern, clustered housing for the Greek community on campus. However, active Greeks and Greek alumni failed to support the concept, and despite extensive efforts and planning, the project never got off the ground.

By the beginning of the 1990s, Alfred University's fraternities and sororities could not meet even the minimal standards set by the university and the national Greek organizations, earning them poor or even "risky" ratings by the nationals. The increased number and severity of infractions prompted the university administration to recommend major fraternity changes to its board of trustees in May 1992. The university set higher, more consistent standards for recognizing Greek chapters as official organizations. A full-time Student Affairs professional was hired to work with the fraternities and sororities. At least one member of each chapter was required to undergo resident advisor (RA) training to create a "more responsible living environment" in houses otherwise devoid of adult supervision. Pledges were required to maintain at least a 2.0 grade point average, and academic standards for Greek organizations were set. All Greek houses were required to have advisors. The university also tightened the requirements for serving alcohol. All parties were to be registered and monitored, with student security at the door and at the party. Students designated for security duty were to check IDs to make sure those consuming alcohol were of legal drinking age. New disciplinary policies, which mandated punishments, were spelled out.

The assistant dean worked with the students on leadership development, standards, and expectations. Students were sent to leadership conferences and offered leadership workshops on campus. A Greek Life Project (1992) was initiated to strengthen the system, followed by Greek Life Benchmarks (1994, revised 1996). A Greek Life Relational Statement was created (1999), as was a Greek Life Code of Pride (1999, replacing the 1996 Benchmarks) with cash rewards for excellence. None of these efforts solved the problems in the Greek system, but all demonstrated an administration committed to helping in many different ways.

Alfred University also offered financial assistance, establishing a $25,000 loan fund to help houses with renovations and guaranteeing bank loans. And for decades the administration subsidized Greek houses by releasing sophomores from the residency requirement and thereby shifting revenue from the university to the Greek organizations. Despite these various efforts by the university, membership continued to decline while alcohol and hazing violations increased. A survey, conducted by a national organization, found higher levels of heavy drinking and illegal drug use among Greek members at Alfred compared to nonmembers.

For a few years after the new standards and policies were put into effect, membership in Greek organizations averaged 23 percent of the student body, but then it began to creep lower again. At the start of the spring 2002 semester, there were a total of 226 members of AU sororities and fraternities, just under 12 percent of the student body.

Hazing continued to be a problem as well. Some initiates, unhappy with their decision, unpledged and found themselves harassed and intimidated; ultimately some even transferred to another university. As a result of hazing and alcohol violations, AU revoked recognition of one fraternity and imposed various forms of suspension on three other fraternities and two sororities. By the spring of 2002, 50 percent of the houses were subject to sanctions.

After the 1998 football hazing incident at Alfred University, the school instituted a new hearing policy for allegations of hazing: to wit, any organization, not just fraternities and sororities, involved in an alleged hazing would have a hearing before a panel of three senior-level administrators. In the interim, if the allegation was against a fraternity or sorority, the pledge process was suspended. If it was another organization, such as an athletic team, the university immediately issued "keep away" orders, barring team members from further contact with the complainants, with the first priority being to keep students safe.

Clearly, there was no double standard in how the football team was treated versus how Greek houses were treated, notwithstanding claims by some alumni to the contrary. What was different was that the student athletes have accountability to the university, something lacking at the Greek houses. Not surprisingly, then, hazing and alcohol violations among varsity athletes were reduced while the numerous previous efforts to reform Greek behavior unsupported by regular and consistent outside supervision failed.

At its February 2002 meeting, the Alfred University board of trustees was informed of a confluence of extremely disturbing events: yet again several Greek houses were charged with violating university policies on hazing and/or alcohol; a fraternity man, Benjamin Klein, had allegedly been the victim of assault by his own Zeta Beta Tau fraternity brothers, and worst of all he had subsequently died. In response to this news about a Greek system suffering from persistent and increasing problems, despite declining membership, the trustees established a Trustee Task Force on Greek Life "to evaluate whether the fraternities and sororities have a future role at our university" and to report to the board at its May 2002 meeting.

Chaired by a former board chairperson, the task force was composed of four trustees, all of whom were Greek themselves: two faculty members, a representative of both the Alumni Association and the Parent's Association (who was also a Greek), and the Associate Provost/Vice President for Enrollment Management.

The goals of the task force were to conduct a fair, objective, and balanced inquiry into the past and present role of Greek life at Alfred University and to determine whether that role was consistent with the mission of the university. To accomplish this, the task force studied data in absolute and relative, as well as historical and contemporary, terms about Greek students versus non-Greek students at AU. They reviewed a number of reports comparing academic performance, drinking habits, and community service among Greeks and non-Greeks at Alfred. They also examined general student interest in joining Greek organizations, as well as interest by gender and ethnicity. They compared Alfred to national data and trends, and reviewed the work of similar task forces at twenty other colleges and universities.

Difficult though the decision was for the committee, the members agreed unanimously that the Greek system should be eliminated as quickly as possible. As quoted in the *New York Times*, "The Greek system is beyond repair," said Robert McComsey, the chairman of Alfred's board. Despite the valuable experiences it offered its members, the Greek system as a whole had deteriorated significantly over time even though the administration made numerous attempts to support and strengthen it. The system required a disproportionate amount of time and resources for the benefits it affords a small group of students, hurt relations between the university and the community, and sometimes worked to the detriment of its voluntary participants. President Coll's successor, Charles M. Edmondson, remarked, "It takes a determined and courageous group of trustees to do this, because Greek alums are vocal." Dr. Edmondson instructed that the board's directive be implemented quickly and fairly.

Some Observations

It is doubtful that the elimination of Greek life has completely eradicated hazing from Alfred University. The way the Alfred community discusses hazing has changed drastically over the past two decades and now reflects the foundational values of the institution. Each year brings in a new class of students that have to be taught that Alfred's traditions do not include hazing. We don't simply talk about the horrors of hazing, but discuss how we lost valuable members of our community to this misguided effort to create special meaning to their group. Like any other prevention effort, the fight never ends.

In closing, hazing has robbed our community of our most precious commodity, the lives of two students. While we cannot bring them back to life, we have endeavored to honor their memory by working tirelessly to spare others from this pain experience. The consistent lessons learned from this several-decade journey to address hazing are:

- Every school and organization that includes teenagers and young adults needs to have an enforceable antihazing policy and year-round prevention education.
- Groups and teams need to be trained on how to create positive team-building initiations. Not only for those participating in the group, but also for those adults entrusted to supervise them.
- We as a society need to send an unequivocal message that we do not condone hazing and that we are approachable and want to intervene.
- Our youth are yearning for initiation opportunities, but when left to their own imagination, without our involvement, they tend to haze. Their intent is noble, it's the process they choose that is misguided.

NORM POLLARD is Dean of Students at Alfred University, a licensed mental health counselor, and certified Title IX investigator. Pollard was author with Nadine Hoover on a seminal study of hazing among athletes and hazing in high schools in the United States.

Attorney John B. Stanchfield, a personal friend to Mark Twain, advised
the likely Cornell University culprits in the homicide of cook Henrietta
Jackson to refuse to testify in a sensational investigation held in 1894. Photo
courtesy of Chemung County Historical Society, Elmira, NY.

Charles W. Wason was seriously injured in a fall from a cliff
while taking Cornell Kappa Alpha Society pledge Mortimer
M. Leggett on a traditional walkabout in an area known for
its gorges. The blindfolded Leggett also fell and died soon
after hitting the ground. Wason, a successful businessman
later in life, became a generous donor to Cornell. Photo
courtesy of Cornell University Division of Rare and
Manuscript Collections.

Francis Walter Obenchain died following a blow or blows delivered by an unknown assailant during a traditional battle at Purdue University between first-year students and sophomores beneath the school's water tower. Obenchain's father privately consulted a coroner to ascertain his son's true cause of death. Photo from 1914 Purdue University *Debris* (yearbook). Courtesy of Purdue University Libraries, Karnes Archives and Special Collections.

Hazing was seen as entertainment in comic books of the early twentieth century, such as *Tip Top Weekly*. The popular Dick Merriwell character stepped up in the nick of time to protect a hazed freshman.

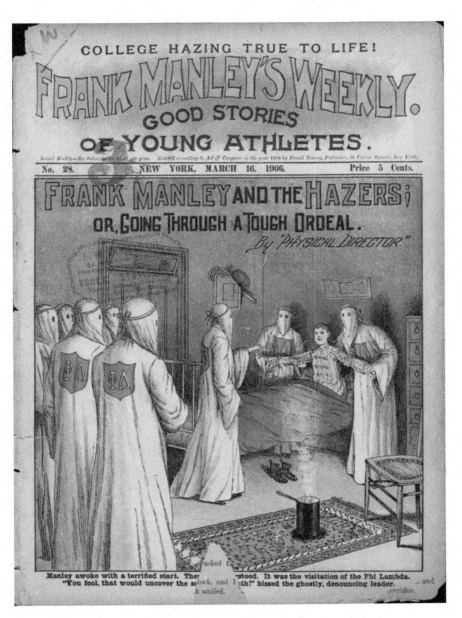

One of the common hazing practices at the turn of the twentieth century found
upperclassmen in robes storming the room of a freshman. Note the headline on the comic
book: "College Hazing True to Life."

Yearbooks of nearly all, if not all, schools celebrated hazing in Greek Life and freshman-sorority hazing. This was the 1946 Franklin College *Almanack (above and facing)*. Photo courtesy of Franklin College School of Journalism.

WE SWAT AND SWING

There's something traditional about paddles and proms . . . something distinctly democratic in the fraternity symbol that reminds us of the right of free men to organize groups. The gay, rhythmic beat of a swing band is a symbol to us of our youth and our college career.

"Get that floor dusted, pledge." [They're probably not so mean as they look!]

The rustle of taffeta, the nostalgic odor of gardenias, black bow ties . . . these will always remind us of "a heavenly time a perfect evening."

Many University of Nevada, Reno, athletes belonging to the subrosa fraternal club Sundowners, which held many initiations in public and in full view until John Davies died from alcohol poisoning in 1978 at Pyramid Lake. No one was charged in the death. Photo courtesy of Edd Lockwood.

Chuck Stenzel died at Alfred University in 1978 when members of Klan Alpine encouraged or coerced him into drinking copious amounts of alcohol. When additional Greek tragedies and incidents occurred at Alfred, the school shut down its Greek system and became a bastion of hazing research. Photo courtesy of Eileen Stevens.

Eileen Stevens was the most important antihazing advocate in the United States in 1978 and for two decades afterward. Her tireless efforts to get a tough hazing law in New York State eventually proved successful. Linda Gray played the part of Eileen Stevens in the movie *Moment of Truth: Broken Pledges*. Photo courtesy of Eileen Stevens.

Joe Bisanz was a recruited baseball player in high school. His career ended at Indiana University because of an injury. After enduring hazing, he enjoyed fraternity life, but died suddenly after a holiday party under circumstances questioned by his parents. Photo courtesy of Valerie Bisanz.

Hank Nuwer, author headshot.
Photo courtesy of Dennis Cripe,
Franklin College Pulliam School of
Journalism.

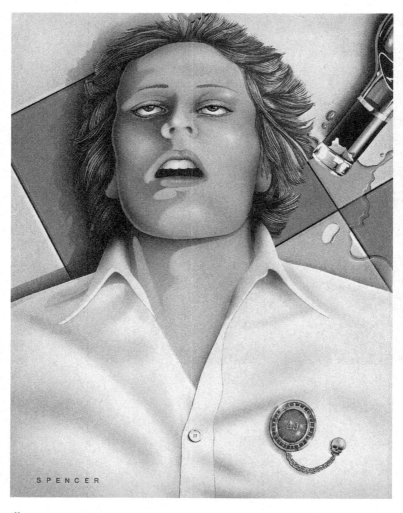

Illustration accompanying Nuwer's Dead Souls article.

Dead Souls of

Not long ago the deadly excesses of fraternity initiations seemed just quaint reminders of the past, but the problem is back again with some tragic results.

Hank Nuwer is a freelance writer living in Los Angeles.

Thirty miles from Reno, under a star-drilled desert sky, a lone pickup truck grinds to a halt alongside the Pyramid Lake Highway. Three men slide out of the cab and stagger to the back of the truck. All wear black felt hats adorned with a yellow patch that depicts a setting sun. The three grin at the sight that greets them: five youths, their clothing flecked with vomit, are sprawled across the floor like bags of cement.

The five are ordered to get up, and four struggle to comply by easing their way down from the tailgate to the road. One remains on the truck bed, a dark-haired giant wearing a thick Fu Manchu mustache. The three youths with hats are amused and clamber aboard to wake him. They laugh drunkenly as they shake him.

Suddenly, one youth tears open the limp young man's coat and puts an ear to his chest. All laughter ceases. The only sound is the whistling wind that bends back the sagebrush as it passes.

The dead youth was John Davies, a 23-year-old University of Nevada football player. His death concluded a three-day drinking spree required for admission into a suspended, but still active, campus club called the Sundowners. In 65 hours, Davies and four other pledges were forced to consume 18 quarts of hard liquor, 16 gallons of wine and vast quantities of beer. Much of the alcohol had been poured down the throats of pledges by Sundowner members. When Davies's body simply gave out from what the coroner termed "an acute alcoholic overdose," his blood alcohol count was a massive .421. In Nevada, a person is legally drunk with a .10 reading.

A second Sundowner pledge, Gary Faulstich, was hospitalized the same night Davies died. His blood alcohol count registered .456. Faulstich suffered a complete respiratory arrest, ceased breathing and was kept alive only with specialized hospital equipment. Had he not made it to Reno, there is no doubt he too would have died.

A grand jury investigating the case determined that the five pledges had been pummeled, ridiculed, cursed and in-

timidated "by approximately 10 of the [30] Sundowner members . . . with the apparent encouragement of the membership." All five had been forced to consume flaming glasses of Everclear, a 190-proof grain alcohol used to prepare flaming duck. Faulstich proved unable to master the art of swallowing the substance and was burned on the chest.

Over three million college men belong to 406 national fraternities in the United States. Many more are members of splinter fraternal and social groups, particularly at the two-year colleges. Conservatively, one million youths will have pledged this fall. All must satisfy initiation requirements that include hazing practices varying from mild to severe. If repeated past tragedies are an indication, at least one fraternity will prematurely halt its Hell Week ceremony after tragedy strikes.

At the time of this incident, I was a graduate student and lived just off campus near the Little Wal, the Sundowner bar where much of the forced drinking occurred. Several times that fatal weekend, I saw Sundowner pledges being hazed. Always they were accompanied by the live chickens that tradition mandates they steal. Although I was not present at the Wal tavern the night Davies died, I had attended this portion of the Sundowner initiation two years before.

At that time, despite the general bedlam in the place, a not unpleasant sense of conviviality was apparent. Nearly everyone in the bar was drinking heavily, and, on occasion, shots of unlit Everclear were ordered. These were drunk, not only by pledges, but by member Sundowners and at least one young woman. A fellow clad in a dark shirt was sprawled across the spit-streaked floor alongside a small pool table. No one in the packed bar took notice of him except whenever he was nudged out of the way for a pool shot. Evil-looking fluid oozed from the young fellow's nose and mouth.

Watching his inert form and fearing he might be dying, I finally approached a Sundowner acquaintance, initiation or not, and expressed concern for the youth's safety. The Sundowner assured me that the boy was fine but did take the stricken youth outside for some air. This incident, and the death of John Davies, have preyed on my mind. My own experiences as a fraternity member of Sigma Tau Rho fraternity at the State University College of New York at Buffalo were not atypical. Sig Tau was an elite fraternity

HELL WEEK

by HANK NUWER

Illustrations by Spencer/South Design

Hank Nuwer has written on hazing for forty years. This article on fraternity deaths (p. 52–53) was published in 1978 after two years of research. *Human Behavior.*

Lianne Kowiak's son Harrison Kowiak died in a hazing at Lenoir-Rhyne University. She was the winner of HazingPrevention.Org's Hank Nuwer Anti-Hazing Award for her tireless work on antihazing efforts. Photo courtesy of Lianne Kowiak.

Harrison Kowiak. Photo courtesy of Lianne Kowiak.

Harrison, Emma, Brian, and Lianne Kowiak. Photo courtesy of Lianne Kowiak.

Debbie Smith, founder of the AHA! Movement, is pictured with her son Matt, husband Greg, and younger son Travis. Matt Carrington died from water intoxication in a fraternity hazing at Chico State. Photo courtesy of Debbie Smith.

HazingPrevention.Org founder Tracy Maxwell has been awarded numerous awards for her work with cancer survivors and with hazing awareness. She is pictured here with former HPO board members Dave Stollman and Dave Westol. Photo courtesy of Tracy Maxwell.

14 How Schools May Have Facilitated and Operationalized Hazing

An Interview with Peter F. Lake

Hank Nuwer

An expert in tort liability and higher education law, Peter F. Lake holds the Charles A. Dana Chair at Stetson University. He is a school safety legal expert and the director of the Center for Excellence in Higher Education Law and Policy. Lake, a graduate of Harvard Law School, has written many influential articles and books, most notably *The Rights and Responsibilities of the Modern University*.

Hank Nuwer: I did a history of Cedar Crest College way back in 2004.[1] The all-female school once upon a distant time published a "Customs Book" that mandated freshman hazing. There were kangaroo courts and beanie wearing and making fun of people's dancing. For example, there was a first-year student named Bird, and so of course upperclassmen had her float around pretending to be flying. So the first question is this: In the old days there were such things as Customs Books. So do schools bear some responsibility for hazing being inculcated in the system and culture?

Peter F. Lake: I think there is a great tradition of how things play forward in the twenty-first century. I think that's what is starting to emerge is the hidden history of hazing, and as a result of research such as yours we understand how hazing actually was more built into the culture with intentionality instead of just simply tolerated and permitted by some schools. I think the narrative that a lot of people have, whether it is true or false, is that hazing was sort of tolerated behavior at the margins of institutions. We're seeing clear evidence that some institutions actually facilitated it and even operationalized it. For example, when I went to Wake Forest University for the first time and some of the old [fraternity] houses had party rooms, and still do actually, architecturally built into the basements so that they were clearly designed to have activities intended to involve alcohol that would be out of sight of public viewing. They were literally building hazing spaces and spaces for underage drinking. So it's part of our history that we're uncovering. It's apparent that some actually built customs into their systems. There is some responsibility to take ownership of who we were and what was done so we can move forward.

NUWER: The Masons certainly had rooms in their basements that were set up with metal goats for initiations, paraphernalia, things on the wall that were there clearly to initiate new members. That Masonic influence went over into the fraternities even in initiation ceremonies and rituals.

LAKE: It's fascinating. It really is.

NUWER: I'm going to go back to my research from 1988 to 1989 for *Broken Pledges* and compare that to your book *The Rights and Responsibilities of the Modern University*, second edition.[2] I didn't hear the term "deliberate indifference," but I certainly heard of the concept from several lawyers. So do you think the greater influence on Title IX protections may make "deliberate indifference" go the way of the dodo, or is it still present in some schools?

LAKE: I do think we have moved substantially into a facilitator experience for most institutions. I think Title IX has been a clear example of legal changes that literally force you out of that mode if you have any residual proclivity to engage in that approach to management. It's sustainable. The new approach does not permit you to do something more than be deliberately indifferent; the reaction requires mandates that are at least consistent with reasonable care.

NUWER: Title IX deals with sexual slurs, unwanted touching, but I remember the interviews I did in the eighties. A librarian in central Indiana who was almost in tears when he admitted pledges had to kiss another pledge's bare butt on order, or when I interviewed Larry Lockridge and he said the chapter his father, author Ross Lockridge, was in at Indiana University had pledges read pornography and they were ridiculed if they had an erection. So those are certainly Title IX offenses that if they occurred today would be definitely actionable.

LAKE: Oh, yes, that's the sort of thing today that would automatically draw an investigatory response, and most likely well beyond that as well. Some of that behavior is just straight-up criminal now and [other] crimes that were just not well articulated in the 1980s are now. I think that is something else, Hank, that is a backdrop to your work—that the legal system has become more precise regarding sex crimes and sex violations—things there weren't names for or weren't articulated well but now are like exploitation. I still have to have this conversation with people who say in the 1970s there were no stalking laws. The idea that someone could stalk you? Well, you wouldn't have a legal remedy for it. You wouldn't be able to go to a criminal prosecutor and get any sort of protection. It's amazing to people whose lives have been lived in the '90s, aughts, and teens to realize what was occurring on campuses just before they hit the planet.

NUWER: Exactly. And with high school athletics, with thirteen- and fourteen-year-olds, we are seeing sodomies committed. It's bad enough that the acts were committed, but then to have a prosecutor in Arkansas say, well, there was no sexual pleasure, so no charges. A prosecutor in northern Illinois—same thing. Or another one, when there was sexual touching through underwear, a prosecutor said he didn't want to ruin the lives of these young men, the defendants, with their stupid horseplay. He said that "I agree it was wrong, but no, I don't want to prosecute." It's going to take time to change all that.

LAKE: There is no question that we're in a new era. I was just speaking to a group last week, and I said that I assumed in organized male contact sports in high school and college that coaches would naturally cast aspersions on your sexual orientation. I didn't have a coach that didn't do that. That was just considered good coaching at the time. Now it's not sustainable. Look at [former Indiana basketball coach] Bobby Knight. It wasn't that long ago that he was being really physically and mentally abusive, and it was considered good coaching; that's what you have to do to win.

NUWER: When I interviewed him for a magazine article he had just put a tampon into a player's locker.

LAKE: There you go. I guess for him it was a step forward. I mean some of these folks just would not have made the transition into modern education.

NUWER: Next question. As you say so articulately in *The Rights and Responsibilities of a Modern University*, with college law, with respect to any special responsibility for college students, except in some special cases such as campus invitee visits and some residential hall situations is evolving—the idea that having a special responsibility, you say, will continue to evolve in the twenties and thirties. My question, from your perspective and a campus-safety perspective, is how can landmark hazing cases, such as *Furek v. Delaware*, be tightened and improved in terms of a special responsibility?[3]

LAKE: Probably the most basic thing I would say is to move away from the idea that you need special relationships to create safety responsibilities for college students. That is, in itself, a conceptual leap that I think we need to take. The case I would draw attention to is that Nova Southeastern case where the Florida Supreme Court unanimously dealt with an assault situation [and found a duty beyond a need to warn about attacks in a parking lot, but to actually take reasonable cautions to protect the plaintiff].[4] They pointed out something that is really fundamental that you have a duty not just because of a special relationship if risks exist but because you have created an environment.

NUWER: I was thinking about the case of a female volleyball player at SUNY Geneseo who was injured after an alcoholic initiation party where she allegedly left to get back to her room on her own. I was wondering if a university has even more of a duty if it recruits an athlete, went after her, and invited her to campus, and then they actually put money in the form of tuition into that person? Would they have more of a duty to that person than to a walk-on player?

LAKE: That's fascinating. Athletic cases are particularly tricky because on one hand you have the reasonable care to make the program as safe as it can possibly be with a school-sponsored activity. However, there are special circumstances in the case of athletes who are voluntarily participating. If you rely on the tort system alone, it won't do very much to do that. So generally, any athlete, whether a walk-on or recruit, assumes ordinary risk in a sport. . . . But generally, yeah, you're on the right track when you are talking about an unusual case and assumption of risk beyond the ordinary risk of the sport. When you create a program like the volleyball team, well, you created that, and so the risks associated with that are ones we have, not because you have a special relationship, but because we're generating risks due to our own activities.

NUWER: Over time I have watched several failed attempts to get a uniform federal hazing bill passed. These were all, in my opinion, flawed in definition, wording, and recommended penalties. I don't know if this is a bright light or not, but hazing expert Elizabeth Allan testified before the US Senate Committee on Health, Education, Labor, and Pensions. . . . In the past there was no chance to get a federal hazing bill passed. Maybe that can change.

LAKE: I think, Hank, over time, and probably beyond our lifetimes, the pressure to recognize a baseline of college safety that applies throughout the United States will see a federal mandate of some kind eventually come to fruition. We will see a comprehensive articulation of a core civil-rights basis for public safety. I think one of the problems with student safety law right now is that it is mostly based on fifty states' individual tort laws with a little bit of overlay of federal safety law on top of that. It's such an incoherent patchwork quilt that only an expert could begin to give people rational advice on how to operate in that world. You and I know not to send our kids to the universities in Alabama to join the Greek system because of their primitive hazing law, and we know the state of Florida has one of the more aggressive laws. But how many parents know that? Most people figure that stuff out only after they have been hurt, and that it actually would have made a huge difference if I went to school in Wyoming, Florida, Kansas, or California. California right now is going to the Supreme Court on fairly significant grounds. It's now said on premises, public schools have no duty to protect students from violence perpetrated by other students in the classroom. What an almost outrageous thing to tell people—when you come to California, if one kid stabs another in the classroom you don't have to do anything about that.

NUWER: If a university eliminates pledging, will it eliminate a lot of the hazing?

LAKE: I doubt it. I think it will just find a way to go someplace else. I think the root causes of hazing are so pernicious that you might be able to block a little of it for a while, but I think you'd have some unofficial way of recreating what has gone on before. I do think part of the solution to hazing is recreating the initiation process in some way, but I think it goes much deeper than that. Of course you and I have talked about this many times. I think there is something in human brain development that creates a sort of proclivity to hazing behavior, especially in certain stages of development. A *Chronicle of Higher Education* piece by Eric Hoover kind of haunts me because he makes this point that we've thrown a lot of stuff at hazing, and it keeps coming back, so how do we really get underneath it?[5] I applaud efforts to try to find a solution, but I have become overcautious about becoming overly optimistic. I've seen delaying pledging or eliminating pledging and any number of techniques, and I don't think any of them in and of themselves have eliminated the phenomenon.

NUWER: We have had Help Week instead of Hell Week.

LAKE: I don't think the Department of Education has been keeping up with the times. We're seeing a little more prevention focus directly tied into Title IX and that's a good thing, but I still see absurdly underfunded prevention efforts at a lot of campuses across the country. It is amazing to me that we have lost that energy in realizing that $10,000 in a prevention program can save a million dollars in litigation and human injury and tragedy.

NUWER: Yes.

LAKE: You know one of the main themes of my work is to try to transmute higher education from a reactive to a preventative mode, and it takes risk management generally to do that. I think there is a culture shift on a fundamental level that is going to have to return. I think our institutions were built to actually be reactive and not preventative. It sort of goes with our DNA as to how we run our businesses. It's going to take some real hard business work to get us to flip the polarities nationally to get us more focused on prevention and less on reaction. We've seen millions of dollars in reactive strategies at the University of Virginia, and you think, gosh, if we had put anywhere near that kind of money into prevention you wouldn't have half the things go on that did go on. I lay a lot of this at the feet of the federal government. The great hope for advancement in our field is interdisciplinary science. Taken from the best minds we can find that work in these areas.

NUWER: Is there anything I didn't have the wit to ask you?

LAKE: Not really, Hank. Any time I talk about hazing I emphasize that hazing is not just a Greek phenomenon, and it shows up just about every place on campus, from bands to athletic groups to faculty. There is something going on in human development, particularly in that age between the teen years and the late twenties, that is very interesting. Trying to pick out one group to be blameworthy from a public health perspective is probably part of the problem. It doesn't do any good to vilify anybody over this. It's like a fatal disease. It's a public health crisis that has spread over our public learning environment. Calling out one group as particularly nefarious isn't exactly working. I do think the work you're doing is very important because the one thing about this public health crisis that makes it so interesting to me is that it has a tendency to hide itself. Like sexual assault, hazing is a close cousin. It tends to go underground and people don't want to bring it forward. We won't be able to address this public health challenge until we can get information and talk about it in a scientific and rational way. I applaud your work. It takes a lot of painstaking effort to root around and find what you are finding.

PETER F. LAKE is Professor of Law, Charles A. Dana Chair, and Director of the Center for Excellence in Higher Education Law and Policy at Stetson University College of Law. He is a graduate of Harvard Law School and author of the seminal *The Rights and Responsibilities of the Modern University*.

15 A Fraternity Model

Addressing Campus Alcohol Misuse and Abuse

Edward G. Whipple and Robert A. Biggs

THE GENERAL COUNCIL of Phi Delta Theta International Fraternity adopted a revision to its risk management policies in March 1997 known as alcohol-free housing. Specifically the governing board's policy stated, "All chapter facilities and properties in Phi Delta Theta Fraternity shall be alcohol-free at all times and under all circumstances." The decision was a bold, dramatic transformation of the visionary General Council to return the fraternity to its core principles.

The Phi Delta Theta alcohol-free housing policy was to be implemented by July 1, 2000. The fraternity provided all of its chapters with housing—including lodges or "spaces" as well as outdoor areas—sufficient time to adjust and transition operations to be in compliance. It became the obligation of each individual chapter to enforce this policy and to hold those accountable that might violate it in accordance with local bylaws and the Code of Phi Delta Theta. Alcohol-free housing did not and does not imply "prohibition" of alcohol use. The fraternity did expect, however, that all chapters would comply with college or university regulations, as well as local, state, and federal laws.

Implementation Strategies

When Phi Delta Theta announced its revised risk management policy regarding alcohol-free housing, fewer than twelve chapter facilities were already alcohol-free. An announcement to students, parents, alumni, university officials, and the media stated this: "By the year 2000, every chapter of Phi Delta Theta will have alcohol-free facilities or it will not continue to exist as a charter group." The decision about this initiative was taken very seriously, and each chapter of Phi Delta Theta was expected to take whatever specific steps were necessary to reach this goal.

Through a series of financial incentives offered by the international fraternity, several chapters voluntarily implemented alcohol-free housing prior to the deadline. Others followed, and by June 2000 all but thirty of some 165 chapters with facilities had adopted the alcohol-free housing policy. The fraternity developed a resource guide containing information on recruitment, social alternatives, enforcement procedures, education, and support materials to help alumni and students with the implementation of this policy. In addition, the fraternity made available additional information at its summer leadership programs and regional alumni summits concerning techniques to successfully implement the alcohol-free housing policy. As a consequence, all Phi Delta Theta International Fraternity chapter facilities were alcohol-free by the deadline.

Reasons for Alcohol-Free Housing

The Fraternity articulated seven key reasons for the implementation of alcohol-free housing facilities: (1) to return the focus to the founding principles, (2) to combat an alcohol-dominated culture, (3) to improve members' academic performance, (4) to stop the deterioration of chapter facilities, (5) to slow the rising cost of liability insurance, (6) to meet the needs of today's college students, and (7) to reinvolve alumni members.

Results and Trends from Alcohol-Free Housing

Articulating these seven key reasons for implementation of alcohol-free housing facilities expectations meant that the fraternity expected to see positive results associated with each reason. A renewed focus on the fraternity's cardinal principles (i.e., friendship, sound learning, and rectitude) became the driving force behind an alcohol-free housing policy. Because it was felt some Phi Delta Theta chapters and members had drifted from the fraternity's true purpose and the founders' vision, a realignment of the organization's values was needed.

Such realignment has occurred with the help of alcohol-free housing. Today, Phi Delta Theta members are succeeding in and out of the classroom. Over 12 percent of Phi Delta Theta chapters were recognized during the past year for achieving the top grade point average on their respective campuses. Over the past sixteen years, the fraternity's elevated academic standards led to implementing a chapter minimum-GPA standard, such as a 2.5. Phi Delta Theta at this time expects both the GPA standard and member performance to continue to increase. Outside of the classroom, members remain leaders on campus.

Phi Delta Theta remains committed to leadership development conferences and emerging online technologies. More than two thousand students and alumni in 2015 and 2016 participated in online education, which enables the fraternity's educational message to reach a high percentage of the membership. Over twenty-five hundred individuals have attended on-site programs (e.g., Kleberg Emerging Leadership Institute, Presidents Leadership Conference, Recruitment Workshops, and the Chapter Advisory Board Summit) throughout the 2015–2016 academic year. Ninety-two percent of Kleberg Emerging Leaders Institute attendees have become officers within the organization. An ever-growing list of student leadership successes can be found on the fraternity's website, PhiDeltaTheta.org.

While definitions vary, most would agree that rectitude can be explained as "doing the right thing." Of the three Phi Delta Theta cardinal principles, rectitude proved the foundation for the transition to alcohol-free housing. Through the value of rectitude, the fraternity expected its student and alumni members to hold one another accountable.

When alcohol-free housing was announced, many were concerned that Phi Delta Theta would attract fewer members, resulting in a declining membership. The data over time refutes this concern. Over sixteen years later, the fraternity has experienced steady growth in numbers of chapters and colonies as well as student members. In 2000, the fraternity had 165 chapters, and in 2016, over 190 chapters. Phi Delta Theta is indeed growing and spreading its cardinal principles to a greater number of students. In 2000, the fraternity had about eight thousand undergraduate members. In 2015, it boasted nearly thirteen thousand members. In 2000, the average chapter size was forty-four members; today, the average chapter size is sixty-five members.

A Sharp Decline in Hazing

With the Phi Delta Theta focus on its core principles and away from alcohol, the fraternity has experienced fewer incidents of hazing, especially on Bid Night, Big Brother Night, and Initiation. The student members have realized that Phi Delta Theta is not a social fraternity, but rather a leadership fraternity where members truly care about helping one another ensure a healthy and safe fraternal experience.

With the adoption of alcohol-free housing, members now approach new member education with the attitude that it is their duty to assimilate the new candidates into fraternity membership instead of have them experience a "rite of passage." This is exemplified in the new member oath that states in part, "I will strive in all ways to transmit the fraternity to those who may follow after, not only not less, but greater than it was transmitted to me."

The data is clear; alcohol-free housing does make a difference in all aspects of fraternal life and while this policy is not perfect, it has differentiated Phi Delta Theta from other fraternities for values-based students seeking a family of fraternal lifelong relationships as undergraduates and alumni in a leadership laboratory.

Positive Implications of Alcohol Reform

During the past sixteen years, the number of new members has increased from about three thousand to more than five thousand. A growing fraternity has many benefits, but one is critical: a larger fraternity equals more services and resources for its membership to propel the organization forward. Alcohol consumption, and specifically the misuse and abuse, correlate with poor academic performance in a college environment. Alcohol affects the ability of undergraduates to adhere to the mission of universities and to an important principle of fraternal organizations, academic achievement. In 2000, the year alcohol-free housing was established, the average Phi Delta Theta chapter GPA was 2.73. Only eight Phi Delta Theta chapters were recognized for achieving the top GPA on their respective campuses. In 2016, the average GPA among Phi Delta Theta chapters was 3.10, and twenty-two chapters achieved the top GPA on their respective campuses. Alcohol-free housing has provided Phi Delta Theta members a clean, safe, and quiet atmosphere to focus on studies, and the resulting outcome clearly is an enhanced academic performance.

Financial Matters

In 2009, the General Council of Phi Delta Theta implemented a minimum standard regarding academic performance for all chapters of the fraternity to ensure that the upward trend in academic performance continued. To recognize and acknowledge academic achievement by student members across North America, the Phi Delta Theta Foundation allocated over $214,000 in undergraduate scholarships and grants and graduate fellowships to over 194 members in 2015. In total, the foundation now has granted more than 3,577 scholarships and fellowships exceeding $4.7 million.

The deterioration of living facilities correlated to the misuse and abuse of alcohol and was a major concern for Phi Delta Theta prior to the implementation of alcohol-free housing. The fraternity's facilities were steadily worsening due largely to behavior at social events. At the time, alumni were unwilling to donate funds to chapter facilities that were not maintained properly. As a result of the shift to alcohol free-housing the past fifteen years, donors to Phi Delta Theta housing have invested millions of dollars.

Funds supporting chapter houses and their transition to alcohol-free environments have also been a priority of the Walter B. Palmer Foundation, formed to provide capital for property acquisitions and improvements. Since 2000, $6.6 million has been loaned to make chapter improvements, making Phi Delta Theta facilities more attractive and safer to potential members, brothers, and alumni. Accordingly, the fraternity's chapters actively recruit members into a facility that they can be proud of and showcase to parents and visitors.

One of the greatest benefits to the membership of Phi Delta Theta concerning alcohol- free housing has been reduced insurance cost. Such savings occur because facilities are considerably safer than they were in prior years. Before the implementation of alcohol-free housing, Phi Delta Theta incurred sharply increasing insurance premiums resulting from a long history of incidents caused by a high-risk living environment. Safer environments, afforded by alcohol-free housing, have resulted in the fraternity's insurance claims decreasing dramatically. Prior to the implementation of alcohol-free housing, Phi Delta Theta averaged 12.4 claims per year due to alcohol issues; this number has decreased to 4.4 claims per year over the past fifteen years, which equates to a 64 percent drop. Looking at average dollars spent per year on insurance claims, Phi Delta Theta has experienced a 94 percent decrease. From a whopping $413,378 pre–alcohol-free housing, the annual expenditure was a mere $24,477 in post–alcohol-free housing.

While a safer environment within Phi Delta Theta facilities allows members to focus on leading their chapters instead of dealing with what went wrong at the last social event, the greatest effect is on the cost of membership. Since implementation, Phi Delta Theta has seen a continual decrease in liability insurance costs for its members. According to a 2015 survey, the average insurance rate for fraternities is $165 per man, while the Phi Delta Theta current rate is $90 per man, the second lowest of all fraternities. This savings allows Phi Delta Theta to offer an affordable fraternity experience to more college-age males.

Phi Delta Theta's stance on alcohol helped rid it of a reputation for being an organization where college students easily obtain alcohol. Approximately 65 percent of the fraternity's current initiated and new members are under the age of twenty-one. Accordingly, Phi Delta Theta determined that an alcohol policy for its facilities had to reflect the reality that a small number of members were of legal drinking age.

According to Neil Howe and William Strauss in *Millennials Rising*, today's students exude the following characteristics: closeness with their parents, commitment to grades and performance, involvement with extracurricular activities, orientation to community service work, and technological competencies. They also prefer secure, regulated environments.[1] A Centers for Disease Control survey found that more college freshmen are not drinking any alcohol.[2]

Phi Delta Theta understood, as it understands today, the characteristics of college-age students and has proactively created an environment for them to thrive and succeed.

Since introducing alcohol-free housing, Phi Delta Theta has experienced an unprecedented increase in alumni support. Financial contributions have increased and alumni are donating more time to chapter support. Phi Delta Theta currently has 270 percent more advisers working with chapters than in 1997: from three hundred prior to the implementation of alcohol-free housing to over thirteen hundred today. Such involvement has provided a wider base of support for chapter leadership and has demonstrated to undergraduate members that Phi Delta Theta truly is a "Fraternity for Life," helping the student members become the greatest version of themselves.

While it is believed that local contributions also have increased, we can certify that during the same time period, the Phi Delta Theta Foundation has experienced its best years. The foundation has seen alumni contribute at record levels since alcohol-free housing was introduced. In fact, since 1997, the Phi Delta Theta Foundation has had nine of its highest giving years in history and increased its endowment to a record level.

As Phi Delta Theta grows and new members are inducted into the fraternity, educating students about the reasons for and the benefits of alcohol-free housing will continue to be a vital piece of the fraternity's educational strategy. The policy is still unique within fraternities and sororities, and our newest members generally have questions regarding how it affects their chapters. These questions become difficult to answer if existing members are not well versed in discussing the policy. Today, the membership is better at such conversations, but the fraternity must continue to educate undergraduates and alumni about the overwhelming benefits.

Phi Delta Theta is a leader in the fraternity community with a comprehensive alcohol-free housing policy. Other fraternities have implemented other varieties of alcohol-free housing policies, but many of them apply only to new chapters or include exemption policies. Phi Delta Theta remains committed to an all-inclusive policy, believing that successful implementation can only be reached with a consistent standard for all members.

In 1997 and in subsequent conversations since, the General Council has recognized that exemptions to alcohol-free housing would only lead to a counterproductive and complicated culture within Phi Delta Theta—a culture focused around the right to drink alcohol. The experience of other fraternities with exemptions to alcohol-free housing has borne this out.

While an exemption policy may seem like a harmless reward to good performance, its results become detrimental to the development of chapters. A constant cyclical trend emerges when a chapter is motivated to achieve strong overall performance for the privilege to consume alcohol in their facility. Many other fraternities with exemption policies have witnessed their "good" chapters deteriorate to the point where they no longer qualify for the exemption. The pursuit of this exemption often becomes the central focus for chapters, detracting from their core values and central focus as a fraternity.

Additionally, other fraternities have shared concern about the "law of unintentional consequences" whereby additional work is created for students, alumni, and staff to evaluate an exemption application noting the reporting of incomplete and inaccurate information. The time, effort, and resources spent to apply for and monitor exemptions holds both chapters and the general fraternity back from focusing on issues at hand and leadership development. It is the hope of Phi Delta Theta that other fraternities join in the alcohol-free housing movement and help alleviate the alcohol issues that fraternities still face.

For alcohol-free housing to work on a specific campus, Phi Delta Theta relies on the institution for support. Colleges and universities have a wide range of views and institutional policies regarding alcohol-free housing. The majority of campuses where Phi Delta Theta chapters exist is supportive of the fraternity's policy and see it as a benefit to the organization and to the campus. When campus-based professionals help support and communicate the fraternity's policy, Phi Delta Theta sees greater success. On the other hand, some campuses discredit the policy, do not see its merits, and do not support enforcement. In many of these cases, a demise of the Phi Delta Theta chapter has occurred, thus minimizing the opportunity for return. The fraternity must continue to build relationships with college and university host-campus administrators.

It was inevitable that a percentage of the fraternity's chapters and general membership would not agree with the tough decision to implement alcohol-free housing, and Phi Delta Theta had to be comfortable with losing some support. Nineteen years later following the announcement and sixteen years following the policy's initial implementation, the fraternity still faces some undergraduate and alumni resistance.

Resistance from chapters generally stems from the environments around them. If the Phi Delta Theta chapter is the only fraternity on campus with alcohol-free housing, members may view the situation as a roadblock rather than a competitive advantage. If the campus is unsupportive of the policy, accountability diminishes and negative consequences may not be visible to the chapter. If influential and visible alumni from a chapter are unsupportive of the policy, two situations generally occur: (1) the chapter is influenced by the resistance and is poorly advised, or (2) the chapter stands up to the alumni resistance and risks what they believe to be alumni support. The second situation is much tougher for students to face and therefore less likely to happen.

The resistance issue has and will take time to solve. The solution, however, is clear—recruiting the "right people." Phi Delta Theta must continue to teach undergraduates the recruitment skills and practices to successfully recruit members who understand the philosophy behind alcohol-free housing; members who value the policy, enjoy its benefits, and help the chapter move forward rather than backward is paramount. This practice holds true for alumni volunteers too because it impacts the quality of advising that undergraduates receive.

The results of an alcohol-free housing policy have enabled Phi Delta Theta to proactively look to the future. Because of the success of its alcohol-free housing, the fraternity has been able to proactively develop a long term plan call Phi Delt 2020 that addresses the following questions:

Growth and Expansion
- How can Phi Delta Theta help its chapters reach healthy levels of membership?
- How can Phi Delta Theta become a member of, or return to, fraternity communities at well-respected college campuses that embrace our three cardinal principles?

Educational Programming
- How can Phi Delta Theta best educate its members, both in person and online?
- How can the Phi Delta Theta educational message reach more members?

Communication and Branding
- How can Phi Delta Theta best tell its story to others?
- How does Phi Delta Theta's communication strategy facilitate this message?

Chapter Support
- How can Phi Delta Theta best support its undergraduate chapters?
- How does the Phi Delta Theta staff and volunteer structure facilitate this support?

Chapter Operations
- How can Phi Delta Theta undergraduate and alumni officers become better educated?
- What technologies can Phi Delta Theta use to efficiently achieve its goals?
- How can Phi Delta Theta improve the quality of its housing stock?
- What risks remain pertinent to the organization, and how does Phi Delta Theta work against them?
- What standards will help Phi Delta Theta move forward?

Fundraising and Revenue
- How can Phi Delta Theta help cultivate major gifts that strengthen the financial foundation of the fraternity?

What alternative sources of revenue besides member dues and fund-raising dollars can help Phi Delta Theta continue to grow and be a leader among all Greek-letter organizations?

Conclusion

Phi Delta Theta is proof that a fraternity with alcohol-free housing can not only survive on today's college campuses, but also thrive. The fraternity has experienced positive results regarding the seven key reasons for implementing an alcohol-free housing policy and expects such results to improve annually. Phi Delta Theta still faces important issues associated with alcohol-free housing, but the fraternity responds swiftly to take corrective measures such as was done in 2017 after Louisiana State University prospective member Max Gruver perished. We believe all issues can be resolved with time and the commitment of the fraternity's alumni and student leaders. While Phi Delta Theta is planning for what is to come in the years ahead, members, young and old alike, should be proud of the progress that has been made to date.

EDWARD G. WHIPPLE is Vice President for Campus Life at Willamette University. He holds a doctorate from Oregon State University and is a member of the Phi Delta Theta General Counsel.

ROBERT A. BIGGS is Executive Vice President and CEO of Phi Delta Theta Fraternity and President of the Phi Delta Theta Foundation.

16 A Realistic Approach to Public Relations for Fraternities in Crisis

Ray Begovich

YOUR DAY IS busy, as usual, but humming along smoothly in your national fraternity headquarters office, or in your student affairs office, or in your oak-paneled college president's office.

Then you get the news—maybe by phone, by text, by email, or by someone rushing breathlessly into your workspace. Or maybe the first time you hear the news is from, well, the news—a reporter calling for comment on the incident that just happened.

Even worse, you don't get the news where you work. You're awakened in the middle of the night at home to be informed of a problem at the *Pick Your Greek Letters* fraternity house.

And, as you well know, such problems can escalate to the deadly serious: pledge Scott Krueger taken off life support at MIT; pledge Tucker Hipps at Clemson, allegedly abandoned by brothers and dead beneath a bridge; Tim Piazza at Penn State, close to death and no brother calling 911, and a Baruch College pledge beaten to death by his supposed chapter friends. You've read the damning article by Caitlin Flanagan in the *Atlantic*. Flanagan wrote this: "Clearly, the contemporary fraternity world is beset by a series of deep problems, which its leadership is scrambling to address, often with mixed results. No sooner has a new "Men of Principle" (Beta Theta Pi) or "True Gentlemen" (Sigma Alpha Epsilon) campaign been rolled out—with attendant workshops, measurable goals, initiatives, and mission statements—than reports of a lurid disaster in some prominent or far-flung chapter undermine the whole thing."[1]

Suddenly you're dealing not only with the problem itself, whatever it may be, but also with communications involving a dizzying array of "publics"—parents, students, members of the fraternity, members of other Greek organizations, faculty, staff, alumni, neighbors, community leaders, advocacy groups, journalists, social media, politicians, government agencies, coroners, lawyers, and police officers. Ouch.

All at once you've dropped all appointments in your crowded schedule to tackle a public relations nightmare. You've seen it again and again at other institutions. You know that many problem situations caused by others put you, the professional, under the microscope by clumsy, inappropriate, delayed, or even nonexistent communications.

Public relations efforts must be strategic and sustained at all times. Crisis upon crisis must be fairly, ethically, and quickly managed.

What follows are basic communications tips for those whose work involves Greeks. Please note that the basics discussed in this section are broad management considerations and reminders, and are not intended to be steps in a how-to manual for a campus-chapter public relations chairperson. Plenty of such manuals exist for chapters across the country.

Following the basics is commentary intended to go a bit beyond PR tips—as important as they are—and provide realistic context for how public relations may best be perceived in relation to the extremely serious problems caused by some fraternity members, even as the majority perform philanthropic works, party responsibly, respect their houses, and graduate to take on responsible roles as politicians, attorneys, educators, and, yes, public relations experts.

PR Basics

As you read, rate the tips below in the context of your personal opinions and your organization's realities using the following categories:

- Got it, we already do that.
- Good idea, we need to work toward that.
- I agree, but I don't see it really happening here.
- No thanks, not helpful, not practical.

Develop a Strategic Communications Plan

A strategic communications plan is not merely a list of ideas. A strategic plan identifies target audiences and desired outcomes. Then it specifies both the broad-based strategies and detailed tactics to be used in striving to achieve the outcomes. There are, essentially, two types of strategic communications plans: one type is for long-term reputation management and another is for short-term, issue-specific campaigns. Reputation management refers to the day-to-day strategically smart communications conducted in sync with wider organizational goals. A campaign, however, has specific start and end dates, and focuses on an issue, policy, development, or change that must be communicated effectively. For both situations, it's crucial to stick with the plan to see it all the way through— organizations far too often ignore the plan once it's approved.

Develop a Crisis Communications Plan

Excellent crisis communication tips are a dime a dozen—make that a dime a million—on the internet. They're easy to find and easy to study. However, fraternities and organizations related to them need their own crisis communications plans because, especially when it comes to fraternities, the cliché about a crisis is true: "It's not a matter of *if*, but *when*." You'll want a specific crisis communications plan that is customized to your organization, to your specific area of oversight. If you're in a Greek organization, invest in the development of a professional crisis communications plan tailored to you. If you're in college or university student affairs, work with your institution's communications office in creating a specific fraternity/sorority crisis communications plan, or, at the very least, try to be included in your institution's overall plan. Hint: Crisis communications plans must be practiced using real-world, potential scenarios at least annually.

Be Honest, Clear, and Quick when Working with Journalists

Forget spin. Tell the truth, tell it well, and tell it in time to meet news deadlines. A great deal of truth can be told without violating student privacy or organizational confidentiality. Remember that a negative news story about a fraternity is not the problem. The real problem is the despicable, destructive, dangerous, and even deadly behavior in which some fraternity members engage. Don't think of reporters as automatic enemies; think of journalists as being among the heroes of our society, deserving of respect and admiration. Yes, you will be driven batty at times by the tone, structure, or focus of news stories. Accept the reality that you won't have much influence on those elements; however, you can and should request that factual inaccuracies be corrected.

Treat Student Journalists as You Would Treat the Pros

Far too often campus journalists are viewed as a second-class tier of reporters, not as important as the local, statewide, regional, or national reporters who may be covering a story related to your fraternity. A crucial PR best-practice idea is to treat that inquiry from the campus news reporter with the same responsiveness and seriousness you would treat an inquiry from the *New York Times*. A national or regional journalist assigned to cover a fraternity incident on a particular campus may well scan student and local news coverage as part of preliminary research. The student article may appear high up in a Google search. And remember, some day that student reporter may indeed be working for the *New York Times*. Respect and fully support a free, vibrant, and engaged student news media.

Use Your Own Communications Tools, Especially People

Invest in the people and resources needed to develop and maintain a professional communications operation as a key element of organizational management. Make sure that your PR personnel—be it a team of communicators or a sole staff member—is "at the table" when key organizational issues are discussed. That way, you can not only use them as sounding boards for how decisions will play out in public, but also as resources who can infuse elements of ethical, open communications into organizational policy. Provide and use technologically up-to-date resources to communicate with journalists and directly to target audiences. If you have bad news to deliver about fraternity activities, deliver it using your own communications tools—social media, website, direct communications (speeches, mailings, in-house publications), and media relations.

Don't Lawyer-Up Your Communications Language

Receiving and heeding counsel from attorneys is crucial. However, when working with attorneys to prepare written communications—statements, news releases, etc.—fight to keep the language clear, simple, and understandable for all audiences. Avoid legalese. Also, there may be good reasons, especially in a crisis, why your attorney should speak publicly for you, for example, to comply with court orders to ensure a fair trial. However, remember that, in general, when the public sees your lawyer talking, the assumption is that you're guilty, that you're hiding something, that you're sleazy, slimy, and scared. When possible, and especially in a crisis, the top executive should be the public face of the organization.

Focus, Focus, Focus on Internal Communications

"Internal" refers to the communications you do with insiders of your organization as opposed to communicating with external audiences. Help your fraternity members, employees, and colleagues be good ambassadors for your organization. They can only be good ambassadors in their informal communications with family, friends, and acquaintances if they are well informed. Invest the time and dollars needed for the people and tools needed to communicate well and consistently with internal audiences. And don't be afraid of hammering home the same messages over and over again through various internal communications media—repetition is crucial to learning. Hint: Always assume that your internal communications may become external communications; so work to ensure that your internal news and training messages would do you proud if they appeared on the front page of *USA Today*.

Get Media-Trained

Fraternity or college/university officials who may possibly find themselves, either proactively or reactively, being interviewed by a journalist should first have been "media-trained." That means using your communications professionals on staff or an outside consultant to provide training that not only helps interviewees deliver their points as effectively as possible, but also provides insights into how journalists work and the importance of what journalists do. Don't try to manipulate reporters (it will backfire), but do get trained on how to best help journalists tell accurate stories in accurate contexts, always with the understanding that the journalist is in control of the story. Help the journalist think of you as a good, accurate, open, responsive, and trustworthy source.

A New Approach

A common concern for professionals whose work, in part or in full, involves college fraternities are the negative news stories and social-media commentary generated when things go bad—when all the high-minded mission statements, noble philanthropic endeavors, and valuable leadership experiences crumble into insignificance when frat guys behave badly.

"Can't we," many who work with or care about fraternities lament, "fix our PR problem?" The short answer is no, they can't.

That's because fraternities don't have a PR problem. They have deeply rooted cultural and operational problems that inevitably grow into public relations nightmares that increasingly dominate the images and impressions society has of social fraternities on college campuses. Those PR nightmares keep recurring despite consistent efforts to communicate all the legitimate good that fraternities do for their members, their colleges, and their communities.

So, fraternities don't really have PR problems. The real problems are the all-too-frequent incidents of sexual assault, sexual harassment, hazing, racism, binge drinking, alcohol poisoning, property destruction, loutish behavior, injuries, and deaths. PR is a wisp of nothingness compared to such overwhelmingly serious real issues.

An old adage still tossed around these days by communications professionals is that if your factory makes bad widgets, no amount of PR can save you. Obviously that's hyperbole; we all know businesses doing well whose products or services are below par. Yet, that old saw remains useful. It helps drive home a point young PR professionals learn early in their careers—that serious, strategic communications efforts (PR, for short) often drive positive changes in organizational culture and operations. Or, at least ideally, the PR would be more effective if the rest of the organization could keep pace with it, if management allowed the PR function to not only communicate policies, activities, and accomplishments, but to also become the conscience of the organization and thus help solve serious (granted, seemingly insurmountable) recurring problems.

However, traditions die hard . . . very hard. "The way we've always done it" becomes "the way we're always going to do it." But a more positive public image of fraternities will never come about by simply continuing to hammer home messages of philanthropy, leadership, and networking. A better public image will only come when fraternities use PR to help stop the totally unacceptable fraternity actions and attitudes.

Also, those who want to improve the behavior of fraternity members must understand that they face an uphill battle against deeply ingrained and constantly repeated pop culture images of what fraternities are and mean. Nevertheless, the communications battle must be waged—not for the preservation of fraternities, but out of simple human compassion, with the outcome of preventing anyone else from becoming a victim of harmful behavior in a setting related to higher education.

It's time to use every tool of public relations, not superficially to try to improve the public image of fraternities, but to drive meaningful and permanent internal changes to culture and operations, to change the very mind-sets about what it means to participate in fraternity activities. To do so will require investments in strategic communications campaigns—nationally, on campuses, from fraternity headquarters, and even within individual houses—aimed at internal fraternity audiences, with the desired outcome being a dramatic reduction in the number of dangerous incidents happening in fraternity settings. If PR can be used to bring about important cultural, operational, and mind-set changes within the fraternity universe, then external image problems will improve, and, more important, lives will be saved.

RAY BEGOVICH teaches as a Pulliam School of Journalism faculty member at Franklin College.

17   A Sorority Hazing Hero Incurs the Wrath of Alums

Sarah Wild

It was my first time on TV. I think most people would feel pretty nervous. You know, being in front of the camera where hundreds, maybe even thousands, of people will see you. Will you stutter? Are you wearing the right shirt? What if you freeze up and forget what you're talking about? Luckily, this wasn't like me. Being a singer since the age of eight, I didn't really experience "stage fright," especially if I only had to *talk* in front of an audience. There was no harmony, no right tune I needed to sing. All I had to do was tell my story. Sure, it felt a little weird; who would have thought? My life is news!

The story was for a local news station in the city of Plattsburgh, New York, where I was wrapping up my final semester of graduate school. Graduation was only a few days away, and I was being interviewed about my sorority and an award I had received about six months earlier: the Hank Nuwer Anti-Hazing Hero Award sponsored and voted upon by the board of HazingPrevention.Org. When you tell someone that you're going to be interviewed on TV about hazing you experienced, most people are pretty intrigued. Because of mainstream media, many individuals immediately expect some horrific, brutal, near-death story, but not all hazing experiences look like that. My story didn't look like that. It's not a one-size-fits-all ordeal.

The news interview lasted a matter of minutes. I briefly explained some of the hazing that took place while I was joining my chapter in the fall of 2009, sharing that most of what we experienced was psychological hazing. Wrapping up the interview, I was also cognizant of articulating that after two years, my chapter had moved away from those detrimental behaviors. After all, who wants to be the girl who goes on TV to say your sorority sucks. My sorority didn't suck. My sisters didn't suck. Hazing sucked, and that was that. A couple quick questions, and it was over before I knew it. A few short days later, I sat attentively, staring at the TV screen. Two minutes and fifty-two seconds later, the story concluded. I called my mom, feeling proud.

I hadn't always been a fan of sororities. Freshman year I actually made fun of the other women around me joining these organizations. I joked with my roommate about how idiotic they were. "If you're going to join a sorority, you might as well actually try to join a *good* one," I'd say, as I noticed some of my friends heading off to recruitment events for the "pretty" sorority. At the time, my depiction of a "good" sorority was one where the members excelled academically, philanthropically, socially—women that were exceptional leaders on campus. As a newer student, I wasn't sure if that type of sorority actually even existed. I mean, sure, some sorority women helped me carry my things into my dorm on move-in day, but does that make them good people? A year later, I surprised even myself when I called my mom to tell her the news: I was jumping on the sorority bandwagon. Five years later, and I can still remember her exact response: *"Are you sure you want to do this?"*

Thinking back, I don't recall feeling taken aback by my mom's comment. It showed that she trusted my judgment (as she usually did), but she also seemed to have hesitations about what I might be exposed to through this sorority experience. Most freshman students coming to college have heard, at one point or another, the stereotypical stories about the frat boys and sorority girls: the drinking, the hazing, and the common sexual-themed partying. It continues to be what consumes the media today, even if fraternities and sororities have tried to move away from that culture, once so popular in the '70s and '80s. As an eighteen-year-old, I'll admit, I was a little worried too, but after attending a few recruitment events with Delta Phi Epsilon sorority, the sisters told everyone that there was no hazing. It was against rules. It was against their values. *Great!* I thought. *No more worries there!*

That was . . . until the first time it happened.

Only a week into my new member education process, which my sisters commonly referred to as "pledging," the hazing began. My experience was entirely psychological hazing, and I remember being very surprised the first time it happened. *Why are they being so mean to us?* I thought. A few weeks in to the pledging process, I can remember walking down the steps into the dark sorority house basement thinking, *why am I doing this?*

It was frustrating. As new members, we were made to feel that we were not good enough, that we were "less than." We had to prove ourselves to be a part of the sisterhood, a part of this continued tradition. It was not an experience I would wish on anyone. It was not sisterhood.

When I describe my experience as a sorority woman now, I commonly will share that it was the best thing I did for myself in college, but it was also the most challenging. I met some incredible individuals and gained leadership experience beyond my years, but it was not easy, by any means. Barely six months after my initiation into the organization, I became president of my chapter, something very uncommon for someone so fairly new. At the time, I envisioned the challenge to be easier than it actually turned out to be. I thought: *No big deal. I'll just become president, fix everything, and be on my way!* I'd always been brave and fairly confident as a young woman, so I pushed full steam ahead.

I did everything I could to remove the hazing behaviors that were taking place within my organization. Even with the amazing support from my on-campus fraternity/sorority advisor and continued guidance from the sorority's International Headquarters professional staff, I soon realized that eradicating the behaviors engrained in my chapter was a monstrous task to take on. But if I wasn't going to try and stop it from happening, who would? And so I did.

On Saturday, May 11, 2013, I graduated with my master's degree in student affairs counseling. I walked at graduation, packed up my apartment, and made the four-hour trip back to my hometown. Greeted by four loving dogs (my mom clearly experienced empty-nest syndrome), I raced up the stairs and plopped down on my bed, ready to relax, when I received a strange text message from one of my sisters: "I can't believe [deleted name] would say those things about you."

My heart dropped to the pit of my stomach. *Huh?* I thought, frantically responding, "What are you talking about?"

She told me to open my laptop and read the posts on my chapter's alumnae Facebook page. *Great*, I thought. *I literally* just *got home. What could have happened in only four hours?*

I flipped open my computer, and clicked open the page. It began: "After watching this news clip about my beloved Delta Phi Epsilon, I have a few questions: 1. Did the women in the pictures found in this clip give their permission to be put on the news?"

Something is wrong here, I thought. The tone, the snide questions, the language. Her "beloved?" I rolled my eyes. This was just one more alumna, like many, that hadn't done much of anything to support the chapter or the greater organization since she graduated. As I continued to read, I felt a pang of nervousness. I *hadn't* gotten permission from my sisters to include their photos in the news interview. The reporter asked me very shortly before the interview to gather photos of my sorority experience, so I chose ones with the people I cared about most, not actually noticing that some of the photos shared, I would later learn, weren't so flattering, and maybe not the best choice. *Shoot*, I thought.

The post went on: "2. I congratulate Sarah on succeeding with antihazing efforts and feel she has made a name for herself that will eventually lead to a wonderful position with student life at a university. However, would she still have the same recognition without including the details of her pledging experience?"

What was interesting to me about this statement was this: I barely shared *any* details of the hazing that I experienced in my news interview. I hardly even touched the surface of what we all experienced, let alone any of the anxiety, fear, and frustration all of us as new members felt during our pledging process. This alumna also seemed to imply that I was telling my story to capitalize on my own accomplishment, clearly only focused on the advancement of myself. On the advancement of *myself.* "She has made a name for herself . . ." Yes, I thought it would be *fun* to try and convince sixty-five women to stop hazing their new members. I thought it would be *enjoyable* to tear apart twenty-plus years of sorority "traditions" so that two-thirds of my sisterhood could actively hate me. It truly was a *pleasure* to take on such an easy task, and it's clear I was doing it to receive a good pat on the back. I felt like I could breathe fire.

I was angry, very angry. I didn't *ask* to receive this award. I didn't set up the news interview, and I certainly wasn't sharing my story to "make a name for myself." I clenched my teeth hard. *The only reason this story even exists is because you helped continue this hazing,* I thought to myself.

Looking back, I think I was so infuriated by this question posed for all of the internet to see because this woman was manipulatively fooling readers into believing that she was proud of my accomplishments. She then carefully invites the rest of her alumna crew to respond, invoking their thoughts and reactions: "3. If you were an alumna of this sorority, how would you feel? How would you feel if you were one of the girls in the pictures?"

Let me tell you, it worked. The comments flooded in. Here are a few:

> "I wouldn't trade my pledging experience for anything and gained amazing friends from it. I learned a lot about myself and what I was capable of achieving. Call it hazing . . . I call it a learning experience!"
>
> "Why would you drag your sorority through the mud after you leave?"
>
> "We were the elite, where a bid was earned, not given."
>
> "Depledges are the worst. Ever. Well, I can think of something worse then quitting the sorority you pledge to."
>
> "I just watched this video with another sister and we both agree we are disgusted with how you portrayed our sorority."

These were my *sisters,* those who were grown adults . . . parents . . . teachers . . . many of which I didn't know and had never met. Ripping me to shreds on the internet. You would have thought that I just set the sorority house on fire. How *dare* I expose the sorority's secrets? Our traditions? Hours passed and comments continued to flow in. No longer were these comments about the interview, or the award, or even about the chapter, but it was my character that came into question. *My* character.

I did my best to respond to some of the posts as calmly as I could, working to share my perspective and my rationale for the interview. I spent hours carefully crafting my responses to come across as polite and collected, and to articulate my thoughts so that my sisters would understand why the behaviors were so detrimental, and why I, and others, wanted these behaviors to end.

It was no use. The comments continued:

"Congratulations on making quite the change, spilling our secrets, and exposing photos of your 'sisters.' I guarantee that besides myself, there's plenty of Deephers that wouldn't trade our 'dazed and confused' era for the new 'come one, come all' era."

"If you didn't like it, then you should have quit. How dare you discuss the sorority on the news like that. Boohoo. You didn't have to join or stay or do anything you didn't want to do. The doors aren't boarded up. Start your own sorority; don't bash mine."

"I sure hope you have hung up your letters because a real Deepher would never do that and anyone who does, doesn't belong in letters."

I cried that night, my first night home from college. I cried the next day too. Not quite the way I had imagined celebrating my completion of graduate school, but this type of backlash from alumnae of a fraternity/sorority aren't out of the ordinary. My alumnae viewed my actions as betrayal, and there were no words that I could say that would change their minds. I was verbally beaten down for trying to do good, for trying to prevent other future new members from feeling like they weren't good enough. But it didn't matter. I had shared the sorority's secrets.

It's been five years since I faced the backlash from many of my sorority sisters, when I shared with them that we would no longer be participating in hazing behaviors. It's been three years since the alumnae from my chapter chewed me up and spit me out on the internet. But the sadness and feelings associated with the challenging times still remain present in my mind. Many nights I lie awake wondering how I could have done things differently, better. I play everything over in my head again and again.

Thinking back, I'm still proud of my accomplishments, and I'm proud of the progress my sisters have made in moving away from the hazing culture that once engulfed our sisterhood. I know I did the right thing—whether some of my sisters and alumnae think so or not. Unfortunately, sometimes, when you stand up for what you believe in, you may end up feeling like you are standing alone.

SARAH WILD is a certified counselor based in North Carolina with a professional background in fraternity/sorority advising and career counseling.

18 How Reforms and Reformers Played a Role in Changing a Hazing Culture

Allison Swick-Duttine

In OCTOBER 1998 I began my professional career working with fraternities and sororities at the State University of New York College at Plattsburgh where hazing was rooted in the institution's culture. Nothing I learned in graduate school student-affairs counseling prepared me for the impact that hazing has on its victims and the campus culture.

My experience as an undergraduate sorority member at Marshall University was positive and hazing-free. I had heard hazing horror stories but had dismissed them as exaggerations or isolated episodes. Plattsburgh had started some intensive work on changing the hazing culture as the result of a Greek Task Force in 1991, but the work had primarily been focused on policy development and enforcement. These important first steps in a long-term plan had the unintended outcome of driving the hazing behaviors underground.

The hazing that occurred at SUNY Plattsburgh was highly secretive. The identities of new members, as well as the new member educators, were guarded. The length of the new member process was undisclosed. Above all, an unwritten agreement by fraternity and sorority members promised revenge, even wrath, to those who spoke out against the abusive and humiliating treatment that a newcomer endured to join some organizations.

With retaliation a certainty, the campus culture simply was not conducive to reporting hazing abuses. If new members reached out for help, I had to meet them where they wouldn't be seen meeting me. Each story was the same. They wanted to stop hazing, but they didn't want anyone to know that they had reported it. They feared for their safety and worried about being socially ostracized. Sometimes they depledged and were harassed by the members of their new-member group (and often by other fraternity/sorority members as well) to the point that transferring was their only option. Other times the reported Greek chapters ran initiation immediately, and the former victims never again spoke of their concerns.

Over the next several years, Plattsburgh developed multiple strategies to prevent and intervene in hazing. These included:

- Educational initiatives included a focus on replacing hazing practices with activities and traditions that focused on positive member and group development.
- An amnesty period was created to allow groups to ask for help from the college in overhauling their new-member processes. After the amnesty period, students were instructed that the penalties would increase for hazing violations and could include charges against individuals, as well as the group.
- Desirable behavior was reinforced through recognition programs, peer-led education, and special privileges for groups who disclosed their new-member processes to potential members before asking them to join.
- The college's conduct philosophy morphed from being strictly punitive in nature (e.g., being suspended without privileges for a year) to assigning developmental sanctions to help the group change the behavior.
- A lot of work was done through the fraternity/sorority governance councils to instill a sense of community standards and accountability. It became the norm for groups to hold one another accountable to mutually agreed upon standards.
- The onus of hazing prevention education was shifted partially to student fraternity/sorority members so that they were able to craft the messages, share their successes, and define their systems of standards and accountability.
- New fraternities/sororities with members who were vocally antihazing were added to the community.

The needle started to move slightly. It became no longer taboo among students to discuss new-member education processes or hazing. Many groups began to ask for help to overhaul their new-member programs. More groups became vocal about their commitment to an antihazing education process. All of these were positive signs that the community was moving in the right direction—and then a hazing death occurred within a chapter best described as a renegade chapter. As a member of Phi Epsilon Chi would later admit, the only rule was there were no rules.

In 2003, freshman Walter Dean Jennings III decided to join this unrecognized former local fraternity despite the fact that pledging it was against college policy. He died from hyponatremia (water intoxication via depleted sodium levels) the night before he was to be initiated into the underground group. I am often asked if the changes in the hazing culture at SUNY Plattsburgh began as a result of this student's death. The answer is no. While this tragedy likely accelerated our results, the college and its fraternity/sorority community had already laid the foundation that helped make hazing an undesirable behavior. The most apparent outcome was that our students saw firsthand that something bad really could, and did, happen as a result of hazing.

In the ensuing years, the frequency and severity of hazing decreased in most Plattsburgh groups. Whereas the previous generation's experience consisted of hazing throughout the entire new member process, hazing began to be reserved for "special occasions" (e.g., big/little night, initiation, and so on). Activities such as drop-offs, kidnapping, forced consumption of alcohol, and sleep deprivation became less common. Lineups, verbal harassment, and activities intended to embarrass new members were still common. Our students knew that the college did not tolerate hazing. It was not endorsed as part of the fraternity/sorority experience as it once was. We had the legend of a death to illustrate the danger. But it was still there.

I share the evolution of SUNY Plattsburgh's hazing prevention efforts to illustrate my point that the culture needed to change in order for students to feel safer in asking for help. While there were many courageous individuals who helped change the hazing culture since the task force of 1991, it was not until twenty years later that students began stepping forward to completely reform their organizations. I will share the stories of two of these students, how they attempted to reform their organizations and how they responded to the backlash they experienced as a result.

Sarah's Story

I do not recall knowing Sarah very well before she turned to me to help her end hazing in her sorority. However, when she became frustrated that her sisters did not all respond positively to her ideas to change their new-member education program and started to experience verbal retaliation, she asked if I would meet with her. Sarah initially came to me because she didn't think she wanted to be president of her chapter any longer. As we discussed why she was so disheartened, I learned that hazing was at the root of her dissatisfaction.

I worked with Sarah to help reinstill her confidence that she had the talents to lead her sorority through this transition. We explored her options and decided to enlist the assistance of the national organization and of those members who agreed that hazing needed to stop. We scheduled a meeting between the members who supported the changes, a representative of the national organization, and myself to talk through what was happening in the organization, why it was happening, and what their plan would be to create the desired changes and to get buy-in from other members.

Although several members who did not necessarily support the elimination of hazing attended the meeting, they remained respectful and listened to different perspectives while sharing their concerns. Other members expressed their outrage through personal attacks on Sarah.

Sarah received text and Facebook messages from sisters who told her that she was destroying the sisterhood. Some members completely stopped talking to her and many will not speak to her now, even five years later. The most vicious verbal attacks came from some senior members during their senior ritual that attacked Sarah's character in front of the entire chapter. Not a single person in the room said a thing to stop them.

Ultimately, Sarah and her sisters were successful in removing the degrading and unnecessary activities from their new-member education program and replacing them with positive traditions. As a result, Sarah received the Hank Nuwer Anti-Hazing Hero Award from HazingPrevention.Org. Unfortunately, this wasn't the happy ending that Sarah had envisioned. When the alumnae members found out about the award through a news story that was posted online, the backlash continued.

I recently asked Sarah, now a higher-education administrator herself, why she persisted in trying to create change in her sorority when she faced so much resistance and retaliation. "I didn't want any future members to join and have a negative experience like I did," she said. "My sister was about to enter college and I didn't want her to experience that if she chose to join. I never want anyone to feel less than [good]. Once you know something is wrong, you know it is wrong and you have to do something about it."

On the other hand, Sarah did receive a lot of encouragement as she tried to create change. She recalls that members of other fraternities and sororities were particularly encouraging to her and gave her the confidence to continue the fight. She also says that she received texts and Facebook messages from time to time from women in her sorority who were too afraid to speak up but thanked her for everything she did to change the organization for the better.

Tyler's Story

Even before Tyler joined a local fraternity at SUNY Plattsburgh, his perception was that hazing was part of the pledging experience, and so he wasn't surprised when it began. Although he willingly participated, he recalls feeling that it was meaningless and "kind of evil." When the pledge process was over, Tyler was not one of the newly initiated members who looked forward to hazing the next group. It just didn't make sense to him, he says. "I wasn't really against hazing, I was just kind of indifferent."

Tyler began to become engaged in the larger fraternity/sorority community, attending leadership trainings and participating in conversations with his peers from other organizations about the purpose of fraternal organizations. "I started to realize that my fraternity wasn't a values-based organization," he said. Still, he wasn't bothered much by that realization because he had joined his fraternity because he was attracted to the partying and drinking that was its primary focus. He began to view Greek life as a leadership opportunity that he could be involved in on campus while still using his fraternity as a social outlet.

The more that Tyler was challenged by his peers outside his fraternity and by college staff members on his behaviors that were incongruent with the purpose of fraternity, the more he started to come to the realization that he was being a bystander. "What my group was doing wasn't victimless," he says. "It was having an impact on the rest of the fraternal community."

Tyler felt that he needed to choose a side, and he came to me for help. Tyler disclosed everything that happened in his fraternity's new-member process, much of which was physical and psychologically brutal. Because I perceived that student safety was a concern, I told Tyler that we needed to involve university police in this conversation. We also began a conversation about options for a long-term strategy to change what was occurring in his fraternity. Tyler got to work having conversations with other members in the fraternity that were opposed to hazing. That is when the backlash began.

"Hazing was something my fraternity really valued and was proud of—they even kept detailed records of hazing activities," he said. "Outdoing the last generation's hazing was the legacy you wanted to leave in the fraternity."

There was also strong alumni support of hazing. When alums heard that there was a possible mutiny, they tried to intimidate Tyler and to remind him of his place.

Members who were intoxicated began to get into physical altercations with Tyler. His room in the fraternity house was trashed and his possessions were broken or stolen. Verbal assaults occurred frequently. Tyler also experienced harassment from people in other organizations who were proponents of hazing.

These interventions did not deter Tyler, and he continued conversations with some of his brothers. He was able to get some of them to acknowledge the need for change, but they weren't as vocal, likely because they began to see the backlash and did not think that stopping hazing was worth the personal consequences.

"My short-term goal was to stop the hazing," said Tyler. "The long-term goal was to recruit like-minds and to get in at least two pledge classes that hadn't been hazed." This plan started to work but the hiccup was that many people in the fraternity did not graduate on time and were in the chapter for five, six, or more years. Couple this with the fact alumni were highly involved in chapter decision-making, and hazing proved very difficult to eradicate.

Ultimately Tyler was able to get the hazing to stop, but he believes that was partially because the fraternity knew they were under supervision by the college. They did not want to lose their recognition.

"The alumni used the lack of hazing as a rationale for why newer members were not living up to their responsibilities and then the newer members began to wish that they had been hazed so they would be like everyone else," Tyler said. "Once that was ingrained into their minds, they weren't necessarily opposed to hazing future groups of new members."

All through this experience, Tyler says that he was stressed, depressed, and constantly questioned if he was doing the right thing. When I asked Tyler recently why he persisted, he said, "I really bought into the fact that hazing was detrimental to my organization and that it was wrong in general. I felt that I had come so far and there was no going back—I was committed."

Tyler also was the recipient of a Hank Nuwer Anti-Hazing Hero Award from HazingPrevention.Org. He was frequently asked to share his story by the media and was interviewed on NPR's *All Things Considered*.

After Tyler left SUNY Plattsburgh, a new member heard the NPR interview in a class and brought it to the attention of the alumni. Tyler was immediately blocked from the fraternity's Facebook group and received a text message from an alum saying that he was blackballed and was not to contact any members or attend any fraternity functions.

"This was upsetting to me because after all the time and energy I had invested into the fraternity, being blackballed was perceived to be my legacy," he said.

Tyler says to this day, more than five years later, his attempt to reform the hazing culture in his fraternity and the retaliation he received as a result still have an effect on him. He only talks to a few fraternity brothers. "I can't just meet up with one of them without checking to see if another brother is going to be there so that I can avoid an altercation," he said. "At the very least, the situation would be unpleasant."

Other Stories of Retaliation

In preparing to write this essay, I spoke with several Greek-life professionals and alumni to hear their experiences with hazing reformers. Much of what I heard about the retaliation was reminiscent of the experiences my former students detailed earlier: verbal abuse, cyber-harassment, physical altercations, threats to personal safety, acts of intimidation, destruction of personal property, and social ostracizing.

All of this stress comes at a cost for many hazing reformers. Many report that their academic work suffered, their physical and mental health was negatively affected, and their social standing in the campus community lessened. So how do university and national headquarters staff members support these reformers in their efforts to eliminate hazing? The colleagues I spoke with identified the following concepts as most effective:

- As student development practitioners, we know that not all students are coming from the same place of maturity. Work with ten hazing reformers and you are likely to experience as many different paths to the same desired outcome. Helping student reformers shape a path that works for them requires knowledge of student development theories and an understanding of how to support growth in various domains: cognitive, social, physical, and emotional.[1]

- Student-affairs practitioners frequently search for best practices from other institutions. While this may prove helpful in understanding the complexity of hazing reform, it is important to note that institutional culture may play a significant role in determining how members perceive and respond to hazing.[2] Organizational culture may also play a critical part in if and how students attempt to reform hazing from within. In short, a successful method at one institution may not lead to the positive results at another.

Examples of a few variables that may affect the outcomes of hazing reform are the following:

- The institution's expectations of the role of the fraternity/sorority professional: Is the role of the advisor to be a disciplinarian or a student-development coach? Are these professionals looked at as culture change experts or are they simply policy and compliance enforcers? Are professionals required to report hazing disclosed by members of the perpetrating group to student conduct officials for adjudication, or are they permitted the flexibility to work with those students to affect change from within the organization?
- The experience level of those fraternity/sorority professionals: Is the Greek-life advisor position an entry-level position or does the institution require significant previous experience? Does the institution provide the professional development opportunities for professionals to become prevention strategists?
- The way the institution handles hazing investigation and adjudication: Are victims of hazing protected as well as the victims who experience other forms of violence on campus may be? Are group sanctions punitive in nature (e.g., removing privileges) or are they designed to help individuals and groups transform? Are individuals held responsible for hazing or are just groups held responsible?
- The perceived hazing norms on a specific campus: In the National Study of Student Hazing, Elizabeth Allan and Mary Madden found that 69 percent of students said they were aware of hazing behaviors occurring on their campus. These perceived norms may influence the extent to which students choose to participate in and/or tolerate hazing.[3]

A widely publicized hazing-prevention strategy that includes students in the development of solutions may give students wishing to reform hazing the incentive to take action. Too often our hazing strategies are focused on one-time educational presentations or enforcing compliance with state, organizational, and institutional policies. Students often hear once or twice a year the message that "hazing is not tolerated." However, research has suggested that this is not the most effective message in and of itself.

The most effective violence prevention programs come from systematic planning efforts that involve multiple partners working together. Linda Langford recommends using multiple, coordinated and sustained strategies to prevent hazing and ensure that programs, policies, and services are coordinated and synergistic.[4]

Allan and Madden recommend designing comprehensive prevention efforts that focus on helping students develop an understanding of power dynamics so that they can identify hazing, understand the role coercion and Groupthink can play, recognize the potential for harm, generate strategies for building the group that do not involve hazing, align group behavior with purpose and values, develop skills to handle resistance to change, and develop critical-thinking skills needed to make ethical judgments in the face of moral dilemma.[5]

It is critical that students be involved in the development and implementation of these strategies. While the ideal situation would be that students wishing to reform hazing would ask for help from a fraternity/sorority professional, 95 percent of students that participated in the aforementioned National Study of Student Hazing said they did not report their hazing experiences to campus officials. They most frequently talked about their hazing experiences with friends, another group member, or family. This illustrates the importance of creating opportunities for like-minded people to have a safe space to share their experiences and to test possible solutions.

In talking to Sarah about her story, shared previously, she mentioned that being connected to conversations with other students who were attempting to eliminate hazing as critical to developing her confidence. She specifically referenced private lunchtime meetings that I arranged with her and members of other fraternities and sororities who were trying to stop hazing in their own organizations as helpful and appreciated. Other professionals told stories of students who felt validated and empowered when they were connected with others who held the same beliefs about hazing as they did. Many students first connect with like-minded individuals when they attended national leadership experiences, but it can be important for them to have similar experiences when they return to their own campus.

A similar theme that came up in my conversations with other professionals was what fraternity/sorority professionals could do to provide an environment that felt safe for students to disclose their experiences and ask for help. Part of the sense of safety may come from feeling that they can trust the advisor to help them come to a solution without fear of others finding out. If an institution requires that all hazing reports are immediately investigated and adjudicated, the students may feel that they are giving up control of the strategy and outcomes. However, if the advisor is permitted to coach the student through some options, challenge them to identify and follow through on solutions of their choosing, and to provide them with supportive environments to assist in the reform, all colleagues that I spoke with felt that this would result in a larger number of students being willing to report and reform hazing.

I have worked at SUNY Plattsburgh for twenty years. I have learned that changing a hazing culture takes patience, persistence, and a lot of time; but more importantly, it takes the investment of students who step up to be the initiators of change. Through the efforts of students like Sarah and Tyler who were persistent in the face of retaliation and personal sacrifice, I have seen our campus culture shift from one where hazing was an expectation for joining a fraternal organization to one where hazing organizations are the outliers and are held accountable by a community of their peers.

ALLISON SWICK-DUTTINE is Director of Fraternity/Sorority Life at SUNY Plattsburgh. She was a founding board member and a past president of HazingPrevention.Org.

19 Hazing Hides in Plain Sight

An Open Letter to Hazers from a Nationally Known Speaker

David Westol

You'd think they—the hazers, of course—would have figured it out by now. That they would have done the math. Run the numbers. Used reductive and deductive reasoning. Maybe listened more than talked. Dialed up the 4-1-1 on this aspect of hazing.

The question? Why in the world would you let people—nonmembers, people outside of your team, sorority, fraternity, club, or organization—know that you are engaging in hazing?

I have been giving a presentation entitled "Forty Ways to Detect Hazing" for about ten years. And ironically, at least to me, this session generates more complaints and criticism from those who attend than other presentations that I make that involve much more direct attacks on hazing and hazers.

I often pose a line of questioning to undergraduates during the "Forty Ways" presentation along the lines of "Would you set up a booth on campus and sell beer? How about marijuana? Adderall? Would you walk up to a professor and strike her in the face on campus? Take a hammer and pound on a parked car in front of hundreds of your fellow students?"

Of course the responses are, "No way, dude. We'd be arrested . . . investigated . . . kicked out of school."

"Okay," I say, "then why would you commit a misdemeanor—not to mention a felony under certain circumstances and in a few states—by hazing your newest members in front of hundreds if not thousands of people?"

Silence is the default response.

Hazing . . . hiding in plain sight.

Members of hazing chapters, teams, and other organizations go to great lengths to emphasize secrecy, stealth, and silence—"Nobody says nothin'!" Just as they bend the truth in telling new members that "everyone has gone through this" (prove it, I say) or "this goes back to when we were founded" (prove it, I say).

Of course they can't prove it. But a passionate belief in hazing allows them to dismiss logic and fact as trivial challenges.

So with all that focus upon secrecy and stealth, why would a hazing organization put the hazing out there for all to see?

A psychologist or sociologist might answer that in terms of the need for hazers to be recognized, even if that recognition is negative in context. It is as though the hazers—those who are firmly committed to hazing—are not satisfied with hazing. They are compulsive about revealing it to others so that the reputation of the hazing organization (and, by the way, their individual reps) as "tough" or "demanding" is perpetuated and expanded.

Let's take a look at some examples.

* * *

I was at a campus in the Northeast recently. I met with the Interfraternity Council (IFC) officers for several hours one afternoon. Two of the IFC officers—from the same chapter—contributed little to the conversation. They had checked out even before I had arrived. I did learn that their chapter has twenty-three pledges . . . oops, new members (one corrected the other) and that they had "the best rush on campus . . . biggest pledge class on campus."

That night I'm watching the women and men enter the large and brightly lit room for my Greek Week presentation. A tall, thin man wearing glasses and a serious expression enters followed by twenty-three younger looking men. The tall man—I'm thinking a junior—positions himself about four rows of chairs from and facing the back of the room. He then begins snapping his fingers and pointing to indicate where the younger-looking men are to sit. The young men, like nine-year-olds who have been chastised by the vice principal, meekly take their seats. In contrast to hundreds of other students, they neither speak nor interact with each other or, heaven forbid, other students not in the chapter they hope to join. They sit facing forward in abject silence.

The tall man is the new-member educator. The twenty-three younger men are the pledges. From that chapter. Of course.

I look sideways at the campus professional. She winces and says, "I know."

And, by the way—those two guys on the IFC? They aren't there to lead. They are there as an early-alert alarm system. Anything that suggests that the chapter will be investigated would be discussed by the IFC or overheard in the fraternity or sorority advisor's office, right?

Hazing . . . hiding in plain sight.

* * *

About four years ago I was at a campus in the Midwest, attending a session for new Greek members. There are hundreds. Thirty-two young men from a large and well-known men's national fraternity enter in single file. They are dressed identically in blazers, khakis, white shirts, and identifiable ties. Each carries his pledge manual in his right hand and at an odd angle. The leader of the new members—I assume the president or pledge educator—waits until they are lined up with chairs and then, attempting to imitate someone from the military, says, "SEATS!" in a loud soprano voice. The thirty-two men sit in unison. They stare straight ahead.

I pound on pledge-class unity during my presentation. Is this how members act, dress, think, speak, conduct themselves . . . all in the same way? Of course not. Our organizations are premised upon individuals brought together by common beliefs and oaths. Our strength is in our diversity under our values and ideals. We are strong because we think differently from each other.

On the way out I walk behind two members of the blazer brigade. One turns to the other and said, "I'd like about five minutes with that guy!" I was about to step forward when the other new member said it for me. "What would you tell him?" And the first guy was silent.

The chapter was closed three years later. Hazing should be your first guess as to why.

* * *

An athletic team is sanctioned for hazing. How was it discovered? Easy. The team members who "coordinated" the activities sent the freshmen out on "quests" or "missions." The freshmen had to visit certain places, have their photos taken doing certain things, obtain certain items from women athletes . . . no, not their lacrosse sticks.

Of course this was at night. Of course they were working with a time limit. Of course some of the freshmen considered this a challenge—a test of their commitment—and took things too far. And, of course, they were reported. Welcome to probation. Plain sight, men.

* * *

A chapter in my own fraternity used the time-honored practice of requiring new members to carry things "at all times," including a twenty-five-pound dumbbell. A new member was awakened early one morning in February. Emergency at home . . . father . . . heart attack . . . guarded condition. Translation: Get home. Airline ticket is at the airport. Three members offer to drive him. But no one thinks to say, "Ditch the weight, dude."

The freshman tries to get through TSA with a dumbbell in his backpack. Uh, nope. When challenged, he says, "This is the weight of my fraternity! I must carry it at all times!" The TSA folks are unimpressed. The young man goes home. The dumbbell stays. An alert TSA agent calls the school. The dean calls me. I call the chapter president and say, "Welcome to probation . . . and do you understand, Mr. President, that there were four dumbbells in that car? One in the backpack and the three members whose clue bags held nothing but lint and mouse droppings." The president, to his credit, offered no defense.

* * *

Women skipping across campus holding hands. Women stepping off the sidewalk in deference to a member walking toward them. Greetings that are artificial and staged but only used by new members for current members. An older member walks up to a group seated in the student center, and a new member leaps to her feet to give up a chair. Yep. That isn't being polite. That's a requirement, Pledge.

* * *

I was at a premembership review meeting for a chapter of a men's national fraternity once. Members and others were filing into the living room of the chapter house. A consultant who had visited the chapter twice during the previous semester tapped me on the shoulder. "Watch the young guys to your left," he whispered.

I did. There was a grouping of couches in the center of the room, and there were spaces on the couches remaining for people to sit as meeting time approached. A young member stood up from the floor where he had been sitting and took a seat on a couch next to two older members. There was room for four, in my opinion. The older member to his left leaned over and whispered something to him. The young member got up, moved to his right, and perched on the armrest of the couch. The older member gestured with a hand. Nope. The young member returned to his seat on the floor.

I learned the next day that new members could not use the couches "at any time." Why? They hadn't earned the "right" to sit there.

* * *

Carrying weights in a backpack . . . all freshmen or new members carrying their backpacks in the same manner . . . mandating that new members wear an insignia "at all times"—all of this in plain sight. Because what idiot, other than a hazer, would demand that wearing a tiny bit of metal or plastic "at all times" would have significance when members don't wear their badges "at all times"?

In the days when pledge paddles were being used by many chapters it was easy to pick out the hazing programs. Pledges would enter with their paddles sticking out of their backpacks—like a convoy of submarines with wooden periscopes. Why do you have to have your paddle with you at all times? No one ever answered that question. Why don't members carry their paddles with them at all times? No one ever answered that question. What is accomplished by carrying a piece of wood around? Well, you understand. No . . . I do not, actually.

And listen hard for the word "encouraged," as in "members are *encouraged* to wear . . ." fill in the blank with an arbitrary item/ribbon/tag/color. Yeah. Right. *How's that fashion statement working out for you?*

Want to know which chapters are hazing in the fraternity and sorority community? Arrange for a speaker to talk about hazing. And watch where chapter members sit in a large room or auditorium. The hazing chapters will sit as far back as possible. Even if there is a large gap between themselves and the other chapters. They are compulsive about this. They don't want to be there, but they also want everyone else to know that they ain't buying what some dumb speaker is selling. So they sit as far away as possible. They will talk, text, and tweet. Audibly. Why? Because they want everyone to know that they haze and that they aren't listening.

Parents and others, ask this: "Does your chapter/club/team engage in hazing?"

Listen hard for the answer.

If the answer is *"Oh, our university has a policy against hazing"* or *"Oh, our national organization has a policy against hazing"* then that chapter, club, or team is hazing. The members are sending you a coded message. *Get your son or daughter out of there.* If you can't run, walk quickly. If they were truly hazing-free they'd tell you that in blunt terms. Instead, they—the hazers—are asking you to use deductive reasoning. If there's a policy in place, that means "er, ah, I suppose that there is enforcement," which means "er, ah, then we're OK! Right?" Right?

Nope. If someone is injured, then the hazers will say, "Well, there was a policy . . ."

* * *

An alumna advisor is returning to her car, which is parked along the proverbial Greek Row on a medium-size campus. It is 11:30 p.m. She is exhausted after helping her chapter with recruitment. It's a Monday night in the fall. Monday Night Football is playing loudly on TVs in chapter houses. As she walks past men's chapter houses she can hear yelling and cheering in sequence with game action.

And then she hears yelling of a different sort coming from the basement of one fraternity house as she walks by.

She describes the yelling as "mean-spirited . . . cruel . . . angry . . . profanities."

She whips out her microcassette recorder, tapes what she is hearing, and circles the chapter house while carefully staying off the property (she is an attorney and knows better). She hears nicknames of members. She observes what appear to be flashlight beams "dancing" on the wall of the room in the basement. She has the audio tape transcribed and forwarded to the chapter's national headquarters along with her detailed and helpful description.

The chapter president gets a phone call. After establishing that he has at least twenty minutes to speak, the topic is addressed. And, after attempting to play hide the ball with generalized noncommittal and nonspecific answers for a few minutes, the chapter president admits that a lineup was occurring.

You make it easy, pal. You make it easy for us. And thank goodness we have women and men who are willing to step forward and report what hazing violations they see in plain sight.

* * *

Members of an honorary society eagerly describe their "pledgeship" to a campus newspaper reporter at a prestigious institution located along the East coast. They want the reporter to know that they had to memorize everyone's birthdates, heights, and other critically important information so that when asked they could rattle off the "rundown" without a mistake or error. If they couldn't or didn't . . . gosh, they had to try it again.

* * *

Oh, and hazers, don't let me forget: Please keep taking the phones of new members. Parents will immediately begin calling the university or the national headquarters to ask, "How come I can't communicate with my child?" Dang good question. The hazers will say, "We're just trying to get them to concentrate!" Right. *Yep. Another cultlike chapter gets busted.*

* * *

Oh, and don't let me forget the chapter Facebook page! You know, the one that doesn't exist. Like your shadow officers. Keep putting up photos and comments about the new members. That makes for great evidence. And you millennials have added depth and breadth to the time-honored phrase that a picture is worth a thousand words.

* * *

Let's change, hazers. Stop requiring new members to use the back door—don't you think neighbors and others are checking that out? How about the community service projects where only freshmen from your organization or chapter show up? Oops. I forgot. The freshmen have to "prove" themselves and that means being demeaned.

Sometimes I feel compelled to ask, "If you're going to haze, why don't you keep it a deep, dark secret? Why do you advertise it? Why do you put it out there for all to see? Why do you publicize a practice that will eventually lead to an intervention . . . sanctions . . . suspension or revocation of the charter . . . civil and/or criminal litigation . . . or the loss of a season or a career?"

But I know the answers.

Logic and leadership are the last places a hazer wants to go. If logic played a role then hazing would vanish. If leadership were important, the hazers would lead by example.

Besides, the hazers *want* to be known as hazers. They like it. They perceive themselves as undergraduate versions of a formidable military drill instructor. They want their chapters to be known as "tough" and "challenging," even though hazing has the exact opposite effect—hazing makes it easy to join and even easier to stay in.

They want to be able to stand with another hazer and talk in code—"*Wait 'til they go through the white volcano*"—and impress the women who are listening to their manliness. In reality, they are saying, "We're bullies and we pick on guys who can't or won't fight back, but that doesn't matter because we're bullies."

Message to hazers: Keep on going. Hazing in plain sight is great because it makes it painfully easy for those of us who oppose hazing to figure out which teams, groups, clubs, Greek-letter organizations, and others are hazing. If you won't *stop* hazing, then keep doing it in plain sight. You're doing us a solid favor. And with all the phones and videos and audio recording devices out there . . . well, you make it easy to bust you.

There is, however, *one* smart choice offered to you.

Don't haze.

And finally enjoy a truly rewarding fraternity experience that your founders *did* envision.

DAVID WESTOL, JD, is the founder of Limberlost Consulting, providing strategic planning and consulting to campuses, organizations, and foundations. He is also a former executive director of Theta Chi fraternity and once served as an assistant prosecuting attorney in Kalamazoo County, Michigan.

20 Hazing and University Ethics

The Need for Faculty Involvement and Guidance

James F. Keenan, SJ

In her compelling essay in *Atlantic Monthly*, "The Dark Power of Fraternities," social critic Caitlin Flanagan acknowledges that fraternities "raise millions of dollars for worthy causes, contribute millions of hours in community service, and seek to steer young men toward lives of service and honorable action." But, she adds, "They also have a long, dark history of violence against their own members and visitors to their houses, which makes them in many respects at odds with the core mission of college itself."[1]

While noting that hazing causes but a small fraction of the harm that fraternities bring, Flanagan reports in her year-long investigation that "lawsuits against fraternities are becoming a growing matter of public interest, in part because they record such lurid events, some of them ludicrous, many more of them horrendous. For every butt bomb, there's a complaint of manslaughter, rape, sexual torture, psychological trauma." While she notes in the *Atlantic* feature that most of these suits are settled somehow and never make it to trial, still "the material facts of these complaints are rarely in dispute; what is contested, most often, is only liability."[2]

Referring to a series of articles on fraternities by *Bloomberg News*'s David Glovin and John Hechinger—who noted in a 2013 article that since 2005 more than sixty people have died in incidents linked to fraternities, twenty-four of them freshmen—Flanagan adds in the *Atlantic* that the figure is "dwarfed by the numbers of serious injuries, assaults, and sexual crimes that regularly take place in these houses."[3]

When I started this project in the spring of 2012, I read the following article on April 10, 2012, about police responding to a noise complaint in the Boston neighborhood of Allston. The story helped me to see the human face of those affected by fraternities' hazing.

> Police sought criminal complaints Tuesday against 14 suspects accused of beating and binding five Boston University students and then covering them in hot sauce and honey as part of a fraternity hazing scheme.

Early Monday morning, police responded to a noise complaint in what could have been another loud, late-night house party, on an Allston street notorious for them.

Police found a circle of students shivering in the cellar, bound, in their underwear and doused in honey, hot sauce, chili sauce, and coffee grounds.

"All five were shivering and horrified and [had] fearful looks on their faces," police officers wrote in a report.

When an officer asked the students if they were ok, one shook his head no as tears fell down his face.

When the condiments were washed off, police could see that welts covered their backs.[4]

I realized that these young men who were beaten, humiliated, and frightened beyond belief were no different than the students in my own classes. I wondered how many faculty in the Boston area, for instance, would refer to the local incident in their classes. For instance, of those teaching ethics in the greater Boston area (there have to be easily a hundred courses in ethics taught in any semester at Boston-area universities), would there have been even one professor who thought the local scandal about twenty-year-old students being brutalized by fellow students merited even a minute of comment?

If any faculty mention it, they don't write about it. For all those who have written on hazing, few wrote as faculty. One was Winton Solberg, a historian who wrote an essay on hazing at his university, "Harmless Pranks or Brutal Practices? Hazing at the University of Illinois, 1868–1913." There he compares the styles and decisions by two very different presidents and notes that by 1913 the practice of hazing had run its course thanks to the president "who demonstrated that educational leadership made a difference. He was responsible for the policy that participation in hazing of any kind could lead to dismissal from the university." While suggesting that those who haze are bullies, Solberg notes that though "hazing was long a serious problem in higher education," college and university histories rarely do more than make fleeting references to the subject." When it comes to brutal campus practices, administrators, like their faculty, brush aside such events affecting their campus.[5]

Hank Nuwer, a professor at Franklin College's Pulliam School of Journalism, is another faculty member addressing the ethics of university life. In 1990, he published *Broken Pledges: The Deadly Rite of Hazing*, a study that begins with the death of pledge Chuck Stenzel at Alfred University in 1978, but then covers so many instances of fraternity and sorority hazing that we begin to appreciate the practice's pervasiveness. Eleven years later he wrote *Wrongs of Passage: Fraternities, Sororities, Hazing, and Binge Drinking*, in which he focused on the historical roots of hazing in the United States and both the Greek system and non-Greek organizations that have coercive drinking as a constitutive part of their hazing.[6]

In *The Hazing* Reader (2004), Nuwer provides many foundational insights and concepts for understanding the ethical issues of hazing through a collection of fifteen essays. First he reproduces Irving Janis's essay "Groupthink" in order to help us understand the effectiveness of a collective and how it thwarts the concerns of individuals. Janis explains:

> I use the term "Groupthink" as a quick and easy way to refer to the mode of thinking that persons engage in when they are deeply involved in a cohesive in-group, when the members' striving for unanimity overrides their motivation to realistically appraise alternative courses of action. "Groupthink" is a term of the same order as the words in the newspeak vocabulary George Orwell used in his dismaying *1984*—a vocabulary with terms such as "double think" and "crimethink." By putting groupthink with those Orwellian words, I realize that groupthink takes on an insidious connection. The inviolousness is intentional. Groupthink refers to a deterioration of mental efficiency, reality testing, and moral judgment that results from group pressures.[7]

In the introduction to the Janis essay, Nuwer appropriates the term, applies it to university fraternities, and therein mints a new word, "Greekthink." Nuwer writes: "I adapted the term 'Groupthink' to become 'Greekthink,' a reference to the less common, but more dangerous, fraternal groups that engage in reckless behaviors and pledging rituals, display near-delusional feelings of invincibility, fail to heed individual member's or their national executives moral qualms in the interest of group unanimity, put a newcomer in harm's way, and demonstrated post-incident denial in the face of clear-cut evidence that they have erred. Likewise, the theory helps explain why pledges will risk death for esteem, backslapping, and bonding with a fraternity chapter." Nuwer reports, too, that when he explained to Janis the connection that he made, Janis remarked, "All of us are very hungry for that sort of thing. None of us can get enough of it."[8]

Nuwer's use of "Greekthink" helps us to appreciate the effectiveness of group identity on college campuses. Helen Lefkowitz Horowitz, author of *Campus Life*, comes close to it when she describes the abiding loyalty of college men when they are at war with the faculty. But Nuwer goes further in describing how Greekthink suppresses the moral instinct and the ethical judgment. Certainly, as Nuwer himself acknowledges, Greekthink occurs not only in fraternity houses; it belongs to any campus collective (think sports, even residential college, or any other student group) that seeks to reduce itself to an identity, that is to a unanimous group, and therein pledges loyalty to one another above any moral claim. It is the culture of the college male.

In a lengthy essay for Nuwer's *Reader* titled "Hazing and Alcohol in a College Fraternity," former Indiana University doctoral student James C. Arnold tells the story of studying for four years the use of alcohol by a local chapter of a fraternity (pseudonym INS) at a Midwestern public university. He sums up how the perpetual use of alcohol at the fraternity wove into the hazing rituals, destroying any semblance of a moral order or a capacity for ethical judgment:

> If one accepts the hypothesis that INS (and groups like them) can be accurately described by an addictive organization model, then perhaps the ingrained, dysfunctional behaviors of the group can be better understood. The continuing central importance of alcohol to the group can be compared to an individual alcoholic/addict seeking the next "fix." And the perpetuation of hazing practices and rituals—which go on, as does alcohol use, after many educational and intervention attempts—fit into the "ethical deterioration" characteristic of an addictive organization. It is my belief that hazing is abusive and wrong—and only an organization whose ethical and moral foundation had significantly eroded could permit such activity to exist.[9]

In the face of the collapse of any moral order, Arnold concludes: "This all comes down to the moral question: How ought we (as campus administrators, fraternity executives, and others) to be in a relationship to a fraternity? It stands to reason we should not continue our roles as codependents and maintain this addictive system; instead we need to change this unhealthy relationship."[10]

Arnold's work is disturbing in that it helps us to see that the fraternity itself, coupled with its collective dependence on alcohol, leads to an eroding of any moral impulse to change.[11] It has a strong spiraling downward effect. Not only that, but Arnold maintains that universities are often complicit in their implicit tolerances of a hazing chapter's practices. We could add that the faculty's disinclination to address any of the ethical issues of these practices on their own campuses places them as, at best, passive witnesses to these collective actions. The downward spiral happens on their watch.

Nuwer's website (HankNuwer.com) includes videos related to hazings, accounts of pledge deaths, narratives of grieving parents testifying against hazing, and strategies for banning hazing. There, too, he offers his own definition of hazing: "An activity that a high-status member orders other members to engage in or suggests that they engage in that in some way humbles a newcomer who lacks the power to resist because he or she wants to gain admission into a group." Along with all this, Nuwer maintains a record of student deaths related to hazing. Beginning with a class hazing death in 1838 at Franklin Seminary in Kentucky, he names more than two hundred student hazing deaths, roughly a quarter having occurred since 2000. While many of these in the early twentieth century were related to freshman-sophomore "rushes," we can see as we enter the twenty-first century the spiraling downward effect suggested by Arnold's essay.

Two other faculty authors merit our attention. Elizabeth Allan read *Broken Pledges* and was so profoundly motivated by Nuwer's account of Chuck Stenzel's hazing death at Alfred University and his mother's grief that she dedicated herself to dismantling hazing practices. She was the lead investigator of "Hazing in View: College Students at Risk, Initial Findings from the National Study of Student Hazing." In this study of more than eleven thousand responses to surveys at fifty-three colleges and universities, Allan defined hazing as "any activity expected of someone joining or participating in a group that humiliates, degrades, abuses, or endangers them regardless of a person's willingness to participate." Her study found the following:

- Fifty-five percent of college students involved in clubs, teams, and organizations experience hazing.
- Hazing occurs in, but extends beyond, varsity athletics and Greek-letter organizations and includes behaviors that are abusive, dangerous, and potentially illegal. Alcohol consumption, humiliation, isolation, sleep deprivation, and sex acts are hazing practices common across types of student groups.
- There are public aspects to student hazing, including 25 percent of coaches or organization advisors were aware of their groups' hazing behaviors; 25 percent of the hazing behaviors occurred on campus in a public space; in 25 percent of hazing experiences, alumni were present; and students talk with peers (48 percent) or family (26 percent) about their hazing experiences. In more than half of hazing incidents, a member of the offending group posts pictures on a public web space.[12]

Today, besides teaching at the University of Maine, Professor Allan is one of the founders of StopHazing.org, which has the mission to eliminate hazing through education. The website claims, "StopHazing now serves as a resource for accurate, up-to-date information about hazing for students, parents, and educators and helps to educate more than 30,000 visitors a month." Since the inception of StopHazing.org, Nuwer has been a regular columnist and contributor.[13]

Allan also contributed two notable essays to Nuwer's 2004 *Hazing Reader.* In "Initiating Change: Transforming a Hazing Culture," Allan writes with Susan Van Deventer Iverson, a professor of higher education leadership at Manhattanville College, about the successes that they had on other campuses in working against a hazing culture. These authors are concerned with the underlying cultures that promote students to act wrongly in a collective manner. Significantly, they do not think of hazing as an event as much as a culture that promotes practices that lead to catastrophic events. Describing cultures "loosely defined as the shared assumptions, beliefs, and normal behaviors (norms) of a group, they examine how students exist in these cultures."[14]

Allan and Iverson recognize the need students have for trying to understand how to confront a moral quandary when they have one. This presupposes, however, that in terms of human development, students understand the goods that are at stake. Invariably students are primarily concerned about relationships, and loyalty and fidelity are important values for those relationships. Ought those values be contested or confronted when one's circle of friends intends to endanger another? Though students might study in their ethics classes some methods of moral reasoning or case studies regarding the world of ethical choices in a variety of professions, rarely do they engage directly the cases that affect them as university students, mostly because neither faculty nor administrators have university ethics on their radar.

Allan and Iverson found that hazing cases helped students to understand newer ethical issues because it "forces them to reexamine values and beliefs in the face of challenging moral situations." They report that students who became involved with antihazing efforts are precisely the students who "experienced dissonance as a result of a moral dilemma related to hazing—and this dissonance contributed to their motivation to take action." Students learned their lessons not in the classroom but in the singularity of their own experience. Their crisis occurred as they recognized an "opportunity to speak out against hazing but also wanted to preserve their membership in the hazing organization." They truly faced "the moral dilemma when they realized that their silence was making them complicit with the problem of hazing and, in turn, contributing to an environment that placed others in danger."[15]

Students who spoke out about their experiences of having been hazed and having hazed, of going through the delusional and humiliating practices of hazing, only could do so by being transparent about their participation in them and by subsequently repudiating them. They in turn became, in a manner, role models for others who recognized the dilemma but did not know how to resolve it. The accompaniment that these role models provided in time prompted the development of a counterculture, a group of rebels against the hazing culture.

In "Hazing and Gender: Analyzing the Obvious," Allan looks first at sorority hazings but turns to the commodification of women's bodies to be the object of men's desires. Here she notes that women often collaborate or initiate the staging of hazing episodes that humiliate women with men as witnesses, and there she identifies the "paradox of sexism": "Women themselves actively participate in sustaining the 'object' status of other women."[16]

Along with the objectification of women, she finds homophobia also embedded in the culture of hazing and therein attempts to identify the subject of manliness that presides over these cultural themes. Similarly, she sees much of the contours of hazing humiliations aiming for practices that objectify women and debase homosexuality. For this she turns to the question of what constitutes the underlying campus culture that promotes collective practices of humiliation and asks readers to recognize how "rigid and narrow versions of gender work in tandem with homophobia to create environments that are more likely to tolerate and perpetuate hazing practices." She invites us to be committed to promoting common ethical stances and practices across university campuses that promote respect for all people, especially across the vicious prejudices that are based on race, gender, and social class.[17]

Clearly in the general ethical wasteland of college campuses where student life is not a concern of faculty and where college men and women collectively engage in increasingly disturbing practices of humiliation while outsiders take cover, Solberg, Nuwer, Allan, and Iverson stand as models of intellectual engagement of the ethical challenges that face the American university. They also show us that faculty can in the classroom, on the internet, on campus, or through publishing enter into university ethics with some effect. Yet the entire challenge of hazing cannot be met by so few faculty. They need others to stand with them and their students.

JAMES F. KEENAN, SJ, holds the Canisius Chair at Boston College and is Director of the Jesuit Institute. He is the author of *University Ethics: How Colleges Can Build and Benefit from a Culture of Ethics.*

21 Understanding Hazing in the Perilous World of *Guyland*

An Interview with Michael Kimmel

Hank Nuwer

DURING HIS DISTINGUISHED career as a pioneering scholar in gender studies and State University of New York sociology professor, Michael Kimmel has tackled hazing as an important gender topic. He is well known for his contributions to the literature on hazing for insights published in his book *Guyland: The Perilous World Where Boys Become Men*.[1] Here he reflects on some of his conclusions.

HANK NUWER: Does belonging to a fraternity count as a defined stage of life? Is hazing a way young males struggle to be viewed as men in their peers' eyes?

MICHAEL KIMMEL: Fraternity membership is an institutionalized form of just one of many different ways in which adolescent men resolve the quest for both manhood and community. Belonging and feeling like a grown-up are the two qualities they are seeking in that membership. But there are dozens and dozens of ways men have invented over the decades to resolve those questions and to facilitate that quest, so to speak. Fraternities are just one. Sport teams and military service and becoming an apprentice—there are lots of different ways. I think fraternities have become, in the twentieth century, dependent on a kind of leisure class. A class that doesn't necessarily find membership and identity through individual hard work but rather in the leisure of an American college campus.

NUWER: After all these years of doing work on hazing, I cannot understand the fifty-seven-year-old alumnus who will attend a hazing practice or the twenty-eight-year-old who was a ringmaster at a hazing where someone eventually dies. Can you explain the thinking of these alumni?

KIMMEL: That is what psychologists call "attribution error." What the attribution error is in this case is that you attribute some effect from the wrong cause. When men say it was my experience in that fraternity, being hazed, that made me what I am today, the men who say that are almost certainly wrong. What made them men was not having been tortured by men about a year older than they were in order to prove their masculinity by forms of degradation, humiliation, and torture, but rather their original class position, their parents' income, their parents' education, the college they went to, and the resources that the college had. So almost certainly it had nothing to do with those experiences of being tortured; it had a lot to do with what sociologists call your "family of origin." But that predictor of who you become is from, after all, who your parents are. There is far, far less interclass mobility as we like to think there is in the United States. Secondly, I think it a product of what we like to call the "Stockholm syndrome" in social psychology. The Stockholm syndrome is when you have been tortured and in prison and you come to identify with your torturer rather than with the other tortured people. So, for example, the only rational response to being hazed in a fraternity is "this is so awful I will never do this to someone else," but somehow, young men come out of that experience with the exact opposite. They come out saying, "I can't wait to do this to the next person." Now, how did they come to identify with their tormentors? That is a real psychological trick. You have to tell them that they are not worthy, and by going through this degradation and humiliation they become worthy. Or that their old self is debased and vile, and they have to be reborn into a new organizational/business self through this process of initiation. Now, if this doesn't sound familiar, you're not a Christian, because that is the model of the Christian baptism—a symbolic death by drowning of the old self and the symbolic rebirth, being pulled out of the water, of the new self in the body of Christ. So, all of these models—initiation, hazing, baptism—all share the demand that the old self be somehow destroyed and the new self, the corporate self in the organization, is the one that matters. When these guys say that is what made me the man I am today, they are following a very old tradition. It is not at all unique to any of these organizations, but that doesn't make it psychologically any less problematic.

NUWER: What you are saying reminds me of my readings from Bruno Bettelheim and his experience in terrible concentration camps.

KIMMEL: Yeah, sure. No question.

NUWER: One thing that Sigma Alpha Epsilon has done out of self-preservation is to get rid of pledging, or to cut it down to a four- or five-day period. The University of South Carolina was set to outlaw pledging, but the USC president vetoed it, perhaps attesting to the power of alumni.

KIMMEL: That's an interesting one. I didn't know about that. So, yeah, this is a problem on college campuses. It goes far beyond the individual fraternities in that these alums through the misattribution of cause earmark much of their funding contingent on the maintenance of the fraternity system as it was when they were there. Everyone remembers their own experience as far more brutal than the current one. So they're saying, "You guys are just pussies—we really did it right. We really tortured these guys." Which also ups the ante for the contemporary ones. Now it is true that when the presidents of universities say they will move against the fraternities and rein in some of these excesses, the alums respond by saying we won't continue to fund you. Which ought not to be as big a problem in a public university like the University of South Carolina as it might be at Colgate or Dartmouth.

NUWER: Yes, that is true. And I have done interviews after a death in which an administrator actually will say, "You know, the hazing wasn't as bad as some other."

KIMMEL: Sure, it's scary.

NUWER: You visited Kappa Alpha Sigma at Northwestern University while speaking there. Is it possible a fraternity chapter might support gender equality?

KIMMEL: That's what they say. I have no reason to doubt it. Sure, why not. There is nothing inherent in its form that determines terrible content. There are a lot of different ways I can imagine fraternities and sororities being voices for good.

NUWER: There is definitely a backlash against members and chapter presidents who try to eliminate hazing in the chapter. Would there be a backlash against males in a fraternity who regard themselves as feminists?

KIMMEL: No, first of all, guys join fraternities to be with guys that they like. So I don't think that would be a particularly big problem. Having guys who are supporters of gender equality in your fraternity and who are willing to intervene makes your fraternity a lot safer.

NUWER: It does, it does. I teach *Guyland* in a senior seminar, and I had a female student with the question as to what you hope to accomplish with *Guyland* in terms of making men better husbands, fathers and mates, employees, and citizens?

KIMMEL: My goal in this is not to get men to be any different. It is to get them to be more authentically themselves. I have a seventeen-year-old son. Let me tell you what I know talking with him and his friends. I ask what it means to them to be a good man. They tell me it means to be a good father and honest and responsible and have integrity and put others first—sacrificing and being a good provider—all of that stuff. Do those qualities of honesty and integrity come to your mind when I say, "Man the fuck up, and be a real man." They say no, that means never show your feelings, play through pain, suck it up, get rich, get laid—so here is what I believe: I believe men are often asked, in the name of proving their masculinity, to be a real man to distance themselves from what they believe it takes to be a good man. That every man that I know has been in some way invited to betray his own ethics in the name of proving his masculinity. When you don't stand up for the person who has been bullied or harassed. When you don't say the right thing. When you don't confront your friends when they do something wrong. When you go along with it and you say nothing. In my mind, we all have those moments. We don't get to look at ourselves in the mirror the same day and say, "Ah, what a good man you are." Because we know we betrayed our own values. So in answer to your student's question, I don't want men to be different; I want men to remember who they actually are. What they believe about themselves as far as being good men. And I believe, Hank, this is true around fraternities as well. I don't support the abolition of fraternities. I say, get me your charter. OK, show me the part where you get women so drunk that they are unconscious and we can fuck them. And it's not there. It's nowhere in their charter. I say, well maybe there is something else in your charter. Like we're men of honor; we're good citizens. We believe in service. Maybe that's there. They say, "Oh yeah." OK, I don't want you to live up to my idea of masculinity; I want you to live up to yours. You're betraying your own charter, your own code. I don't want you living up to mine; I want you living up to yours. So in answer to your student, I'm not interested in changing men—I am interested in them becoming more authentically themselves.

NUWER: That's a wonderful answer. So the next question comes from Matt Deeg, who is a graduate teaching assistant at the University of Kansas. He wonders if you have considered whether biology plays a factor with guys in Guyland?

KIMMEL: Sure, I thought of it. I thought about it a lot. In fact, the first chapter, by far the longest in my book, is a consideration of all the biological evidence that says males and females are so fundamentally different. But by biology what does he mean? Does he mean different brains? In which case coeducation would never be successful. Because if we had really different brains we couldn't read the same book or listen to the same lecture, or do any of those things where we are supposed to be so biologically different. So that can't be it; so it must be testosterone. It must be that testosterone is such a driver of men, but that begs the question: If it's true that testosterone is the driver of all this, why is it not universal? Why are there so many societies that don't have a rape culture? Where guys basically love and respect women. Don't they have testosterone in equal amounts? So if you're going to make a biological argument, you better make damn sure that it is categorical and not just a distribution. My feeling is there is nothing categorical about it. Biology gives us the raw material, but society tells us the shape of what that will look like and the mobilization into social interaction. And it gives us the morality of whether or not that is OK. The biology argument goes this way: Men are so much more violent and so aggressive. Anyone who believes that would definitely be voting for Hillary Clinton and vote to replace every man in every single position—national, international, state, and local—with women. Because we know men would be far more likely to engage in war. Therefore, you wouldn't want them to run the country because they decide by testosterone. I don't believe in the biology argument, and I don't think the person who asked the question does either, because if he did, we would replace all the men in power and replace them with women.

NUWER: On an NPR radio program, I once called hazing an equal opportunity disgrace, because there are deaths in the Asian fraternities, the black fraternities, the Caucasians. For example, in the Asian-American fraternities, we have had three deaths from beatings. In the Philippines, all fraternity deaths are from beatings, and there is a tremendous amount. How does this fact that all groups have deaths play out in terms of race?

KIMMEL: I think it is an indication of the way the dominant forms of masculinity are adapted and engrained by marginal groups. Like, if this is the definition of masculinity, we can do it too because we are real men. It breaks my heart when I see that Michael Jordan and members of his [Omega Psi Phi] fraternity were branded as part of their hazing at the University of North Carolina. Why? Because branding is something that slave owners did to slaves. It would be like if a Jewish fraternity would tattoo a number onto your body. It is unconceivable and I cannot actually believe they would do this. It is the most accepting of racist ideas that you can possibly imagine. I think it is inevitable that if this is the way the dominant model says this is the way you prove your masculinity, we can embrace it and we can do it even more. We're real men and we can do it even better.

NUWER: I'd like you to address these many cases where women in sports or sororities require their so-called rookies or pledges to do risky things, or to demean them in front of male athletes or fraternity members, or have them consume excessive amounts of alcohol.

KIMMEL: Women can be real men, too. If this is how we set the standard and this is what we say it looks like to join, then everyone who wants to become a member of some club, like women athletes, or women police officers, or women soldiers, will use what men do, because women have set the terms for that.

MICHAEL KIMMEL is author of *Guyland: The Perilous World Where Boys Become Men* and author or editor on more than twenty books on gender studies. He is Professor of Sociology at the State University of New York, Stony Brook.

22   A Cold Case

How Did Joe Bisanz Die?

Hank Nuwer

> Father teach us to tread the paths of honor and truth.
> —Indiana University Pi Kappa Alpha house prayer

STRONG AND COORDINATED, Joe Bisanz once hit a home run that cleared a fence and hit the fifty-yard line of an adjacent football field. He once chased a deer through the woods near his suburban Chicago home. He dreamed of being a rock-and-roll drummer, but hated what drugs did to Kurt Cobain.

"I will never end up dying by myself," he wrote in a high-school essay.

After enrolling at Indiana University in the fall of 1997 to study finance, Joe gained membership into Pi Kappa Alpha (Pike) and two national honor societies. Valerie Bisanz, his mother, says she wasn't pleased Joe pledged Pike, fearing he and his dad overplayed the professional advantages accrued from Greek life. Mrs. Bisanz wanted nothing to interfere with the ethical development she said made her son "such a good human being and such a good spirit."

Like others in his pledge class, Joe went through hazing—even though IU and Pi Kappa Alpha headquarters absolutely forbid it—to "earn" his membership. He endured "pledge showers," attic confinement, housecleaning, and shouting. He drank alcohol in spite of being underage.

"All you guys are welcome to the Pi KA barn dance," wrote one officer to Joe's class. "You don't have to work at it. You just get drunk."

In spite of pledging obligations for a chapter proud of its hazing and alcohol consumption, Joe Bisanz pulled good grades. "I must be absorbing [my schoolwork] through my pillow," he joked to his family.

After Pike accepted Joe, a few fraternity members resented his Jeep and Abercrombie & Fitch sweatshirts. But Joe bonded with many others, including the chapter's athletes. People said he never broke his word. When an injury ended his dream of playing baseball for the Hoosiers, he supported his friends at IU by going to their events and cheering them on. Member Alex Howell once said that he even regarded Joe as a natural for chapter president. Some Pike brothers called Joe a "great listener," "unselfish . . . with an overwhelming heart," "always kind, always positive," and someone who "knew the true meaning of friendship and brotherhood."

Valerie and Gary Bisanz call Joe "the all-American kid." He was a "good kid," stresses Valerie, recalling how he used to make a point of saying goodnight after high-school dates because he knew she'd be waiting up for him.

A driven man who works long hours, Gary Bisanz says that Joe was like his paternal grandfather—a decent, caring individual. An aunt observed that Joe loved baseball, academic challenges, and visiting older relatives. A former girl-friend's mother said she felt her daughter was safe with Joe.

Joe was a comfort to Valerie as her marriage to Gary dissolved. After older brother, Keith, suffered a brain injury in an Illinois car accident (two of his passengers died), Joe made his mother promise to pull the plug if he were ever pronounced brain-dead.

The Party

On December 12, 1998, Joe and some other Pike sophomores were preparing to throw a Christmas party that evening. That afternoon, Joe phoned his mother. Valerie Bisanz says her son complained that he'd seen fraternity members with drugs. He didn't name names.

The house was decorated for the holidays and food was served. While many members skipped the party, some upperclassmen were there. Although the house was on probation for an alcohol violation (someone had thrown a can of beer at an IU policeman), at least one adult Pike broke the law to purchase alcohol, according to IUPD records. Spiked eggnog, wine, beer, rum, and gin were at the party. Joe had two rum bottles in a fridge, but IUPD never learned how he obtained them.

That evening, Joe got dressed, selecting a sea-blue dress shirt, gold-and-red tie, and charcoal pants. He took new shoes out of a box. He seemed in good spirits.

Photographs taken at the party show Joe grinning amid brothers and with his date. Afraid of drug contamination (his dad warned him not to drink from open containers), Joe sipped juice and lower-proof Parrot Bay rum from his trademark white-and-red travel mug. He may also have sipped wine from the community stash, or so fraternity brothers later recollected.

Timeline Toward Death

At 12:30 a.m., Joe's date left for home. She wanted to keep things platonic. Joe was disappointed, but not depressed, a party-goer recalls. He visited several rooms to visit with friends.

Joe's roommate, Larry Hsia, would later say that at 1:00 a.m., Joe was "slightly drunk." But an hour or more after that, Joe guarded the door of a communal bathroom for a female friend and chatted with a brother in the hallway outside his room, 208. Neither heard him slur nor saw him stagger.

Before going to bed, Joe hung his clothes in his closet, put his shoes back in their box, and set his alarm for 10:30 a.m. Fraternity friends said Joe planned to lift weights and study the next day.

At an indeterminate time, Alex Howell entered Joe's room. Howell left either after Joe went to bed on his own or after he helped a woozy Joe get in bed, according to differing IUPD interviews.

Howell later returned to Joe's room with Andy Baer, where they found Joe on the floor, dressed in shorts. Vomit was near the bed and on furniture.

Howell patted Joe on the cheek and splashed him with water. Baer ran to a brother's room as Howell screamed for help. Adam Auffart responded and tried to resuscitate Joe, as three or four others came into room 208.

Auffart blew twice into Joe's mouth. He tried to revive his fraternity brother.

Another member took over who, though not certified, knew the rudiments of CPR. More brothers pushed into the room and hallway.

Police Respond

Police records show Auffart called 911 at 2:55 a.m. IUPD recorded a response for "medical assistance."

The first IU officer arrived at the 1012 East Third Street house just before the rescue team pulled up. Joe was not breathing and he lacked a pulse. Parts of his skin had turned a ghastly blue. He had abrasions on his face and one leg. A bandage covered a splinter in his left fourth finger (party pictures show no bandages on Joe's hand). The source of these injuries, and time they occurred, is unknown.

Word that Joe had collapsed reached people in the party rooms, creating bedlam. Police ordered distraught members away from 208 and into a meeting room.

IUPD phoned a police superior and then Dean of Students Richard McKaig. A junior IU staff member went to the house.

The rescue team restarted Joe's pulse. An ambulance took him to a Bloomington Hospital. A physician measured Joe's temperature at 93.9. The doctor noted an abrasion on Joe's chin.

Although Joe had a pulse at first and took a few good breaths, he started frothing at the mouth and was transferred to a critical care unit.

Meanwhile, in suburban Chicago, police located Gary and Valerie Bisanz, occupying separate residences following their divorce. Nevertheless, they sped together to Bloomington. Upon arrival, according to Gary, "I looked into his eyes and I knew, I knew, he was gone."

About 2:00 p.m., Joe suffered cardiac arrest, held on, and then endured another seizure. A ventilator breathed for him. A doctor told the Bisanzes Joe was probably brain-dead.

Valerie remembered her promise to Joe not to continue life support. At 2:51 p.m., Joe Bisanz perished.

The Cleanup Crew

Room 208 was cleaned as if a member had gotten sick—not been found, as Joe had, without a pulse or unable to breathe. Police typically follow routine, possible-homicide procedures at the scene of an alcohol or drug overdose where a death has occurred or someone is in a coma. Such procedures are recommended by standard texts like James C. Garriott's *Medicolegal Aspects of Alcohol* and Spitz and Fisher's *Medicolegal Investigation of Death: Guidelines for the Application of Pathology to Crime Investigation*.

Because forensic laboratories are frequently called upon to perform alcohol analysis in legal cases where death or serious injury has occurred, medical and police investigators are advised by Garriott and Spitz to observe hard-and-fast rules for collection and storage of specimens. Ideally, vomit gets preserved, areas where the victim has been are taped off-limits, and surfaces are covered so a medical examiner can later try matching them to the victim's abrasions.

Pike member Shaun Scott told a reporter that Joe just "got sick."

This explanation helps account for IUPD's activities following Joe's collapse. An inspection on IUPD records reveals no suspicion on any officer's part that anything other than an accident due to drinking occurred. True, some officers cleared fraternity members from room 208 and conducted interviews with some of the members and guests. But other IUPD interviews were conducted weeks, even months, after Joe's death.

Police also allowed roommate Larry Hsia, several other fraternity members, and (according to a senior member's statement) an IU staff member to clean up the scene, including Joe's vomit and mug. IUPD told Gary Bisanz there was no broken furniture in the room. But, on being pressed by Gary, Hsia is said to have disclosed that two broken computer stools had indeed been in the room and disposed of during the cleanup.

Police snapped photos of the tidied-up room, but none of the scene where Joe collapsed. A small amount of Joe's rum was retrieved and tested fine in the lab—but Joe may have sipped more than rum that night. A bent fan blade in Joe's room was collected, but it could have been wiped clean by someone unknown to police.

Police records do not show who gave the OK to clean up. Dean of Students Richard McKaig, nationally known for his efforts to achieve Greek-life reforms, in a phone interview reiterates that nothing suggested to police that anything other than an alcohol overdose occurred. The first priority for campus police, he says, is to save a person's life under challenging circumstances. There was no way for police or staff to know Joe would die when the ambulance carried him away, for he had regained a pulse.

Enough Alcohol to Kill Him?

Using a visual estimate of 175 pounds (Joe's parents estimated his real weight at 195–198 pounds), Bloomington hospital officials estimated that Joe's blood-alcohol content was .206—twice the legal level for driving, but almost positively not enough to kill him.

Could Joe have rapidly ingested the rest of his rum or some other form of alcohol in his room and triggered respiratory distress? Or after Joe's date (who told police she had sipped from Joe's mug without ill effect) left, could he have consumed a hard-to-detect drug, like gamma-hydroxybutyrate (GHB), the so-called "date-rape drug," causing him to overdose? Could Joe have died from a physical defect, perhaps triggered or aggravated by alcohol?

If anyone at the Pike house knows, he failed to respond to emailed and telephoned requests for an interview. The views of chapter members have to be pieced together from what they told IUPD.

Valerie Bisanz is talking. "Joe didn't die of alcohol," she asserts.

Nor, say both Bisanzes, would he willingly take drugs. They cite Joe's anti-drug history and roommate Hsia's insistence that Joe was always drug-clean. Upon admission to the hospital, Joe was given a basic drug screen that proved negative for detectable drugs.

But that screening likely would not show rave- and party-scene GHB or similar substances. Some use GHB for a cheap high and some males slip it to women for nonconsenting sex because the drug blots out short-term memory. GHB takes about twenty minutes to cause a rush, and it eludes drug testing after the user urinates. GHB can be deadly when used to excess, with alcohol, or other drugs. Heavy vomiting, followed by respiratory meltdown is not uncommon. Dead male Greeks have been found to have GHB in their systems at Louisiana, Michigan, and Ohio State Universities.

The best chance IUPD would have had to determine what killed Joe would have been by collecting his urine and blood samples for sophisticated lab analysis. An autopsy by a forensic pathologist could have looked for organ failure or elevated GHB levels. Neither was done. Samples were taken by hospital doctors to look for detectable drugs like cocaine, but they were later destroyed.

After Joe died, a medical doctor who assisted the Bisanzes at Bloomington Hospital asked Valerie and Gary to take back their signed, witnessed autopsy request.

The Bisanzes, worn out by their traumatic experience, failed to insist the autopsy be carried out. The doctor informed the family that Joe had "asphyxia secondary to aspiration of gastric contents." In other words, Joe's inhaled vomit caused—or strongly contributed to—his death.

The doctor, returning my phone call, was cooperative but would not discuss case details. Her report said she had explained Joe's probable cause of death and that the family had an "understanding" of what likely killed him.

More Questions

Coroner George E. Huntington of Monroe County, who had previously been employed as chief of IUPD, filed paperwork stating that Joe's death had been caused or exacerbated by a "well-elevated level of alcohol." On December 14, Huntington, a doctor, and an IUPD officer examined the body, taking X-rays of the skull. No head injuries were found. However, an MRI, which can reveal the presence or absence of soft-tissue trauma, was not administered.

Huntington's sworn coroner's report stated that the cause of death was "asphyxia secondary to aspiration of gastric contents." However, the funeral director who arranged Joe's showing saw enough amiss to jot down some notes. "Several small areas of trauma needed to be attended to," wrote Paul E. Chominski. He described the placement and type of facial abrasions.

On October 7, 1999, with permission of a Waukegan, Illinois, coroner, the Bisanz family exhumed Joe's body. The autopsy found no death-causing injuries—though decomposition can, in fact, interfere with diagnosis. Joe's heart was enlarged, raising the remote possibility that an irregular heartbeat led to death, but he was likely disease-free.

More important, the Illinois report contradicted conclusions of the doctor and Coroner Huntington: "While there was a small amount of foreign matter in the lungs, there was no evidence of significant amounts of foreign matter or of a significant acute inflammatory response associated with this foreign matter in the lungs. This makes significant ante mortem (before death) aspiration of stomach contents unlikely. Finding vomitus in the mouth and airways is a common postmortem (after death) finding often not associated with aspiration. Where true aspiration has occurred there is normally a significant inflammatory response in the lungs, especially when there is a period of survival time as seen here."

Did alcohol alone kill Joe? The forensic pathologist, agreeing with Valerie, thought not. While elevated enough to make him stagger, the amount should not have been enough to kill a healthy young male, wrote Dr. Mark J. Witeck and two colleagues. Toxicological tests showed elevated GHB in Joe's system, along with ethanol, but without samples taken in life, no definitive conclusions were possible.

In other words, Joe "died of undetermined causes," according to Witeck.

The second autopsy might have been unnecessary had there been a first autopsy in Bloomington. A forensic pathologist then could have tested for GHB without embalming and decomposition limiting the diagnosis. Dr. Michael Clark, a forensic pathologist who examined the hospital's handling of Joe's case upon the request of police investigators, concluded that "an autopsy should have been performed anyway" to erase any doubts regarding Joe's demise.

Witeck's report, however, suggested no wrongdoing on the part of Coroner Huntington, IU staff, Pike partygoers, the doctors who treated Joe, or Bloomington Hospital.

Back at the Fraternity

IUPD received minimal cooperation from the Pike brothers. Quite often after a fraternity death, members and pledges stonewall police and university staff. "The amount of alcohol(ic) beverages is undetermined at \this time," one officer wrote. "None of the members would give any information on where the alcohol was purchased."

After Joe's death, his chapter failed to delete his name from a house group email list that the Bisanz family had access to. Soon after Joe died, Howell wrote an email, congratulating the dead Joe on making national news. A brother on December 14 outlined four points to tell police regarding the presence of alcohol in the house and other matters. A Pike officer maintained that there was nothing anyone could do to the house if members stuck together.

Email also revealed that Pike members agreed to keep future hazing to a minimum, lest a dean stumble upon activities.

After viewing the email, Dean McKaig, now retired, said there really wasn't much more he could do to the fraternity without strong evidence of additional wrongdoing. "When the chapter comes up for review, we'll take a long hard look at what they have to say," said McKaig.

The Bisanzes object to McKaig's decision to go lighter on the chapter than he had on some other IU chapters where infractions but no death occurred. In February 1999, the Pike chapter was prohibited from functioning as an organization, but members continued to live in the house. To the Bisanzes, the destruction of evidence undercut IU's written policy against having liquor consumed in houses by underage members. According to an *Indiana Daily Student* story, McKaig's decision not to expel the chapter ran counter to a recommendation to do so by the Office of Student Ethics.

Pi Kappa Alpha's international office did not investigate. According to the now-board chairman Raymond Orians, "We did encourage a thorough investigation by all the proper authorities, and we fully cooperated with those authorities, particularly officials at Indiana University."

Indianapolis Bureau of Criminal Investigations

In 1999, as the case stalled, the Bisanzes complained to the Indianapolis Bureau of Criminal Investigations. Gary and Valerie criticized IUPD's follow-up investigations on the case.

Although months had passed since Joe's death, Indianapolis Detective Sgt. Brooks B. Wilson interviewed party attendees and reviewed IUPD's handling of the case. Wilson reported that IUPD did not seal and photograph room 208 because they thought they were doing a "routine inquiry" and failed to recognize "the seriousness of the situation." According to Wilson's report, the issue of date-rape drugs can never be addressed with certainty.

Wilson, in an interview at his office with me, expressed empathy for Joe's parents' pain but said his independent discussions with chapter members and party guests made him conclude that Joe's collapse likely came from the influence of alcohol consumed over the course of the night.

Wilson told me that after talking to members, he saw nothing to suggest that Joe experimented with drugs. Nor did Wilson's talks with Howell and other partygoers lead him to conclude that anyone slipped GHB into Joe's drink. Asked about one Pike's contradictory statements to IUPD, Wilson said that he recalled the partygoer tried to be "cooperative," but had too much to drink to provide coherent recollections.

Wilson criticized one or two partygoers who contacted the family with what he called hearsay about drugs such as GHB they thought Joe might have taken. Wilson said he concluded that definitive findings could not be made given the cleanup of party materials and vomit.

The Bisanz family wanted the state attorney general to look over Wilson's report and to evaluate IUPD procedures following Joe's death. Gary Bisanz wanted the attorney general to let him know which ranking officer gave the OK to clean the Pike house. Neither request was fulfilled by Indiana state officials. No charges ever were filed against Pike members, and none were even ranked persons of interest.

Where We Are Today

Valerie Bisanz says the death of her son has tested her faith in the world, but didn't destroy it. Some day, she believes, someone will give her a more complete account of what happened to Joe. For now, she perceives the chapter's attitude to be, "Too bad, so sad, but let's move on."

"I don't care so much about redeeming Joe now," says Valerie. "Joe didn't need redeeming—he was a parent's dream. I just want the truth. I can't believe fraternity policies are more important than the human spirit."

Valerie and Gary Bisanz never got the answers they sought from Joe's fraternity brothers who professed they loved him. None of the Indiana Pike members have contacted Valerie Bisanz to shed light on the mystery.

Although the death of Indiana University fraternity member Joe Bisanz was in no way hazing related, these events occurring after his death show how unlikely it is for a hazing chapter like his or that of the late Tucker Hipps at Clemson University to be totally forthcoming with police, school officials, and even, or maybe especially, with the grieving family. Seldom does a fraternity chapter known for its hazing conduct all its other activities in a fashion approved by the institution or national fraternity. Parties get thrown that are unregistered, underage drinkers find it easy to fill a red cup, and neighbors complain of noise and litter.

The case grew cold. There was no way a civil suit against the chapter or IUPD would have been successful given the dearth of evidence. A defense lawyer would argue that no one could testify with certainty what killed Joe. That lawyer would pin the death on Joe himself—saying Joe could have spiked his drink, died of alcohol alone, or been brought down by his enlarged heart. Friends and brothers would be called to testify about any drinking Joe did in his life. It would be pointed out that all contraband was destroyed and that no partygoers were charged.

Nonetheless, Valerie has held out hope that one of Joe's Pike brothers or someone at that party might one day come forward with facts heretofore undisclosed and reopen the closed case.

"What would you do," Valerie asks, "if it was your son?"

HANK NUWER is a professor in the Franklin College Pulliam School of Journalism. He has written *The Hazing Reader* (IUP) and *Wrongs of Passage: Fraternities, Sororities, Hazing, and Binge Drinking* (IUP).

23   Women and a Feminine Leadership Style Can Defeat Hazing

Tracy Maxwell

"THE WORLD WILL be saved by the Western woman." When the Dalai Lama, who also referred to himself as a feminist, said this during the 2009 Vancouver Peace Summit, he perhaps could not have known how far and wide his statement would be quoted, and the terrific impact it would make. Amy O'Brian of the *Vancouver Sun* also quoted him as calling for "increased emphasis on the promotion of women to positions of influence."[1]

What exactly did he mean? Feminist and author Annie Burnside, in a *Chicago Now* blog post, opined that Western women have the time, influence, education, availability, inclination, and relative affluence to do the consciousness-raising required to shift the planet in significant ways. That amid the violence, destruction, and conquest (and yes, the invention, progress, and innovation too) of a masculine power structure, the rising of the feminine—not just women, but a more feminine style of leadership—would usher in a renaissance.[2]

Forbes magazine published an interview in 2014 by Silicon Valley entrepreneur Victor W. Hwang with scientist Janet Crawford suggesting that feminine leadership traits such as connectivity, communication, and collaborative sharing are the future of business. "The data are strong. Research out of MIT suggests that group intelligence is correlated with the number of women on a team. New research from Gallup found that retail stores with more gender diversity experienced a significantly higher revenue growth rate. Research from Catalyst found that Fortune 500 companies with the highest percentages of women board directors produced an average of 66 percent higher return on investment than those with the least," said Crawford who delivers workshops called "The Surprising Neuroscience of Gender Inequity."

Crawford went on to say, "Both men and women can exhibit feminine leadership qualities, but the tendency, both biologically and culturally, is for women to embody them more. These include a host of characteristics such as long-term and global perspective taking, nurturing, empathy, conversational turn taking, credit distribution, inquiry, networked thinking, etc. Promoting feminine leadership is less an issue of male vs. female, but a question of whether we are overlooking qualities that may be crucial to navigating twenty-first-century business challenges." She also cited results of a global survey of sixty-four thousand people in thirteen countries, in which two-thirds of respondents (both genders) ranked feminine leadership traits as essential to solving today's most pressing problems in business, education, government, and more.[3]

Along this same vein, is the Circle of Sisterhood Foundation, founded in 2010 by Ginny Carroll. The premise was that a movement of privileged, educated, and affluent sorority women could use their collective financial clout and acumen to enable females in the developing world to overcome poverty and oppression. By 2016, the Circle has assisted women in twenty-two countries on four continents, awarded grants of more than half a million dollars, and built eleven schools. At the same time, the foundation engaged students and staff on more than two hundred campus communities and educated countless people about the global issues affecting the target population.[4]

In my twenty-five years working in and around higher education, I have repeated often to students what I was taught. I say that sorority women at the local level have the power to change the face of a fraternity and sorority community by standing up for their values, by refusing to participate in events or activities that are mean-spirited, dangerous, or demeaning to women and/or men, and by exercising their leadership. Over time I have personally observed the activism and accomplishments of undergraduate women on campuses across North America.

In 2015 this could be seen on a national scale when sororities began pulling their support for a sexual assault bill, which they had previously spent hundreds of thousands of dollars lobbying on behalf of. That turnaround occurred after many advocacy groups contended such a bill would make women less likely to report sexual violence because it would require them to file criminal charges in order to trigger a campus investigation.

The remainder of this chapter will share examples of how women and feminine styles of leadership have led to positive change in communities around the world. It will also highlight my belief that another turnaround for the better has occurred with sorority groups committed to eradicating hazing and how this effort can be nurtured and furthered even more.

Masculine Versus Feminine Leadership

It is important to note right from the start that this essay is not about the failures of men. It seeks to demonstrate instead the role of a new style of leadership, one that comes naturally to women, but can be utilized by males as well, in meeting the unique needs of the twenty-first century. Around the world, various projects and studies demonstrate the effectiveness of women's leadership when barriers are removed and gender equality is fostered.

The book *Half the Sky: Turning Oppression into Opportunity for Women World-wide* by Nicholas Kristof and Sheryl WuDunn details the disadvantages of women in developing countries but also shares stories of heroines who have bravely stood up to oppressors and helped their peers escape situations equivalent to slavery. The authors describe how entrepreneurial women have formed economic cooperatives in their communities and helped improve health care and educational opportunities for women and children. Through a combination of stories and statistics, the authors paint a vivid picture of problems and solutions. Their book has sparked women's leadership programs and inspired new projects around the world, such as the aforementioned Circle of Sisterhood. In an interview with the *Huffington Post*, coauthor Kristof said, "There is some pretty robust evidence that shows that it does matter when you have women leaders at the local level."[5]

Years before *Half the Sky* was published, an MIT study documented successful projects led by women in various parts of the world. These included Nepalese women who protected local trees because they knew of their importance to their children's future, and also Kenyan women spearheading a greenbelt around Nairobi to give city dwellers access to parks. The study found that "women are capable of initiating innovative processes in situations of difficulty and stress." Further, at the individual level, "women are more flexible and better equipped to manage change, are better multitaskers, are solidarity- and community-minded, more networked than hierarchical, and an important source of creative and imaginative ways of adapting to changing circumstances . . . ways that don't always follow rules accepted at the social level."[6] All of these projects demonstrated the importance of long-term thinking, community-mindedness, and the sacrifices women are willing to make in order to secure a better future.

Feminine Leadership in Hazing Prevention

The early pioneers of the antihazing and/or hazing-education movement were men—Hank Nuwer, Dave Westol, Walter Kimbrough, Ricky L. Jones, and Mike Dilbeck, among others. Nuwer brought hazing into public awareness with his investigative journalism, as well as maintaining the then first and only database of hazing deaths to show that the problem in Greek Life was far more extensive than previously known. Kimbrough and Jones wrote books uncovering and criticizing hazing in black Greek-letter organizations, as well as explaining the behaviors accompanying such hazing. Westol, a former assistant prosecutor and onetime director of Theta Chi, used his legal skills to travel the country and put on his simulated hazing-on-trial courtroom presentation. Dilbeck, a videographer, creating three of the most-viewed educational videos about hazing prevention.

Risk management approaches, while necessary in the early days of the movement to demonstrate potential legal ramifications, utilized a more masculine-style scare tactic, that in my opinion has proven to be less effective over time than the more collaborative, inclusive, preventative, and transformational approaches largely in use today. What the pioneers and today's hazing education professionals had in common, however, was the insistence that hazing prevention be based on the best science available.

In opposition to more response-driven, masculine prevention efforts that focused on policies, enforcement, and legal remedies, many women and male feminists today tend to favor the employment of a mostly transformational approach.[7] Such an approach emphasizes promoting strongly collaborative prevention practices, a focus on moral development, and efforts at changing organizational culture. These include researchers Elizabeth Allen and Mary Madden, consultants Kim Novak and Linda Langford, myself as the founder of HazingPrevention.Org, and current HPO Executive Director Emily Pualwan. Then and now, there have been activists, mainly mothers whose sons died from hazing, who try to convince college audiences by telling their personal tragedies.

There are also some prominent men at the forefront of the modern movement, including academics Tim Marchell, Dan Wrona, Gentry R. McCreary, Norm Pollard, and Travis Apgar. Their characteristics in common, aptly described by researchers John Gerzema and Michael D'Antonio, include the following traits: passionate, flexible, intuitive, future-oriented, loyal, reasonable, collaborative, and empathetic. While research does not prove feminine leadership styles to be best in every organizational situation, it did seem to suggest that in our current worldwide evolution, this moment is especially poised to appreciate and benefit from a leadership style that is based upon values more often fostered by women.[8]

Pioneering Work with HazingPrevention.Org

In 2007 when I founded HazingPrevention.Org, I had no clue what I was doing. The prevention movement was (and still is) so new that there weren't really any proven practices to follow. I relied heavily on my feminine leadership instincts to build partnerships and collaborations with individuals mentioned above. My intent was to formulate a strong and diverse board of directors and to sponsor relationships with a variety of national organizations representing fraternities and sororities, athletes, student affairs professionals, and academics.

Apart from my job description, my empathy for hazing victims and their families led me to spend hours on the phone supporting, advising, and counseling victims and families. Many of those relationships continue and remain one of the most rewarding aspects of my career. My passion for the job carried me through challenges such as organizational cash-flow and funding issues, more work than one person could manage, and uncertainty about how to proceed to make the organization continue, let alone prosper.

Because the HazingPrevention.Org board and I were convinced that furthering the organization and stoking the prevention movement was important, we developed long-range strategic plans and a succession strategy that included employing the services of a management company. Through all of this, remaining flexible was crucial. When the media or victims called and there were deadlines to be met, some projects had to wait in order to bring attention to the cause. The job required constant multitasking, and my feminine leadership abilities helped me navigate a truly uncertain path with passion and immediacy. A decade after its founding, HazingPrevention.Org spearheads the hazing education movement with its publications, national awards, advocacy, and know-how.

Two Success Stories

By sharing the stories of two women who changed the hazing cultures in their communities, I hope to provide inspiration for addressing hazing in anyone's corner of the world, regardless of whether or not he or she holds a formal leadership role. I will refer to these two women by their first names only as Stacy and Jackie.

Stacy and Jackie were both called to address hazing in their respective camping and Greek Life communities. Jackie didn't hold a formal leadership position at the time that she, as simply a student, began important conversations about hazing in her community. Stacy, on the other hand, did have a prominent title when she took steps toward changing a culture at summer camp. Though the settings and their prominence in their respective communities were vastly different, the two women took a similar approach, invoking values and creativity to challenge the status quo. I'll start with Stacy's story, which readers may recognize in part from chapter 4.

Stacy was a camp director in Kentucky when she was called to take action on some long-standing camp traditions after she realized the harm they were causing. "Thankfully it did not involve the campers, but it did involve teenage staff, and it affected them for years. I know because (years earlier) I was one of those teenage staff members who went through it," she said. "Looking back, I am thankful that the hazing I experienced did not escalate and didn't cause physical harm. It did produce some emotional scars for a number of young women, and when I came back to camp a decade later as director, I was determined to get the camp back on the right track, giving girls the experiences and self-confidence to excel in their lives."

Stacy remembers being hesitant her first summer at camp, crying on the shower house steps before dinner one night. She was comforted by a counselor named Andy who gave her a piece of gum (camp contraband), and from that moment on, she was hooked, coming back to multiple sessions each summer for the next several years before joining the CIT (Counselor in Training) program and then becoming a staff member.

"As a long-time camper, I thought I knew every camp activity, but my first year on staff I heard buzz about "Ooga Booga" and how all new staff members would be inducted that session. The campers had fun being in on the mystery and teasing the staff throughout the week about what was going to happen to them," Stacy said.

The night of the activity, the new staff was separated from the campers and taken down to the shower house under the charge of one of the junior counselors. Since the junior counselor had previously participated in the initiation, she was to keep Stacy and others distracted and harassed until it was their turn to go up to the lodge. At this point the staffers were blindfolded and told to sit on the cement floor. They were not allowed to speak to one another and if they did, the punishment was to be sprayed with a garden hose. At first Stacy tried to go along with this event in good humor, but inside she was confused and thrown off balance.

The self-titled "Shower House Bitch" continued to laugh, curse at the staffers, and spray Stacy and the others until they were soaked. "By the time I was called up to the lodge I was holding back tears. I was then standing in front of all the campers, trying to figure out the point of all this and following the motions of the 'leader' of the activity. Turns out, the point of the entire thing was to get the new staff to sit on a wet sponge. I was too wet to even get the joke when the campers all started laughing," said Stacy.

Stacy thought her reaction to the Ooga Booga hazing practice was unique and didn't talk to anyone else about it at the time. It wasn't until years later at a camp reunion that former staffers shared their traumatic experiences of this same activity, regardless of what year they experienced it. "It was heart-breaking that a camp I loved so dearly was the source of so much pain and shame for so many strong young women," she said. "I wasn't very popular my first year as camp director. I knew the camp, its history, its traditions, and the hazing that had occurred there. I had experienced some of it firsthand, and I had decided to do something about it."

Stacy Takes Action

Stacy credits the education she received about hazing in an National Panhellenic Conference sorority as a foundation for her determination to eliminate all forms of this harmful practice at camp. Her camp administrator supported her to make hazing a black-and-white issue with no remaining gray areas, and she began by asking current staff members to make a list of camp traditions. Then she asked them to identify how each tradition supported one of the four overarching program goals: (1) Develop to their full potential, (2) Relate to others with increasing understanding, skill, and respect, (3) Develop a meaningful set of values to guide their actions and provide for sound decision-making, and (4) Contribute to the improvement of society through the use of their abilities and leadership skills, working in cooperation with others.

The conversation flowed easily for some of the songs and games as they easily fit into the program goals, but not surprisingly the staff had a difficult time rationalizing how some of their favorite activities built the campers' sense of self-worth. Nonetheless, they began to get frustrated wondering why they couldn't just "have fun" without having to think about the deeper reasons they were there.

Stacy got pushback for her stance. She began to receive text messages and angry voicemails and anonymous posts on her blog that challenged and even threatened her. She recalls that it took all of her internal strength, as well as the support of her friends and advisor, to not give in. She kept blogging, researching, and talking to other students about her antihazing beliefs, and she went back to her fraternal values again and again.

"The ideal of noble womanhood reminded me that I was a strong woman with a network of strong women behind me, and I had the stage," she said. "I knew this conversation was important and needed to happen, and since I had some influence with my peers, I kept exerting it, and having difficult conversations with anyone who would listen. I wouldn't stop, sit down, or give in to the pressures to stifle my beliefs."

In time, the camp staff conversation began to revolve around a favorite song, believed by Stacy to inappropriately single out campers, mimic physical hazing, and put a spotlight on these behaviors in front of the entire camp during meals. What surprised her was that when the staff couldn't provide any connection between this song and the stated program goals, they began to whine and complain instead.

"Holding firm to the four program goals was the key to our success," Stacy said. "If the activity did not promote one or more of those goals, it was not to be done at camp."

An unexpected positive impact of this process was the impact on new staff members. They appreciated the opportunity to create new traditions and felt as though they were adding value to the camp.

Jackie's Experiences

Jackie entered sorority life as a sophomore at the University of Maryland, Baltimore County, and expected to be hazed. Instead, she said she was "showered with sisterly love," and describes an educational experience that included role modeling and inspiration to become the kind of woman she wanted to be. She felt completely accepted for who she was, and at the same time had a strong desire to be better. The love and sense of community she experienced were perhaps the foundation for her future activism as she saw what was possible in a new-member process, but it didn't begin until a few years later when she was a senior and a former chapter president.

While a sorority member at the Baltimore-Maryland campus, Jackie sat in the front row nodding in agreement with an invited hazing-education speaker. Much of what she was hearing from the stage resonated with her, and she said she felt empowered. Her campus advisor approached her after the talk to ask how she felt about the behavior of the fraternity/sorority community. She confided to her advisor that in Greek Life there were scavenger hunts that included theft and sexual exploitation, head shaving, sleep deprivation, lots of drinking, pledge interviews, and signature books, and that was just the stuff she knew about! Some chapters seemed proud of their exploits, she said, bragging about hazing exploits on Facebook; others tried to hide it and denied hazing was even happening.

As she chatted with her advisor, she felt challenged to do something about hazing. Even though her organization didn't haze their members, she knew sorority women, including herself, had participated in the antics and initiations of the fraternities, and she decided in that moment to stop going along with them, and to try to convince others as well.

"I remember a conversation with one of my pledge sisters just a few weeks after initiation when she said she was so glad we weren't hazed because she would have walked away. I thought, 'she must not have wanted it as much as I did,' because I would have done pretty much anything to be part of a sisterhood. It took me almost my entire collegiate career as a sorority woman to realize how wrong I was in that moment," Jackie said.

Jackie started her crusade by sharing the following post on her blog:

Don't Help Them Haze

Today I was asked to sign a pledge book for the first time this semester. I have made the choice to stand up against this act of hazing and say NO. Upon (my) saying no, the pledge said, "Please. I have to prove to my brothers that I met you."

My question to this organization and to this member is this: What do you have to prove? If your "brothers" trusted you enough to be a member of your organization, if you trusted your "brothers" enough to take a vow to your organization, and to wear your pledge pin, what do you have to prove that you haven't proven already? Why is your word not good enough? Why is my signature better than your fraternity vow?

I hope that my fellow Greeks will think about things like this before signing, before helping these young men (or women) be hazed. Because really . . . is signing helping them not be hazed? Or (is it) helping to perpetuate an organization's tradition of hazing?

I am proud to be a part of an organization that does not haze.

I am proud that I was never hazed (by my chapter or any other Greek).

And I am endlessly proud that I will never participate in hazing.

"I had no way of knowing that this brief post would trigger a much larger conversation on my campus about the tradition and culture of hazing," Jackie said. "My post went viral within our community. Every chapter was talking, guessing, and pointing fingers."

It showed her that one committed person could make a difference and that she was not alone in wanting to change the culture of hazing.

In Conclusion

Both Stacy and Jackie are proud of the actions they took to address hazing in their communities, and both have gone on to positions of leadership in their national organizations and on college campuses, respectively.

Using a leadership style that is more traditionally feminine will bring multiple collaborators together to effect positive change. In particular, women on our campuses have to embrace their ability to influence others to make choices that are community-enhancing instead of community-destroying. Every individual should be safe and free to learn. Empowering and supporting through our collective energy toward a stronger community will make for real, lasting, and positive change.[9]

That change can and will defeat the practice of hazing.

TRACY MAXWELL is the founder of HazingPrevention.Org. She has been working in and around higher education for more than twenty-five years. She currently speaks about hazing for CAMPUSPEAK. Her work as a healing coach assists survivors of hazing and their families.

24   The Purdue Tank Scrap

David Hovde

Class of 1908
On the final eventful night we met around the tank and there were most closely
bound together. For like Spartans of old, we came pledged to win or leave our
bodies on the field (until morning). To record the daring and heroic deeds of
that fateful night would require volumes. Let it suffice to say that not a man
wavered and, although we can record no victory, even our common enemies
admit that we died game.[1]

PURDUE UNIVERSITY, LIKE all colleges and universities, has a long history of
customs and traditions unique to the institution. The nightshirt parade, the
Purdue Circus, the Burning of Miss Indiana, the Cords, the Mechanics Burning, the Nude Olympics, and the Grand Prix are just a few that have come into
being over the years. Some were short-lived and some endured for decades. One
tradition, the Tank Scrap, has to be one of the oddest and certainly the most
violent of all of the Purdue University traditions.

The Tank Scrap was one of many such events that occurred across the country on college campuses, beginning in the early nineteenth century. These events,
called a "rush," "spree," or "scrap," continued on a number of campuses into the
second half of the twentieth century. Most involved some sort of class-on-class
rivalry.[2] These events were at times brutal by modern standards and did result in
injuries and even deaths, but they were so common that they deserved a chapter
in *The Book of Athletics and Out-Of-Door Sports* published in 1895. The author
traced these conflicts back to the ancient Greek Olympics: "When planned upon
a manly athletic basis, and controlled by the spirit of friendly rivalry, it is, perhaps, one of the most exciting contests adopted by the restless college 'men.'
When participated in along the lines of courtesy and courage, it enlists a Spartan
element of honor. It is regarded as a duty, which no loyal class member would
think of shirking. It cements a class union that otherwise would never be formed,
enthusiastically contributed to by the many secret meetings, private conferences,
and careful 'pointers' that precede the day of the contest."[3]

The Purdue Tank Scrap was a free-for-all wrestling match between the freshman and sophomore classes, which involved hundreds of students. The brawl started with a sophomore charge downhill into the ranks of the freshmen. The object was to wrestle down and hog-tie your opponent and then drag him to your camp. Once one side was subdued, the victors were awarded the honor of painting their class year on the tank.

It is interesting to realize that in those days, university administrators and faculty were concerned about these events but rarely stopped them. The violence and injuries on college campuses were not limited to these events. In 1905, for example, it took US President Theodore Roosevelt to threaten banning football entirely by executive order before college presidents took action. During this period, an average of three players a year died on the football field.[4] In 1905, eighteen college football players were killed and 159 injured.[5] Although Roosevelt threatened to ban the game, he, like many at that time, approved of football as it represented manly virtues, rather than just brutal spectacle.[6] These events did have their detractors. In a 1909 article entitled "Hazing," Philip Lutz Jr. described college hazing in its many forms, "so harrowing that one living in the present age of civilization would scarcely believe them American."[7] Similar class rivalries were known to have taken place at Indiana University, DePauw University, Wabash College, Ohio State University, Princeton University, University of Tennessee, Harvard, Pennsylvania State University, and many others. Like the event at Purdue, broken bones, black eyes, and other injuries were common.

The tank was built for the West Lafayette Water Works Company in 1894 on North Salisbury Street in West Lafayette surrounded by farm fields. Students painted the tank with class numerals soon after the tank's construction, beginning with the '97 class year.

Before the tank was built, there were other pranks both on and off campus undertaken by students at the very beginning of the school year. In the 1896 student yearbook *Debris*, there are references to various class vs. class baseball and football games, defacing images on the fence surrounding the football field, and tearing down the class of '95's flag hanging from the tower of University Hall and replacing it with the flag of '96.[8] Class flags were run up the flagpole in front of University Hall and became the target of the other class. Scraps, or fights, between the freshmen and sophomores appear to have been common. They are even known to have occurred in the chapel in University Hall.

In the early years of the tradition, there was not one big event but a series of small group efforts of the sophomores and freshman painting and repainting the tank, almost nightly, beginning at the opening of the classes in September and continued sporadically through the spring and into the summer. In the evening of September 17, 1899, the class of '03 successfully decorated the tank. On September 20, there was another altercation. In this event some freshmen were captured and tied to trees and the sophomores danced around them. On September 21, the two classes met on the corner of Grant and North Streets, near to where the Purdue Memorial Union now stands. The scrap that year lasted two hours with the class of '03 claiming victory. As a result, "'03" appeared on the tank and the class banner was raised on the flagpole. On September 28, "'02" appeared on the tank, but soon after was replaced by "'03." The sophomores again tried to paint the tank, but they were driven away when seven of their number were captured, tied up, and photographed.[9]

The following year sixty-five freshmen were captured, bound, and paraded down to the county courthouse in Lafayette where they were forced to drink the sulfur water from the Lafayette fountain. By this time the faculty, fed up with the whole affair, replaced the "'03" with a "P.U." The seniors' feeling that the faculty had overstepped their bounds quickly replaced the "P.U." with a "'01." The senior interference was welcomed by the other classes and the back-and-forth painting continued until Thanksgiving. One of many detailed descriptions of the calendar of events is found in the 1901 *Debris*:

> The first day of school in its Freshman year the class made a gallant effort to put '01 upon the tank. The attempt was unsuccessful because of the fact that the Freshman [*sic*] present were outnumbered two to one.

> 1. Soon, however, a class election was held and Atkins was chosen president. Then the class was well organized and a second attempt made to paint the tank. After a hard fight the Sophomores were forced to admit defeat, and '01 was placed upon the tank and guarded till the break of day. After daylight, despite all traditions, the Sophomores put back their '00. All through the fall months tank fights were fought, with the result that '01 was generally on the tank. The Sophomores soon learned that the only safe times to put their numbers up were either Saturday morning, when the Freshmen had school work, or Sundays, which custom decrees should be given to other things than tank fights.[10]

> 2. At some point in the first few years of the twentieth century it was determined that one large scrap would be a better option. The winners would then have the honor of painting their class year on the tank and it would not be disturbed for the rest of the academic year. Although all parties agreed on the idea of one large official Tank Scrap, there were other activities associated with it. Up to 1913 there were small group skirmishes and preliminary scraps. Generally they occurred somewhere on campus, some were planned and others were spontaneous. The Class of '02 reported two "skirmishes" before the major event. The only recorded incident involving a firearm occurred during the 1902 scraps. Apparently a group of freshmen stole a sophomore's painting equipment and took it to a freshman's off-campus room. Discovering the location of the apartment, a group of sophomores attempted a raid. They were stopped by the "cold, icy stare" of a .32-caliber revolver in the hands of the landlady that "promptly cooled their ardor."[11]

At the very beginning of the school year the freshman class, with junior advisors, and the sophomore class, with senior advisors, met separately to discuss strategy and tactics for an upcoming scrap, choose a class yell, and elect a scrap leader, a yell leader, and a treasurer. Another annual task was to secure permission to hold the event from Purdue's president. On the days prior to the official scrap the freshmen and sophomores practiced knot tying and memorized passwords. Freshmen also tried to force the sophomores out for preliminary scraps by capturing lone sophomores and painting them. At times this involved removing the sophomores from streetcars or setting up roadblocks and stopping cars going across the Wabash River. Upon capture the victims were stripped and doused or dunked head first into pails of paint. An example of the freshmen's prescrap activities is described in a 1910 *Purdue Exponent* article. The two victims were sophomore *Exponent* reporters:

> Two reporters on a peaceable mission were summary "jerked" from the west bound car at the foot of the hill and in the face of vain protests, threats, and assumption of official dignity on their part, were divested of their wearing apparel and clothed in a coat of paint of indescribable colors. Joseph in his many-colored coat certainly had nothing on the two wayfarers who emerged from the ordeal only to face one still more interesting from the spectator's standpoint. One of the unfortunates by the name of Laird was called upon to engineer the business end of a pump handle until the trough in the West Side livery barn was full to overflowing. Then young Laird, a bonny-haired giant, gave exhibitions in aquatics and won a round of well-deserved applause by his fancy swimming and high diving. Laird emerged from his exhibition breathless and shivering and was allowed to escape clad in his scanty garb.[12]

The night of the big event, the official Tank Scrap, had become one of the major annual events on campus. By 1907, the standard practice for the freshmen was to start assembling by the call, "Freshmen Out!" They gathered behind the Civil Engineering Building early in the evening. Sophomores assembled an hour later at Stuart Athletic Field. The freshmen then marched through West Lafayette singing and chanting the class yell. Class yells included such inspired poetics as:

Rip! Rah! Razoo!
Zip! Boom! Bazoo!
Wah! Hoo! Hullabaloo!
Ninety-Seven! Old Purdue![13]

When the freshman arrived at the tank they took up positions downhill from their target. In the 1908 battle, the freshmen dug shallow trenches to deter the sophomore charge. Around 2:00 a.m., the sophomores arrived accompanied by rockets and roman candles. Upperclassmen acted as marshals, keeping the crowd off the field of battle. After a period of yelling, singing, and chants the battle was opened at the firing of a signal rocket. The sophomores then charged down the hill into the freshmen ranks. Some of the sophomores' charges were in the form of a flying wedge, a T formation, or in Napoleonic lines of battle. Generally, both sides held men in reserves in case the battle turned against them. In some years the brawl lasted a couple of hours and in others, such as the 1907 battle, it was over in twenty-five minutes with the victory going to the sophomores who captured and chained 347 freshmen. Once the upperclassmen declared the winner, the next phase of the event was the parade into downtown Lafayette and the ceremony at the courthouse where the losers were made to pay homage to the winners. The losers were decorated with paint before the parade began.

By 1905 it was customary to have a band lead the procession off the field of battle, but the 1905 scrap was memorable in many other ways. From start to finish it took two hours and twenty minutes. The entire event took place in a rainstorm. The freshmen had been on the field beginning at 6:00 p.m., but it was 2:10 a.m. before the sophomores established their camp. Because the site was, in places, six inches deep in mud, the sophomores were overly cautious. The upperclassmen had little patience for their caution. For an hour the upperclassmen and freshmen hurled accusations of cowardice before the sophomores finally advanced in a Napoleonic line of battle. It was 4:30 a.m. before the freshmen were declared victors. The freshmen had an easier time getting captives into their camp since it was downhill and nearly impossible for the freshmen captives to be escorted up hill. The freshmen merely had to launch the captives downhill in the slick mud. A final rush by the remnants of the sophomores was overwhelmed and the sophomore camp was secured.

1. In 1908, to make the event safer, the faculty and student council agreed that the scrap would begin at 7:00 p.m. Also beginning that year, after the defeated had been securely chained and painted, they were paraded in a snake-like procession to Stuart Field where a large bonfire was lit and all the bleachers filled up with spectators. The event no longer ended at the Tippecanoe County Courthouse. After being paraded around the fire the losers were forced to perform dances, leapfrog, a crawling race, the sophomore yell as well as Purdue yells, and other antics all to the accompaniment of drums. One year, a freshman was stripped, covered in paint and "required" to give his interpretation of Vaudeville performer Eva Tanguay's Dance of the Seven Veils.[14]

2. Over the years, tactics on both sides changed. One of the most creative was that of the freshmen class during the 1904 scrap. The freshmen built a raft before the event and placed it in the tank, which apparently did not have a roof at the time. Two freshmen spent the night onboard with the intent to dislodge the sophomores' ladders and painters with water and sticks. After the freshmen were defeated, the two continued to resist. Since by tradition the winners had to paint the tank before daylight to make the win official, the victors went to the West Lafayette pumping station and bribed the engineer

with ten dollars to flood the tank, thus making it dangerous for the inhabitants. After abandoning the tank, the two joined their defeated and chained
classmates who were forced to encircle the tank and get thoroughly drenched
as the water flowed over them.[15]

As the event evolved rules were established, expanded, and modified. By
1901, it was established that no weapons of any sort were to be used and no fisti-
cuffs. Knives had been introduced to cut friends free from bondage. To prevent
this padlocks and chains were introduced in 1902 to replace the ropes. Finally, in
1905, official rules were published.

At present the only rules are those of tradition, which may be briefly stated
as follows:

1. None save freshmen and sophomores shall engage in the contest.
2. It shall occur in the night and end before daylight on the morning of the first
   football game on Stuart Field.
3. No contestant shall use any weapons, nor be permitted to strike with his fist.
4. The class having the fight won on the morning above mentioned shall be
   declared the victors and their numerals remain on the tank at least through
   the football season.
5. In case the fight is declared a draw, the numerals actually on the tank shall
   declare the victors.[16]

Besides weapons, another issue was the sheer size of the event. Because of
the ever-increasing class sizes, the event was becoming more difficult to control:

Again, we have outgrown the time when the fight can be conducted in the old
slipshod manner. Henceforth some rules must be laid down which will govern
the conditions of the combat and these rules must be made and enforced by
the upperclassmen. The growth of the university and consequent enlargement
of the classes have added greatly to the interest in the event, but they have also
added greatly to the attendant dangers. It is becoming more apparent each
year that the plot of the ground on which the clash usually takes place is not
well adapted to the purpose. It is cut up with small ditches and gullies and
sometime a serious accident will occur.[17]

It was not just the classes that were getting bigger, but the crowd as well.
By 1904 the crowd that came to observe the event numbered in the thousands.
As many as six to ten thousand people attended the 1907 event. One reporter
stated that the crowd began to assemble by 6:00 p.m., but the event itself did
not begin for another six hours. In the meantime, wienerwurst and peanut
vendors made a great deal of money. There were complaints of members of the
crowd interfering with the event rather than just observing as well, so the following year upperclassmen formed a shield between the scrappers and the

public—and this precaution continued. Upperclassmen were appointed as marshals to make sure the rules were followed. The number of marshals increased over time.

By 1904 the Tank Scrap was making news on a national level and it must have made both the administration and some parents anxious. One highly exaggerated Indianapolis newspaper article reported thirty students injured.[18] After the 1904 event, Purdue President Winthrop E. Stone addressed the student body, condemning the practice in the strongest terms: "The 'Tank Scrap' in its present aspect is intolerable and indefensible. The entire University is charged with the grave responsibility of purging itself from all cause for future criticisms in this connection. What is to be done is a matter for deliberation, but it can be stated without hesitation that this contest must cease to disturb the peace of the Community and the work of the University; it must be shorn of brutality and meanness; it must become an affair of the students and not a public spectacle."[19]

President Stone presided over the university during the height of the scrap and during that time it was regularly condemned. Yet, it only got bigger, more complex, and popular. Prior to Stone's tenure, the city had ceased fining the students for damages, and police and medical staff were made available to assist in the event. Concern over the reputation of the Tank Scrap and how it reflected on Purdue was always on someone's mind. The faculty at various times tried unsuccessfully to end the tradition. One of the most interesting somewhat tongue-and-cheek editorials in the *Exponent* noted that the event was being reported in newspapers across the country. According to the editorial writer, since the Tank Scrap was, "the most unique and the most widely known college custom in the United States," the university should be proud and the participants should keep "upon the same high plane."[20] The wry "editorial" continued:

Preliminary scraps are now coming off nightly and we hope those connected with them will bear in mind that the annual class fights are not pitched battles between ruffians, but rather friendly contests between gentlemen. It is not necessary to say, "Pardon me, but I am going to knock your block off," or "Pray excuse me while I jam your face in the mud," but go quietly about the business with a grim determination to win without brutality. A little courtesy shown a man bound and helpless while hundreds of feet are stepping on his face will go a long way toward making a freshman love Purdue and Purdue men.[21]

Typically, a number of students required medical attention after these events. Concussions, broken rib, smashed collarbones, and sprains were not uncommon. They were so common, in fact, that one of the first items of business for the freshman and sophomore classes at the beginning of the school year was to raise enough money to cover the expected medical expenses. Newspapers eagerly reported detailed accounts of the injuries. One famous injury involved a member of the marching band. According to school lore up to the Tank Scrap he was a fifer. After he had his teeth knocked out during the scrap, he became a drummer.[22]

1. The event attracted attention in newspapers outside of Indiana and these accounts were often exaggerated. For example, a 1901 *New York Times* article was entitled "Two Students May Die."[23]
2. In the same paper, three years later, there was a report of thirty students with injuries such as a broken collarbone, a wrenched spine, and internal, head, and chest injuries.[24]
3. In 1904, one Ohio paper reported five students killed.[25]
4. The students who viewed the Tank Scrap as an honored tradition had little time for off-campus reporters who covered the event and exaggerated the violence and injuries. In 1909, one Lafayette reporter was confronted by the students who threatened to "mop the earth" with him if he reported the injuries. The students had to be restrained from doing him harm. In this particular year concern over injuries were justified. One student sustained serious injuries to his left side and had to be removed from the field. Another was kicked under the chin. The cut he received was not the only injury. He became so delirious it required six fellow students to restrain him. Finally a doctor had to anesthetize him in order to examine his injuries. He was later hospitalized.[26]

Neither of these students completed their freshman year and never returned to Purdue. One later graduated from a nearby college and became a major donor to that institution.

5. The 1913 event was the most controlled event in the history of the Tank Scrap. Parents were complaining and it was giving the university negative publicity. In recent years both students and spectators had received serious injuries. One spectator during the previous year fell thirty feet from a tree and landed in the midst of the melee.[27]
6. The rules were expanded due to pressure from the faculty. Both the number of participants and the crowd was getting so large that it was becoming more and more difficult to control peoples' actions. Participants would now be searched for contraband weapons, such as knives, before entering the field of battle. Rubber-soled tennis shoes were required. During this year there was an option to be excused from involvement due to a heart condition or if one were physically disabled. The university physician was authorized to examine students free of charge at their request and certify whether a medical issue excused them from participating. The university hoped to avoid lawsuits.[28]

On the night of the scrap, vehicles were banned from the campus, and no one was allowed to park on Salisbury Street, which ran along the event grounds. Five sheriff's deputies were on hand. As in previous years, a wire fence was erected around the field of battle to keep the crowd from joining the fight.

Neither the *Exponent* nor the local papers reported the usual activities, such as roving bands of freshmen capturing and painting sophomores. So, it appears that the rules were complied with. The preliminary fight was won by the sophomores and little negative information was reported other than the standard injuries due to the wind being knockout of some of the participants.

The 1913 scrap was one of the shortest and, on the surface, tamest in the history of the event—but it turned deadly. It lasted only fourteen minutes, but despite all the precautions, what everyone feared would happened, finally did happen. Sophomore Francis W. (Frank) Obenchain of South Whitley, Indiana, lay dead on the field. The initial story stated that he was seen by one of the upperclass marshals and, still breathing, was immediately carried to an aid station and soon after moved to his room in the Phi Kappa Sigma fraternity house. The doctors on site assumed heart failure and despite all their efforts he was pronounced dead. His death was announced to the procession heading for Stuart Field and the students immediately dispersed.

1. The local coroner and deputy coroner both examined the body and determined no marks of violence were present on the body. They reportedly found a goiter and obtained a history of previous heart trouble from a local physician who had been treating him for the condition. No autopsy was performed at the request of the father who suspected a cover up.[29]
2. Once the body was returned to South Whitley, Indiana, five Fort Wayne physicians performed an autopsy and discovered that Obenchain had died of a broken neck. Specifically, there was a dislocation and fracture of the first cervical vertebra that nearly severed the spinal cord. The physicians also claimed to have discovered finger marks behind the ears.[30]

Various witnesses later gave conflicting statements about what they saw happen to the victim. No one was ever accused of a crime or identified as the person responsible. The day after the 1913 Tank Scrap, the entire university body assembled in Fowler Hall and with a unanimous vote ended the tradition.

The Tank Scrap was fiercely defended by the students during its two decades of existence. They did not look upon the event as hazing. To them it was an important means of social bonding, a rite of passage, and a claim to manhood. The faculty and administration alike had a strongly held view of the event, claiming that it presented a negative impression of the institution. However, for decades, even after 1913, the Tank Scrap was remembered fondly in Purdue publications.

DAVID M. HOVDE is Associate Professor of Library Science and Research and Instruction Librarian at the Virginia Kelly Karnes Archives and Special Collections Research Center at Purdue University Libraries.

25 A Blueprint for Greek Reforms

How to Establish an Antihazing Task Force with Concrete "Good First Steps" to Change a Hazing Culture

Travis T. Apgar

I CAN RECALL THE morning of February 25, 2011, with vivid detail. It appeared to be a typical winter morning in Central New York. I woke to snow, dressed for the cold, and headed out to clear the drive. After I went back into my house to warm up, I received a call from the Cornell University dean of students. He informed me that I was needed on campus as soon as possible. George Desdunes, one of our students, had died from alcohol poisoning. The dean began to describe the details: where the student was found in a fraternity house, the cleaning men who located him, and his condition when discovered. I learned that the death might have been related to hazing. I was stunned.[1]

As a higher-education student affairs professional, I have spent my career working to increase access to college, to offer students an enriching environment within which to pursue academic successes, and to prepare students to be well-rounded, positive contributors to a global society. In addition to the primary responsibilities of recruiting, retaining, and graduating students, higher-education professionals like me are challenged to address issues such as campus and student safety, the proliferation of technology and social media, the abuse of alcohol and other drugs, acts of discrimination and bias, and the economic challenges of society, our institutions, and of course the students. Early in my career I noticed how little attention was paid to the topic of hazing—still seen largely back then as benign, humorous, or just "students being students." Through personal experiences, as an undergraduate student and later as a student affairs professional, I knew I had to do what I could to advance efforts to abolish the practice. As I began to educate myself on the topic, I came to view Cornell University as an institution leading with innovative ideas and initiatives in the hazing prevention effort.

Cornell University is among the first, if not *the* first, institution to have developed a website dedicated to the education and prevention of hazing.[2] Skorton

Center for Health Initiatives Director Timothy Marchell and his colleagues publish a comprehensive online resource dedicated to this topic. The site educates visitors with definitions, policies, and laws; describes the range of behaviors that form the continuum of hazing; poses the arguments for and against hazing, including perceived costs and benefits; offers resources and references on hazing including alternative activities and organizations that work to mitigate hazing; and details studies that explore the prevalence and form of these hidden practices. The student leadership of the self-governing fraternity and sorority community of Cornell collectively decided that transparency was necessary to end hazing practices and created what became known as the "Sunshine Policy." This policy states the "misconduct that exhibits hazing and/or a threat or disregard for students' mental or physical health and safety" will be made public. Every instance in which a Cornell student organization or team was found responsible for hazing since 2004 has been listed publically on the searchable site at http://hazing.cornell.edu and http://http://groupmisconduct.cornell.edu.

As a member of the Cornell University staff, I became directly involved in the university's expanded efforts to eliminate these behaviors. I believed, and the data supported, that we were making progress. Perhaps it was naiveté that dreadful morning in February 2011, or a moment of denial, but despite having spent countless hours developing hazing prevention programs at Cornell and many other campuses as a consultant, I hadn't prepared myself for a hazing death to occur within my community.

The dean's statement momentarily put me on my heels. I hung up, went to the fraternity house, and interacted with police and members of the fraternity to piece together the details of what may have occurred. Instead of educating about hazing, I now found myself working the other side of a hazing death, helping to put together the response. I was much less familiar with the best practices in responding to a hazing-related death. In the days, weeks, and months that followed, I struggled with the question, "If it can happen here, where we have invested as much, if not more than anywhere else, can we realistically end hazing?" The answer came in the form of a challenge.

On August 23, 2011, the *New York Times* published an op-ed titled "A Pledge to End Fraternity Hazing" written by David J. Skorton, then Cornell University president.[3] In it he shared details about the hazing death of our student, and how that tragic loss of life convinced him that we must address the long-outdated practices of hazing by challenging the most basic of fraternity traditions: pledging. To pursue the end of pledging was a provocative choice. He acknowledged that hazing is not unique to fraternities and sororities, noting that fraternity and sorority organizations possess redeemable qualities.

Dr. Skorton challenged the international fraternity and sorority communities as well as those on our campus to eliminate the pledge period, the platform on which hazing most often occurs. He had concluded that pledging and the activities defined as hazing had become synonymous. He declared that if we were to eradicate hazing, we would have to reconstruct the manner in which students join these organizations. The process to bring people in as new members would have to offer activities and experiences meeting the legitimate goals and desired outcomes of the historical pledge process, but we would not tolerate any form of hazing or other questionable activities.

In the weeks following the op-ed, we began to map the process for which this work would be done. President Skorton invited students to put forward ideas for alternatives to hazing/pledging, but a workable plan needed to be refined, structured, and facilitated. A group representative of the stakeholder populations was formed, called the Recruitment, Acceptance, Retention, and Education Task Force (RARE).

The Cornell Fraternity and Sorority Member Education Working Group

A top-down directive was issued by the university president to end the practice of pledging, and a bottom-up approach was chosen as the means to meeting the challenge to identify alternative methods for welcoming new members into fraternal organizations that were "free from humiliation, degradation, or any other form of hazing." The makeup of the RARE Task Force was carefully planned to include representation from the key stakeholder groups.[4]

Launched in the fall of 2011, the task force consisted of twenty-four members, representing undergraduate students, fraternity and sorority alumni, international fraternities and sororities, subject-matter experts, university faculty, and administrators.[5] The group to be most directly affected by the change, students, made up the majority of the task force. There were fourteen chapter presidents, council officers, and members from various class years selected to provide insight and input across the community. Among the fourteen were the presidents of each of the undergraduate governing councils (Interfraternity Council, Multicultural Greek Letter Council, and Pan-Hellenic Council), student leaders determined to be influential community leaders (such as chapter presidents as well as current and former council officers), and finally second-year or third-year students who could offer the perspective of the general member and would maintain membership over multiple years to provide continuity of student input.

Alumni members made up the second-largest representative group. They represented the stakeholders who had a significant investment of time and financial resources, and largely represented the owners of the physical houses within the system. Each of the three alumni advisory groups (Alumni Panhellenic Advisory Council, Alumni Interfraternity Council and Alumni Multicultural Greek Letter Council) had a representative.

The task force engaged William Sonnenstuhl, PhD, who serves as Associate Professor of Organizational Behavior and Director of Graduate Studies for the Cornell University School of Industrial and Labor Relations. Professor Sonnenstuhl's current research focuses on college drinking. His current book, *The Misperception of College Drinking: Pluralistic Ignorance and Campus Life*, and his expertise in the areas of alcohol and substance abuse, prevention and treatment, complex organizations, organizational deviance, and organizational change made him well suited to provide the task force with both research-based and practice-proven strategies for addressing culture change.

Considering the desired outcome was to end a ubiquitous historical practice of fraternities and sororities, the task force invited two international fraternity executives to participate and provide the perspective of that stakeholder group and key partners. In addition, a number of key international organization leaders were consulted over the course of the year from which the task force worked to collect information and construct recommendations.

Finally, a staff member within the Office of Fraternity and Sorority Affairs and I served on the task force as topic authorities, to represent the university as a stakeholder, and provide the group with logistical support.

Working Group Process

The Cornell Fraternity and Sorority Member Education Working Group, as the task force was initially referred, convened in the fall semester of 2011. We worked collaboratively over the course of one calendar year to respond to the president's challenge to "end pledging" by examining recruiting and initiation processes so as to develop an appropriate alternative process to welcome new members and to more broadly put forth recommendations to positively change the culture to remove hazing. Additional parameters provided to the group included the expectation that the new process would be free of any form or possibility of degradation, humiliation, or any other form of hazing; the recruitment and welcome of new members would occur on a platform of mutual dignity and respect in which members and those seeking membership would be equals; and all new-member activities would align with the values of the organization and the Cornell community. Cochair people were identified to lead the working group; these were an undergraduate student leader and an alumnus of an interfraternity council organization. Upon organizing, the working group identified their immediate key objectives to be to:

- Identify causes of and behaviors/traditions that result in a culture of hazing.
- Research history, best practices, and experts for ideas for reforms.
- Develop alternatives that welcome new members free of degradation, humiliation, and all other forms of hazing.
- Enable and provide resources to chapters to create their own unique, safe, and effective new-member processes.[6]

The group also defined the outcomes they would consider to be successes as "the elimination of all negative recruitment and membership activities, including all mental anguish, physical injuries, and deaths caused by hazing and/or negative new member orientation activities."

Upon focusing on their objectives and goals, the group renamed themselves. In consideration of the key aspects of their mission, the group chose the Recruitment, Acceptance, Retention and Education (RARE) Task Force.

The members of the RARE Task Force educated themselves on the theories and explanations of the reasons groups employ hazing activities. They worked to understand the root causes, such as identification with aggressors, need for belonging and intimacy, symbolic interactionism, fear of rejection, perceived power, lack of alternatives, and misperceived community norms. They did this so the task force would be better equipped to identify healthy and positive alternatives that would be generally accepted by the community.

In formulating a set of recommendations, the task force also identified as critical the need to raise the level of expectation of behavior in order to elevate the performance of members of the community, and in turn the community as a whole. They declared that to be a member of a fraternity or sorority is to be a leader, a scholar, a person of character, healthy, and one who can inspire others. That membership in a fraternal organization is and should remain a lifetime privilege and, as such, criteria for selection and retention should set a high standard for membership. It was stated that raising the level of performance and expectation can build a stronger experience for each member, developing over time a high-performing community of organizations focused on the core principles of each organization and contributing to the external goal of achieving the mission of the university.

Recommendations for Change

In the spring semester of the 2012 academic year, the task force submitted a draft report, including a list of recommendations for change, to the Cornell University Fraternity and Sorority Advisory Council. Having received feedback, the group worked over the summer months and in mid-Fall 2012 presented a final report detailing how the group used their time, the process for developing conclusions, what recommendations they considered but did not put forward, and the recommendations they submitted for consideration by the university. The recommendations were as follows:

1. Create and implement the One Greek Cornell Community Experience. The aim was to develop an experience for all students interested in fraternity and sorority life made up of components addressing academics, personal character, leadership development, service to community, and personal fitness.

2. Modify the new-member process. The goal was to eliminate the pledge process and offer organizations a limited time period to welcome new members.
   a. Require a written new-member education plan from each organization that provides transparency and defines positive "rites of passage." Such a plan must be approved annually by national, alumni, and/or faculty advisors.
   b. Shorten the duration of time in which the welcoming period may occur so as to focus the organization in educating new members on what is truly meaningful, and to limit opportunity for hazing activities.
   c. Require chapters to adopt a four-year membership education model, planning the ongoing education and development of members over the course of the time they are undergraduates.
3. Focus on academic excellence. Because academic excellence is a key value among Cornell students, this aim was intended to create proper alignment between the university and Greek chapters.
   a. Create "rites of enhancement," including academic performance, that recognize students and encourage chapters to perform.
   b. Require new and existing members, and chapters, to maintain minimum GPA at all times, with careful monitoring during an intake process.
   c. Defer the recruitment of prospective members who fail to meet the minimum GPA for at least one semester, until performance improves.
   d. Adopt a suspension-of-status process for members or chapters below the minimum academic standards.
   e. Implement a mentorship program to encourage members to excel.
4. Motivate chapters to intentionally plan and deliver ongoing development opportunities for members through chapter-defined four-year education models.
   a. Each chapter would adopt a new-member education program based on national requirements.
   b. There would be a strong preference for four-year education models offering chapter-focused, new-member education, including the following:
      i. Leadership development training for sophomores and juniors;
      ii. Leadership, risk management, professional, and career development education for juniors and seniors; and
      iii. Education and/or training for all members on bystander intervention related to high risk behaviors.
   c. Leverage breadth and depth of university and community for programs that add ongoing value to members beyond social agenda.
5. Recommend that new and "at risk" chapters with houses be required to have an advisor live in the facility to provide a heightened level of guidance and advice to the self-governing organization while in transition as a new group, or as the group works to reform underperformance.

a. There is a need to define "at risk" chapters. For example, these chapters may display all or some of the following: low performance tier ratings, failure to address audit findings, recruiting challenges, financial issues, or reported incidents.

b. It was agreed that a minimum four-year period of commitment for advisors be recommended.

c. Certain criteria will not be required for well-performing chapters or chapters without houses.

d. Chapters must move ahead with requirements to develop job descriptions, recruitment criteria and process, training and development, quality control, insurance coverage, and cost and funding models.

e. The task force agreed there was a need to explore funding alternatives for houses lacking the monetary resources to meet the requirement.

6. Expand self-governance concept to include alumni. Alumni have long been viewed as a cherished and strategic component of a strong fraternity and sorority experience at Cornell.

a. Each chapter must have a minimum of three active advisors per chapter, with at least one being a local resident. It is preferred that at least one advisor be an alum, but this is not necessarily required.

b. Alumni training must comply with national guidelines.

c. Exceptions may be granted to small chapters and new interest groups to have a minimum of one active advisor.

d. It is encouraged for chapters to recruit faculty and experienced individuals, especially if alumni network is insufficient.

e. Chapters must participate in risk management audits.

f. Chapter advisors should serve on alumni advisory groups.

g. Participate in interviews of new leaders and exit interviews.

7. Hire a hazing specialist for all campus organizations and athletic teams. There is a need to recruit a recognized leader capable of delivering to Cornell standards and national mandates. This position should do the following:

a. Lead the implementation of these recommendations.

b. Develop research and measurement processes to evaluate successes of initiatives and efforts.

c. Promote National Hazing Hotline and national legislation encompassing both physical and psychological hazing.

d. Develop "Real Life, Real Hazing" film of Cornellians and access similar, existing "powerful" tools for education and awareness.

e. Create bystander intervention training, preparing individual community members who can conduct chapter-wide education on how to identify and intervene successfully in hazing and other high-risk behaviors.

8. Create a risk management council. It is recommended there be developed a council of alumni, student leaders, and staff tasked with providing ongoing assessment of chapter performance and poised to intervene with the alumni and student leadership of an organization that demonstrates underperformance or the risk of underperformance.

9. Set university standards for Greek chapters. The mandate is to develop a clear list of expectations for fraternities and sororities and a comprehendible process for evaluation. The recommendation is that the university do the following:
   a. Revise the current end-of-year reporting performance tier-rating process.
   b. Create ratings based on shared values.
   c. Incorporate chapter objectives and written intake-plan deliverables.
   d. Expand performance ratings from the present tier system to four tiers to improve differentiation of results.
   e. Enhance ease of use through web-based or phone application reporting.
   f. Initiate quarterly reviews undertaken by chapter officers, alumni advisors, and council officers to be reported annually to national organizations (if applicable) and the university.
   g. Subject underperforming chapters to alumni advisor and risk management council audits.
   h. Recognize improving and excellent-performing chapters specifically with rewards through the expanded council-initiated incentive program.

10. Provide funding necessary for transformation. Motivation can come from tragedy, but it can also come from exciting new programs, resources, and incentives. Hazing prevention programs, including reforms and alternatives to hazing "rites of passage" in new-member processes, require sustained development resources and funding. Funded and unfunded mandates from the university, once finalized, can lead to funding discussions among nationals, alumni, and undergraduates.

It was further recommended by the RARE Task Force that cultural change can take an extended period of time, and with that considered and for the maximum opportunity of successful implementation, these recommendations, along with parallel or incorporated initiatives, should be phased in over an acceptable period of time. The report and recommendations were accepted by President Skorton as "a good first step" in our work to eliminate hazing.

University Implementation

The work of the RARE Task Force provided a tremendous launching point for significant structural changes, programmatic offerings, and cultural interventions.

The university accepted this thoughtful and thorough report and considered what was presented through the framework detailed in Linda Langford's 2008 working paper entitled "A Comprehensive Approach to Hazing Prevention in Higher Education Settings."[7] This framework, with techniques backed by results and science that have been proven effective in preventing violence on college campuses, was adapted by Langford to take the issues associated with violence in the form of hazing into consideration. Her working paper outlines principles and a process, which can be customized for the educational institution and the needs of the community. The key actions for a comprehensive antihazing initiative are as follows:

1. Identify and address multiple contributing factors.
2. Conduct a "local" analysis.
3. Include prevention, early intervention, and response components.
4. Use multiple, coordinated, and sustained strategies.
5. Make sure programs, policies, and services are coordinated and synergistic.
6. Ensure that each component of the initiative has clearly defined goals and objectives that are informed by data and research.
7. Build collaborations.

Additionally, Cornell has adopted a public-health model in developing and instituting a strategic framework for addressing hazing in a comprehensive manner.

This model demonstrates the multiple interventions deployed across settings to comprehensively address the culture of hazing.[8] It informs the public and guides the work internally. It is comprehensive in approach, including an array of interventions to address the salient antecedents or intermediaries of the specific problem of hazing.

The recommendations and additional guidance were provided by the RARE Task Force along with input put forward by the Cornell University Fraternity and Sorority Advisory Council, the Cornell University Council on Hazing Prevention, content experts, and various university staff, administrators, and departments. All the preceding filled out the Cornell Model for Transformational Change. All initiatives were prioritized by immediate need for implementation, foundational necessity, and/or anticipated impact on hazing culture. The priorities were implemented in three phases between October 2012 and December 2014.[9]

Model for Transformational Change: Phase 1, 2012–2013

1. Transition to Total Membership Development Model
   - Maximum four-week new-member orientation.
   - Chapter creates development opportunities for all members of the organization for the duration of their undergraduate experience.

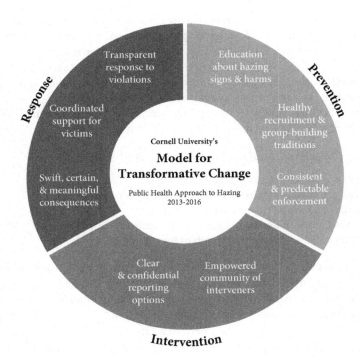

Fig. 25.1. A working model that attempts to change a perceived hazing culture into hazing-free and responsible student groups.

2. All membership programs must be approved by international organization and alumni.
3. Goal is to require timely, predictable, and meaningful adjudication of infractions.
4. Transparency of outcomes is essential. Create website (www.groupmisconduct.cornell.edu) to help students and families understand the culture of any group or team in which they are considering membership.
5. Increased individual preparedness needs to be implemented. Critical for success is bystander intervention training.
6. Increased alumni involvement for support and prevention.

Model for Transformational Change: Phase 2, 2013–2014

1. Enhanced Advising: Increasing the presence of a more-experienced adult through the addition of alumni/chapter advisors who are local, or live-in advisors for those organizations with houses.

2. One Greek Cornell Community Experience: Create a shared experience for those students interested in learning about Cornell Fraternity & Sorority Life in the form of academic, service, social, or educational activities.
3. Access to Houses: Required access to houses for health and safety purposes would eliminate, among other abuses, admission of under-the-drinking-age visitors and strangers that could prove a security problem.
4. System-Wide Incentives: Self-governing councils will identify ways in which to incent organizations/members to increase positive community contributions.

Model for Transformational Change: Phase 3, 2014–2015

1. Increase value of chapter evaluation process.
2. Develop plan to expand antihazing efforts across campus.
3. Institutionalize alumni and advisor support.
4. Establish uniform and consistent communications with alumni.
5. Identify consistent academic standard for the system.

Between 2012 and 2015 all initiatives were implemented, some ahead of schedule. Key initiatives, such as the transition to a Total Membership Development Model—specifically those objectives associated with organization new-member orientation programs—were fully realized and persist as the current practice. Others, such as the development of a One Greek Cornell Community Experience and the formation of a Risk Management Council have either been initiated and unsuccessful, or continue to be developed.

Measured Outcomes

We have used both quantitative and qualitative means to assess the impact of these efforts. The quantitative data is derived from surveys, such as the Membership Activities in Student Clubs, Organizations and Teams (MASCOT) Survey, which measures personal hazing experiences, perceived attitudes of peers on the topic of hazing within the Cornell community, and the perceived prevalence of hazing practices within the Cornell community. This instrument was administered in spring 2013 (a full year after the transition from the pledge to the orientation model). At that time, results indicated that 39 percent of all Cornell students had experienced at least one activity that would be considered hazing as a result of their membership in an organization, group, or team, with higher rates for those belonging to a fraternity, sorority (48 percent), or varsity sport team (47 percent). In spring 2015, following two years of intensive prevention programming, heightened community intervention capabilities, and establishing more predictable, timely, and meaningful responses to hazing, the MASCOT Survey was readministered. It demonstrated a reduction of all students reporting having experienced at least one activity that is considered hazing to 31 percent. Even more significant were the reductions measured by those who belong to a fraternity or sorority (35 percent) or a varsity sports team (30 percent). There was also a reduction measured with those students identifying as belonging to an "other" group, but not a fraternity, sorority, or varsity sport (25 percent compared to 31 percent in 2013). The most dramatic reductions occurred in the areas we at Cornell have focused our efforts: fraternities, sororities, and athletics. While reduction was measured among students identifying as belonging to an "other" student group, it was limited in comparison, perhaps a reflection of the limited focus on hazing prevention more broadly.

Between 2012 and 2015 we observed an increase in the number of reports submitted alleging hazing occurring within the fraternity and sorority community. Conversely there has been a measured decrease in the number of organizations that have committed an infraction. Overall, in 2011, six out of ten fraternities and sororities had violated the hazing policy in the preceding ten years. Between 2005 and 2015, the total fell very slightly to five out ten chapters.

In October 2015, prior to her death from colon cancer which occurred later that year, Cornell University President Elizabeth Garrett addressed several hundred student and alumni fraternity and sorority members attending the Eighteenth Andrew Dickson White Annual Summit for Greeks on this topic. She acknowledged the success in significantly reducing the prevalence of hazing, but made clear that she, nor any member of the Cornell community, should be satisfied until the practice of hazing departs the campus altogether.

Post-implementation Observations

In reflection of this work, and in consideration of others who may pursue similar reform efforts, there are several observations to share, generated from discussions with those directly involved and those who have arrived following the work or provided critique.

- Resources, be it people, funding, hardware or software, is necessary for some initiatives to be successful. If no new resources are committed to campus-based initiatives, they must be reallocated away from other important programs, which may negatively impact the community.
- Clear and up-front communication of expectations and processes with members of the task force is imperative. Those who are leading the task force must have a clear understanding of the expected process and be aware that there may be shifts and changes to that process, if that is where reforms lead.
- Regular, ongoing communication of implementation, direct assignment of ownership of initiatives, and coordination of the plan would help to avoid redundancies and splinter efforts disconnected from comprehensive strategy. This is a waste of resources that could be best used directly within the coordinated effort.

- Having the direction and ongoing support from the former university president and his cabinet provided our group with leverage to influence colleagues and other community members to collaborate. A timely, strong, but measured response took advantage of the worst possible situation and made what was thought of as next to impossible, possible—ending pledging.
- A high-functioning work relationship between offices sharing ownership of various aspects helps to avoid making difficult work manageable. Clarity on who owns and is responsible for various responsibilities is a key to maintaining these relationships.

Conclusions

The process and framework are generally applicable as they have been proven successful in use at a volume of institutions. There is no way to know if the specific recommendations and initiatives generated by the process at Cornell University are transferable. There may be fidelity of success if it is found that specific circumstances, challenges, and practices, such as the pledge process, have strong similarities between the communities, otherwise each institution must consider the unique qualities and components of its own culture and environment. At the least, the framework utilized provides a clear structure and the necessary components any higher-education institution community must consider and address if a comprehensive cultural change is to occur.

TRAVIS T. APGAR served Cornell University as the Robert G. Engel Senior Associate Dean of Students from 2006 to January 2017. An authority on hazing prevention, he is currently Assistant Vice President and Dean of Students at Rensselaer Polytechnic Institute.

26 Hazing and the Law and Litigation

What You Need to Know

R. Brian Crow and Colleen McGlone

THE DEARTH OF hazing litigation seems at odds with the continued prevalence of hazing, particularly considering forty-four states by August 2017 have passed antihazing statutes. Therefore, it is fitting to ask why the criminal prosecution of hazing, as well as civil litigation involving hazing, continues to occur so infrequently. Further, the study of how antihazing legislation has evolved is essential, as is the understanding of how courts and the legal system are interpreting and applying antihazing statutes. Finally, it is important to review how state legislators hope to change the ways that college and university fraternal organizations, athletic teams, bands, and some high school students are changing the techniques of initiating new members.

In order to focus on legislative and litigation developments around hazing, one must first examine possible reasons hazing still exists. That hazing persists in sport and other organizations is a function of three main concepts: (a) that it creates team cohesion and unity; (b) that it shows who on a team is dominant; and (c) that it proves commitment to the team.[1] While on the surface theories (a) and (b) seem to be in direct contrast to one another, this dichotomy is often cited by hazers who believe that new teammates should be subservient to veterans in order to improve or maintain team cohesion. This flawed assumption is deeply rooted in sport. Veteran athletes who are involved as perpetrators of hazing often were victims of hazing in previous seasons. They justify further hazing of new or prospective teammates under the false guise of tradition or hazing rituals increasing team cohesion. Reframing the mindset of these players and coaches is a critical part of eradicating hazing behavior.

Justin Burns contends that hazing is not just an act, but "an intent, reason, or goal behind an act that makes the mental state unique."[2] While this claim is not new, it will do the reader well to be reminded of these unique mental processes that make prosecution of hazers a challenge. The two reasons are that (1) there is a definite power relationship between the hazer and the hazed, and (2) "hazers suspend notions of morals and ethics to justify behavior as that of the group and not of the individual."[3]

Hazing and Criminal Law

Of the forty-four states that have criminalized hazing, many consider hazing a misdemeanor usually carrying a fine between $10 and $10,000 and jail sentences between ten days and one year, usually far less than the maximum. In six states (Illinois, Idaho, Missouri, Texas, Virginia, and Wisconsin) hazing that results in death or "great bodily harm" is categorized as a felony. Interestingly, most of the states that carry criminal laws regarding hazing do not require teachers, coaches, or administrators to proactively try to prevent hazing. However, in Alabama, Arkansas, Massachusetts, New Hampshire, South Carolina, and Texas, the state imposes a duty on school personnel to report hazing.[4] In addition, as will be discussed in this essay, a 2016 Pennsylvania law also holds high school administrators culpable if they fail to educate students about hazing and fail to report violations. In fact, the Alabama statute states "(c) No person shall knowingly permit, encourage, aid, or assist any person in committing the offense of hazing, or willfully acquiesce in the commission of such offense, or fail to report promptly his knowledge or any reasonable information within his knowledge of the presence and practice of hazing in this state to the chief executive officer of the appropriate school, college, university, or other educational institution in this state. Any act of omission or commission shall be deemed hazing under the provisions of this section."[5]

Nicholas Bittner in 2016 wrote extensively on litigation that occurs after hazing, and in doing so provided a comprehensive chart depicting current state antihazing laws. His analysis clearly shows the level of inconsistency in state statutes, and it is notable to mention that civil causes of action are rarely mentioned, and that some of the statutes only apply to college students. This chart by Bittner will be referenced often in this chapter.

In addition, Bittner provides an insightful commentary on the current state of antihazing litigation: "Antihazing laws are frankly too little, too late, and do not provide criminal or civil penalties, responsibility, or liability to any meaningful degree. Change must occur at both the state and the federal levels. There must be uniformity, proper recognition of the broad scope of what constitutes hazing, and recognition that the individuals most at fault are not necessarily the ones holding the paddle or the bottle of alcohol."[6]

Another legal scholar, Brandon W. Chamberlin, stated the sad reality in dealing with hazing prosecution and civil lawsuits is that "the rare cases in which hazing laws provide a benefit over general criminal statutes are the very cases in which the hazing laws are most vulnerable to legal challenge."[7]

Table 26.1

State	Misdemeanor	Aggravated Result or Risk	Failure to Report	No Defense of Consent	Student Perpetrator Only	Third-Party Liable	Civil Action	Inchoate Liability	Mental or Social Harm	Reckless Risk of Harm	Higher Education Only
AL	X		X			X		X	X		
AZ				X	X	X		X	X		
AR	X		X		X	X		X	X		
CA	X	X					X	X			
CO	X							X			X
CT	X			X				X	X		
DE	X			X				X	X		
FL	X	X	X	X				X		X	
GA	X			X				X			
ID	X		X		X	X		X	X		
IL	X	X	X							X	
IN	X	X								X	
IA	X	X		X				X		X	
KS	X							X		X	
KY								X	X	X	X
LA				X		X		X	X	X	
ME									X	X	
MD	X			X				X	X	X	
MA	X	X	X	X		X		X	X	X	

Constitutional Law

Constitutional claims have had limited success and victims typically initiate the litigation citing the due process clauses of the fourth and fourteenth amendments. In *Hilton v. Lincoln Way High School*, a hazing ritual took place in which the new band members were kidnapped and taken to the woods where they were forced to participate in a "Ku Klux Klan"–type of ceremony. Hilton asserted that the hazing ritual violated her Fourth Amendment right because of an illegal seizure termed "kidnapping."[8] The court heard that there was a history of unconstitutional conduct that school officials contributed to, and thus ruled in the favor of Hilton.[9]

In *Nice v. Centennial Area School District*, Nice brought suit claiming his Fourteenth Amendment rights had been violated during a hazing incident when he was held down by a teammate during an initiation. The hazing act that occurred in this case involved a tenth-grade wrestler who was victimized by a number of different kinds of hazing activities. Furthermore, under 42 U.S.C. 1983, public institutions can be held liable for monetary damages and injunctive relief.[10]

Under 42 U.S.C. 1983, a hazing victim can attempt to sue a school official if the official was directly involved in the hazing or if an official failed to prevent the hazing. Of course, the plaintiff must show the official was acting within state law and that the victim's constitutional rights were deprived, noted Bittner in his article titled "A Hazy Shade of Winter." [11]

Using the standards set forth under 42 U.S.C. 1983, victims of hazing have sought relief stating that the hazing violated one of their federal rights. In *DeShaney v. Winnebago*,[12] the U.S. Supreme Court reasoned that a student's right to bodily integrity is a constitutionally protected interest. In order to prevail with this type of claim, the plaintiff must prove that the defendant acted with deliberate indifference in regards to the student's individual constitutional rights by failing to prevent harm when there was previous knowledge of harmful situations occurring.

In *Meeker v. Edmunson*, the Fourth Circuit found that even though a wrestling coach was not directly involved in hazing beatings, the fact that he directed other students to administer the abuse was enough to constitute "direct action." When looking at third-party actors in terms of a 1983 claim, Bittner again found evidence that, while difficult, a successful claim is possible:

> In the context of ß 1983, the Third Circuit emphasized the Supreme Court's holding that third-party state actors can be liable for injuries caused by another when the "defendants, with deliberate indifference to the consequences, [establish] and [maintain] a policy, practice, or custom which directly [causes a] constitutional harm." Other courts have addressed this theory of inaction.

The Sixth Circuit listed the elements a plaintiff must prove to succeed on this theory; 1) the existence of a clear and persistent pattern of . . . abuse by school employees, (2) notice or constructive notice on the part of the School Board, (3) the School Board's tacit approval of the unconstitutional conduct, such that their deliberate indifference in their failure to act can be said to amount to an official policy of inaction, and (4) that the School Board's custom was the 'moving force' or direct causal link in the constitutional deprivation.[13]

A 2007 case involving two members of Kappa Alpha Psi fraternity based at Florida A&M University (FAMU) hinged on the legal definition of "serious bodily harm." This was the first case in Florida to utilize the Chad Meredith Act, named after the University of Miami student who died in 2001 as a result of drowning during a Kappa Sigma hazing. The act makes distinctions between misdemeanor and felony hazing charges based on bodily harm. The defendants received a jail sentence of two years for the hazing incident, but after some time was served, an appellate court reversed the convictions.[14]

In 2011, also at FAMU, band member Robert Champion was beaten to death in a hazing incident on a band bus in which fifteen band members were charged with hazing and various criminal acts. The alleged ringleader of the hazing received the longest sentence of sixty-six months while the majority of the defendants were sentenced to community service and probation. The conviction was under appeal to Florida's highest court in February, 2018.

In *Alton v. Texas A&M University*, Alton claimed to have been beaten repeatedly as part of a hazing ritual. He filed suit against the attackers, who were also students, and the officials and faculty advisor, claiming his rights had been violated.[15] The court addressed this issue in the case of the nonstudent officials who had tried to take action to stop the hazing incidents: "In sum, the officials' conduct must be measured against the standard of deliberate indifference." Therefore, Alton had to establish the following to be successful in his claim: "(1) The officials learned of facts or a pattern of inappropriate hazing behavior by a subordinate pointing plainly toward the conclusion that the subordinate was abusing the student; (2) The officials demonstrated deliberate indifference toward the constitutional rights of Alton by failing to take action that was obviously necessary to prevent or stop the abuse; and (3) The officials' failure caused a constitutional injury to Alton."

Alton was not able to successfully prove that the officials acted with deliberate indifference and the court granted the defendant qualified immunity.

Federal Law

There is currently only one federal statute that deals directly with hazing, an 1874 military law, although new federal legislation is under consideration in the fall of 2017. Otherwise, heretofore, federal law currently overlooks the issue of hazing altogether. Federal antihazing law has been proposed, but prior to 2017 has never made it to the floor of either the US Senate or House of Representatives. Some federal claims, then, have been filed under a violation of Title IX. In claims of same-sex hazing, invoking Title IX is one strategy that is gaining momentum.

To be liable for damages, a school district must have actual knowledge of the harassment, which is often attributable to the knowledge of a school employee who has the power to stop the abuse. After gaining that knowledge, the school district is liable under Title IX if it acts with deliberate indifference, or if its response or failure to respond "is clearly unreasonable in light of the known circumstances."[16]

In *Seamons v. Snow,* the trial court denied, and an appeals court affirmed, the dismissal of a victim's Title IX complaint because the victim had not stated the hazing was sexually harassing.[17]

State Law

As the number of reported hazing incidents has increased, so has the number of states that have passed legislation to deter hazing from occurring. To date, forty-four states have distinct hazing laws, each with varying components. The states of Alaska, Hawaii, Montana, New Mexico, South Dakota, and Wyoming do not have specific hazing laws in place. However, these states do have related statutes that may be utilized when hazing has occurred. While each of the states has different legal elements contained within the hazing laws (see chart above), there are three basic similarities within the state laws. Each state statute includes:

1. Language that clearly identifies a specific type of harm
2. A statement that relates to or alludes to being a member in some sort of group or organization
3. Statement that a hazing act is perpetrated to a distinct group of individuals (students, athletes, club members, etc).[18]

Variation among these state laws include what type of charge can be filed as well as the type of punishments that may be utilized, which may include a fine, imprisonment, or both depending on the state and the severity of the hazing incident. In the states that have antihazing statutes, the laws are often imperfect. Often the states developed these statutes as a reactionary measure following a tragic hazing act that received attention. This reactionary response often leads to statutes that are not fully developed.

Furthermore, hazing is often not well defined or is constricted in terms of scope. For example, Michigan law may be overbroad as it attempts to define hazing:

> "Hazing" means an intentional, knowing, or reckless act by a person acting alone or acting with others that is directed against an individual and that the person knew or should have known endangers the physical health or safety of the individual, and that is done for the purpose of pledging, being initiated into, affiliating with, participating in, holding office in, or maintaining membership in any organization. Subject to subsection (5), hazing includes any of the following that is done for such a purpose: (i) Physical brutality, such as whipping, beating, striking, branding, electronic shocking, placing of a harmful substance on the body, or similar activity. (ii) Physical activity, such as sleep deprivation, exposure to the elements, confinement in a small space, or calisthenics, which subjects the other person to an unreasonable risk of harm or that adversely, affects the physical health or safety of the individual. (iii) Activity involving consumption of a food, liquid, alcoholic beverage, liquor, drug, or other substance that subjects the individual to an unreasonable risk of harm or that adversely affects the physical health or safety of the individual. (iv) Activity that induces, causes, or requires an individual to perform a duty or task that involves the commission of a crime or an act of hazing.[19]

Many anti-hazing statutes fail to recognize that hazing activities can lead to emotional and mental harm, and none take into account the intent to harm. In many instances, hazing has resulted in athletes experiencing symptoms like depression, feelings of guilt, anxiety, and hopelessness.[20] The athletes who experience these symptoms following a hazing incident have little recourse when seeking relief under these statutes. Other definitions, like one from Louisiana, fail to recognize that hazing may take place on athletic teams and address only fraternal organizations.[21]

Ohio Antihazing Statute, An Example

Legal researcher Justin Burns provided an in-depth analysis and interpretation of the shortcomings of the Ohio law, which unfortunately are also found in many other state antihazing statutes. Burns claimed Ohio's statute is flawed in two ways: because it focuses on *initiation* into *organizations*, and also because it overlooks the *motivation* and *intent* behind hazing.[22]

As in many states, Ohio's antihazing statute makes hazing a strict-liability offense, which means the mental state of the perpetrator(s) is not a factor in whether a crime was committed. Burns contends that this shortsighted approach overlooks hazing research that shows hazing is motivated by "a mind-set of power over another, influence, and authority." He also asserts that because hazing is a fourth-degree misdemeanor, hazing may not be charged absent other criminal charges. Burns writes, "But as a stand-alone crime, the statute may not be sufficient to address the real hazing problem. In many instances, existing criminal statutes already cover harassment and violent hazing. Murder and assault are already crimes, just as are kidnapping and theft. . . . In fact, not a single Ohio hazing case could be found where the government charged hazing without some other offense attached for the same incident."

In summary, Burns contends that Ohio's antihazing law fails to deter future hazing, and it ignores the motivation and intent of hazers.

Pennsylvania State Law Updated 2016

In 2016 the Pennsylvania legislature passed, and the governor signed, an updated antihazing law. The previous law, on the books since 1986, only applied to colleges and universities. The new law, which many believe was passed in response to several severe high school hazing incidents within the state, will apply to middle and high school students as well.[23]

Civil Action Permissions

Four states directly mention that a hazing victim can bring a civil lawsuit against either the person who has committed the hazing or the organization to which the hazed individual was seeking entry. For example, California's Penal Code 245.6 PC reads: "The person against whom the hazing is directed may commence a civil action for injury or damages. The action may be brought against any participants in the hazing or any organization to which the student is seeking membership whose agents, directors, trustees, managers, or officers authorized, requested, commanded, participated in, or ratified the hazing."

Liability: Failure to Report

One of the most interesting content areas regarding hazing laws is a clause addressing failure of authorities and others to report. This is an important factor considering that hazing seldom occurs in a vacuum and others who may not be active participants in a hazing incident may have known about, heard about, or witnessed the incident. A total of seven states have included some sort of failure-to-report clause in the hazing statutes. In South Carolina, the statute reads, "It is unlawful for any person to knowingly permit or assist any person in committing acts made unlawful by Section 16-3-510 or to fail to report promptly any information within his knowledge of acts made unlawful by Section 16-3-510 to the chief executive officer of the appropriate school, college, or university."[24]

In Illinois, the punishment for not reporting hazing is more severe than those imposed on the individuals who conduct the hazing. The punishment includes up to one year of incarceration and up to $5,000 in fines.

The New Hampshire state law also includes failure-to-report language, and it states in part, "A natural person is guilty of a class B misdemeanor if such person . . . being a student, knowingly submits to hazing and fails to report such hazing to law enforcement or educational institution authorities."[25] In other words, a person such as a pledge who was hazed can be charged criminally if he or she does not report the hazing.

Third-Party Liability

Third-party liability is addressed specifically in hazing laws in seventeen states. Third-party liability is typically explained as when someone other than the individual who has performed the act of hazing can be held liable for the incident. This could be a result of someone who knew hazing was going to occur and did nothing to stop it, or someone who witnessed the event and failed to take steps to deter the event. The State of Idaho uses this within their hazing statute as an example.[26]

Emergent or Inchoate Liability

A total of twenty-four states have statements within the hazing statutes that address individuals who have knowledge regarding a hazing conspiracy, attempt, plan, or inducement.

Elements of Risk

Many states have multiple statements regarding harm and risk as elements within the law. Forty states have addressed the risk of harm within its hazing laws in some form. Risk is generally contained within one of three different categories: (1) *aggravated risk/result*: fifteen states, (2) *social and/or mental harm*: twenty-four states, and (3) *reckless endangerment*: thirty-one states. In Florida, for instance, the reckless endangerment clause addresses physical harm: "A person commits hazing, a third-degree felony, punishable as provided in s. 775.082 or s. 775.083, when he or she intentionally or recklessly commits any act of hazing as defined in subsection (1) upon another person who is a member of or an applicant to any type of student organization and the hazing results in serious bodily injury or death of such other person."[27]

Educational Status

In fourteen states the wording of the laws include specific statements regarding educational status. In fact, a total of seven states address hazing only when a *student* has been the perpetrator of the act. In addition, seven states address hazing only in higher-education settings and those focus mostly on Greek organizations. In Kentucky, for example, the state hazing laws address hazing only in the context of higher education and mandates that universities adopt policies that prohibit hazing.[28]

Civil Law

Plaintiffs who pursue civil action for hazing offenses may do so under the auspices of civil antihazing statutes, constitutional law, and tort law. The legal statutes under which remedy has been sought include *in loco parentis*, negligence, assault and battery, harassment, vicarious liability (*respondeat superior*), and premise liability claims.

Several states offer specific terms for what relief may be sought after hazing has transpired. For example, in Ohio the law states, "Any person who is subjected to hazing . . . may . . . sue for injury or damages, including mental and physical pain and suffering, that result from the hazing." This law is novel because it allows suits to be filed against administrators, employees, and faculty who could or should have been aware of the possibility of hazing but failed to take action to stop its occurrence.[29]

Tort Law

Under tort law, the hazing victim must prove that wrongdoing occurred on the part of the defendant who caused some type of damage and/or injury. Intentional tort claims are cited frequently in hazing litigation. Several cases have included tort claims of negligent infliction of emotional distress, intentional inflection of emotional distress, assault and battery, negligence, and vicarious and premise liability. For example, in *Brueckner v. Norwich*, a twenty-four-year-old ROTC student filed suit against Norwich University after being enrolled for only sixteen days subsequent to being subjected to several incidents of hazing. A lower court found the institution liable for assault and battery, negligent infliction of emotional distress, intentional infliction of emotional distress, and negligent supervision. In the case, upperclassman ROTC members who were charged by Norwich with the responsibility to "indoctrinate and orient 'rooks'" through various activities committed the hazing episodes. The university trained these cadets on how to fulfill this role.[30]

Brueckner reported the hazing to university officials prior to leaving the institution. Records indicate that the university had been aware of persistent hazing problems involving the ROTC program; however, they did not take any action to alter the training programs offered on campus and left the upperclassmen "virtually unsupervised." The jury awarded the plaintiff both compensatory and punitive damages based on the conclusion that the university had made the decision to remain ignorant of the hazing activities.

Respondeat Superior

The Supreme Court of Vermont upheld a lower court's ruling utilizing *respondeat superior*, stating that the university was vicariously liable for the actions of the students because they were acting within the scope of their employment. The scope of *respondeat superior* specifies that an employer may be held accountable for tortuous acts of an employee during the span of the employment.[31]

The implementation of *respondeat superior* can also apply to a national chapter of a fraternal organization, although the implementation of this doctrine has been inconsistent at best. Jared Sunshine found that an agency relationship between a national fraternity and its local chapter that is similar to a master-servant relationship can exist in the eyes of the law.[32]

This was important in *Ballou v. Sigma Nu General Fraternity*. L. Barry Ballou was a student at the University of South Carolina who died in a hazing, and the fact that he was hazed while pledging the Sigma Nu fraternity was hardly questioned. The court, however, grappled with who should ultimately be responsible. As Sunshine writes:

> A lawsuit ensued against Sigma Nu's national organization, which the jury found liable (imposing a quarter of a million dollars in damages); the national promptly appealed the verdict. On appeal, Sigma Nu conceded that the local members were its agents, arguing instead that the actions that led to Ballou's death had exceeded the scope of its agency. The court then made several salient observations in the course of rejecting Sigma Nu's argument. First . . . it noted that the scope of agency embraces not only those acts authorized expressly and by implication, but also those done with apparent authority. Second, it drew attention to the fact that although Sigma Nu prescribes a specific program of initiation, it does not prohibit supplementation of that program, as was apparently done in Ballou's case. Third, it emphasized Sigma Nu's interest in the initiation of new members into its brotherhood, the ultimate purpose of the activities that led to Ballou's death. Fourth, it concluded that Ballou's submission to the chapter's onerous requirements demonstrated its apparent authority, seeing as he "placed himself at the local chapter's disposal on hell night only because he wanted to become an active brother of Sigma Nu." Having recited these findings, the court found that the local was acting (at least) within the apparent scope of its authority as the national's agent for admitting new members.[33]

The court found the national chapter responsible for Ballou's death because of its relationship with him, not its relationship with the local chapter, and that it had apparent, if not actual, authority over the local initiation process. Sunshine summarizes eloquently, "Even if a national flatly prohibits any hazing, the fact that a servant violates its master's guidelines does not eliminate the national's liability."

Negligence

The issue of negligence is often reviewed in hazing cases and is typically the principal way plaintiffs bring suit. The issue at hand in most negligence claims is whether the defendant owed the plaintiff a duty. In the case of *Knoll v. Board of Regents*, "the threshold inquiry in any negligence action is whether the defendant owed a plaintiff a duty."[34] As the court noted, reasonable minds may disagree as to the duty owed a student by a university in circumstances where hazing occurs off campus. However, it further concluded "the university owes a landowner-invitee duty to students to take reasonable steps to protect against foreseeable acts of hazing, including student abduction on the university's property, and the harm that naturally flows therefrom."

Many college administrators believe that they cannot be liable for what happens outside of school hours or off campus grounds because the students are of legal age. However, some courts have been willing to hold schools accountable in hazing cases on the basis that the university had a responsibility to protect students from foreseeable injuries, including those resulting from acts of hazing. In *Morrison v. Kappa Alpha Psi Fraternity*, the court of appeals held that it did not matter that the students were of legal age and presumably could take care of themselves. Regardless, the school had a duty to watch over the behavior of the fraternity because they had a known history of hazing.[35]

In a similar case, *Furek v. The University of Delaware*, the court held that while the doctrine of *in loco parentis* has not typically held up in college and university settings, it is applicable in hazing cases where "there is direct university involvement in, and knowledge of, certain dangerous practices of its students, the university cannot abandon its residual duty of control." This line of reasoning cannot be discarded in situations where the university has implemented policy to abate hazing practices. In fact, by issuing policy the school or university itself acknowledges it has a duty to protect students from hazing.[36]

Furthermore, the courts that have followed this line of reasoning have explained or justified their positions, often stating that the schools themselves are not under the same influence and can both foresee and recognize the possible risks associated with hazing from a more-educated standpoint than the general student body. Moreover, the courts state that often the rookies or students being initiated do not fully understand the risks often associated with various acts of hazing. The *Morrison* case illustrates this by stating, "The pledging process to join a fraternal organization is not an activity which an adult college student would regard as hazardous." This statement is echoed by research findings indicating that students often perceive that they will be isolated from peers or not be accepted into the group or by the group if they do not go along with the initiation process or hazing.[37]

Courts have held schools accountable for injuries resulting from acts of hazing when the institutions, administration, or officials have had knowledge of hazing occurring within their scope of jurisdiction. In *Chappel v. Franklin Pierce School District No. 402*, the court held that since there was a known tradition of hazing occurring at the school, the school could be held responsible for a hazing injury. The court found that the school was liable because the faculty advisor knew of and helped plan the activities that resulted in the injury. In addition, in *Chappel* the court identified that a connection existed between the school and the off-campus hazing. The court based this connection on the fact that the school had some control over the event. The reasoning included the fact that all clubs that were planning off-campus activities were required to submit the activity for approval, and that provides a subtle signal that an institution has knowledge of hazing activities involving students.[38]

Negligent Supervision

An institution can be found to be vicariously liable for injuries occurring as a result of hazing activities if it is found that the damage resulted from negligent supervision. The *Morrison* court found this to be the case, stating that the university's failure to keep an eye on student activities was directly related to the resulting injury.

As established, institutions of higher education are not typically considered the insurer of student health and well-being. However, judges have imposed institutional liability for breach of a duty of care associated with the role of the institution as a landlord responsible for the safety of campus residents and invitees.[39] Courts have frequently recognized the institutional obligation to provide a safe environment.

The most recent extension of liability under this theory is that associated with the duty to foresee the likelihood of a third-party assault that would endanger the safety of the student. This potential for institution-as-landlord liability was evident in the case of *Mullins v. Pine Manor College*. In this case, a female student used this claim after being abducted and sexually assaulted. The court ruled in favor of the plaintiff, finding the university, as a landowner, was negligent.[40] Furthermore, in the *Furek* case, the university was held liable for the resulting injuries under the premise of landowner–invitee theory.

In *Knoll*, the court did not limit the duty to on-campus facilities; it extended the standard to property off-campus. Here, a student was injured while trying to get away from being hazed. The hazing activity was taking place off campus; however, the court articulated, "The University could have foreseen various forms of student hazing on its property, even though [the fraternity] failed to disclose the pledge sneak event, including typical fraternity abductions and the consequences that could reasonably be expected to result from such activities." In both cases, the duty was imposed based upon the fact that the university could have and should have been able to foresee that the hazing acts may occur.

Application of In Loco Parentis

The courts have grappled with the application of *in loco parentis* standards for many years in cases that involve student safety, including incidents of hazing. The legal doctrine of *in loco parentis* describes a relationship that is similar to that of a parent and child without legal formality that is generally temporary in nature.[41] History shows that prior to the 1960s, the legal system recognized a duty on the part of college and university administrators to stand "*in loco parentis.*"

In *Bradshaw v. Rawlings*, an off-campus sophomore-class party was planned with a faculty advisor who cosigned a check for the purchase of alcohol. The students who attended the party arranged for their own transportation to and from the party. After the party, a student was involved in an automobile accident that rendered him quadriplegic. The appellate court reversed the lower court's decision in favor of Bradshaw. The appellate court cited that colleges could not be the insurer of student safety even when an employee had been part of the planning process.[42]

In *Beach v. University of Utah*, a professor was present at an off-campus party following a field trip in which students were drinking. The alcohol consumption continued during the van ride back to the field trip's campsite, and a student wandered off and fell from a cliff. In this case, the court refuted the duty of the college to keep students safe, reasoning that college students were old enough to vote and be tried as adults. In this case the court set a standard that the university was a "bystander" to student misconduct and that no duty was owed to these students because they were "adults."[43] These cases set the standard that college and universities would not be found to have a legal duty to protect students as previously held under the doctrine of *in loco parentis*.

The milieu changed again during the 1990s. During this time courts broadened their range regarding potential institutional liability in regards to student safety and behavior. After the bystander era and to the present day, the courts have seen a switch once again in the progression of the duty-owed standard. These cases often use the landowner liability standards that establish that schools as landowners do in fact have a duty to protect students under certain conditions.

Hazing Education

Educational institutions at all levels may not place much emphasis on hazing prevention because most state laws do not require them to do so, a situation that will change exponentially should the 2017 "Report and Educate Campus Hazing" (REACH) federal hazing legislation (or similar federal proposed legislation in the future) become law and mandate education.[44] Many state laws identify hazing in regards to the perspective of the student but fail to address the role of the institution itself in the prevention of hazing.

The lack of educational oversight regarding hazing was adjudicated in the State of South Carolina. This follows the death of Clemson pledge Tucker Hipps whose parents alleged that he died as a direct result of hazing. (The parents of Hipps were awarded $250,000 from the university by the courts.) At the crux of this *Tucker Hipps Transparency Act* is that the law now requires South Carolina's public colleges and universities to post online any misconduct violations that have been imposed on any fraternity or sorority. It is the hope that by making these infractions public that students may avoid engaging with these organizations or at least give them the information to make more informed choices about the history of the organization before becoming involved. This law is aimed at making college fraternities and sororities safer in the future. The impact of this law is yet to be known. However, this may pave the way for other states to move in the same direction and even possibly expand the reach by requiring all organizations to post violations publicly.

Another recent action taken in the State of South Carolina involves a proposal at the state's flagship institution, the University of South Carolina, to abolish all pledging within its Greek Life system. However, what would have been regarded as a groundbreaking proposal was postponed by direct order of the USC president until 2017 or later. (Editor: As of December 2017, the reform movement appears to have been quashed by USC's president.)

Defenses

When colleges and universities find themselves at the center of a hazing lawsuit, the two defenses most frequently utilized are assumption of risk and sovereign immunity.

Many cases cite the use of assumption of risk as a defense, some more effectively than others. In *Siesto v. Bethpage Union Free School District* the court suggests that a student athlete assumes the risks of injury that are inherent in sport; however, this assumption of risk does not indicate they assume the risk of being injured due to hazing.[45]

In 1998, the Alabama Supreme Court in *Barran v Kappa Alpha Order* found that a fraternity pledge named Jones, an Auburn University student who lived in the Kappa Alpha fraternity house and was subjected to hazing for two years before flunking out of school, assumed the risk of being hazed. Jones had sued KA and its members for assault and battery, and the trial court dismissed most of charges saying he assumed the risk by (1) knowing the risks, and (2) voluntarily subjecting himself to them. An Alabama Court of Appeals reversed the decision, stating that hazing was negligence per se and therefore assumption of risk could not be a defense. The defendants appealed, and the Supreme Court of Alabama reversed the Appellate Court decision, saying that Jones had continued to assume the risk of being hazed by staying in the fraternity house long after other pledges had left.

Consent Is Not a Defense

Another of the more interesting clauses and statements that many states use when addressing hazing is a statement that indicates that "consent is not a defense" in hazing occurrences. Consent or willingness to participate is somewhat challenging because many inductees do not consider the possibility of being hazed until they are hazed. The problem with these components of the statutes is that the "victims" typically do not have enough information given to them before the hazing occurs to give any type of informed consent. Furthermore, while they may "voluntarily" participate in the hazing activities, they may do so only out of the fear of repercussion.

Conclusion

Antihazing statutes continue to be applied inconsistently across state boundaries in the aforementioned forty-four states that currently have these laws. While changes have been made recently in Pennsylvania and South Carolina, the majority of laws have been in place for decades. As more of these laws are being utilized in prosecutions and civil cases, it is hoped that stiffer penalties, more broad and clear definitions, and more consistent findings will occur. It is also possible that federal antihazing legislation in the form of the 2017 REACH proposal (or a similar federal proposal in the years ahead should REACH fail to pass Congress) will be enacted at long last.

R. BRIAN CROW is Professor of Sport Management at Slippery Rock University. He has presented and written extensively on hazing in sports and is an expert on sports law.

COLLEEN MCGLONE is Associate Professor of Recreation and Sport Management at Coastal Carolina University. Her PhD is in Sport Administration from the University of New Mexico.

27 Smokeouts and Smokescreens

Military Hazing

Hank Nuwer

Wᴴɪʟᴇ ᴍᴀɴʏ ᴀ tree has been pulped for publications related to congressional investigations concerning hazing in the service academies, few government publications have addressed military hazing despite hazing-related suicides, psychological meltdowns, physical abuse, tawdry line-crossing ceremonies, navy chief horseplay, and revenge beatings known as smokeouts conducted by senior troops taken against "slackers" that sleep at post or underperform. Often the punishment is accompanied by racial slurs aimed at minorities.

That all changed in 2016 when the US Government Accounting Office published its lengthy "Department of Defense and Coast Guard: Actions Needed to Increase Oversight and Management Information on Hazing Incidents Involving Servicemembers."[1] Finally, verifiable research on hazing in the armed services was released that demonstrated, officially, what long had been suspected: the Department of Defense was largely uninformed about hazing, particularly in the Coast Guard, where little or no tracking of incidents was in place to determine if problems were getting better or worse.

The military has been rocked by the suicides of young soldiers that fell asleep on guard-duty or otherwise were adjudged deficient and subjected to being "smoked"—beaten, chewed out, and subject to endless grueling labor—as punishment. Internet chat groups have been flooded with messages from veterans that insisted one recruit's negligence could mean the deaths of several servicemen.

- On March 18, 2016, Raheel Siddiqui, a twenty-year-old Muslim and son of a Pakistani father, killed himself in a forty-foot barracks stairwell fall after a drill instructor, already under investigation for alleged brutality, slapped the recruit at Parris Island.
- In 2010, Army Specialist Brushaun Anderson, who had been hazed horrifically in Iraq, killed himself.
- In 2011, after enduring taunts about his Chinese ancestry from superiors and his peers for six weeks, nineteen-year-old soldier Danny Chen shot and killed himself in an army guard tower.

- In April 2011, a young marine of Chinese ancestry killed himself after being brutally punished for falling asleep on guard-duty in an area of Afghanistan known to be infested with Taliban. Lance Cpl. Harry Lew, twenty-one years old, was, among other things, brutally punched in the back of the head after a sergeant informed other marines in the unit that Lew needed "smoking" to punish him in the middle of the night. Lew killed himself with a single shot. Lew's suicide prompted his aunt, California Representative Judy Chu, to persuade the first-ever congressional hearing to investigate hazing and other abuses in all military service areas. This led to a thorough investigation by the Government Accounting Office (GAO) that found all service areas were deficient in their tracking methods. In 2016, Rep. Chu testified before the House Armed Services Committee, calling for far more stringent oversight on hazing by the Department of Defense.

The Cautionary Tale of Joe Branson

My own investigations into Coast Guard and other types of military hazing for a book and *American Legion* magazine article showed me that these incidents can be as cruel, demeaning, frightening, and senseless as anything fraternity males can envision. Prior to the 2016 GAO report, any member of Congress that wanted full transparency into military hazing incidents had to rely on heavily redacted investigations prompted by a congressional inquiry.

My work was driven by an inquiry launched by then senior Republican Senator Richard Lugar of Indiana with the assistance of Senator Dan Quayle and Senator Dan Coats. The concerns of Lugar, Quayle, and Coats had been inspired by the sexual hazing nightmare aboard a Coast Guard cutter of an eighteen-year-old National Guard enlistee named Joe Branson of Muncie, Indiana, and fueled by subsequent investigative journalism by the *Indianapolis Star* that led me to contact Joe Branson and his wife, Tammy, for interviews.

Senators Take Action

At the behest of Sen. Lugar, the Coast Guard looked into Branson's case. A single investigator questioned the crew, but many participants lied, an admiral later said. Had the Branson case resulted in impartial congressional hearings of the Coast Guard, questions about the sodomizing of enlistees would elicit questions that would have targeted at least five ringleaders. Branson showed me a psychological assessment performed on him by the Michigan-based counseling centers that concluded that without his severe hazing, "there is nothing in Mr. Branson's history that he would not have . . . made an adequate adjustment to the Coast Guard." The assessment found he had a happy childhood, no problems in high school, and that all acting out he did occurred only after he was hazed and then hounded by certain *Mesquite* crew. The assessment said any retaliation of Branson toward other crew was consistent with the way a victim of abuse may act out.

Antihazing activists would call Branson's fight to get authorities to believe him a second hazing. The heavily redacted documents sent to the senators made it clear that the Coast Guard's command disagreed. Superiors felt Branson had brought many troubles on himself by resisting the attempts to haze him.

Hazing Traditions

The US Navy's best-known initiation ritual, the Order of Neptune, occurs when a newcomer to the equator (a "pollywog") is put through many silly and sometimes demeaning paces by the veteran shipmates ("seabacks" or "shellbacks") that make up King Neptune's court. As long as a pollywog doesn't resist, the ceremonies are accompanied by merriment, cross-dressing, the serving of inedible foods, sliding across a deck strewn with garbage, and the kissing of the king's grease-covered belly.[2]

Deaths aboard shipboard happen on occasion while a vessel crosses the equator. In my online list of hazing deaths, I list the electrocution of shipfitter Jack P. Jarosz in a "crossing the line" ceremony after he touched the electrified trident of King Neptune. In 1946, two teenagers aboard the SS *Frederick Galbraith*, a working vessel, perished when made to consume a lethal amount of saltpeter while crossing the equator.

Both the US Navy and the Coast Guard traditionally employed shipboard initiations to accompany the promotions of officers. The Coast Guard's crossing ceremonies had certain defined rituals for "landlubbers" crossing the Arctic Circle or, in the case of Branson, the Great Lakes for the first time.

On July 15, 2005, the Department of Navy Secretary disseminated a letter detailing what constituted hazing by definition:

> Hazing is defined as any conduct whereby a military member or members, regardless of service or rank, without proper authority causes another military member or members, regardless of service or rank, to suffer or be exposed to any activity which is cruel, abusive, humiliating, oppressive, demeaning, or harmful. Soliciting or coercing another to perpetrate any such physical contact among or between military members; it can be verbal or psychological in nature. Actual or implied consent to acts of hazing does not eliminate the culpability of the perpetrator.[3] Hazing can include, but is not limited to, the following: playing abusive or ridiculous tricks; threatening or offering violence or bodily harm to another; striking; branding; taping; tattooing; shaving; greasing; painting; requiring excessive physical exercise beyond what is required to meet standards; "pinning;" "tacking on;" "blood wings;" or forcing or requiring the consumption of food, alcohol, drugs, or any other substance.[4]

Horrific Hazing

The eighteen-year-old Branson's nightmare began on June 23, 1986, when the *Mesquite* found itself with a new skipper, Lt. Commander Thomas M. Conlon. The following August, Conlon was approached by two veterans. They asked permission to hold a kangaroo court, which they said was similar to a chief's initiation. However, the subsequent investigation revealed that for at least two years, the initiation rituals included nudity, sexual innuendo, and simulated sex.

Conlon maintained that he had no reason to question the two; they generally were regarded as among the best seamen on the *Mesquite* with recent "Sailor of the Quarter" commendations. Conlon conceded that he was "vaguely aware" of the tomfoolery that went along with ship crossings. No complaints were filed with Conlon that August, and so he rubber-stamped a request to hold a second ceremony on November 11, 1986, while the *Mesquite* was under way from Charlevoix, Michigan, to Sturgeon Bay, Wisconsin. The cutter's log registered temperatures in the midtwenties. Cumulus clouds predominated. Winds blew up to fourteen knots. Waters were calm.

The hazing early in the day was mild, perhaps a performance for Commander Conlon that no one was taking the fun too far. One enlistee wore a garbage sack. One carried a "Lick Me" sign and was slavered upon by petty officers. Two were made to wear makeshift rat and whale costumes. Branson wore his undergarments over his regular work clothing.

Between 1800 and 1900 hours a message piped over the public address system that said initiation was about to begin in the crew's lounge. "Better hide," the speaker warned. Branson was afraid. For days older shipmates had intimidated the chunky, red-haired enlistee. "We're going to get you," they vowed. Branson asked a friend to help him squeeze inside a locker, and the accomplice slapped a lock on the door. Another worried initiate hid in the weather entry on the buoy deck. The other initiates lined up and later told the investigator they were not afraid. Like many fraternity pledges, they welcomed the ritual that would make them full-fledged seafarers. They stripped and were led into the makeshift court.

An angry posse stalked the ship. They easily found the first man in his hiding place, but Branson took an hour to find and only after his accomplice gave his location out. "Your ass is mine," one yelled outside the locker, while another ran to fetch bolt cutters. They put him in a headlock, stripped and blindfolded him, and dragged him by the arms into the lounge. Three spat tobacco juice on him as he entered. They shoved him before the designated Prince of Punishment, a junior petty officer wearing a T-shirt bearing the image of a satanic music group.[5]

"People were pretty wound up," the prince admitted to the investigator. Branson was tried and convicted. They shoved him into a tub of ice water filled with refuse from a spittoon. Like others before him, he sat at least ten minutes in the bath. Crew members took his hands and clamped them to an electrical device called a "megger." The Prince of Punishment called the megger a lie-detector machine. A medical corpsman stood by, but he made no effort to halt the shocking of Branson. In addition to the prince, the court held a mock judge, prosecutor, defense attorney, bailiff, and jurors. At first the shocks tingled, but enough repetitions made them smart "like ants on your fingers," one enlistee would say.

The blindfolded Branson was initiated with the others who were wrapped in toilet paper and made to eat the "apple of truth," an onion.

The seamen displayed an unquenchable thirst for sadism. They squirted Branson with warm water and coffee from a syringe. "Oh, no, don't piss on him," someone called in mock horror. The inquisitor was later told a crewman got carried away and did, in fact, urinate on Branson. Other initiates were mauled and pawed as a shutter-happy camera bug clicked away, supplying incontrovertible evidence that could have hanged the crew had the Coast Guard called for court-martials. A number of men were penetrated in the buttocks with carrots that had been coated with axle grease, clearly a felony crime if prosecuted in a court of law.

The crew squeezed liquid soap onto the bodies of the seven blindfolded initiates. "He came on you, he came on you," roared the hazers. One man was made to lick Crisco off a hazer's palm and told he had consumed donkey ejaculate. One crew member tried to halt the proceedings. "Give the kid a break," he urged, and he was thrown out of the lounge for his protest.

One clicked scissors close enough to an enlistee's genitals to shear pubic hair.

A group surrounded the nude Branson. "Where is your dick?" one screamed, pretending it was too small to see. "Did you bring your pecker?"

"How many times a day do you jack off?"

"Do you give good head to guys?"

"Are you a homosexual?"

The sailors showed no mercy. They accepted only answers that demeaned the initiates.

"You can't have sex with a woman, can you?"

"Yes, sir. I can." One thousand volts shocked a leg or arm.

They called him a faggot when he cried the demanded no instead.

Branson was mauled and his blindfold slipped. He saw the faces of his tormentors, including the man working the voltage device.

Branson "admitted" having had sex with men. They made him stroke a sausage and simulate oral sex. When he tried to refuse, a reveler jammed it in Branson's mouth and pumped it in and out. They hollered despicable things at him and demanded to know if he had had sex with the CO.

Branson's nightmare went on and on. They dyed his genitals with purple surgical dye. They packed bearing grease into his ears, hair, and genitals. At last some of the hazers began to feel disgust as the initiation had degenerated into torture. They fed him a grog made of disgusting ingredients and then a whole egg. He had to jump up and down to break the egg, then swallow it, and then they made him cluck like a chicken.

"Want something a little sweeter?" They fed him globs of shortening filled with sugar, hot sauce, and tobacco spit.

Branson tried to defy his tormentors. He vomited out the disgusting substances, and he laughed aloud as they groaned their disgust, and the prince expelled him from the court. Once outside, Branson was spared the final indignity. The other hazees were given weights on a string and told to toss the Shackle of Truth, the "joke" being that the lines to their genitals secretly had been cut.

Once that was done, the Prince of Punishment cheered and congratulated the hazees. Branson and five others were welcomed as full crew members. One enlistee got a thumbs down from the prince.

Post-Traumatic Stress

That night Branson felt less a part of the crew, not at all accepting. A strictly raised Catholic, he felt disgraced, angry, and betrayed. He informed an officer that he wished to file a grievance. The commanding officer ordered future initiations canceled.

"Snitch," his mates called him. He began to throw ice at the perpetrators. He started to drink. He got into fistfights. His superiors wrote him up and labeled him a troublemaker. His closest shipmates avoided him. All he could talk about was the abuse they tried to forget. One made it his job to bully Branson full time, flicking boogers into the enlistee's food in the mess hall.

About this time, Branson's brother John visited the ship and Joe broke down. Branson called his parents. Arthur J. Branson, the father, appealed on December 17, 1986, to Senator Lugar, then a powerhouse as a ranking senator, and to Senator Quayle, a rising star who would become the next US vice president, and himself a National Guard member.

Mesquite officers retaliated immediately. They blasted Branson in a service record write-up. Lt. Commander Joseph W. Bodenstedt opined that Branson was a troublemaker unfit for further service and ordered him to be medically evaluated. "This command's opinion is that [Branson] is too immature to continue in the USCG," Bodenstedt wrote in a confidential report obtained by *Indianapolis Star* investigative reporter R. Joseph Gelarden. "Branson is an individual prone to tearful outbursts. These outbursts are embarrassing and frustrating to him and the source of ridicule on the part of some crew members."[6]

Branson talked to a Coast Guard bigwig sent out to assess facts, but the investigator himself had endured an initiation and gave no support, according to Branson. The *Mesquite*'s commanding officer, Lt. Conlon, denounced Branson for "always making a big deal out of everything." Branson was on the verge of being drummed out of the Coast Guard without access to medical treatment, but Senator Lugar intervened, and Branson was discharged with access to counseling. The Coast Guard's final word in Branson's file was that his immaturity, antagonism, and poor attitude contributed to the seaman's alienation from his shipmates. No one at the brass level would concede that the initiation had thrown the young man into an icy skid.

Senators criticized the chain of command after Branson met with Coast Guard medical staff who blamed the hazing, not Branson, for his acting out. "It is my opinion that Branson has suffered a serious indignity in the hazing and because he is a . . . snitch, (Branson) is being hounded by some of his peers and supervisors," wrote Dr. Martin J. Nemiroff of the Public Health Service, refuting Bodenstedt's allegations.

Elizabeth Sullivan at the Woodland Counseling Centers agreed with that assessment, writing a medical report that said Branson "has been scapegoated" and should have received treatment for post-traumatic stress as soon as he reported the initiation. Although Branson received a promotion, the hounding from fellow sailors who learned of his so-called tattling made it difficult for him to function. Armed with the medical reports, Lugar and Coats wrote the Coast Guard a no-nonsense memorandum that began, "We are outraged."

Action swiftly followed the ultimatum by the Indiana senators. On April 19, 1989, Rear Admiral Arnold M. Danielsen addressed the hazing that had tarnished the career of a commander and ended the career of a crewman. In part of his statement, he said, "Unfortunately, the event had deteriorated two years earlier to include total nudity, sexual/homosexual innuendo, and simulated oral sex," wrote Danielsen in a summary. "Initiations are by their nature in bad taste, but the initiation here is a graphic example of going too far. They should not have been demeaning, gross, crude, and lewd."

Branson went public. The *Indianapolis Star* ran a string of investigative articles. Branson and his wife, Tammy, also spoke with me at length for my first book on hazing.

The Coast Guard had dismissed the original investigation as flawed, because several of those interviewed were found to have downplayed crucial facts. The inquiry became serious, and investigators from Cleveland and Milwaukee flung new questions at the crew and Conlon. Admiral Danielsen threw the book at the perpetrators but failed to ask for court-martials. "I am troubled by those few members who did not cooperate and have lied outright to (the investigator) about these matters," said Danielsen in a formal report, specifically mentioning the commander and the petty officer that played the prince. "Such conduct by anyone, especially by a petty officer, is appalling."

Douglas MacArthur on the Stand

Perhaps the best example of how difficult it can be for authorities to get to the bottom of military hazing is the case of Douglas MacArthur. When he was a plebeian, or "plebe," at West Point at the turn of the twentieth century, MacArthur found himself in a hazing controversy. In his book *Reminiscences* he said this about hazing—that it "was practiced with a worthy goal, but with methods that were violent and uncontrolled."

MacArthur was one of dozens of West Pointers commanded to testify at a congressional court of inquiry ordered by President William McKinley in December 1900. The hearings had two purposes: to deduce whether hazing had caused the death of a young cadet named Oscar Booz of Bristol, Pennsylvania, and to determine if hazing was rampant at West Point. The court of inquiry doubted whether Booz's death by illness could be pinpointed as hazing-related, but upperclassmen had harassed, beaten, and forced him to chug undiluted pepper sauce. However, when that special committee (made up of six members of the House of Representatives) finished its report, it was clear that violent and dangerous hazing was common at West Point.

The committee concluded that cadets who were famous Americans' sons—including MacArthur and Philip Sheridan Jr.—were particularly targeted. Sheridan, for example, was forced to mount a broomstick and mock his father's victory at Winchester, yelling "Turn, boys, turn, we are going back."

MacArthur, son of a brigadier-general who gained fame during the recent war with Spain, would one day become one of the most famous and controversial generals in history. In 1900, however, he was a not-so-robust youth facing an inquisition. Previous testimony from members of the beast barracks, where plebes began their education, revealed that MacArthur had been brutalized often. One time his body had convulsed, and he begged a friend to stuff a rag in his mouth lest he cry out and be viewed as weak.

While giving testimony, MacArthur, ranked number one in his class, refused to name the upperclassmen that had hazed him, and he denied the rag story. Then he lied on the stand and said his only two hazers were two cadets already drummed out of West Point, claiming reports of hazing at the institute were "very much exaggerated indeed."

The committee presented MacArthur a list of hazers and fifty-nine hazing practices that had come from cadet testimony. "My father and mother had taught me those two immutable principles—never to lie, never to tattle," he wrote in *Reminiscences*. "But here was a desperate situation for me. If the court insisted and ordered me to reveal the names, and I refused to obey the order, it would in all likelihood mean my dismissal and the end of my hopes and dreams."

The turning point came during a recess. As he tried to regain composure, a note from his mother was pressed into his hand. She had written him a note in verse that encouraged him to remain silent. MacArthur's behavior shows how difficult it is for any military inquiry to learn the truth about hazing practices. Encouraged by his mother, he would not blab. He would deny, deny, and leave the committee with the crumbs of information given by other cadets. His smokescreen worked. The committee dare not expel the son of a military genius, a youth with the best academic record at West Point to boot. Douglas MacArthur returned to West Point as a superintendent between 1919 and 1922, outlawing some of the worst practices. But not even MacArthur could eliminate the ritual of hazing at the United States Military Academy.[7]

Blaming the Victim

Another reality of military hazing is that in the end it is the victims who continue drawing the blame. They should have been tough enough to withstand the abuse and to get the satisfaction of hazing the next recruits. Lt. Bodenstedt defended his crew to the end. "The treatment [Branson] received was no different than a half-dozen other members," Bodenstedt told a reporter. Bodenstedt left the *Mesquite* but was given a comparable change of command to the cutter *Bramble*.

Conlon's response was one of defensiveness. "I received an administrative censure, a service record entry," Conlon told an *Indianapolis Star* reporter on May 14, 1989. "I expect it to affect my career." Conlon enrolled at the Naval Postgraduate School and graduated with an advanced degree in 1992.

Instead of the initiation succeeding in welcoming Branson, it separated him from all on ship. As for the USCGC *Mesquite*, there is no evidence that heavy hazing made the shipmates better sailors. Disaster struck the *Mesquite* after Conlon was replaced.

On December 4, 1989, the *Mesquite* traveled in high waves and heavy winds as it tried to retrieve a buoy twelve feet above the bottom that was placed there to warn other ships of low waters. (Buoys must be removed before waters ice over and the markers are lost). The commander and crew botched the task and ran the vessel into a rocky reef in Lake Superior at the tip of Keweenaw Peninsula in Michigan. Cold waters flooded the cutter as it rocked and locked in place on the shoal. The crew, officers, and skipper abandoned ship, and the *Mesquite* became a military disgrace. Joe Branson could have been there stuck on the rocks had he kept quiet about his initiation. An investigation of *Mesquite* operations was ordered by Rear Admiral Richard Appelbaum. The crew that had humiliated Branson now was vilified for the unpardonable sin of sinking a cutter.

Winter storms and accumulating ice further devastated the grounded cutter. There was no saving the ship. Rescue crews sprang into action to remove nineteen thousand gallons of fuel that could have devastated the Michigan coast if leaked. The Coast Guard used a barge to tug the *Mesquite* into deeper lake waters and then buried the vessel at sea in 1990.

Those in charge of the ship—Captain John Lynch, engineering officer James Thanasiu and deck officer Susan Subocz—were reprimanded by a board of inquiry for poor navigational performances in allowing the *Mesquite* to drift and assigning too few crew members to keep vigilance over the ship's position. Commander Lynch was tried in a court-martial on two counts. The Coast Guard found the skipper guilty of vessel negligence but innocent of dereliction of duty. He was punished with a loss of seniority in September 1990. Ensign Subocz was fined $1,000. Chief Thanasiu resigned from the Coast Guard but was reprimanded nonetheless.

"What a lot of people don't realize is how many hours you work when you're on a ship like that," former *Mesquite* seaman John Kramer told a Michigan reporter, blaming fatigue for the errors that sank a $37 million dollar ship. "[The *Mesquite*] was the best unit I ever served on, and [its crew was the] best group of people I ever served with."[8]

HANK NUWER is a professor in the Franklin College Pulliam School of Journalism. He has written *The Hazing Reader* (IUP) and *Wrongs of Passage: Fraternities, Sororities, Hazing, and Binge Drinking* (IUP). Editor's note: In 2017, the Marines introduced sweeping reforms after a successful Camp Pendleton court martial in December 2017 concluded that subordinate troops had been victimized by a superior.

Notes

Introduction

1. H. Hedge, "University Reform," *Atlantic Monthly*, September 1866, 296+.

1. Dead to Rites

1. T. H. Waterman, *Cornell University: A History* (New York: University Publishing, 1905), 1.
2. "Freshman Banquet: A Merry Night Spent Feasting," *Cornell Daily Sun*, February 21, 1894.
3. The details of the mayhem in the kitchen, as well as court transcript excerpts later in this chapter, all come from testimony in the coroner's inquiry.
4. So wrote an *Ithaca Daily Journal* reporter on February 22, 1894.
5. "Was It Murder?" *Ithaca Daily Journal*, February 24, 1894.
6. Ibid.
7. "Mrs. Jackson's Funeral," *Cornell Daily Sun*, February 24, 1894.
8. Mark Goldman, *Bishop Timon and Immigrant Catholics in Buffalo* (Albany: State University of New York Press, 1984), 78–81.
9. Ruth Stahl, "More on the Dingens Diary, 1895," *Treasures* (blog), February 13, 2003, http://www.isledegrande.com/treasures2003.htm. Ruth Stahl, "The Valentine's Day Fires," *Treasures* (blog), February 20, 2003, http://www.isledegrande.com/treasures2003.htm.
10. Ruth Stahl, "Red Top Plus The Two-Headed Calf," *Treasures* (blog), January 23, 2003, http://www.isledegrande.com/treasures2003.htm. Joseph Dingens, "Red Top Diary" (unpublished), Buffalo and Erie County Historical Society Archives, Mss. A00–119.
11. "Obituary," *The Catholic Union and Times*, September 26, 1907.
12. "C. L. Dingens," *Buffalo Evening News*, February 24, 1894.
13. "Dingens Called Home," *Ithaca Daily Journal*, February 28, 1894.
14. "The Cornell Banquet Affair," *Buffalo Evening News*, February 26, 1894.
15. "Four Arrests," Associated Press, March 2, 1894.
16. "Guilty Student Ready to Confess," *New York Times*, February 23, 1894.
17. Ibid.
18. "Confession Coming: One of the Cornell Students will Make a Clean Breast," *Ithaca Daily News*, February 28, 1894.
19. "A Bill Against Hazing," *Cornell Daily Sun*, March 1, 1894.
20. *New York Times*, March 2, 1894.
21. Ibid.
22. "Contempt of Court," *Ithaca Daily Journal*, May 3, 1894.
23. "No Indictments," *Cornell Daily Sun*, May 17, 1894.
24. People ex rel. Taylor v. Forbes, 143 N.Y. 219 (1894).
25. Richard H. Wels, "Fifth Amendment Precedent," *Cornell Alumni Newsletter* 57, no. 6 (May 15, 1935): 521.

2. Hazing in Fraternities and Sororities

1. Aldo Cimino, "Predictors of Hazing Motivation in a Representative Sample of the United States," *Evolution and Human Behavior* 34 (2013): 446–452.

2. See also Aldo Cimino, "Fraternity Hazing and the Process of Planned Failure," *Journal of American Studies* (December 2016): 1–23.

3. Lionel Tiger, *Men in Groups* (New York: Random House, New York, 1969). Revised as "Males Courting Males" in *The Hazing Reader*, ed. Hank Nuwer (Bloomington: Indiana University Press, 2004), 14–18.

4. Irving Janis, *Victims of Groupthink* (Boston: Houghton Mifflin, 1974).

5. Hank Nuwer, *Wrongs of Passage: Fraternities, Sororities, Hazing, and Binge Drinking* (Bloomington: Indiana University Press, 1999), xxiv–xxv.

6. Alan D. DeSantis, *Inside Greek U.: Fraternities, Sororities, and the Pursuit of Pleasure, Power, and Prestige* (Lexington: University of Kentucky Press, 2007), 6.

7. Elliott Aronson and Judson Mills, "The Effect of Severity of Initiation on Liking for a Group," *Journal of Abnormal and Social Psychology* 59 (September 1959): 177–181.

8. Margaret Thaler Singer and Janja Lalich, *Cults in Our Midst* (San Francisco: Jossey-Bass, 1995), 4–36.

9. "Hazing and Alcohol in a College Fraternity" by James C. Arnold, in Nuwer's *The Hazing Reader*, 51–105.

10. James C. Arnold, "Hazing and Alcohol in a College Fraternity," in *The Hazing Reader*, ed. Hank Nuwer (Bloomington: Indiana University Press, 2004), 51–105.

11. John van Maanen and Edgar Schein, "Toward a Theory of Organizational Socialization," *Research in Organizational Behavior* 1 (1979): 209–264.

12. Arnold, "Hazing and Alcohol in a College Fraternity," 105. See also Anne Wilson Schaef and Diane Fassel, *The Addictive Organization* (New York: Harper One, 1988).

13. Stephen Sweet, *College and Society: An Introduction to the Sociological Imagination* (Upper Saddle River, NJ: Pearson, 2001). Revised as "Understanding Fraternity Hazing" in *The Hazing Reader*, ed. Hank Nuwer (Bloomington: Indiana University Press, 2004), 1–13.

14. Thomas Leemon, *The Rites of Passage in a Student Culture* (New York: Teachers College Press, 1972).

15. Ricky L. Jones, *Black Haze: Violence, Sacrifice, and Manhood in Black Greek-Letter Fraternities*, rev. ed. (Albany: State University of New York Press, 2015).

16. Susan Lipkins, *Preventing Hazing: How Parents, Teachers, and Coaches Can Stop the Violence, Harassment, and Humiliation* (San Francisco: Jossey-Bass, 2006), 19–26.

17. Arnold van Gennep, *The Rites of Passage* (Paris: Noutery, 1909).

18. Harold H. Kelley and John W. Thibaut, *The Social Psychology of Groups* (Hoboken, NJ: Wiley, 1969).

19. Hank Nuwer, *Broken Pledges: The Deadly Rite of Hazing* (Atlanta: Longstreet, 1990), 286–294.

20. Nuwer, *Broken Pledges*, 119–120.

21. E. J. Allan and M. Madden, "Hazing in View: College Students at Risk, Initial Findings from the National Study of Student Hazing," (2008), 3–17, http://www.stophazing.org/wp-content/uploads/2014/06/hazing_in_view_web1.pdf.

22. Hank Nuwer, "Greek Letters Don't Justify Cult-Like Hazing of Pledges," *Chronicle of Higher Education*, November 26, 1999.

23. Nuwer, *Broken Pledges*, 286–298.

24. Hank Nuwer, "What's the Life of a Dead Fraternity Pledge Worth?" *Orlando Sentinel* op-ed, July 11, 2012.

25. Elizabeth Allan, "Hazing and Gender: Analyzing the Obvious," in *The Hazing Reader*, 252–274.

26. Christopher Bollinger and Hank Nuwer, 2009, "Hazing" in *Violence Goes to College*, ed. John Nicoletti, Sally Spencer-Thomas, and Christopher Bollinger (Springfield, IL: Charles C. Thomas), 185–203.

27. David Skorton, "A Pledge to End Fraternity Hazing," *New York Times*, August 23, 2011.

3. A Need for Transparency

1. Caitlin Flanagan, "The Dark Power of Fraternities," *Atlantic Monthly* 313, no. 2 (March 2014). available at https://www.theatlantic.com/magazine/archive/2014/03/the-dark-power-of-fraternities/357580/.

2. Fraternal Information and Programming Group, *FIPG Risk Management Manual* (Indianapolis, IN: FIPG, 2013), https://websites.omegafi.com/omegaws/fipg/files/2015/02/FIPG_MANUAL.pdf.

3. Henry Wechsler et al., "Correlates of College Student Binge Drinking," *American Journal of Public Health* 85 (July 1985): 921–926.

4. National Center on Addiction and Substance Abuse at Columbia University, "Wasting the Best and the Brightest: Substance Abuse at America's Colleges and Universities," March 2007. The study found 89 percent of fraternity and sorority members drink compared to 67 percent of nonmembers, and 64 percent of Greeks binge drink compared to 37 percent of nonmembers.

5. United Educators, "Facts From United Educators' Report, Confronting Campus Sexual Assault: An Examination of Higher Education Claims," 2015, https://www.naicu.edu/docLib/20150218_United_Educators_Sexual_Assault_infographic.pdf.

6. John D. Foubert, Johnathan T. Newberry, and Jerry Tatum, "Behavior Differences Seven Months Later: Effects of a Rape Prevention Program," *Journal of Student Affairs and Practice* 16 (8) (2007): 784–807. See also Catherine Loh et al., "A Prospective Analysis of Sexual Assault Perpetration: Risk Factors Related to Perpetrator Characteristics," *Journal of Interpersonal Violence* 20 (2005), http://jiv.sagepub.com.

7. Jacqueline Chevalier Minow and Christopher J. Einolf, "Sorority Participation and Sexual Assault Risk," *Violence Against Women*, May 19, 2009, http://vaw.sagepub.com/content/15/7/835.abstract. See also M. Mohler-Kuo et al., "Correlates of Rape While Intoxicated in a National Sample of College Women," *Journal of Studies on Alcohol* 65 (January 2004), https://www.ncbi.nlm.nih.gov/pubmed/15000502.

8. See "Hazing Deaths," HankNuwer.com, http://www.hanknuwer.com/articles/hazing-deaths.

9. James R. Favor & Company, http://www.jrfco.com/ABOUTUS/HistoryofCompany/tabid/193/Default.aspx.

10. Virginia Tech Review Panel, "Mass Shootings at Virginia Tech: Report of the Review Panel" (August 2007), https://governor.virginia.gov/media/3772/fullreport.pdf.

11. Ibid., 81.

12. Ibid., 82.

13. Ibid.

14. For example, see "For Parents," *Penn State Fraternity and Sorority Life*, accessed June 13, 2016, http://studentaffairs.psu.edu/hub/greeks/forparents/faq.shtml; "Fraternity and Sorority Life: Frequently Asked Questions," Kansas State University, accessed June 13, 2016, https://www.k-state.edu/fsl/parents_families/faq.html.

15. "For Parents," *Penn State Fraternity and Sorority Life*.

16. Laura Ly, "Former Penn State Fraternity Member Alleges Harsh Hazing in Lawsuit," CNN, June 9, 2015, http://www.cnn.com/2015/06/08/us/penn-state-fraternity-hazing-lawsuit.

17. Carley Mossbrook, "Sexual Assault at Off-Campus Fraternity Reported to Penn State Police," *Daily Collegian*, March 23, 2016, http://www.collegian.psu.edu/news/crime_courts /article_8dc99c68-f14d-11e5-ae81-bf748352fe59.html. Note that the report was the tenth sexual assault reported since the beginning of the semester on January 11.

18. David DeKok, "Dad Sues Penn State, Says Son Committed Suicide After Hazing Ritual," *Reuters*, December 16, 2015, http://www.reuters.com/article/us-pennsylvania-hazing -suicide-idUSKBN0TZ0CO20151216.

19. Barbara Miller, "Kappa Delta Rho Fraternity Expels 38 of Its Members in Wake of Penn State Scandal," *Penn Live*, June 8, 2015, http://www.pennlive.com/midstate/index.ssf/2015/06 /kappa_delta_rho_fraternity_exp.html.

20. Cornell University, "Fraternity & Sorority Life," accessed June 10, 2016, http://dos .cornell.edu/fraternity-sorority-life.

21. Cornell University, "Fraternity & Sorority Life, About Us," accessed June 10, 2016, http:// dos.cornell.edu/fraternity-sorority-life/about-us.

22. Cornell University, "2012–2013 Annual Report: Office of Fraternities, Sororities, and Independent Living, Fraternity & Sorority Advisory Council," http://fsacannualreport.imirus. com/Mpowered/book/vfsacar14/i1/p1.

23. Cornell University, "Hazing.Cornell.edu: A Revealing Look at Hidden Rites, Incidents," accessed June 13, 2016, http://hazing.cornell.edu/hazing/incidents.

24. Ibid.

25. Cornell University, "Report an Incident," *Student and Campus Life*, accessed June 21, 2016, https://scl.cornell.edu/about-us/report-incident. The link to Cornell's hazing prevention website is easy to miss in the middle of this web page.

26. For example, see University of Virginia, Office of the Dean of Students, Fraternity & Sorority Life, "Chapter Conduct History," accessed June 10, 2016, http://www.virginia.edu/fsl /chapter-conduct-history; University of Minnesota, Office for Fraternity & Sorority Life, "Current and Past Sanctions," accessed June 13, 2016, http://www.fsl.umn.edu/discipline/current&past .html; Sigma Alpha Epsilon, "Chapter Health & Safety History," accessed June 13, 2016, http:// www.sae.net/2013/pages/resources/2013-parents-chapter-risk-management-history.

27. Cornell University, "Report an Incident."

28. University of Virginia, "Chapter Conduct History."

29. Ibid.

30. See University of Virginia, "Chapter Conduct History," at http://www.virginia.edu/fsl /chapter-conduct-history/.

31. T. Rees Shapiro, "U-Va Swim Team Hazing Case Dismissed After Settlement," *The Washington Post*, March 29, 2016, https://www.washingtonpost.com/news/grade-point /wp/2016/03/29/u-va-swim-team-hazing-case-dismissed-after-settlement.

32. Ibid.

33. Russell Westerholm, "Soy Sauce Overdose Nearly Killed University of Virginia Student," *University Herald*, June 7, 2013, http://www.universityherald.com/articles/3473/20130607/soy -sauce-overdose-nearly-killed-university-virginia-student.htm.

34. Cornell University, "Report an Incident."

35. For example, see Jillian Rayfield, "Wesleyan Sued Over 'Rape Factory' Frat," *Salon*, October 7, 2012, http://www.salon.com/2012/10/07/wesleyan_sued_over_rape_factory_frat.

36. 20 US Code § 1092(f).

37. "Intersection of Title IX and the Clery Act," accessed June 13, 2016, https://notalone.gov /assets/ferpa-clerychart.pdf.

38. Know Your IX, "The Clery Act in Detail," accessed June 10, 2016, http://knowyourix .org/the-clery-act-in-detail.

39. See 20 US Code § 1681(a).

40. American Law Institute, "Conscious Misrepresentation Involving Risk or Physical Harm," *Restatement of the Law, Second: Torts* (2016), § 310 states the following: "An actor who makes a misrepresentation is subject to liability to another for physical harm which results from an act done by the other or a third person in reliance upon the truth of the representation, if the actor (a) intends his statement to induce or should realize that it is likely to induce action by the other, or a third person, which involves an unreasonable risk of physical harm to the other, and (b) knows (i) that the statement is false, or (ii) that he has not the knowledge which he professes."

41. American Law Institute, "Negligent Misrepresentation Involving Risk of Physical Harm," *Restatement of the Law, Second: Torts* (2016), § 311 states the following: "(1) One who negligently gives false information to another is subject to liability for physical harm caused by action taken by the other in reasonable reliance upon such information, where such harm results (a) to the other, or (b) to such third persons as the actor should expect to be put in peril by the action taken. (2) Such negligence may consist of failure to exercise reasonable care (a) in ascertaining the accuracy of the information, or (b) in the manner in which it is communicated."

42. American Law Institute, "Fraudulent Misrepresentation Causing Physical Harm," *Restatement of the Law, Second: Torts* (2016), § 557A states the following: "One who by a fraudulent misrepresentation or nondisclosure of a fact that it is his duty to disclose causes physical harm to the person . . . of another who justifiably relies upon the misrepresentation, is subject to liability to the other."

43. American Law Institute, "Liability for Fraudulent Misrepresentation," *Restatement of the Law, Second: Torts* (2016), § 525, comment (b).

44. Consider, for example, University of Pennsylvania's assertion to parents that "fraternities and sororities are the perfect environment for this safe 'letting go' [between students and parents]" (Office of Fraternity & Sorority Life, "Welcome to OFSL's Parents' Page," University of Pennsylvania, accessed June 13, 2016, http://www.vpul.upenn.edu/ofsl/parents.php).

45. For example, see McGrath v. Dominican College of Blauvelt, New York, 672 F. Supp. 2d. 477 (S.D.N.Y. 2009), which was a lawsuit against Dominican College for the sexual assault and subsequent suicide of a female student alleging that failure to disclose and adequately deal with sexual assaults on campus intentionally misrepresented the safety of the school's campus to induce students to enroll.

46. American Law Institute, "Liability for Fraudulent Misrepresentation," *Restatement of the Law, Second: Torts* (2016), § 525, comment (b).

47. American Law Institute, "Representation Misleading Because Incomplete," *Restatement of the Law, Second: Torts* (2016), § 529.

48. Ibid., comment (a).

49. For example, under California law, "though one may be under no duty to speak as to a matter, if he undertakes to do so, either voluntarily or in response to inquiries, he is bound

not only to state truly what he tells but also not to suppress or conceal any facts within his knowledge which materially qualify those stated. If he speaks at all he must make a full and fair disclosure" (Sullivan v. Helbing, 226 P. 803, 805 [Cal. Dist. Ct. App. 1924]). See also Zinn v. Ex-Cell-O Corp., 306 P.2d 1017, 1025 (Cal. Ct. App. 1957), which describes, "One situation is where the defendant, who has no duty to speak, nevertheless does so. In such a case he is bound to speak truthfully and to speak the whole truth."

50. Zinn v. Ex-Cell-O Corp., 306 P.2d 1017, 1025 (Cal. Ct. App. 1957).

51. 73 Pa. Stat. Ann. § 201-1–201-9.3 (2016).

52. 344 U.S. 1 (1952).

53. For example, see University of Pennsylvania's "Welcome to OFSL's Parents' Page" (note 44 above).

4. Shame

1. Brad Land, *Goat: A Memoir* (New York: Random House, 2005).

2. J. van Raalte, A. Cornelius, D. Linder, and B. Brewer, "The Relationship Between Hazing and Team Cohesion," *Journal of Sport Behavior* 30, no. 4 (December 2005): 491–507.

3. Brené Brown, *Daring Greatly: How the Courage to be Vulnerable Transforms the Way We Live, Love, Parent, and Lead* (New York: Gotham Books, 2015), 196.

4. Ibid., 76.

5. All past and current editions of the National Hazing Prevention Week resources can be read online at www.HazingPrevention.Org.

6. Leslie Shelton, "The Heart of Literacy: Transforming School-Induced Shame and Recovering the Competent Self," (unpublished dissertation, Union Institute and University, 2001).

7. J. P. Tangney, S. A. Burggraf, and P. E. Wagner, "Shame-Proneness, Guilt-Proneness, and Psychological Symptoms," in *Self-Conscious Emotions: The Psychology of Shame, Guilt, Embarrassment, and Pride*, ed. J. P. Tangney and K. W. Fischer (New York: Guilford, 1995), 343–367.

8. R. F. Baumeister and M. R. Leary, "The Need to Belong: Desire for Interpersonal Attachment as a Fundamental Human Motivation," *Psychological Bulletin* 117 (1995): 497–529.

9. Shelton, "The Heart of Literacy."

10. Eliza Ahmed and Valerie Braithwaite, "Shame Management and School Bullying," *Journal of Research in Crime and Delinquency* 40 (2004): 445–473.

11. Elizabeth Allan and Mary Madden, "Hazing in View: College Students at Risk, Initial Findings from the National Study of Student Hazing," 2008, http://www.stophazing.org/wp-content/uploads/2014/06/hazing_in_view_web1.pdf.

12. David R. Hawkins, *Transcending the Levels of Consciousness: The Stairway to Enlightenment* (Carlsbad, CA: Hay House, 2006), 33.

5. Sexual Hazing

1. Anthony Cohen, *Self Consciousness: An Alternative Anthropology of Identity* (New York: Routledge, 2002).

2. Norm Pollard and Nadine C. Hoover, "Initiation Rites and Athletics: A National Survey of NCAA Sports Teams, Final Report," Alfred, NY: Alfred University, 1999, http://www.alfred.edu/sports_hazing/docs/hazing.pdf.

3. Jeffrey Jensen Arnett, "Emerging Adulthood: A Theory of Development from the Late Teens through the Twenties," *American Psychologist* 55, no. 5 (2000): 469.

4. Hank Nuwer, *Broken Pledges* (Marietta, GA: Longstreet, 1990), 50.

5. Erik H. Erikson, *Identity, Youth, and Crisis* (New York: Norton, 1968).

6. Laura Robinson, *Crossing the Line: Violence and Sexual Assault in Canada's National Sport* (Toronto: McClelland & Stewart, 1998).

7. Nadine C. Hoover and Norman J. Pollard, "Initiation Rites in American High Schools."

8. Caroline F. Keating, Jason Pomerantz, Stacy D. Pommer, Samantha J. H. Ritt, Lauren M. Miller, and Julie McCormick, "Going to College and Unpacking Hazing: A Functional Approach to Decrypting Initiation Practices Among Undergraduates," *Group Dynamics: Theory, Research, and Practice* 9, no. 2 (2005): 104.

9. Nuwer, *Broken Pledges*, 115.

10. Philip G. Zimbardo, Christina Maslach, and Craig Haney, "Reflections on the Stanford Prison Experiment: Genesis, Transformations, Consequences," in *Obedience to Authority: Current Perspectives on the Milgram Paradigm*, ed. Thomas Blass (New York: Taylor & Francis, 2000), 193–237.

11. Eric Anderson, Mark McCormack, and Harry Lee, "Male Team Sport Hazing Initiations in a Culture of Decreasing Homohysteria," *Journal of Adolescent Research* 27, no. 4 (2012): 427–448.

12. Jay Johnson, "Through the Liminal: A Comparative Analysis of *Communitas* and Rites of Passage in Sport Hazing and Initiations," *Canadian Journal of Sociology* 36, no. 3 (2011): 199–227.

13. Jay Johnson and Margery Holman, "Gender and Hazing: The Same but Different," *Journal of Physical Education, Recreation & Dance* 80, no. 5 (2009): 6–9.

14. Doe v. Rutherford County, No. 3: 13-0328 (M.D. Tenn. Apr. 24, 2014). See also Anne DeMartini, "Sexual Hazing or Harassment Is a Title IX Violation," *Journal of Physical Education, Recreation & Dance* 87, no. 4 (2016): 53–55.

15. Susan P. Stuart, "Warriors, Machismo, and Jockstraps: Sexually Exploitative Athletic Hazing and Title IX in the Public School Locker Room," *Western New England Review* 35 (2013): 377, 395–396.

16. Stuart, "Warriors, Machismo, and Jockstraps," 392.

17. Anderson et al., "Male Team Sport Hazing Initiations," 430.

18. Jennifer L. Waldron and Christopher L. Kowalski, "Crossing the Line: Rites of Passage, Team Aspects, and Ambiguity of Hazing," *Research Quarterly for Exercise and Sport* 80, (2009): 291–302. See also Michael A. Messner and Donald F. Sabo, *Sexual Violence and Power in Sport* (Freedom, CA: Crossing River, 1989).

19. Anderson et al., "Male Team Sport Hazing Initiations," 429.

20. Arthur G. Miller, Barry E. Collins, and Diana E. Brief, "Perspectives on Obedience to Authority: The Legacy of the Milgram Experiments," *Journal of Social Issues* 51, no. 3 (1995): 1–19.

21. Waldron and Kowalski, "Crossing the Line," 292.

22. Stuart, "Warriors, Machismo, and Jockstraps," 392.

23. Aldo Cimino, "The Evolution of Hazing: Motivational Mechanisms and the Abuse of Newcomers," *Journal of Cognition and Culture* 11, no. 3–4 (2011): 241–243.

24. Ibid.

25. Johnson and Holman, "Gender and Hazing," 6.

26. Ibid., 7.

27. Anderson et al., "Male Team Sport Hazing Initiations," 432.

28. Brett G. Stoudt, "You're Either In or You're Out: School Violence, Peer Discipline, and the (Re)Production of Hegemonic Masculinity," *Men and Masculinities* 8, no. 3 (2006): 273–287.

29. Stuart, "Warriors, Machismo, and Jockstraps," 391.

30. Anderson et al., "Male Team Sport Hazing Initiations," 431.

31. Ibid.

32. Ibid.

33. Stoudt, "You're Either In or You're Out," 281.

34. Anderson et al., "Male Team Sport Hazing Initiations," 429.

35. Hank Nuwer, *Wrongs of Passage: Fraternities, Sororities, Hazing, and Binge Drinking* (Bloomington: Indiana University Press, 2001), 31–39.

6. Ill Met by Moonlight

1. Charles V. P. Young, *Cornell in Pictures: 1868–1954* (Ithaca, NY: Cornell University Press, 1954), 25.

2. Letter from M. D. Leggett to the editor of the *New York Times*, October 21, 1873.

3. The details and facts in this essay were taken from testimony delivered by members of Cornell's Kappa Alpha Society at a two-day coroner's inquest in Ithaca, New York, October 12 and October 16, 1873.

4. *A History of Cornell University* by Morris Bishop, Ithaca: Cornell University Press, 1962, 132. (Bishop was, for many years, a holder of the endowed Kappa Alpha chair at Cornell); the author published his claim that Legget's blindfold had been removed before the fall. Also without evidence was Bishop's claim that Leggett perished because he was lost, "unfamiliar with the topography," and trying to find his way home with the aid of two Kappas, presumably Wason and Lee. Bishop may have failed to read the coroner's inquest transcript or may have forgotten important witness testimony while writing the university history.

5. "The Midnight Initiation," *Nashville Tennessean,* October 19, 1873.

6. "Untitled," See Andrew Bradford, *American Mercury* 946 (February 14, 1738).

7. Edward.

8. All this was recorded by Lyman Pierson Powell in the 1893 book *History of Education in Delaware.*

9. "The Death of Young Leggett," *Washington Evening Star,* October 17, 1873, 1.

10. Cornell historian Morris Bishop chauvinistically rebutted one such fabrication of Leggett's demise in a 1968 letter he wrote to a *New York Times* book-review editor. "In her review of Elspeth Huxley's memoir, *Love Among the Daughters* (September 22, 1968), Anne Fremantle quotes the author as asserting that a Cornell student, during a hazing ritual, 'plunged to his death in the ravine naked, save for a jockstrap, carrying a bowl of goldfish.' Nonsense, my dear lady! Some Cornellian was pulling your pretty leg."

11. Letter from M. Leggett to the editor of the *New York Times*, October 21, 1873.

12. Ibid.

8. Hazing and Gender

1. Michael S. Kimmel, *Angry White Men: American Masculinity at the End of an Era* (New York: Nation Books, 2013).

2. See, for example, the research from L. C. Ball, R. A. Cribbie, and J. R. Steele, "Beyond Gender Differences: Using Tests of Equivalence to Evaluate Gender Similarities," *Psychology of Women Quarterly* 37 (2013): 147–154; Kimmel, *Angry White Men*; P. Kivel, *Boys Will Be Men: Raising Our Sons for Courage, Caring, and Community* (Gabriola Island, BC: New Society, 1999); H. T. Reis and B. J. Carothers, "Black and White or Shades of Gray: Are Gender Differences Categorical or Dimensional?" *Current Directions in Psychological Science* 23, no. 1 (2014): 19–26; and E. Zell, Z. Krizan, and S. R. Teeter, "Evaluating Gender Similarities and Differences Using Metasynthesis," *American Psychologist* 70, no. 1 (2015): 10–20.

3. L. Finley and P. Finley, "They're Just as Sadistic as Any Group of Boys! A Content Analysis of News Coverage of Sport-Related Hazing Incidents in High Schools," *Journal of Criminal Justice and Popular Culture* 14, no. 2 (2007): 197–219.

4. E. J. Allan and M. Madden, "Hazing in View: College Students at Risk, Initial Findings from the National Study of Student Hazing," 2008, 3–17; http://www.stophazing.org/wp-content/uploads/2014/06/hazing_in_view_web1.pdf.

5. Ibid., 5.

6. Ibid., 9.

7. Ibid., 17.

8. Nadine C. Hoover, "National Survey: Initiation Rites and Athletics for NCAA Sports Teams," August 30, 1999, http://www.alfred.edu/sports_hazing/docs/hazing.pdf.

9. Kevin Cokley et al., "Developing an Instrument to Assess College Students' Attitudes toward Pledging and Hazing in Greek Letter Organizations," *College Student Journal* 35, no. 3 (2001): 451–456.

10. D. L. Shaw and T. E. Morgan, "Greek Advisors' Perception of Sorority Hazing," *NASPA Journal* 28 (1990), 60–64. For an additional examination of views of women, see H. Holmes, "The Role of Hazing in the Sorority Pledge Process," (unpublished doctoral dissertation, State University of New York at Buffalo, 1999).

11. Allan and Madden, "Hazing in View," 14, 33.

12. Hank Nuwer, *Wrongs of Passage: Fraternities, Sororities, Hazing, and Binge Drinking* (Bloomington: Indiana University Press, 2001), 140–158; Hank Nuwer, *High School Hazing: When Rites Become Wrongs* (New York: Grolier, 2000), 16.

13. Nuwer, *Wrongs of Passage*, 31–56.

14. Nuwer, *High School Hazing*, 36.

15. See E. Anderson, M. McCormack & H. Lee, "Male Team Sport Initiations in a Culture of Decreasing Homohysteria," *Journal of Adolescent Research*, 27 (4), 2012, 1–22; H. Nuwer, *Broken Pledges* (Atlanta: Longstreet Press 1990), 50; Nuwer *Wrongs of Passage* (1999) 2001, 32–40; Nuwer, *High School Hazing* (2000), 42–57; L. Robinson, *Crossing the Line: Violence and Sexual Assault in Canada's National Sport* (Toronto: McClelland & Stewart, 1998), 65–97. See also Peggy R. Sanday, *Fraternity Gang Rape: Sex, Brotherhood, and Privilege on Campus* (New York: New York University Press, 2007), 38; Stephen Sweet, "Understanding Fraternity Hazing: Insights from Symbolic Interactionist Theory," *Journal of College Student Development* 40, no. 4 (1999): 355–363; and Lionel Tiger, *Men in Groups*, 2nd ed. (New York: Marion Boyars, 1984), xv–x, 3–21.

16. Sanday, *Fraternity Gang Rape*, 33–40.

17. Sandra Lipsitz Bem, "Gender Schema Theory: A Cognitive Account of Sex Typing," *Psychological Review* 88, no. 4 (1981): 354–364. See also S. L. Bem, *The Lenses of Gender: Transforming the Debate on Sexual Inequality* (New Haven, CT: Yale University Press, 1993).

18. Michael Kimmel and Amy Aronson, eds., *Men and Masculinities: A Social, Cultural, and Historical Encyclopedia*, vol. 1, (Santa Barbara: ABC Clio,) 2004: xxiv.

19. Ibid., 504.

20. The term "hir" is used as a gender-neutral version of the pronouns "his" and "her." It is used in this context in an effort to be inclusive of transgender or gender queer (those who do not identify with socially constructed genders as they currently exist) individuals. See M. E. O'Neil, E. H. McWhirter, and A. Cerezo, "Transgender Identities and Gender Variance in Vocational Psychology: Recommendations for Practice, Social Advocacy, and Research," *Journal of Career Development* 34, no. 3 (2008): 286–308. Hazing, while sometimes shaped by gender binaries, is not a problem isolated to either end of the gender spectrum. See also E. S. Abes, S. R. Jones, and M. K. McEwen, "Reconceptualizing the Model of Multiple Dimensions of Identity: The Role of Meaning-Making Capacity in the Construction of Multiple Identities," *Journal of College Student Development* 48, no. 1 (2007): 1–22.

21. Bem, *Lenses of Gender.*

22. M. Frye, *Politics of Reality: Essays in Feminist Theory* (Trumansburg, NY: The Crossing, 1983); M. S. Kimmel, "Masculinity as Homophobia: Fear, Shame, and Silence in the Construction of Gender Identity," in *Race, Class, and Gender in the United States: An Integrated Study,* ed. Paula S. Rothenberg (New York: Worth, 2016), 81–93.

23. Michael Kimmel, Guyland: The Perilous World Where Boys Become Men (New York: HarperCollins, 2009).

24. Kimmel, *Guyland.* 20, 24.

25. Ibid.

26. Ibid.

27. D. S. David and R. Brannon, *The Forty-Nine Percent Majority: The Male Sex Role* (Reading, MA: Addison Wesley, 1976).

28. Kimmel, *Guyland*, 2008, 20–28.

29. Ibid., 18–33.

30. Ibid., 13–15.

31. Ibid. 3, 13–15.

32. H. Dohnt and M. Tiggemann, "The Contribution of Peer and Media Influences to the Development of Body Satisfaction and Self-Esteem in Young Girls: A Prospective Study," *Developmental Psychology* 42, no. 5 (2006): 929–936. See also A. E. Field et al., "Peer, Parent, and Media Influences on the Development of Weight Concerns and Frequent Dieting among Preadolescent and Adolescent Girls and Boys," *Pediatrics* 107, no. 1 (2001): 54–60.

33. Nuwer, *The Hazing Reader,* 282.

34. A. Howard and E. Kennedy, "Breaking the Silence: Power, Conflict, and Contested Frames within an Affluent High School," *Anthropology & Education Quarterly* 37, no. 4 (2006): 347–365.

35. Nuwer, *Broken Pledges,* 266; Nuwer, *Wrongs of Passage* (1999), 31–36, 94–95; Nuwer, *High School Hazing* 17–18.

36. P. Y. Martin and R. A. Hummer, "Fraternities and Rape on Campus," *Gender and Society* 4 (1989): 457–473.

37. J. L. Pershing, "Men and Women's Experiences with Hazing in a Male-Dominated Elite Military Institution," *Men and Masculinities* 8, no. 4 (2006): 470–492.

38. Allan and Madden, "Hazing in View, 29."

39. Martin and Hummer, "Fraternities and Rape on Campus," 457–473.

40. "Understanding Fraternity Hazing," in Hank Nuwer, *The Hazing Reader,* (Bloomington: Indiana University Press).

41. Robinson, *Crossing the Line,* 66.

42. A. Cimino, "The Evolution of Hazing: Motivational Mechanisms and the Abuse of Newcomers," *Journal of Cognition and Culture* 11 (2011): 241–267.

43. N. Krieger and E. Fee, "Social Class: The Missing Link in US Health Data," *International Journal of Health Services* 24, no. 1 (1994): 25–44.

44. L. M. Waldron, "Girls are Worse: Drama Queens, Ghetto Girls, Tomboys, and the Meaning of Girl Fights," *Youth & Society* 43, no. 4 (2011): 1298–1334.

45. M. Stombler and P. Y. Martin, "Bringing Women In, Keeping Women Down: Fraternity Little Sister Organizations," *Journal of Contemporary Ethnography* 23, no. 2 (1994): 150–184.

46. J. Kilbourne, *Deadly Persuasion: Why Women and Girls Must Fight the Addictive Power of Advertising* (Lexington, KY: Lexington Volunteer Recording Unit, 2000).

47. R. A. Rhoads, "Whales Tales, Dog Piles, and Beer Goggles: An Ethnographic Study of Fraternity Life," *Anthropology & Education Quarterly* 26, no. 3 (1995): 306–323.

48. A. Robbins, *Pledged: The Secret Life of Sororities* (New York: Hachette, 2005).

49. Nuwer, *High School Hazing*, 38–41.

50. Waldron, "Girls are Worse," 1298–1334.

51. Quoted in Nuwer, *Wrongs of Passage*, 180. See original in Paula Giddings, *In Search of Sisterhood* (New York: William Morrow, 1998), 8–9. See also Giddings, 18, 243, 284.

52. P. H. Collins, *African American Feminist Thought: Knowledge, Consciousness, and the Politics of Empowerment* (New York: Routledge, 1991).

53. G. S. Parks, S. E. Jones, R. Ray, M. W. Hughey, and J. M. Cox, "[A] Man and a Brother: Intersectionality, Violent Hazing, and the Law," (legal studies paper, Wake Forest University, 2014), 66; http://ssrn.com.prxy4.ursus.maine.edu/abstract=2409764.

54. Ibid.

55. P. Ruffins, "Fratricide: Are African American Fraternities Beating Themselves to Death?" *Diverse Issues in Higher Education*, July 11, 2007, http://diverseeducation.com/article /8216; Nuwer, *Broken Pledges* (1990), 207–221; and Nuwer *High School Hazing* (1999), 106–114. See also Nuwer's Hazing Prevention Blog at http://hanknuwer.com for an ongoing list of hazing incidents in all fraternal groups of all races.

56. M. A. Messner, "Masculinities and Athletic Careers," *Gender and Society* 3, no. 1 (1989): 71–88.

57. Ibid., 72.

58. J. Katz, *Macho Paradox: Why Some Men Hurt Women and How All Men Can Help* (Naperville, IL: Sourcebooks, 2006).

59. H. Holmes, "The Role of Hazing in the Sorority Pledge Process," (unpublished doctoral dissertation, State University of New York at Buffalo, 1999), 81.

60. L. Langford, "A Comprehensive Approach to Hazing Prevention in Higher Education Settings," Higher Education Center Working Paper, US Department of Education's Higher Education Center for Alcohol and Other Drug Abuse and Violence Prevention, 2008, http:// files.eric.ed.gov/fulltext/ED537679.pdf.

61 J. Johnson and J. W. Chin, "Seeking New Glory (D)Haze: A Qualitative Examination of Adventure-Based, Team Orientation Rituals as an Alternative to Traditional Sport Hazing for Athletes and Coaches," *International Journal of Sports Science & Coaching* 11, no. 3 (April 28, 2016): 327–341.

9. Listening to the Voices of the Hazed

1. J. W. Blassingame, *The Slave Community: Plantation Life in the Antebellum South* (New York: Oxford University Press, 1979).

2. R. Jones, *Black Haze: Violence, Sacrifice, and Manhood in Black Greek-Letter Fraternities*, 2nd ed. (Albany, NY: SUNY Press, 2004), 11.

3. Ibid.

4. W. Kimbrough, *Black Greek 101: The Culture, Customs, and Challenges of Black Fraternities and Sororities* (Madison, NJ: Farleigh Dickinson University Press, 2003).

5. Stephanie M. McClure, "Improvising Masculinity: African American Fraternity Membership in the Construction of a Black Masculinity," *Journal of African American Studies* 10 (2006): 57–73.

6. R. W. Connell, *Masculinities*, 2nd ed. (Berkeley: University of California Press, 2005), 152.

7. Ibid.

8. Michael S. Kimmel, *Manhood in America: A Cultural History*, 2nd ed. (New York: Oxford University Press, 2006).

9. Patricia Hill Collins, *Black Feminist Thought: Knowledge, Consciousness, and the Politics of Empowerment*, 2nd ed., (New York: Routledge, 2000). See also P. H. Collins, *Black Sexual Politics* (New York: Routledge, 2005).

10. McClure, "Improvising Masculinity."

11. Connell, *Masculinities*, 83.

12. Ibid.

13. J. Katz, *Tough Guise: Violence, Media & the Crisis in Masculinity* (video from the Media Education Foundation, 1999).

14. Jones, *Black Haze*, 49.

15. Ibid.

16. Ibid.

17. Tyra Black, Joanne Belknap, and Jennifer Ginsburg, "Racism, Sexism, and Aggression: A Study of Black and White Fraternities" in *African American Fraternities and Sororities: The Legacy and the Vision*, ed. T. L. Brown, G. S. Parks, and C. M. Phillips, (Lexington: University of Kentucky Press, 2005), 363–392.

18. Jones, *Black Haze*, 57.

19. Ibid.

20. Brown et al., *African American Fraternities and Sororities: The Legacy and the Vision*, 447.

21. Jones, *Black Haze*.

22. Brown et al., *African American Fraternities and Sororities: The Legacy and the Vision*.

23. Ibid.

24. Ibid.

25. H. Nuwer, *Broken Pledges: The Deadly Rite of Hazing* (Atlanta: Longstreet, 1990), 118.

26. Collins, *Black Feminist Thought*, 176. See also Collins, *Black Sexual Politics*.

27. O. Patterson, *The Cultural Matrix: Understanding Black Youth* (Cambridge: Harvard University Press, 2015).

28. W. Kimbrough, "Should Black Fraternities and Sororities Abolish Undergraduate Chapters?" *About Campus* 10, no. 4 (September/October 2005), 29.

10. Unspoken Sisterhood

1. H. Nuwer, *Wrongs of Passage: Fraternities, Sororities, Hazing, and Binge Drinking* (Bloomington: Indiana University Press, 1999), 211.

2. R. Roberts, "The Sisterhood, Taking on the Old Boy Network," *Washington Post*, September 27, 2003.

3. P. Giddings, *When and Where I Enter: The Impact of Black Women on Race and Sex in America* (New York: Harper Collins, 1984), 90.

4. See Nuwer, *Wrongs of Passage*; W. M. Kimbrough, *Black Greek 101: The Culture, Customs, and Challenges of Black Fraternities and Sororities* (Rutherford, NJ: Fairleigh Dickinson University Press, 2003).

5. J. A. Williams, *Perceptions of the No-Pledge Policy for New Member Intake by Undergraduate Members of Predominately Black Fraternities and Sororities* (doctoral dissertation, Kansas State University, UMI Services, 1992).

6. T. A. Leemon, *The Rites of Passage in a Student Culture* (New York: Teachers College Press, 1972), 172.

7. G. E. Rutledge, "Hell Night Hath No Fury Like a Pledge Scorned and Injured: Hazing Litigation in US Colleges and Universities," *Journal of College and University Law* 25, no. 2 (Fall 1998), 361.

8. K. Cokley, K. Miller, D. Cunningham, et al., "Developing an Instrument to Assess College Students' Attitudes toward Pledging and Hazing in Greek-Letter Organizations," *College Student Journal* 35, no. 3 (2001): 451–457.

9. W. M. Kimbrough, "Notes from the Underground: Despite a Ban, Pledging Remains," *Black Issues in Higher Education* 17, no. 6 (2000): 88.

10. D. Shaw and T. Morgan, "Greek Advisors' Perceptions of Sorority Hazing," *NASPA Journal* 28, no. 1 (1990): 60–64.

11. Nuwer, *Wrongs of Passage*, 179.

12. Ibid.

13. M. Geraghty, "Hazing Incidents at Sororities Alarm Colleges," *Chronicle of Higher Education* 43, no. 41 (1997): 37–38.

14. Walter Kimbrough, *Black Greek 101* (Madison, NJ: Fairleigh Dicinon Press, 203), 58–59.

15. R. Jones, "The Historical Significance of Sacrificial Ritual: Understanding Violence in the Modern Black Fraternity Pledge Process," *Western Journal of Black Studies* 24, no. 2 (2000): 112–124.

16. Kimbrough, "Notes from the Underground," 88.

17. B. Hooks, *All About Love* (New York: William Morrow, 2000), 165–166.

18. C. M. Taylor and M. F. Howard-Hamilton, "Student Involvement and Racial Identity Attitudes among African American Males, *Journal of College Student Development* 36, no. 4 (1995), 330–336.

19. G. D. Kuh and E. J. Whitt, "The Invisible Tapestry: Culture in American Colleges and Universities," in *College Student Affairs Administration*, ed. E. J. Whitt (Needham Heights, MA: Simon and Schuster, 1997), 125–327.

20. D. R. Person and M. C. Christensen, "Understanding Black Student Culture and Black Student Retention," *NASPA Journal* 34, no. 1 (1996): 47–56.

21. For example, see W. M. Kimbrough, "Self-assessment, Participation, and Value of Leadership Skills, Activities, and Experiences for Black Students Relative to Their Membership in Black Sororities and Fraternities," *Journal of Negro Education* 64, no. 1 (1995): 63–73. Also consult D. J. DeSousa and G. D. Kuh, "Does Institutional Racial Composition Make a Difference in What Black Students Gain from College?" *Journal of College Student Development* 37, no. 3 (1996): 257–266.

22. Kimbrough, 2004, 38.

23. C. M. Phillips, "Sisterly Bonds: African American Sororities Rising to Overcome Obstacles," in *African American Fraternities and Sororities: The Legacy and the Vision*, ed.

T. L. Brown, G. S. Parks, and C. M. Phillips (Lexington: University Press of Kentucky, 2005), 341–362.

24. S. B. Merriam, *Qualitative Research and Case Study Application in Education* (San Francisco, CA: Jossey-Bass, 1998), 72.

25. M. Patton, *Qualitative Research and Evaluation Methods* (Thousand Oaks, CA: Sage, 2002), 340.

26. Jones, "Historical Significance of Sacrificial Ritual," 121.

27. R. L. Jones, *Black Haze: Violence, Sacrifice, and Manhood in Black Greek-Letter Fraternities* (Albany: State University of New York Press, 2004).

28. See Jones, "Historical Significance of Sacrificial Ritual," and Nuwer, *Wrongs of Passage.*

11. Sexually Exploitive Athletic Hazing and Title IX in the Public School Locker Room

1. Editor's Note: Professor Susan P. Stuart's original article was some twenty thousand words and had to be trimmed to fit the essay into this volume. I strongly encourage parents, coaches, and administrators, in particular, to read her original article in its entirety online. Please see S. Stuart, "Warriors, Machismo, and Jockstraps: Sexually Exploitative Athletic Hazing and Title IX in the Public School Locker Room," *Western New England Law Review* 35, no. 2 (2013): 377–423. Downloadable at https://works.bepress.com/susan_stuart.

2. R. W. Connell and J. W. Messerschmidt, "Hegemonic Masculinity: Rethinking the Concept," *Gender and Society* 19, no. 6 (2005): 829–859.

3. Section 1681(a) of Title IX reads, "No person in the United States shall, on the basis of sex, be excluded from participation in, be denied the benefits of, or be subjected to discrimination under any education program or activity receiving Federal financial assistance."

4. E. J. Allan and M. Madden, "Hazing in View: College Students at Risk, Initial Findings from the National Study of Student Hazing," 2008, 37; http://www.stophazing.org/wp-content/uploads/2014/06/hazing_in_view_web1.pdf.

5. Laura L. Finley and Peter S. Finley, "They're Just as Sadistic as Any Group of Boys! A Content Analysis of News Coverage of Sport-Related Hazing Incidents in High Schools," *Journal of Criminal Justice and Popular Culture* 14, no. 2 (2007): 197–219, 204.

6. See "25 Bad Hazing Incidents" at HankNuwer.com.

7. See Susan Lipkins, *Preventing Hazing* (Hoboken, NJ: Wiley, 2006). See also Jennifer J. Waldron and Christopher L. Kowalski, "Crossing the Line: Rites of Passage, Team Aspects, and Ambiguity of Hazing," *Research Quarterly for Exercise and Sport* 80, no. 2 (2009): 291–302.

8. Jay Johnson, "Through the Liminal: A Comparative Analysis of *Communitas* and Rites of Passage in Sport Hazing and Initiations," *Canadian Journal of Sociology* 36, no. 3 (2011): 199–227, 208.

9. In Michael A. Messner, *Power at Play* (Boston: Beacon Press, 1992), 88.

10. Ibid.

11. J. van Raalte, A. Cornelius, D. Linder, and B. Brewer, "The Relationship Between Hazing and Team Cohesion," *Journal of Sport Behavior* 30, no. 4 (December 2005): 491–507.

12. Ibid. See also Lipkins, *Preventing Hazing,* 15–16.

13. Johnson, "Through the Liminal," 194–197.

14. Lipkins, *Preventing Hazing,* 15–16. See also Eric Anderson, Mark McCormack, and Harry Lee, "Male Team Sport Hazing Initiations in a Culture of Decreasing Homohysteria," *Journal of Adolescent Research* 27, no. 4 (2012): 427–448. See also http://ericandersonphd.com.

15. Sandra L. Kirby and Glen Wintrup, "Running the Gauntlet: An Examination of Initiation/Hazing and Sexual Abuse in Sport," *Journal of Sexual Aggression* 8, no. 2 (2002): 49–68. See also Leslee A. Fisher and Lars Dzikus, "Bullying and Hazing in Sport Teams," in *Routledge Handbook of Applied Sport Psychology*, ed. Stephanie J. Hanrahan and Mark B. Andersen (New York: Taylor and Francis, 2011).

16. See Lionel Tiger, "Males Courting Males," in *The Hazing Reader*, ed. Hank Nuwer, (Bloomington: Indiana University Press, 2004), 14–16.

17. Johnson, "Through the Liminal," 203.

18. Ibid.

19. Ibid.

20. Jeffrey C. Gershel, Rachel J Katz-Sidlow, Eric Small, and Stephanie Zandieh, "Hazing of Suburban Middle School and High School Athletes," *Journal of Adolescent Health* 32 (2003): 333–335.

21. Johnson, "Through the Liminal," 199.

22. Ibid.

23. Johnson, "Through the Liminal," 223.

24. Ibid., 199–200.

25. Jennifer Waldron, Lynn Quinten and Vikki Krane, "Duct Tape, Icy Hot & Paddles: Narratives of Initiation onto U.S. Sport Teams," *Sport, Education & Society*, 16 (1), 2011, 111–125.

26. Ibid., 292, 297.

27. Johnson, supra note 44, "Through the Liminal," 212.

28. See, for example, Hank Nuwer, *High School Hazing*, (New York: Scholastic, 2000), 31, 37.

29. See also Nuwer, *High School Hazing*, 44; Waldron and Kowalski, "Crossing the Line," 112–113.

30. Waldron and Christopher L. Kowalski, "Crossing the Line: Rites of Passage, Team Aspects, and Ambiguity of Hazing," supra note 28, at 292.

31. Eric Anderson et al., "Male Team Sport Hazing Initiations in a Culture of Decreasing Homohysteria," *Journal of Adolescent Research* (July 4, 2011), 3–4, available at http://www.ericandersonphd.com/journal-articles.php.

32. Kirby and Wintrup, "Running the Gauntlet," 61.

33. Ibid., 60.

34. Waldron and Kowalski, "Crossing the Line," 112–113.

35. Connell and Messerschmidt, "Hegemonic Masculinity," 846.

36. Ibid.

37. L. Hong, "Toward a Transformed Approach to Prevention," *Journal of American Health* 48, (2000): 269, 271, quoting *The Forty-Nine Percent Majority: The Male Sex Role* (eds. Robert Brannon and Deborah S. David, 1976).

38. Connell and Messerschmidt, "Hegemonic Masculinity," 849.

39. Raewyn Connell, "Masculinity Construction and Sports in Boys' Education," *Sport, Education, and Society* 13, no. 2 (2008): 131–145, 137.

40. Waldron and Kowalski, "Crossing the Line," 113.

41. Connell, "Masculinity Construction and Sports in Boys' Education," 133.

42. Michael Messner, "Boyhood, Organized Sports, and the Construction of Masculinities," *Contemporary Ethnography* 18 (1990): 431–432.

43. Holman, *Making the Team*, 52. See also Kirby and Wintrup, "Running the Gauntlet," 61.

44. Anderson and Lee, "Male Team Sport Hazing," 427–448.

45. Kirby and Wintrup, "Running the Gauntlet," 61.

46. Ibid. See also Anderson, 3.

47. Anderson, "Male Team Sport Hazing," 3.

48. Waldron and Kowalski, "Crossing the Line," 113.

49. Connell and Messerschmidt, "Hegemonic Masculinity," 846.

50. Holman, *Making the Team*, 53.

51. Celia Brackenridge, *Spoilsports: Understanding and Preventing Sexual Exploitation in Sport* (London: Routledge, 2001), 15–18, 22–23.

52. Johnson, "Through the Liminal," 206.

53. Waldron and Kowalski, "Crossing the Line," 113.

54. Johnson, "Through the Liminal," 207.

55. Waldron et al., "Duct Tape, Icy Hot and Paddles," p. 120.

56. Waldron and Kowalski, "Crossing the Line," 120.

57. Brackenridge, *Spoilsports*, 91. See also Kirby and Wintrup, "Running the Gauntlet," 51.

58. Anderson, "Male Sport Team Initiations," 5.

59. Johnson, "Through the Liminal," 221.

60. Waldron and Kowalski, "Crossing the Line," 81, 113.

61. Cyd Zeigler, "The 'Gay' Side of Hazing," https://www.outsports.com, May 24, 2006.

62. Helen Jefferson Lensky, "What's Sex Got to Do with It? Analyzing the Sex Violence Agenda in Sport Hazing Practices," in Holman, *Making the Team*," 86–87.

63. According to Glankler v. Rapides Parish School Board, 610 So. 2d 1020, 1029 (Louisiana Ct. App 1992). Stuart previously cited Glankler in Susan P. Stuart, Jack & Jill Go to Court: Litigating a Peer Sexual Harassment Case Under Title IX, 29 AM. J. TRIAL ADVOC. 243 (2005), 274, when she wrote this: "Although charged with the highest degree of care toward children placed in their custody, supervisors at schools are not absolute insurers of the children's safety and cannot be expected or required to prevent them from falling or striking each other during normal childhood play."

64. Johnson v. School District of Philadelphia, 454 A. 2d 1038, 1039 (Pennsylvania Superior Court, 1982).

65. Johnson v. School District of Millard, 573 N. W. 2d 116, 119–120 (Nebraska, 1998).

66. Ibid., Johnson v. School District of Millard, 120.

67. Simonetti v. School District of Philadelphia, 454 A. 2d 1038, 1039 (Pennsylvania Superior Court, 1982).

68. Beckett v. Clinton Prairie School Corporation, 504 N. E. 2d 552, 554 (Indiana, 1987). See also Yanero v. Davis, 65 S. W. 3d 510, 529 (Kentucky, 2001); Prejean v. E. Baton Rouge Parish School Board, 729 So. 2d 686, 689 (Louisiana Court of Appeals, 1999).

69. Podgorski v. Pizzoferrato, No. CV-07-5010288, 2009 WL 3739409, at 5 (Connecticut Superior Court, October 7, 2009).

70. Marc Edelman, "How to Prevent High School Hazing: A Legal, Ethical and Social Primer," *North Dakota Law Review* 81 (2005): 319–321.

71. Kirby and Wintrup, "Running the Gauntlet," 56.

72. Davis v. Monroe County Board of Education, 526 U.S. 629 (1999).

73. Ibid, Davis v. Monroe County Board of Education at 650.

74. Ibid, Davis v. Monroe County Board of Education at 651.

75. Ibid, Davis v. Monroe County Board of Education at 651–652.

76. Title IX is framed on stopping harassment on the "basis of sex," rather than "because of sex" as required under Title VII. Thus, gender-targeted harassment, and not just sexually suggestive behavior, has proved sufficient to proceed under Title IX.

77. Russlynn Ali, "Dear Colleague Letter: Sexual Violence," United States Department of Education, April 4, 2011. Ali's title at the time was Assistant Secretary of Education for Civil Rights. See also Stuart, 271–273.

78. Stuart, 274. See also Halvorson v. Independent School District, No. 1-007, (2008).

79. *Davis*, 526 U.S. 629 (1999).

80. See Oncale v. Sundowner Offshore Services, 523 U.S. 75 (1998); Theno v. Tonganoxie Unified School District No. 464, 377 F. Supp. 2d 952, 963–64 (D. Kansas, 2005).

81. Theno v. Tonganoxie Unified School District No. 464, 377 F. Supp. 2d 952, 963–64 (D. Kansas, 2005). See also Montgomery v. Independent School District No. 709, 109 F. Supp. 2d 1081, 1090-93 (D. Minnesota, 2000).

82. Some of the cases reviewed by the author have had to be cut to do space limitations. For additional cases, including a thorough review of the literature in the State of Indiana, please see Stuart, "Warriors, Machismo, And Jockstraps," https://works.bepress.com/susan_stuart.

83. For references to the Sky View hazing, see Seamons v. Snow, 84 F. 3d 1226 (10th Cir. 1996). Brian could not prove discrimination on the basis of gender (Id2m, 228). However, he was able to proceed on a First Amendment "Freedom of Speech" claim.

84. Lipkins, *Preventing Hazing*, 135–140.

85. Ali, "Dear Colleague Letter."

86. Ibid.

87. Ibid.

88. Editor's Note: One Texas A&M fraternity member lost a testicle to a wedgie. See generally Michal Buchhandler-Raphael, "The Failure of Concept: Re-Conceptualizing Rape as Sexual Abuse of Power," *Michigan Journal of Gender and Law*, 18, no. 1 (2011), 147–228.

89. Michal Buchhandler-Raphael, "The Failure of Consent: Re-Conceptualizing Rape as Sexual Abuse of Power, *Michigan Journal of Gender and Law* 18, no. 1 (2011): 147.

90. Ali, "Dear Colleague Letter."

91. Donna Winslow, "Rites of Passage and Group Bonding in the Canadian Airborne," in Nuwer, *The Hazing Reader*, 2004, 165–166.

92. E. L. Epstein, "Notes on *Lord of the Flies*," in William Golding, *Lord of the Flies* (Berkley, CA: Berkley Publishing, 2003), 287–290.

93. R. W. Connell, "Teaching the Boys: New Research on Masculinity and Gender Strategies for Schools," *Teachers College Record* 98 (1996): 206–212.

94. Christopher Kowalski and Jennifer Waldron, "Looking the Other Way: Athletes' Perceptions of Coaches' Responses to Hazing," *International Journal of Sports Science and Coaching* 5, no. 1 (2010): 87–100, 96.

95. Brian Crow, Robin Ammon, and Dennis R. Phillips, "Anti-Hazing Strategies for Coaches and Administrators," *Strategies: A Journal for Physical and Sport Educators* 17, no. 4 (2004): 13–14. See also Lipkins, *Preventing Hazing*, 94–97; Fisher and Dzikus, "Bullying and Hazing in Sport Teams," 359–361; Waldron and Kowalski, "Crossing the Line," 300–301.

96. Waldron and Kowalski, "Crossing the Line," 89.

12. A Mother's Story

1. For more information please go to www.ahamovement.org and www.wemissyoumatt .com.

2. For the entire text of the *Diablo* story, see http://www.diablomag.com/August-2015 /In-the-Basement-No-One-Can-Hear-You-Scream.

13. How Alfred University Ended the Greek System to Become a Hazing Research Institution

1. Nadine C. Hoover, "National Survey: Initiation Rites and Athletics for NCAA Sports Teams," August 30, 1999, http://www.alfred.edu/sports_hazing/docs/hazing.pdf.

14. How Schools May Have Facilitated and Operationalized Hazing

1. Hank Nuwer, *At the Crest: A History of Cedar Crest College from 1867–1988* (Allentown, PA: Cedar Crest Alumnae Association, 2004).

2. Peter F. Lake, *The Rights and Responsibilities of the Modern University: The Rise of the Facilitator University*, 2nd ed. (Durham, NC: Carolina Academic Press, 2013).

3. Furek v. The University of Delaware, 594 A.2d 506 (Del. 1991).

4. Nova Southeastern University, Petitioner, Cross-Respondent v. Bethany Jill Gross, Respondent, Cross-Petitioner, No. SC94079 (2000).

5. Eric Hoover, "As Deaths Mount, A Question Is Raised: Are Students Hard-Wired for Hazing?" *The Chronicle of Higher Education*, February 12, 2012. Hoover wrote, "If humans are hardwired for hazing, it's also true that colleges are well constructed to perpetuate it."

15. A Fraternity Model

1. Neil Howe and William Strauss, *Millennials Rising* (New York: Vintage, 2000).

2. CDC documents on alcohol use are downloadable at http://www.cdc.gov/alcohol/fact-sheets/underage-drinking.htm.

16. A Realistic Approach to Public Relations for Fraternities in Crisis

1. Caitlin Flanagan, "The Dark Power of Fraternities," *Atlantic Monthly* 313, no. 2 (2014), 72–91; https://www.theatlantic.com/magazine/archive/2014/03/the-dark-power-of-fraternities/357580/.

18. How Reforms and Reformers Played a Role in Changing a Hazing Culture

1. L. Darling-Hammond, "Teacher Learning that Supports Student Learning," in *Teaching for Intelligence*, 2nd ed., ed. B. Z. Presseisen (Thousand Oaks, CA: Corwin, 2008), 92.

2. G. R. McCreary, "The Impact on Moral Judgment and Moral Disengagement on Hazing Attitudes and Bystander Behavior in College Males," (PhD dissertation, University of Alabama, 2012), 73.

3. E. J. Allan and M. Madden, "Hazing in View: College Students at Risk, Initial Findings from the National Study of Student Hazing," 2008, http://www.stophazing.org/wp-content/uploads/2014/06/hazing_in_view_web1.pdf.

4. L. Langford and W. DeJong, *Strategic Planning for Prevention Professionals on Campus*, Prevention 101 Series (Washington, DC: US Department of Education, Office of Safe and Drug-Free Schools, 2008); L. Langford, "A Comprehensive Approach to Hazing Prevention in Higher Education Settings," Higher Education Center Working Paper, US Department of Education's Higher Education Center for Alcohol and Other Drug Abuse and Violence Prevention, 2008, http://files.eric.ed.gov/fulltext/ED537679.pdf.

5. Allan and Madden, "Hazing in View."

20. Hazing and University Ethics

1. Caitlin Flanagan, "The Dark Power of Fraternities," *Atlantic Monthly* 313, no. 2 (2014), https://www.theatlantic.com/magazine/archive/2014/03/the-dark-power-of-fraternities/357580/.

2. Ibid.

3. John Hechinger and David Glovin, "Fraternities Scuttle Proposals to Ban Freshman Rush after Drinking Deaths," *Bloomberg News*, October 15, 2013.

4. Peter Schworm, "Police Seek Charges in Apparent Fraternity Hazing at BU," *Boston Globe*, April 10, 2012.

5. Winton Solberg, "Harmless Pranks or Brutal Practices? Hazing at the University of Illinois, 1868–1913," *Journal of Illinois State Historical Society* 91, no. 4 (1988): 233–259.

6. Hank Nuwer, *Broken Pledges: The Deadly Rite of Hazing*" (Atlanta: Longstreet Press, 1990); Hank Nuwer, *Wrongs of Passage: Fraternities, Sororities, Hazing, and Binge Drinking* (Bloomington: Indiana University Press, 2001).

7. Hank Nuwer, ed., *The Hazing Reader* (Bloomington: Indiana University Press, 2004), 105.

8. Nuwer, *Wrongs of Passage*, 50, 51.

9. Ibid., p. 105.

10. Ibid.

11. Editor's note: Using theorists James Prochaska and Carlo DiClemente's Cycle of Change Model, Rochester Institute of Technology Greek Life staffer Eric Pope has hypothesized that much like a drug addict has to go through a process of determined behavior changes to get clean and sober, a chapter and its members need to go through a similar process of healthy behavior adoptions to refrain from hazing. See also James Prochaska and Carlo DiClemente, "Transtheoretical Therapy: Toward a More Integrative Model of Change," *Psychotherapy* 19 (1982): 276–288, doi:10.1037/h0088437.

12. Elizabeth Allan and Mary Madden, "Hazing in View: College Students at Risk, Initial Findings from the National Study of Student Hazing," 2008, http://www.stophazing.org/wp-content/uploads/2014/06/hazing_in_view_web1.pdf.

13. See, for example, Hank Nuwer's play "The Broken Pledge," at http://www.stophazing.org/blog/the-broken-pledge-a-play-by-hank-nuwer.

14. Elizabeth Allan and Susan Van Deventer Iverson, "Initiating Change: Transforming a Hazing Culture," in *The Hazing Reader*, ed. Hank Nuwer (Bloomington: Indiana University Press, 2004), 256.

15. Ibid.

16. Elizabeth Allan, "Hazing and Gender," in *Hazing Reader*, 289.

17. Ibid., 294.

21. Understanding Hazing in the Perilous World of *Guyland*

1. Michael Kimmel, *Guyland: The Perilous World Where Boys Become Men* (New York: HarperCollins, 2008).

23. Women and a Feminine Leadership Style Can Defeat Hazing

1. Amy O'Brian, "We Need More Effort to Promote Basic Human Values," *Vancouver Sun*, September 27, 2009.

2. Annie Burnside, "The Dalai Lama: 'The World Will Be Saved by the Western Woman,'" *Chicago Now* (blog), July 25, 2012, http://www.chicagonow.com/soul-to-soul-perspective/2012/07/the-dalai-lama-the-world-will-be-saved-by-the-western-woman.

3. Victor W. Hwang, "Are Feminine Leadership Traits the Future of Business?" *Forbes*, August 30, 2014, https://www.forbes.com/sites/victorhwang/2014/08/30/are-feminine-leadership-traits-the-future-of-business/#c68ce99598e5.

4. Information on the Circle of Sisterhood Foundation is available online at https://www.circleofsisterhood.org.

5. Tabby Biddle, "Exclusive Interview with Nicholas Kristof: Women Hold Up Half the Sky," *Huffington Post*, November 14, 2011, http://www.huffingtonpost.com/tabby-biddle/exclusive-interview-with-_6_b_1091593.html.

6. Eleonora Barbieri Masini, "The Creative Role of Women in a Changing World," *Leonardo* 27, no. 1 (1994): 51–56.

7. See James M. Kouzes and Barry Z. Posner, *The Leadership Challenge*, 5th ed. (Hoboken, NJ: Wiley, 2012). Kouzes and Posner defined transformational leadership through thousands of student leadership assessments that built on the work of previous researchers. A transformational style is one in which in which leaders employ charisma and enthusiasm to inspire their followers. This more-feminine style puts emphasis on the values, ideals, morals, and needs of the followers. There is emphasis on changing the existing organizational culture. Instead of a single leader, there are many leaders.

8. John Gerzema and Michael D'Antonio, *The Athena Doctrine: How Women (and the Men Who Think Like Them) Will Rule the Future* (Hoboken, NJ: Jossey-Bass, 2013).

9. Tracy would like to thank the following women for their help with this chapter: Jen Day Shaw, Jackie, and Stacy, the latter two who are referred to in the chapter by only their first names.

24. The Purdue Tank Scrap

1. "The Freshman Class," *Debris* (Lafayette: Purdue University, 1905), 173.

2. Simon J. Bronner, "The Rise and Fall—and Return—of the Class Rush: A Study of a Contested Tradition," *Western Folklore* 70, no. 1 (2011): 5–67.

3. Malcolm Townsend, "A Cane Rush," in *The Book of Athletics and Out-Of-Door Sports*, ed. Norman W. Bingham Jr. (Boston: Lothrop, 1895), 226.

4. Kathleen Dalton, *Theodore Roosevelt: A Strenuous Life* (Westminster, MD: Knopf, 2004), 290.

5. Jack Cavanaugh, *The Gipper: George Gipp, Knute Rockne, and the Dramatic Rise of Notre Dame Football* (New York: Skyhorse, 2010), 83.

6. Bill Reid and Ronald Austin Smith, *Big-Time Football at Harvard 1905: The Diary of Coach Bill Reid* (Urbana: University of Illinois Press, 1994), xvii; Christopher Nowinski, *Head Games: Football's Concussion Crisis from the NFL to Youth Leagues* (East Bridgewater, MA: Drummond, 2007), 101.

7. Philip Lutz Jr., "Hazing in American Colleges," *The World To-Day* 17 (August 1909): 851–858.

8. "History of the Class of '96," *Debris* (Lafayette: Purdue University, 1896), 49.

9. "November," *Debris* (Lafayette: Purdue University, 1898), 213; "October," *Debris* (Lafayette: Purdue University, 1899), 366; "The Tank," *The Purdue Exponent*, November 3, 1897, 14–17.

10. "History of 1901," *Debris* (Lafayette: Purdue University, 1901), 107.

11. "A 32-calibre Argument," *The Purdue Exponent*, September 26, 1902, 9.

12. "Painted and Ducked," *The Purdue Exponent*, September 20, 1910, 1.

13. "Class of '97," *Debris* (Lafayette: Purdue University, 1897), 45; "The Sophomore Class," *Debris* (Lafayette: Purdue University, 1909), 176.

14. "The Tank Scrap," *Debris* (Lafayette: Purdue University, 1910), 63.

15. "Tank Scrap of Other Years," *The Purdue Exponent*, September 21, 1907, 1.

16. http://collections.lib.purdue.edu/traditions/index.php?id=12, citing coverage in *The Purdue Exponent*, October 3, 1902, 8–9.

17. The tank scrap of 1904," *The Purdue Exponent*, September 22, 1904, 12.

18. "The Scrap," *The Purdue Exponent*, September 22, 1904, 18–19.

19. "President Stone Briefly Addressed the Student Body, Addresses, etc. 1904, Box 1, Winthrop E. Stone—president, Purdue University 1900–1921", Virginia Kelly Karnes Archives & Special Collections Research Center, Purdue University Libraries, West Lafayette, Indiana.

20. "The Tank Scrap," *The Purdue Exponent*, September 11, 1909, 2.

21. Ibid.

22. "In the Wake of Purdues," *Debris* (Lafayette: Purdue University, 1924), 435.

23. "Two Students May Die," *New York Times*, September 21, 1901, 11.

24. "30 Hurt in Class Rush," *New York Times*, September 18, 1904, 4.

25. "The Scrap," *The Purdue Exponent*, September 22, 1904, 18–19.

26. Second Year Men Place Numerals on Big Reservoir," *The Purdue Exponent*, September 18, 1909, 2, 8.

27. "Scrappy Sentences," *The Purdue Exponent*, September 21, 1912, 3.

28. "Physical Examination," *The Purdue Exponent*, September 16, 1913, 4.

29. "Sophomore Claimed By Death," *The Purdue Exponent*, September 20, 1913, 1.

30. "South Whitley Youth Came To His Death By Rough Handling," *South Whitley Tribune*, September 19, 1913, 1; "Tank Scrap Claims Victim at Purdue: Frank Oberchain is Killed in the Melee," *South Whitley Tribune*, September 26, 1913, 1; "True Statement of Local Physicians as Cause of Death," *South Whitley Tribune*, September 26, 1913, 1.

25. A Blueprint for Greek Reforms

1. For particulars on the death of Cornell Sigma Alpha Epsilon member George Desdunes, see Michael Winerip, "When a Hazing Goes Very Wrong," *New York Times*, April 12, 2012.

2. Hazing.Cornell.edu, *A Revealing Look at Hidden Rites*.

3. David Skorton, "A Pledge to End Fraternity Hazing," *New York Times*, August 23, 2011.

4. Robert Forness, "RARE Task Force Comprehensive Report," 2012, 11–13, https://www.alumni.cornell.edu/volunteer/documents/Cornell%20RARE%20Livestreaming%20Event%204.27.2012%20Final.pdf.

5. Disclosure: Subject expert Hank Nuwer volunteered by conference call and e-mail without compensation from the RARE Task Force.

6. Forness, RARE report.

7. Linda Langford, "A Comprehensive Approach to Hazing Prevention in Higher Education Settings," Higher Education Center Working Paper, US Department of Education's Higher Education Center for Alcohol and Other Drug Abuse and Violence Prevention, 2008, http://files.eric.ed.gov/fulltext/ED537679.pdf.

8. Ibid.

9. Please consult https://hazing.cornell.edu/cms/hazing/do/council.cfm.

26. Hazing and the Law and Litigation

1. A. Cimino, "The Evolution of Hazing: Motivational Mechanism and the Abuse of Newcomers," *Journal of Cognition and Culture* 11 (2011): 241–267.

2. Justin M. Burns, "Covering Up an Infection with a Bandage: A Call to Action to Address Flaws in Ohio's Antihazing Legislation," *Akron Law Review* 48, no. 1 (2015), article 6.

3. Ibid.

4. M. Edelman, "How to Prevent High School Hazing: A Legal, Ethical, and Social Primer," *North Dakota Law Review* 81, no. 2 (2005): 309.

5. Code § 16-1-23.

6. Nicholas Bittner, "A Hazy Shade of Winter: The Chilling Issues Surrounding Hazing in School Sports and the Litigation That Follows," *Sports Law Journal*, 23 (2016), 211–254.

7. Brandon W. Chamberlin, "Am I My Brother's Keeper?: Reforming Criminal Hazing Laws Based On Assumption Of Care," *Emory Legal Journal* 63, no. 925 (2014): 945.

8. No. 97-C-3872 (1998).

9. R. B. Crow and S. R. Rosner, "Institutional and Organizational Liability for Hazing in Intercollegiate and Professional Team Sports," *St. John's University Law Review* 76, (Winter 2002).

10. Ibid.

11. Bittner, "Hazy Shade of Winter."

12. 489 US 189 (1982).

13. Bittner, "Hazy Shade of Winter," 20.

14. See "Chad Meredith" YouTube documentary video, created by Franklin College Pulliam School of Journalism students at https://www.youtube.com/watch?v=MxwmqUL8jbA.

15. No.98-40338 (1999).

16. S. Stuart, "Warriors, Machismo, and Jockstraps: Sexually Exploitative Athletic Hazing and Title IX in the Public School Locker Room," *Western New England Law Review* 35, no. 2 (2013): 377–423.

17. 84 F.3d 1226 (10th Cir. 1996).

18. Chamberlin, "Am I My Brother's Keeper?"

19. Michigan Penal Code 750.411t (2004).

20. See Greg Graber, "It's Not all Fun and Games," accessed September 04, 2003, http://www.espn.go.com/otl/hazing/wednesday.html. See especially Colleen McGlone, *Hazing in NCAA Division I Women's Athletics: An Exploratory Analysis* (PhD dissertation, University of New Mexico, 2006).

21. Louisiana Revised Statute Ann. 17:1801.

22. Justin M. Burns, "Covering Up an Infection with a Bandage."

23. Justin Heinze, "New Pennsylvania Antihazing Law Will Apply To High Schools, Too," accessed August 8, 2016, http://patch.com.

24. SC Code § 16-3-520 (2015).

25. NH Rev Stat § 631:7 (2015).

26. ID Code § 18-917, amended 2002.

27. FL Code § 1006.63, 2010.

28. KY Code § 164.375, 1986.

29. Ohio rev. Code Ann. 2307.44 (2005); see also Edelman, "How to Prevent High School Hazing."

30. No. 730 A. 2d 1086 (1999).

31. See *Anderson v. Toombs*, 119 Vt. 40, 44–45, 117 A. 2d 250, 253 (1955).

32. J. Sunshine, "A Lazarus Tax in South Carolina: A Natural History of National Fraternities' Respondeat Superior Liability for Hazing," *Charlotte Law Review* 5, no. 79 (2014).

33. Sunshine, "A Lazarus Tax in South Carolina," 26.

34. 601 N.E.2d 757 (1999).

35. 738 So.2d 1105 (1999).

36. 594 A.2d 506 (1991).

37. McGlone, *Hazing in NCAA Division I Women's Athletics.* See also Nadine C. Hoover, "National Survey: Initiation Rites and Athletics for NCAA Sports Teams," August 30, 1999, http://www.alfred.edu/sports_hazing/docs/hazing.pdf.

38. *No. 402,* 71 W.D.2d 16 (1967).

39. D. Pearson and J. C. Beckham, "Negligent Liability Issues Involving Colleges and Students: Balancing the Risks and Benefits of Expanded Programs and Heightened Supervision," *NASPA Journal* 42, no. 4 (2005): 460–477.

40. 389 Mass. 47, 449 N.E. 2d 706, (1983).

41. H. C. Black, *Black's Law Dictionary,* 6th ed. (St. Paul, MN: West Group, 1990).

42. 612 F.2d 135 (1979).

43. 726 P.2d 413 (1986).

44. Edelman, "How to Prevent High School Hazing."

45. E. Staurowsky, "Hazing," in *Law for Recreation and Sport Management,* 3rd ed., ed. D. Cotton and J. T. Wolohan (Dubuque, IA: Kendall/Hunt, 2003).

27. Smokeouts and Smokescreens

1. United States Government Accountability Office, Report to Congressional Committees, "DOD and Coast Guard: Actions Needed to Increase Oversight and Management Information on Hazing Incidents Involving Servicemembers," February 2016.

2. Keith P. Richardson, "Pollywogs and Shellbacks: An Analysis of the Equator-Crossing Ritual," *Western Folklore* 36 (April 1977): 154–159.

3. SECNAVINST 1610.2A Letter, July 15, 2005, https://fas.org/irp/doddir/navy/secnavinst /1610_2a.pdf.

4. Ibid.

5. R. Joseph Gelarden, "Bizarre Initiation Rite Has Coast Guardsman on Brink of Discharge," *Indianapolis Star,* May 14, 1989.

6. Ibid.

7. Douglas MacArthur, *Reminiscences* (New York: McGraw-Hill, 1964).

8. Ryan Bentley, "Mesquite Sunk 20 Years Ago Today," *Petoskey News-Review,* December 4, 2009. The ship was launched in 1943 at a cost of $874,798.

Index

CPSIA information can be obtained
at www.ICGtesting.com
Printed in the USA
LVOW13s1544200218
567273LV00021B/209/P